880 ✓

This book is to be returned on or before the last date stamped below.

−1. MAY 1987		
26. OCT. 1987	~ FEB. 1989	
19. SEP. 1988		
−3. OCT. 1988		
−3. OCT. 1988		
12. FEB. 1989		
		LIBREX

THE CAMBRIDGE HISTORY OF
CLASSICAL LITERATURE

GENERAL EDITORS

Mrs P. E. Easterling *Fellow of Newnham College, Cambridge*
E. J. Kenney *Fellow of Peterhouse, Cambridge*

ADVISORY EDITORS

B. M. W. Knox *The Center for Hellenic Studies, Washington*
W. V. Clausen *Department of the Classics, Harvard University*

VOLUME II PART 3
THE AGE OF AUGUSTUS

THE CAMBRIDGE HISTORY OF
CLASSICAL LITERATURE

VOLUME II: LATIN LITERATURE

THE CAMBRIDGE HISTORY OF CLASSICAL LITERATURE

VOLUME II

PART 3

The Age of Augustus

EDITED BY

E. J. KENNEY

Fellow of Peterhouse, Cambridge

ADVISORY EDITOR

W. V. CLAUSEN

Professor of Greek and Latin
Harvard University

CAMBRIDGE UNIVERSITY PRESS

CAMBRIDGE

LONDON   NEW YORK   NEW ROCHELLE

MELBOURNE   SYDNEY

Published by the Press Syndicate of the University of Cambridge
The Pitt Building, Trumpington Street, Cambridge CB2 1RP
32 East 57th Street, New York, NY 10022, USA
296 Beaconsfield Parade, Middle Park, Melbourne 3206, Australia

First published 1982 as chapters 15–23 of *The Cambridge History of Classical Literature*, Volume II
First paperback edition 1983

Printed in Great Britain by the University Press, Cambridge

Library of Congress catalogue card number: 82-19783

British Library Cataloguing in Publication Data
The Cambridge history of classical literature.
Vol. 2: Latin literature
The Age of Augustus
1. Classical literature – History and criticism
I. Kenney, E. J. II. Clausen, W. V.
880'.09   PA3001
ISBN 0 521 27373 0

CONTENTS

CONTENTS

1
UNCERTAINTIES

Cicero was murdered by the soldiers of Antony and Octavian in December of 43 B.C. In the following year, according to the ancient tradition, Virgil began to write the *Eclogues*. A new age, in both politics and literature, had begun.[1] The period between Virgil's début and the death of Ovid was one of extraordinary and unprecedented literary creativity at Rome. Perhaps no other half-century in the history of the world has witnessed the publication in one city of so many unquestioned masterpieces of enduring significance in so many different fields. Between them Virgil, Horace and Ovid imparted to most of the major genres of poetry what might appear their mature, even definitive, shape. Epic, lyric, elegy, bucolic, didactic, satire, all underwent this magisterial discipline. In prose one monumental undertaking, Livy's history *Ab urbe condita*, survives (in part) to uphold Ciceronian canons of historiography against the influence of Sallust and to leave a permanent mark on the tradition. Only drama and oratory languished in a society in which free speech, at least among the upper classes,[2] was confined within increasingly narrow limits.

In some such manner, simplified by hindsight and the selective operations of taste and chance, what is conventionally called the Augustan Age of Latin literature tends to be presented. Contemporary reality was considerably more complex. The record of lost and fragmentary literature,[3] added to the explicit testimony of our sources, provides evidence of much diversity and experiment, conducted to a counterpoint of sometimes fiercely outspoken criticism and controversy. All the best work of Virgil, Horace and Ovid was experimental and a good deal of it, in the eyes of their contemporaries, controversial. Vilification of Virgil began, we are told (*Vit. Don.* 171–9 B) immediately with the publication of the *Eclogues*. The poet's deathbed wish to have the *Aeneid* destroyed (ibid. 143–53) may well have been due to a more fundamental uneasiness than that arising from its unfinished state. This was, after all, and Virgil must have been well aware of the fact, the most original epic ever

[1] Cf. Du Quesnay (1976) 39–43.   [2] Cf. Cameron (1976) 173.
[3] See below, pp. 180–3, 187–97.

written, not at all what many people would have been expecting after reading the proem to the third book of the *Georgics*; and in spite of Propertius' famous eulogy (2.34.65–6) its success can at the time have seemed by no means secure to the poet.[1] Horace's literary epistles afford vivid, if not always unambiguous,[2] insights into the literary dissensions of the age. Even Ovid, whose earliest poetry (he tells us) took the town by storm, had encountered critical hostility (*Rem. Am.* 387–98) some years before incurring the much more damaging displeasure of the Princeps.

In these respects, then, the Augustan Age did not differ materially from the ages that preceded and followed it. It is in the domain of technique that it may lay claim to a unique status. In the period of almost exactly two centuries which separates the literary début of Virgil from that of Livius Andronicus the Latin language and its native modes of expression had been, by fits and starts as genius came on to the scene, and not without friction,[3] assimilating itself to the metres and forms of Greece. In the work of Virgil and Horace it seems that the process of assimilation has achieved a happy equilibrium: the most characteristic monuments of Augustan poetry display a formally and aesthetically satisfying fusion of new and old, native and alien elements. For the first time since the classical age of Greece the competing claims of technique (*ars*) and inspiration (*ingenium*) were again harmonized. The balance which Callimachus (Ov. *Am.* 1.15.14) and Ennius (Ov. *Trist.* 2.424) had missed, Ovid – and by implication those contemporary writers approved by educated taste – had triumphantly compassed.

As in human affairs in general, so in art, equilibrium is a transitory thing. In the longer perspectives of later literary history Ovid himself, like his contemporary Livy, is a transitional figure, documenting – to use a familiar though fundamentally misleading stereotype – the waning of the 'Golden' and the waxing of the 'Silver' Ages of Latin letters. In Ovid's verse we find consummated the technical legacy of the Augustans to their successors: a common idiom, a poetical *koine*, with affinities to current prose, in which anything could be expressed with ease and elegance by anybody with an ear and the necessary training. Respect for the generic boundary-lines and restraint in the exploitation of the abundant technical resources, subordination of means to ends, self-control: the area in which technique shades into taste, and taste into morals – that was a bequest with less appeal to poets eager to astonish and surprise. Already in the *Controversiae* and *Suasoriae* of the Elder Seneca, whose memories went back to the age of Cicero (*Contr.* 1 *praef.* 11), the incipient domination of the rhetoric which in the view of Wilamowitz was principally to blame for

---

[1] Cf. Kidd (1977), on Hor. *Odes* 1.3 as referring to the boldness of Virgil's attempt.

[2] See, for instance, the interpretations of *Epist.* 1.19 by Fraenkel (1957) 339–50 and G. W. Williams (1968) 25–8.

[3] Cf. on Lucilius *The Early Republic*, pp. 167, 169–71.

the decline of civilization[1] is clearly perceptible. Even before the fall of the Republic, that is to say, the pursuit of rhetorical brilliance for its own sake was tending to obscure the practical ends of public speaking,[2] and the infection was spreading to literature.

After the elimination of Octavian's last rival at Actium in 31 B.C. the Roman world entered on an unexampled period of peace and prosperity. Naturally the official author of these blessings expected his achievements to be reflected in contemporary literature. A tradition of court poetry going back through Theocritus and Callimachus to Pindar and beyond[3] offered obvious models; and in his friend and first minister Maecenas Augustus could call on the services of an intermediary who could bring to bear on the irritable brood of poets (Hor. *Epist.* 2.2.102) an unrivalled combination of tact and munificence – so much so that he still stands for later ages as the type of literary patron. Very little surviving Augustan poetry, however, can be described as court poetry: comparison with Statius' *Silvae* is enough to make the point. Certain poets, notably Ovid and Tibullus, were attached to patrons other than Maecenas; and even Virgil, Horace and Propertius obstinately resisted all inducements to celebrate Augustus and the régime in ways which they could not reconcile with their literary (i.e. Callimachean) consciences. Dissent and reservations may go deeper than that. Although some poems – the 'Roman' odes and the *Georgics* spring to mind – appear to align the poet solidly with current official attitudes and aspirations, it is rarely appropriate to talk of propaganda. The message of the *Georgics* is moral rather than political;[4] and even the *Aeneid*, a poem undertaken, we are told, expressly in order to bring past and present into harmony,[5] strikes a note of resignation rather than of confidence. To what extent signs of disillusion can be detected in the poetry of Horace and Propertius is more problematical.[6] In the case of Ovid, goaded by a cruel and vindictive persecution, resentment finally broke out into overt protest – if irony may be so bitter as to justify the phrase.[7] It would indeed be odd if the political and social stresses and strains of Augustus' long reign[8] were not reflected in the literature of the period, even in the work of writers not basically disaffected. Even if common prudence had not imposed discretion, Virgil and Horace were heirs to a poetical tradition in which a wink was as good as a nod, in which nuance and innuendo were preferred to explicit statement. The hints of independence, of emancipation from officially-approved values, in their work take different forms.

---

[1] Wilamowitz (1928) 73.

[2] Cf. Winterbottom (1974) I viii–ix.   [3] Gow (1950) II 305–7, 325.

[4] Wilkinson (1969) 49–55.

[5] *Vit. Don.* 77–8 B '...et in quo, quod maxime studebat, Romanae simul urbis et Augusti origo contineretur'.

[6] Johnson (1973).

[7] See below, pp. 153–6.   [8] Syme (1939) *passim*.

In Horace uneasiness perhaps expressed itself by what would now be called politely opting out;[1] in Virgil it issued in tortured and ambiguous literary guise. Only Ovid was finally pushed into what bordered on defiance. Paradoxically, the result was some of his sincerest and finest poetry. There is a negative as well as a positive patronage.

[1] Johnson (1973) 174.

2

THEOCRITUS AND VIRGIL

Theocritus of Syracuse, who invented the pastoral, was a Hellenistic poet, a contemporary of Callimachus and Apollonius. Disappointed perhaps in an earlier appeal to Hiero II of Syracuse (*Idyll* 16,[1] a brilliant display-piece), Theocritus migrated 'with the Muses' (16.107) to the great new capital of Egypt, whose lord, Ptolemy Philadelphus, was renowned for his liberality to poets and men of letters. It is evident from *Idyll* 15 that Theocritus was familiar with the city of Alexandria; and from *Idyll* 17 that he gained Ptolemy's favour. He was familiar too with the Aegean island of Cos, Ptolemy's birthplace and home of his tutor Philitas, the coryphaeus, as it were, of the Alexandrian school of poetry. There Theocritus had good friends, Eucritus, Amyntas, the brothers Phrasidamus and Antigenes, all mentioned in *Idyll* 7, the setting of which is Cos; and there he probably met Nicias, the love-sick physician and minor poet to whom *Idyll* 11 is addressed: the Cyclops in love, no longer Homer's blood-curdling monster but 'our Cyclops, old Polyphemus' (7–8), an enamoured country bumpkin. It is tempting to imagine Theocritus in Alexandria, Alexander's city, a city composed of all sorts and conditions of men, Greek and barbarian, with no history, no common traditions, no intimate relationship to the countryside – to imagine him there cultivating a special nostalgia by writing of the Sicilian herdsmen of his youth: a landscape of memory, for it is not known that he ever returned to Sicily.

Theocritus' poetry, or rather his pastoral poetry (for he wrote much else besides), is nostalgic, exquisitely so, as any urbane reflection on a simpler, now remote existence will be. But it is saved from sentimentality by the elegance of the poet's language and his apparent – at times his too apparent – erudition. (Pastoral poetry was never quite to lose this character of learning, except perhaps in its most attenuated derivation from Virgil.)

Here, for example, is a passage from Theocritus' first *Idyll*: the beginning of Thyrsis' lament for the cowherd Daphnis, mysteriously, ruthlessly, dying of

---

[1] Theocritus' poems are indiscriminately called 'idylls', εἰδύλλια – an all but meaningless term having none of its English connotations.

love; a passage imitated by Virgil in his tenth *Eclogue* and by Milton (after Virgil) in his *Lycidas*:

Ἄρχετε βουκολικᾶς, Μοῖσαι φίλαι, ἄρχετ' ἀοιδᾶς.

Θύρσις ὅδ' ὡξ Αἴτνας, καὶ Θύρσιδος ἀδέα φωνά.
πᾷ ποκ' ἄρ' ἦσθ', ὅκα Δάφνις ἐτάκετο, πᾷ ποκα, Νύμφαι;
ἦ κατὰ Πηνειῶ καλὰ τέμπεα, ἢ κατὰ Πίνδω;
οὐ γὰρ δὴ ποταμοῖο μέγαν ῥόον εἴχετ' Ἀνάπω,
οὐδ' Αἴτνας σκοπιάν, οὐδ' Ἄκιδος ἱερὸν ὕδωρ.

ἄρχετε βουκολικᾶς, Μοῖσαι φίλαι, ἄρχετ' ἀοιδᾶς.

τῆνον μὰν θῶες, τῆνον λύκοι ὠρύσαντο,
τῆνον χὠκ δρυμοῖο λέων ἔκλαυσε θανόντα. (64–72)

Begin, dear Muses, begin the pastoral song.

Thyrsis of Etna am I, and sweet is the voice of Thyrsis. Where were ye, Nymphs, where were ye, when Daphnis was wasting: in the fair vales of Peneius or of Pindus? for surely ye kept not the mighty stream of Anapus, nor the peak of Etna, nor the sacred rill of Acis.

Begin, dear Muses, begin the pastoral song.

For him the jackals howled, for him the wolves; for him dead even the lion of the forest made lament.

This translation[1] fails, as any translation will, because it does not represent qualities inherent in the original, of which three may be briefly noted:

Poetic reminiscence: Ἄκιδος ἱερὸν ὕδωρ 'the sacred water of Acis' (69). The Acis is a small stream that rises under Etna and flows into the sea. Theocritus would have known it as a boy; no doubt it pleased him to ennoble it with a phrase out of Homer.

Doric dialect: an artificial dialect largely adapted from previous poetry, though Theocritus' own speech may be involved to a degree; certainly not the 'boorish dialect' Dryden took it for (*The dedication of the Pastorals* (1697); but Dryden rightly sensed 'a secret charm in it which the Roman language cannot imitate'). Given the linguistic sophistication of the poet and, presumably, of his audience, it is probable that some effect of rusticity was intended.

Rhetorical structure: lines 71–2 form a highly stylized period composed of three clauses (a tricolon), the last being the longest; in this case each begins with the same word, an added refinement (anaphora).

This passage, as indeed most of the first *Idyll*, is remarkably elaborate; of the pastoral *Idylls* only the seventh compares with it. Still, even Theocritus' lesser efforts, those that seem closer to the realities of peasant experience, are not at bottom dissimilar. Theocritus' pastoral style or mode, though varying greatly in intensity, is nevertheless consistent: his most penetrating critic – to judge from the catholicity of Virgil's imitation[2] – found it so.

[1] By Gow (1952) 1 9.
[2] But Virgil did not particularly care for *Idylls* 6, 9, 10; see Posch (1969) 17.

6

The *Idyll* begins with Thyrsis complimenting an unnamed goatherd on the sweetness of his music:

> Ἁδύ τι τὸ ψιθύρισμα καὶ ἁ πίτυς, αἰπόλε, τήνα,
> ἁ ποτὶ ταῖς παγαῖσι, μελίσδεται, ἁδὺ δὲ καὶ τύ
> συρίσδες.

Sweet is the whispering music of that pinetree, goatherd, the pinetree by the springs, sweet too your piping.

Casual rustic speech (such is the fiction) is apprehended and, with beautiful precision, fastened in the rhythm of the hexameter.

'Sweet is the whispering music of that pinetree...' Landscape is necessary to this poetry: in Theocritus description is accurate and frequently luxuriant, in Virgil sparse and suggestive. The pastoral landscape is capacious: strange and oddly assorted figures may be accommodated; it is static, a perpetual décor or background against which these figures are set off, and thus it serves to unify what might otherwise seem a discordant collocation of speakers and topics. In this environment of rural fantasy the sophisticated, city-bred poet, poet-scholar in the guise of poet-shepherd, is able to speak with a kind of obtrusive simplicity: he may speak of country things, oftener (in Virgil) he speaks of political events, of love, of poetry. And, meanwhile, goats will continue to behave in their goatish way:

> αἱ δὲ χίμαιραι,
> οὐ μὴ σκιρτασῆτε, μὴ ὁ τράγος ὔμμιν ἀναστῆ.

You she-goats, don't be so skittish, the he-goat will rouse himself.

So ends the first *Idyll*, almost abruptly: after the prolonged elevation of Thyrsis' lament for Daphnis, a moment of earthy humour – and a reminder of the confines of this poetry.

I. VIRGIL AND THEOCRITUS

> Prima Syracosio dignata est ludere uersu
> nostra neque erubuit siluas habitare Thalia.   (*Ecl.* 6.1–2)

My Thalia first condescended to amuse herself with Syracusan verse nor did she blush to dwell in the woods.

A proud claim, made with all the delicate force of which pastoral rhetoric is capable: the claim, that is, of being the first Latin poet to imitate Theocritean pastoral; and made at the beginning of an eclogue which owes little or nothing overtly to Theocritus. Hence two questions: was Virgil indeed the first? and what was the nature of his imitation?

7

Virgil's imitation of Theocritus is restricted mainly, and not surprisingly, to the pastoral *Idylls* (1, 3–11), with the notable exception of *Idyll* 2, Simaetha's incantation, a most unpastoral song which Virgil managed to translate into a pastoral setting (*Ecl.* 8.64–109). Virgil may be thought of as a Roman poet appropriating a province of Greek poetry, formed late and not, as he gracefully insinuates, highly prized. Indications of a Theocritean presence in Latin poetry, or what remains of it, before Virgil are meagre and elusive. So erudite a poet as Parthenius could hardly have been ignorant of Theocritus, a famous Alexandrian who had, moreover, sided with Callimachus against his critics.[1] (Parthenius nowhere uses Theocritus in his Περὶ ἐρωτικῶν παθημάτων, but that instructive booklet had a very limited purpose.[2]) Catullus apparently modelled the refrain in his epyllion (64) on that in *Idyll* 1, and adapted, perhaps after Cinna, a single verse from *Idyll* 15.[3] And there is the curious remark of Pliny the Elder (*N.H.* 28.19) to the effect that Catullus, like Virgil, imitated Simaetha's song; the imitation has not survived. Perhaps Parthenius possessed only a few of the idylls; perhaps his first pupils were not interested in pastoral poetry.

For Catullus and his friends, young poets concerned to be fashionable, to be urbane, 'of the city', the country had no charm; it represented rather the very qualities they despised, in poetry as in manners, the inept, the uncouth, the out-of-date. So the ultimate dispraise of Suffenus, witty and delightful fellow that he is, is this: let him but touch poetry and he becomes country clumsy, clumsier (Catull. 22.14 *idem infaceto est infacetior rure*); and of the superannuated *Annals* by the disgusting Volusius: that they are a mass of country clumsiness (Catull. 36.19 *pleni ruris et inficetiarum*). Not for such poets idealized peasants and pastoral sentiment – even had they read Theocritus.

Virgil was different, as, somehow, Virgil always is. He was born in a rural district not far from Mantua; his father was a farmer, though hardly so poor as the ancient Life (*Vita Donati*) would have him be; more likely a country entrepreneur (a type not uncommon in Italy today) with ambition and money enough to send a gifted son away to school, first to Cremona, where Virgil assumed the *toga uirilis*, the garb of manhood, then to Milan and shortly thereafter to Rome. In later years Virgil owned a house in Rome, on the Esquiline near the gardens of his patron Maecenas. (Why does Maecenas not figure in the *Eclogues*? For it is now clear that Virgil became a member of his 'circle' several years before the Book of *Eclogues* was published.) Most of the time, however, Virgil lived in peaceful retirement at Naples or in Sicily. Unlike Catullus, miserable in Verona (Catull. 68.1–40), Virgil did not long for Rome; he very rarely went there, and when he did he shunned public notice. So far from seeming urbane, he had the look of a countryman about him (*Vita Don.* 8 *facie*

---

[1] *Id.* 7.45–8; cf. Gow (1952) II ad loc.   [2] See *The Early Republic*, pp. 184–6.
[3] See *The Early Republic*, p. 191.

8

rusticana). Of course Virgil's biography will not explain why he wrote pastoral poetry; or why he wrote the ten pastoral poems he did; or why he wrote poetry at all. Still, a serious writer of pastoral poetry must have some affection for the country; and Virgil's deep and abiding affection is evident in all his poetry, even his latest. So it is that a reader will encounter, with the surprised pleasure of recognizing the familiar in a strange place, a passage in the *Aeneid* which puts him in mind of the young poet of the *Eclogues*. *Aen.* 12.517–20, for example: Menoetes, a young Arcadian, a fisherman once, who died in the fields of Laurentum, to whom the doors of the rich and powerful were unknown, whose father was a poor farmer tilling rented land.[1] It is not difficult to understand why Virgil was attracted to Theocritus' pastoral *Idylls*. Were these poems then new in Rome? Or new for Virgil?

From a prefatory epigram it appears that Artemidorus of Tarsus, a grammarian more or less contemporary with Parthenius (but having no known connexion with him), published a collection of pastoral poems:

> Βουκολικαὶ Μοῖσαι σποράδες ποκά, νῦν δ' ἅμα πᾶσαι
> ἐντὶ μιᾶς μάνδρας, ἐντὶ μιᾶς ἀγέλας.   (*A.P.* 9.205)

The bucolic Muses, scattered once, are now together, all in one fold, in one flock.

Did Virgil use this comprehensive edition? Or a separate edition of Theocritus? In any case, he used an edition that contained – by one of the happiest accidents in literature – ten pastoral *Idylls* 'of Theocritus'.[2] To Virgil, a Latin poet after all, it would matter little that Bion and Moschus or other Greek imitators of Theocritus had written pastoral poetry; or that there were pastoral moments, if in fact there were, in the elegies of Gallus: he, Virgil, was indisputably the first Latin poet to make whole poems, *Bucolica*, after the example of Theocritus.

But Theocritus may justly be preferr'd as the Original, without injury to Virgil, who modestly contents himself with the second place, and glories only in being the first who transplanted Pastoral into his own country; and brought it there to bear as happily as the Cherry-trees which Lucullus brought from Pontus.

(Dryden, *The dedication of the Pastorals*, 1697)

Whether Virgil was modestly content with second place may be questioned. Very likely he felt some diffidence at the start (when writing the second and third *Eclogues*, as they were to become), but did he by the time he had almost finished with the pastoral Muse, when he could write:

> Prima Syracosio dignata est ludere uersu
> nostra neque erubuit siluas habitare Thalia?

---

[1] Cf. Clausen (1976).

[2] *Id.* 8 (which Virgil admired) is probably, and *Id.* 9 certainly, spurious; but Virgil could not have known.

9

It may be questioned too whether the transplanting was quite so easy as Dryden's pretty simile – very pretty, and thoroughly Roman in sensibility – suggests: it required some seven or eight years to accomplish.

The relationship of Virgil and Theocritus is extraordinary, a literary symbiosis unparalleled in Graeco-Latin poetry. Comparison as usually proposed, between the *Eclogues* and the pastoral *Idylls*, is unequal and tends to Virgil's disadvantage. Nor can Theocritus' poetic achievement, which is of the highest order, be appreciated as it should be if attention is confined to his pastoral *Idylls*. If such a comparison must be made, then it should be between the whole of Theocritus, on the one hand, and the *Eclogues* and parts of the *Georgics*, at least, on the other.

Virgil was a young poet when he started the *Eclogues*. Much, far too much, has been written (echoes of which still, incredibly, are heard) about the adolescent Virgil, the supposed author of the *Culex* and several other bad or indifferent poems; much less about the young poet of the *Eclogues*, his problems, his successes, his failures. The reason is the *Aeneid*: the lustre of that august and splendid poem has been reflected on to the *Eclogues*, so that the young poet is very hard to see. (If only it might be given to read the *Eclogues* in perfect innocence of the *Aeneid*...) A few perceptive comments have been made about him, not by a professional scholar but by a professional poet, Paul Valéry,[1] who had been persuaded by a friend to translate the *Eclogues* – 'cette œuvre illustre', as he justly terms it, 'fixée dans une gloire millénaire'. By a wilful act of sympathy, by recalling himself to himself as a young poet, Valéry was able to see in Virgil another young poet and speak personally, as it were, of him at a critical phase in his development and that of Latin poetry:

L'homme était jeune; mais l'art des vers à Rome en était au point ou il devient si conscient de ses moyens que la tentation de les employer pour le plaisir de s'en servir et de les développer à l'extrême, passe le besoin vrai, primitif et naïf de s'exprimer. Le goût de produire l'effet devient cause... (p. 214)

Les *Bucoliques*, me tirant pour quelques instants de ma vieillesse, me remirent au temps de mes premiers vers. Il me semblait en retrouver les impressions. Je croyais bien voir dans le texte un mélange de perfections et d'imperfections, de très heureuses combinaisons et grâces de la forme avec des maladresses très sensibles; parfois, des pauvretés assez surprenantes, dont je montrerai quelqu'une. Je reconnaissais dans ces inégalités d'exécution un âge tendre du talent, et ce talent venu à poindre dans un âge critique de la poésie. (p. 216)

Virgil's second *Eclogue* is generally considered his earliest: apart from lines 45–55, a somewhat overfull description of flowers, fruits, and sweet-smelling trees, which may have been added later, it is mostly derived from Theocritus'

[1] Valéry (1962).

eleventh *Idyll*. Here, if anywhere, some infelicity of expression, some awkwardness or incompetence might be looked for.

The love-sick Corydon, denied the favours of the petulant boy Alexis, his master's darling, boasts that he too is somebody:

> despectus tibi sum, nec qui sim quaeris, Alexi,
> quam diues pecoris, niuei quam lactis abundans.
> mille meae Siculis errant in montibus agnae;
> lac mihi non aestate nouum, non frigore defit. (19–22)

I am despised by you, nor do you ask who I am, Alexis, how rich in herds, how abundantly supplied with snowy milk. A thousand ewes of mine roam the Sicilian hills. Fresh milk I lack not, neither in summer nor winter.

Now Polyphemus, Theocritus' old neighbour (and rather too close for the comfort of Virgil's reader here), may preen himself on his pastoral riches:

> ἀλλ' οὗτος τοιοῦτος ἐὼν βοτὰ χίλια βόσκω,
> κἠκ τούτων τὸ κράτιστον ἀμελγόμενος γάλα πίνω·
> τυρὸς δ' οὐ λείπει μ' οὔτ' ἐν θέρει οὔτ' ἐν ὀπώρᾳ,
> οὐ χειμῶνος ἄκρω. (*Id.* 11.34–7)

Yet, such as I am, I graze a thousand sheep, and from these I draw and drink milk, the very best. Cheese I lack not, neither in summer nor autumn, nor in midwinter.

But Corydon... Corydon is a poor slave. Comment on this passage is somewhat embarrassed, and excuses are made.

Polyphemus proceeds:

> συρίσδεν δ' ὡς οὔτις ἐπίσταμαι ὧδε Κυκλώπων,
> τίν, τὸ φίλον γλυκύμαλον, ἁμᾷ κἠμαυτὸν ἀείδων. (38–9)

I can pipe as no other Cyclops here, singing to you, my sweet honey-apple, and of myself.

And Corydon partially follows:

> canto quae solitus, si quando armenta uocabat
> Amphion Dircaeus in Actaeo Aracyntho. (23–4)

I sing as Amphion used to sing when calling the cattle home, Dircaean Amphion in Actaean Aracynthus.

Verse 24 – over which grown men have puzzled their brains – is beautiful nonsense of the most precious Alexandrian sort: 'Le goût de produire l'effet devient cause.'

Corydon continues:

> nec sum adeo informis: nuper me in litore uidi,
> cum placidum uentis staret mare. (25–6)

Nor am I so very ugly: for recently I saw myself on the shore, when the sea was calm and still.

This passage is imitated from Theocritus' sixth *Idyll*, a singing-match between Daphnis and Damoetas,[1] Damoetas impersonating Polyphemus:

καὶ γὰρ θην οὐδ' εἶδος ἔχω κακὸν ὥς με λέγοντι.
ἦ γὰρ πρᾶν ἐς πόντον ἐσέβλεπον, ἦς δὲ γαλάνα...   (34–5)

Indeed I am not so bad looking as they say. For I gazed into the sea recently, it was calm...

Again, comment is somewhat embarrassed.[2] The phrase *nec s(um) ade(o) informis* is itself very ugly with its harsh elisions: technical incompetence? or deliberate artifice? like the description of 'shepherd Polyphemus' (*pastorem Polyphemum*) in the *Aeneid*: *monstr(um) horrend(um) inform(e) ingens...* 'a monster horrible, ugly, huge...' (3.658), where the elisions are obviously expressive. On a note of irresolution this soft impeachment may well conclude.

Intentional imitation (as distinguished from reminiscence, of which the poet may not have been aware) was not looked down on in antiquity, it was looked for; and where found admired, thoughtfully, critically, as the poet intended it should be. The body of literature that might be referred to was not large, and the poet knew very well for whom he was writing – not for the crowd, whose ignorant praise he scorned, but for the discerning few, friends and others who shared his idea of poetry:

> Plotius et Varius, Maecenas Vergiliusque,
> Valgius, et probet haec Octauius, optimus atque
> Fuscus, et haec utinam Viscorum laudet uterque!
> ambitione relegata te dicere possum,
> Pollio, te, Messalla...   (Horace, *Sat.* 1.10.81–5)

May Plotius and Varius, may Maecenas and Virgil, Valgius, may Octavius approve of these poems, and the excellent Fuscus, and may both the Viscus brothers praise them. Flattery aside, I can name you, Pollio, you, Messalla...

For the Alexandrian poets and for their Roman derivatives, imitation involved emulation, poetic rivalry, with no implication of disability or want of inventive-

---

[1] These pastoral names are mostly borrowed from Theocritus and have no hidden significance, except that Tityrus and Menalcas seem occasionally to represent Virgil. The pastoral masque belongs to the later tradition: in Virgil Pollio is Pollio, Varus Varus, Gallus Gallus.

[2] 'It is just possible that a Mediterranean cove might be calm enough to mirror a giant, not possible that it should be calm enough to mirror Corydon' Conington (1881) ad loc. Cerda (1608) ad loc. argues very learnedly to the contrary; but his advice to doubters – that they should go look in the sea for themselves – betrays some exasperation. Marvell diminishes and intensifies the conceit:

> Nor am I so deform'd to sight,
> If in my Sithe I looked right;
> In which I see my picture done,
> As in a crescent Moon the Sun.   (*Damon the Mower* 57–60)

ness on the part of the imitator. So understood, imitation may be taken as evidence both of a poet's confidence in himself and of his esteem for the poet he has chosen to imitate: his aim was not to reproduce but to improve on the original. Virgil's imitations of Theocritus occasionally result in something inferior, rarely, if ever, in anything equivalent; usually the result is something quite different. It is not sufficient to notice places where Virgil uses Theocritus, as commentators routinely do, without enquiring further how or for what purpose he uses Theocritus. These imitations or allusions (a better word, perhaps, as hinting that quality of playful elegance which Horace detected in these poems: *molle atque facetum*[1] | *Vergilio adnuerunt gaudentes rure Camenae* 'To Virgil the Muses who rejoice in the country granted grace and wit' (*Serm.* 1.10.44–5)) – these allusions, then, are not discrete elements: they are, allowing for some failures, fused into Virgil's own composition.

'The title of his first book was Fragments.'[2] The paradox of the Book of *Eclogues* is, that it should contain so many fragments and yet not seem fragmentary. Whoever reads it through will be left with a sense of completeness, Virgilian completeness.

2. THE BOOK OF 'ECLOGUES'

Not only did Virgil compose the *Eclogues*, he also, and to some extent simultaneously, composed the Book of *Eclogues*,[3] a poetic achievement scarcely less remarkable. Virgil was not the first Latin poet to arrange his own poems for publication: Catullus had already done so.[4] But the Book of *Eclogues* differs essentially from Catullus' book of occasional poems: in Virgil's book the design of individual poems has been adjusted to the design of the book as a whole.

The chronology of the ten *Eclogues* had become a subject of learned speculation in late antiquity. Three apparent dates could be extracted from the text: 42 B.C., the land-confiscations (*Ecl.* 1 and 9), 40 B.C., Pollio's consulate (*Ecl.* 4.11–12), and 39 B.C., Pollio's campaign against the Parthini (*Ecl.* 8.6–13). It has recently been demonstrated,[5] however, on historical grounds, that the reference in the eighth *Eclogue* is not to Pollio but to Octavian, not therefore to the year 39 but to the year 35: this year – and not 38 or 37 as heretofore – must now be accepted, with certain literary consequences, as that in which the book of *Eclogues* was published.

---

[1] It will be noticed that Horace associates with the country the very quality (*facetum*) that Catullus denied to it.

[2] Robert Frost (1946), of the apprentice poet, in 'The constant symbol'.

[3] The title *Bucolicon liber* is found only in the explicit of the Medicean MS (fifth cent.). Virgil apparently called his poems (and his book) *Bucolica*, cf. Quint. *Inst.* 8.6.46, 9.2.3, 11.1.56, Suet. *Gramm.* 23, *Vita Don.* 19, 25, 26, 43.

[4] See *The Early Republic*, pp. 193–7.

[5] By Bowersock (1971).

The second and third *Eclogues* may well be the earliest Virgil wrote: both are studiously imitative of Theocritus and both exhibit some technical immaturity. Near the end of the fifth *Eclogue* Virgil refers, in the ancient fashion, to the second and third by quoting part of the opening line of each:

> hac te nos fragili donabimus ante cicuta;
> haec nos 'formosum Corydon ardebat Alexin',
> haec eadem docuit 'cuium pecus? an Meliboei?'

This delicate pipe I will give you first; this taught me 'Corydon burned for the fair Alexis', this same 'Whose flock? Is it Meliboeus'?'

When Virgil had written several eclogues, he decided that *Cur non, Mopse* 'Why not, Mopsus' would be the fifth; and having so decided, added or substituted a few lines to produce a summary effect, an effect of cadence, and thus to define, as will be argued below, the first half of his book.

From line 60 onwards the third *Eclogue* is occupied with a singing-match between two rival shepherds, Damoetas and Menalcas. There is nothing strange about the form of their song, granted the amoebaean convention: couplet responds to couplet with strict partiality; nor, for the most part, about its content: the attitudes struck, the emotions vented are such as seem suitable to imaginary shepherds. But suddenly, rather disturbingly, the real Pollio is intruded into the scene:

> D. Triste lupus stabulis, maturis frugibus imbres,
>   arboribus uenti, nobis Amaryllidis irae.
> M. Dulce satis umor, depulsis arbutus haedis,
>   lenta salix feto pecori, mihi solus Amyntas.
> D. Pollio amat nostram, quamuis est rustica, Musam:
>   Pierides, uitulam lectori pascite uestro.
> M. Pollio et ipse facit noua carmina: pascite taurum,
>   iam cornu petat et pedibus qui spargat harenam.
> D. Qui te, Pollio, amat, ueniat quo te quoque gaudet;
>   mella fluant illi, ferat et rubus asper amomum.
> M. Qui Bauium non odit, amet tua carmina, Meui,
>   atque idem iungat uulpes et mulgeat hircos.
> D. Qui legitis flores et humi nascentia fraga,
>   frigidus, o pueri (fugite hinc!), latet anguis in herba.
> M. Parcite, oues, nimium procedere: non bene ripae
>   creditur; ipse aries etiam nunc uellera siccat.   (80–95)

> D. *A wolf is harmful to the folds, rain to the ripened wheat, a high wind to the trees, to me Amaryllis' ire.*
> M. *A shower is delightful to the crops, the arbutus to the weaned kids, the tender willow to the gravid flock, to me only Amyntas.*
> D. *Pollio loves my Muse, rustic though she be: Pierian maids, feed a heifer for your reader.*

M. *Pollio himself makes new poems: feed a bull that now will butt with his horn and scatter sand with his hooves.*

D. *Let him who loves you, Pollio, come where he gladly sees you too have come; may honey flow for him, and the rough bramble bear spikenard.*

M. *Let him who loathes not Bavius love your poems, Mevius, and may the same yoke foxes and milk he-goats.*

D. *You who pick flowers and the low-growing strawberries, a cold snake, children (run away!), lurks in the grass.*

M. *Don't go too far, my sheep: it's no good to trust the bank; the ram himself even now is drying his fleece.*

Lines 84–91 are unrelated to those which precede or follow and would not be missed were they absent. (Let the reader try the experiment of reading the third *Eclogue* through without these lines: perhaps he will find that it gains as a poem by their absence.) Why then are they present? Because Virgil inserted them when he was shaping his book, after he had decided that *Dic mihi, Damoeta* 'Tell me, Damoetas' would be the third *Eclogue* and the one which honours Pollio, *Sicelides Musae* 'Sicilian Muses', the fourth. Line 89:

> mella fluant illi, ferat et rubus asper amomum

was designed to 'anticipate':

> occidet et serpens, et fallax herba ueneni
> occidet; Assyrium uulgo nascetur amomum.   (*Ecl.* 4.24–5)

The snake shall die, and the herb that hides its poison shall die; Assyrian spikenard shall spring up everywhere.

Virgil nowhere else mentions this rare spice-plant.

Individual eclogues must have been shown or given to friends as they were written, the fourth to Pollio in 40 B.C. surely; but since all ten were published together in 35 B.C., all ten are, in a sense, contemporaneous; and any attempt to determine the exact order of their composition will be illusory. Until Virgil finally relinquished his book, he was free to make changes in it – reworking, adding, deleting – where and whenever he pleased.

The main design of Virgil's Book of *Eclogues* is obvious because Virgil took pains to make it so. (Lesser or partial designs are not however precluded: Virgil is a poet of labyrinthine complexity.[1]) The book is divided into two halves of five eclogues each: 1–5, 6–10,[2] the first containing 420, the second

---

[1] For a description and criticism of the various designs that have been discovered see Rudd (1976) 119–44.

[2] Horace adverts to the design of Virgil's book in his own first book, published about the same time, *Sat.* 1: ten satires, the first of which begins *Qui fit, Maecenas* 'How comes it, Maecenas', the sixth *Non quia, Maecenas* 'Not because, Maecenas'. The impression made by Virgil's book must be the reason why subsequent poets – Horace, Tibullus, Ovid – composed books of ten (or multiples of ten or five) poems.

410 (or 408) lines. The two longest eclogues, the third (111 lines) and the eighth (110 or 108 lines) are symmetrically placed, each being the centrepiece of its half; and in each eight lines have been inserted to flatter a patron who is praised for his poetry: 3.84–91 (Pollio), 8.6–13 (Octavian).

The first word of the first line of the first *Eclogue* and the last word of the last line of the fifth is a poet-shepherd's name, in the vocative case: *Tityre...Menalca*. Tityrus and Menalcas, Virgil's *personae*: such precision of form cannot be accidental. The two names define the first half of the book as tersely as the name Alexis, in the accusative case, rounds off the second *Eclogue*, the first line of which ends...*Alexin*, as does the last...*Alexin*. Did Virgil expect his readers to notice – or, rather, would a Roman reader notice details of this sort? Probably: for he read aloud, slowly, and had been trained from boyhood up in the discipline of rhetoric. However, artifice need not be noticed to be effective, and may be the more effective for not being noticed.

The opening line of the sixth *Eclogue*:

> Prima Syracosio dignata est ludere uersu

suggests a fresh start, and some ancient critics (so Servius affirms) wished to put the sixth *Eclogue* first. Tityrus' name in line 4 (*Tityre*) and especially line 8:

> agrestem tenui meditabor harundine Musam

I will meditate the rural Muse on a slender reed

were meant to recall the opening lines of the first *Eclogue*:

> Tityre, tu patulae recubans sub tegmine fagi
> siluestrem tenui Musam meditaris auena.

Tityrus, you lying there under the covert of a spreading beech, you meditate the woodland Muse on a slender reed.

Virgil, or for that matter any poet schooled in the Alexandrian tradition, rarely repeats a line intact or even slightly varied; and if he does, he does so with a special purpose in mind. Virgil's purpose here is obviously to define the first half of his book and, at the same time, connect it with the second half.

It will be enough to add – although much more might be added to this brief and necessarily superficial description – that as Gallus the erudite Alexandrian is the chief figure of the sixth *Eclogue*, so Gallus the love-sick elegist is the chief figure of the tenth. Again, Virgil's purpose is obvious: to define the second half of his book.

But why a book of ten pastoral poems? a book in which each of the ten is enhanced somehow in its place? in which the ten, taken together, have a collective beauty and sense? The marvellous fact of the Book of *Eclogues* defies explanation. As to the number ten, however, a conjecture is probable: Virgil got the idea from the edition of Theocritus he used, in which there happened to be ten pastoral poems; and this original idea, vague and inchoate as it must have been, he eventually realized, by patient labour, by a slow process of refinement,[1] in the Book of *Eclogues*.

The peculiar charm of Virgil's book is immediately felt but not so readily accounted for: elegance of phrase, a harmony of meaning and music so that the one reinforces the other, artifice evident and unabashed – these and suchlike impressions can be summed up, perhaps, in a single word: style, style in its larger significance, style as displayed by no poet before Virgil. The publication of the Book of *Eclogues* is an epoch in Latin poetry.

3. THREE ECLOGUES

The first

Two shepherds are talking, but not of country things; they talk rather of civil discord and violence, of a possible reconciliation, of the infinite sadness of exile. Meliboeus has lost his farm; as he is driving off the pitiful remnant of his flock he espies Tityrus, canopied from the heat under a beech-tree and carelessly meditating his thankful Muse:

> Tityre, tu patulae recubans sub tegmine fagi
> siluestrem tenui Musam meditaris auena:
> nos patriae finis et dulcia linquimus arua.
> nos patriam fugimus: tu, Tityre, lentus in umbra
> formosam resonare doces Amaryllida siluas. (1–5)

Tityrus, you lying there under the covert of a spreading beech, you meditate the woodland Muse on a slender reed: we are leaving our country and these dear fields. We are fleeing our country: you, Tityrus, easy in the shade, teach the woods to echo fair Amaryllis' name.

This seemingly artless statement consists of two sentences or periods, each a tricolon (the rhetorical structure would be clearer with a comma after *fagi* and *umbra*); and has in fact been contrived with much art:

Line 2: the two adjectives before the main pause or caesura, *siluestrem tenui*, are completed and balanced by the two nouns after the caesura, *Musam...auena*; the implicated word-order is suggestively Alexandrian in technique.

[1] Virgil was a laborious finisher. When he was writing the *Georgics*, he would dictate a very large number of verses every morning, then spend the whole day reducing these to the fewest possible – like a she-bear, he said, licking his poem into shape (*Vita Don.* 22). 'When he was writing the *Georgics*' – that is, when the *Eclogues* had made him famous and his work-habits an object of curiosity.

Lines 3–4: the iteration is extremely pathetic, *nos patriae finis . . . | nos patriam . . .* The contrasting arrangement of the personal pronouns, *tu . . . nos, nos . . . tu*, adds to the intensity of the effect.

Line 5: the two last words echo (*resonare*) to the sense, *Amaryllida siluas*.[1]

No Roman reader had ever heard music quite like this before.

The first *Eclogue* is, in several ways, a strange poem, recognizably Theocritean in manner and yet very different from anything Theocritus wrote: Theocritus excludes the profanity of war and politics from his pastoral demesne. It is a beautiful poem, however, about a harsh and ugly experience that Virgil had suffered with his fellow-countrymen, but only as may be surmised: the first *Eclogue* is not, in any useful sense, autobiography. Virgil's paternal farm, not quite fact and not quite fiction, bears no resemblance to Horace's Sabine villa.

'O Meliboeus', Tityrus answers (the tone deepening):

> O Meliboee, deus nobis haec otia fecit,
> namque erit ille mihi semper deus, illius aram
> saepe tener nostris ab ouilibus imbuet agnus. (6–8)

O Meliboeus, a god has given me this ease. For he will ever be a god to me, often will a tender lamb from my fold stain his altar.

Who is the benevolent young god to whom Tityrus owes his pastoral ease?

> sed tamen iste deus qui sit da, Tityre, nobis. (18)

But tell me, Tityrus, who is this god of yours.

Meliboeus is not told; Tityrus changes the subject: *urbem quam dicunt Romam, Meliboee . . .* 'The city they call Rome, Meliboeus . . .' (19). Ancient readers noticed, and were puzzled: 'The question is why does he, on being asked about Octavian, describe Rome' (Servius). Virgil's poetic tact is here most politic.[2]

The first *Eclogue* cannot have been written, as generally supposed, about 40 B.C. In that year Octavian was a young man of twenty-three, but a young man hated and feared for the depredations in the Po valley and the massacre of Perugia, and more or less openly despised in comparison with Antony. Furthermore, in that year, as may be inferred from the fourth *Eclogue*, Pollio was Virgil's patron (perhaps they met when Pollio was governing Cisalpine Gaul for Antony); and Pollio and Octavian were not then, nor were they ever to be, friends.

The first in an ancient book of poems was usually the last or one of the last written, and served to introduce those which followed.[3] Only on the assump-

---

[1] Cf. Catull. 11.3–4; a similar effect can be heard in *Geo.* 1.486.

[2] See Clausen (1972) 204–5.

[3] *Ecl.* 1 appears to have been designed so as to conform with the design of the book itself: Meliboeus begins with 5 lines, Tityrus answers with 5 = 10; then M. 8, T. 7 = 15; M. 1, T. 9 = 10; M. 4, T. 6 = 10; M. 13, T. 5 = 18 (a slight variation characteristic of Virgil's mature style); M. 15,

tion that it was written in 35 B.C. (or at the very end of 36 B.C.) does the first *Eclogue* become intelligible. In early September 36 B.C. Pompey's son Sextus was utterly defeated at Naulochus, and peace at last seemed secure in the West. In the grateful municipalities of Italy Octavian's statue was set up beside the statues of the customary gods: he became, in Hellenistic style, an 'additional' god. Virgil's first *Eclogue* may be taken as a personal expression of a public attitude; and in this respect compared with his fourth, written in a mood of hope and euphoria after Brundisium.

Time is a relation of experience, and much had happened in the few urgent years during which Virgil was meditating his book. His consulate over, Pollio had gone off to govern Macedonia for Antony; Virgil came to know Maecenas and, somewhat later it would seem, Octavian. Whether imperceptibly or dramatically his position changed – supposing a previous allegiance of some kind had existed. To confound past experience with present is only human; yet Virgil does not forget the anguish of that earlier time. Now, finally, he can represent that experience in pastoral terms and contemplate, in the person of Tityrus, Octavian as saviour and god.

The fourth

By a small irony of history the one eclogue that can be related to a historical event was related to a historic event, and consequently misunderstood for centuries. The modern reader of course understands that the fourth *Eclogue* has nothing to do with the advent of Christ and the peaceable kingdom; he may find, however, that hallowed error is not so easily dispelled, and that it is all but impossible not to overhear, as he reads, the dominant tones of Isaiah 11.6: 'And the wolf shall dwell with the lamb, and the leopard shall lie down with the kid; and the calf and the young lion and the fatling together; and a little child shall lead them.' Something of its grand and sombre repute clings to this brilliant little poem still.

For such it is, exuberantly imaginative, allusive, elusive; serious, tender, playful – a virtuoso performance by a very self-confident young poet, finely calculated, but bewildering with its sudden intensities. The poem was excited by the pact of Brundisium, a political settlement between Antony and Octavian which soon receded into insignificance but which, for the moment, appeared bright with promise. Negotiations were concluded in late September or early October 40 B.C. with the consul Pollio acting on Antony's behalf. Hence:

> teque adeo decus hoc aeui, te consule inibit,
> Pollio, et incipient magni procedere menses. (11–12)

While you, while you are consul, Pollio, shall enter this glorious age and the great months begin their state.

T. 5 = 20. In *Ecl.* 2 Corydon's 'disordered' utterance (4 *haec incondita*) is introduced with 5 lines and ends with 5 lines of self-reproach. To secure this symmetry Virgil amputated the last 3 lines of Polyphemus' complaint in *Id.* 11 (77–9); thus he relates *Ecl.* 2 formally to *Ecl.* 1.

This poetical annunciation seems curiously remote from the political fact: such extravagant reference is typical of the poem and makes it difficult to interpret. And yet, at whatever remove, political fact must be reckoned with.

The poem begins with oracular solemnity: the last age of the Sibyl's spell is now come, a great ordinance of time is born anew (*nascitur ordo*) and with it a wonder-child:

> tu modo nascenti puero, quo ferrea primum
> desinet ac toto surget gens aurea mundo,
> casta faue Lucina. (8–10)

Lucina, chaste goddess, bless the boy, at whose birth the iron age shall first cease and the golden rise up throughout the world.

As this son of time grows slowly to manhood, so will the golden age (for a few traces of aboriginal sin remain) be purified.

The pact of Brundisium was consummated, after the high Roman fashion, with a dynastic wedding: Antony took Octavian's sister, the blameless Octavia, to wife. For contemporary readers of Virgil's poem the vexed question 'Who is the boy?' would not arise. They would know who was meant: the son of Antony and Octavia, and heir to Antony's greatness (17) – the son that never was, a daughter was born instead.[1] Antony claimed descent from Hercules as proudly as Julius Caesar claimed descent from Venus;[2] thus the boy would have been descended on his father's side from Hercules, on his mother's from Venus: a symbol incarnate of unity and peace. Like Hercules[3] (the poem implies) he will be exalted to heaven, there to see gods mingling with heroes (15–16, among them the recently deified Julius?), to banquet with gods and share a goddess's bed (63).

In the year 40 B.C. – on earth – Antony, not Octavian, was the commanding figure; and of this their contemporaries, spectators to the mighty scene, would have no doubt. The modern reader, under the disadvantage of hindsight, must constantly remind himself that Octavian was not yet Augustus nor Virgil yet the poet of the *Aeneid*; that both eventualities were as yet latent in an unimaginable future. Failure of historical perspective distorts much of what is written about the fourth *Eclogue*.

The epithalamium is a potentially embarrassing form of composition. That Virgil conceived of his poem as in some sort an epithalamium is indicated by lines 46–7:

> 'Talia saecla' suis dixerunt 'currite' fusis
> concordes stabili fatorum numine Parcae.

'Speed on such ages' to their spindles the Parcae sang, unanimous by fate's established will

---

[1] All this was forgotten with the years, until Asinius Gallus (Pollio's son) could assert that he was the child. What would his father have said! [2] App. *Bell. civ.* 3.16, 19; also Plut. *Ant.* 4, 36.

[3] The type and model of heroic virtue; the word *heros* occurs 3 times in *Ecl.* 4, but nowhere else in the *Eclogues*. This divine connexion was later appropriated to Augustus even though he was not descended from Hercules, cf. Hor. *Odes* 3.3.9–12, 14.1–4.

– an allusion to Catullus 64, to the song the Parcae sang at the wedding of Peleus and Thetis, whose son was to be the great Achilles.[1] When, some five years later, Virgil decided to publish his 'epithalamium' as an 'eclogue', he prefixed a brief pastoral apologia (1–3); at the same time – hope having been disappointed, circumstances altered – it is likely that he made certain other adjustments. Hence something of the mystery, or mystification perhaps, which readers sense in the fourth *Eclogue*.

The sixth

> cum canerem reges et proelia, Cynthius aurem
> uellit et admonuit: 'pastorem, Tityre, pinguis
> pascere oportet ouis, deductum dicere carmen.'
> nunc ego (namque super tibi erunt qui dicere laudes,
> Vare, tuas cupiant et tristia condere bella)
> agrestem tenui meditabor harundine Musam. (3–8)

When I was singing of kings and battles, Cynthian Apollo tweaked my ear and warned: 'A shepherd, Tityrus, ought to feed fat sheep, but sing a fine-spun song.' Now I (for there will be poets enough wanting to tell your praises, Varus, and recount war's grim story), I will meditate the rural Muse on a slender reed.

This passage can now be understood for what it is: not an autobiographical statement, as ancient scholiasts thought, but a literary allusion, Virgil's pastoral rendering of Callimachus' famous rejection of epic:[2]

> καὶ γὰρ ὅτε πρώτιστον ἐμοῖς ἐπὶ δέλτον ἔθηκα
> γούνασιν, Ἀ[πό]λλων εἶπεν ὅ μοι Λύκιος·
> '.......]... ἀοιδέ, τὸ μὲν θύος ὅττι πάχιστον
> θρέψαι, τὴ]ν Μοῦσαν δ' ὠγαθὲ λεπταλέην.' (*Aet.* 1.1.21–4)

For when first I set a writing-tablet on my knees, Lycian Apollo spoke to me: poet, feed your victim as fat as you can, but your Muse, my good fellow, keep her thin.

Agrestem tenui meditabor harundine Musam: no attentive reader can fail to hear the echo of the first *Eclogue*: *siluestrem tenui Musam meditaris auena*. There the adjective *tenui* is ornamental, necessary rather to the balance of the line than to its meaning. Here, however, the adjective is no mere ornament: it involves a concept of style, the Callimachean concept, and is the Latin equivalent of λεπταλέος (or λεπτός). His pastoral poetry, all of it, Virgil thus obliquely asserts, is Callimachean in nature.

Silenus is a stranger to Theocritean pastoral; an intractable character whom Virgil hardly confines within a pastoral frame of reference (13–30, 82–6).

---

[1] See especially Slater (1912); more generally Tarn (1932) 151–7, Syme (1939) 216–20; and *The Early Republic*, p. 193.

[2] See *The Early Republic*, pp. 181–2.

Traditional features[1] remain: he is the ancient drunkard still, the lover of nymphs and music, gifted with arcane wisdom. Yet Virgil's Silenus – and the Silenus of the sixth *Ecologue* is largely Virgil's – is wondrously changed: he has undergone a Callimachean metamorphosis from forest seer to literary critic.

Virgil's song of Silenus (31–73) originates in Apollonius' song of Orpheus, as Virgil wished his reader to notice: Silenus sings more enchantingly than even Orpheus himself (27–8, 30).

> Ἤειδεν δ' ὡς γαῖα καὶ οὐρανὸς ἠδὲ θάλασσα,
> τὸ πρὶν ἔτ' ἀλλήλοισι μιῇ συναρηρότα μορφῇ,
> νείκεος ἐξ ὀλοοῖο διέκριθεν ἀμφὶς ἕκαστα·
> ἠδ' ὡς ἔμπεδον αἰὲν ἐν αἰθέρι τέκμαρ ἔχουσιν
> ἄστρα, σεληναίης τε καὶ ἠελίοιο κέλευθοι·
> οὔρεά θ' ὡς ἀνέτειλε, καὶ ὡς ποταμοὶ κελάδοντες
> αὐτῇσιν νύμφῃσι καὶ ἑρπετὰ πάντ' ἐγένοντο.
> ἤειδεν δ' ὡς πρῶτον 'Οφίων Εὐρυνόμη τε
> 'Ωκεανὶς νιφόεντος ἔχον κράτος Οὐλύμποιο.   (*Arg.* 1.496–504)

He sang how earth and sky and sea had of old been fitted together in one form, but separated, each apart, the result of a deadly quarrel; and how forever in heaven the stars and the paths of the moon and sun have their steadfast place; and how the mountains rose up, and how plashing rivers with their nymphs and all creeping things came to be. He sang how first Ophion and Eurynome, daughter of Ocean, held sway over snowy Olympus.

Like Orpheus, Silenus begins with the creation of the world, the emergence of living things, primeval figures, Pyrrha, Prometheus; and his song is similarly articulated: 31 *namque canebat* 'for he sang', 41 *hinc* 'hereupon', 43 *his adiungit* 'to these he joins', 61 *tum canit* 'then he sings', 62 *tum* 'then', 64 *tum canit* 'then he sings'. But whereas Orpheus 'stayed his lyre and ambrosial voice' (512) with Zeus still a child in the Dictaean cave, still thinking childish thoughts, Silenus continues on, singing as if there were to be no end of song, singing until 'the evening star advanced in the unwilling sky' (86). He sings distractedly, as it seems, touching on various subjects; in fact, his song is by way of being a neoteric *ars poetica*, artfully concealed, with but a single subject: poetry, as defined by Callimachus (and poets after Callimachus) and as now exemplified by Gallus. That Pasiphae's ἐρωτικὸν πάθημα – Virgil's perfect miniature of an epyllion – and the recondite praise of Gallus' aetiological poem occupy most of the song can only be a reflection of contemporary taste, Virgil's and that of his friends.

Although the sixth *Eclogue* is addressed ostensibly to Varus, the chief figure is obviously Gallus; and readers have therefore sensed an awkwardness or disunity in the poem. The failure of sensibility is not Virgil's, it is the modern

---

[1] Cf. *OCD*² s.v. 'Satyrs and Silenoi'.

reader's, unschooled in Callimachean poetics. The refusal to write an epic poem necessarily involved writing a different poem since the refusal was always made in a poem. Apollo's magisterial rebuke to the poet and the poet's initiation on Helicon: these two scenes are complementary, the one explicitly, the other implicitly, programmatic; and the two occurred together at the beginning of the *Aetia*.

One of the Muses conducts Gallus to the summit of Helicon, where the divine singer-shepherd Linus (pastoralized by Virgil for the occasion) gives him Hesiod's pipes, with these words:

> . . . 'hos tibi dant calamos (en accipe) Musae,
> Ascraeo quos ante seni, quibus ille solebat
> cantando rigidas deducere montibus ornos.
> his tibi Grynei nemoris dicatur origo,
> ne quis sit lucus quo se plus iactet Apollo.'   (69–73)

'These reeds the Muses give you (come, take them), the reeds they gave of old to Ascra's poet, with which he used to sing and draw the stubborn ash-trees down from the mountains. With these tell the "cause" of the Grynean grove, so that there be no wood in which Apollo glories more.'

Apollo will be pleased with Gallus' poem about his sacred grove: at this point the reader may recall how displeased Apollo was with a poem about kings and battles. Now with a conclusive *quid loquar. . .?* 'Why should I speak of. . .?' at the beginning of line 74, Virgil hurries Silenus' song and his own to a pastoral close. The abrupt phrase has the effect of underlining what immediately precedes; and the poet speaks again in his own person, as he did at the outset: *cum canerem reges et proelia.*

That the same poet who wrote *cum canerem reges et proelia* wrote, years later, *Arma uirumque cano* is one of the considerable surprises of literature. The sixth *Eclogue* is an appropriately oblique – but uncompromising – declaration of adherence to the aesthetic principles of Callimachus; no reader at the time could have anticipated that its author would one day write an epic – a didactic or aetiological poem possibly, but not an epic. The *Aeneid* so imposes upon the imagination that Virgil's poetic career is seen as an orderly progression from the lesser to the greater work; it requires a corresponding effort of the imagination to see that it cannot have been so.

3

THE *GEORGICS*

I. POLITICAL BACKGROUND

By 39 B.C. Virgil had joined the circle of Octavian's right-hand man Maecenas. But Antony was still the dominant Triumvir. It was only with the defeat of Sextus Pompeius in 36 and the consequent lifting of the threat of starvation from Italy that Octavian, the man on the spot, brushing Lepidus aside, began to outshine his other colleague, absent in the East. From then on the final showdown, at Actium in 31, became inevitable. The misery of the years following Julius' murder are recalled in Virgil's next work, the *Georgics*, in the magnificent rhetoric of the finale of Book 1, 466–514, which represents the chaos as continuing and the young Octavian as the only hope. But by the time the proems to Books 1 and 3 and the epilogue were composed Octavian has emerged as sole leader, a triumphant candidate for divinity. One major misery had been the ruin of agriculture: small-holders were conscripted for war or evicted to accommodate veterans, many of whom would be less competent farmers even if minded to cultivate land at all.

To what extent was there already an 'Augustan' policy? As to agriculture, we hear of no legislation concerning land-tenure apart from the settlement of veterans. The development of large slave-run estates (*latifundia*), favoured by the geography of Italy and the economic trends of the times, continued. But there was a feeling abroad among thinking people, reflected also by Horace, that a simple, Sabine-type, peasant life was happier and morally healthier, at least for others. It is this that the *Georgics* advocated, its idealism signalized by the astonishing absence of any reference to slavery; and the districts Virgil knew best, the Po valley and the surroundings of Naples, happened to be ones in which the small-holder (*colonus*) still flourished. The attunement of the *Georgics* to future Augustan policy was more moral than agricultural. Nor need we press the words 'your behest, no easy one, Maecenas' (3.41):[1] whatever encouragement may have come from the statesman, its inspiration is clearly literary and personal: it was a labour of love – *singula dum* capti *circumuectamur* amore 'while enthralled by love we are transported from one thing to another' (3.289).

---

[1] See van de Woestijne (1929) 523–30.

24

The poem deals with husbandry in four books – on Crops, Trees, Beasts and Bees. It occupied Virgil till 29 B.C. The set pieces with which it is diversified, though integral to the overall poetic design, seem mostly to have been worked up last. Thus the proem (1.1–42) addresses Caesar (Octavian) as now supreme; the epilogue (4.559–62) and the encomium of Italy (2.136–76) refer to his eastern campaign during the winter of 30/29 (2.170–2); the proem to Book 3 anticipates his triple Triumph of August 29 (ll. 26–36); the encomium of country life (2.458–540) has references that would be topical then (ll. 495–8), and the description of the Corycian's garden (4.116–48) proclaims itself as late in its opening lines. Suetonius tells how Virgil, aided by Maecenas, read the completed poem to Caesar on his return to Italy in the summer of 29.[1]

2. LITERARY ANTECEDENTS

In the *Eclogues* Virgil had established himself as the Roman Theocritus. He had shown an interest in country life to be expected of the son of the Mantuan farm, a concern for evicted peasants in 9 and 1, and for the revival of agriculture in 5. But his singing herdsmen are inhabitants of a 'soft primitive' Arcady of the imagination. He next aspired to be the Roman Hesiod, Hesiod being another poet who had appealed to the Alexandrianizing 'modernists',[2] to 'sing a song of Ascra through Roman towns' (2.176). There are in Book 1 some obvious superficial reminders of Hesiod's *Works and days*, but otherwise his chief relevance is more general, by his insistence on the moral value of relentless hard work performed by the small farmer *ipse manu*.

Another favourite of the Alexandrians and their 'neoteric' followers was Aratus. Virgil, always adept at transfiguring what was suggestive in inferior poets, made much poetic capital out of his *Weather-signs* in 1.351–468. More generally, his attribution of phenomena to divine providence may owe something to Aratus. There is further evidence of specific influence at 2.536–42; the onset of the Iron Age is marked, as in Aratus (*Phaenomena* 127, 132), by the departure of Justice (in Hesiod it was Aidos and Nemesis) and the impious innovation of eating meat (oxen). Even the dry Hellenistic versifier Nicander is laid under contribution, his extant work at 3.391 and 425; and Quintilian (10.1.56) is our authority for thinking that more was owed to his *Georgics* (of which his poem on *Bee-keeping* may possibly have been a part).

But by far the greatest poetical influence, directly and indirectly, was

[1] Suet. *Virg.* 25, 27. We may suppose that Virgil began to study for the *Georgics* well before 36, even if we do not accept J. Bayet's theory (1930) that he composed Book 1 as a Hesiodic entity in 39–37, and then added 2–4 under the stimulus of Varro's prose treatise in dialogue *Res rusticae*, which appeared in 37/6.

[2] '*Neoteroi*'. At *Eclogue* 6.64–71 Gallus, consecrated as poet by Linus, receives as a gift from the Muses of Helicon the pipe they had once given to Hesiod.

Lucretius, whose *De rerum natura* appeared when Virgil was at school. Lucretius would show him how a didactic poem could be moving by its descriptive power and its moral-philosophic fervour. Many passages show specific influence, whether they agree, as in detestation of war, or disagree, as on Stoic providence against Epicurean fortuity in the universe.[1] The attraction of poet for poet is stronger than any difference of mentality and temperament:

> felix qui potuit rerum cognoscere causas...
> fortunatus et ille deos qui nouit agrestis.   (2.490, 493)

Happy the man who has been able to find out the causes of things... Fortunate too is he who has found the gods of the countryside.

Scientific sources

As for agricultural lore, many of Virgil's possible sources are lost.[2] But he clearly used Theophrastus for Book 2, Aristotle for 3 and 4. No Roman would disregard Cato's extant *De agri cultura*, of which we find traces. But paramount was Varro's *Res rusticae*, which appeared in 37/6, just when he was starting work. This dialogue had literary pretensions, and may have suggested certain literary features, such as the opening invocation to twelve gods (cf. Varro 1.4–6). It certainly influenced some technical passages. But above all it is a standing reminder that for any Roman farmer who, *ignarus uiae*, needed technical advice there were real handbooks available, far fuller than the *Georgics*. Those who praise Virgil's knowledge of husbandry should recollect that, while he gives the impression of being a keen countryman, his knowledge may always be second-hand, and that he sometimes gives advice which first-hand knowledge would have precluded. This opens the whole question of the intention and nature of the poem.

3. INTENTION AND NATURE OF THE POEM

Seneca (*Epist.* 86.15) said pertinently that Virgil was interested in what could be said most gracefully (*decentissime*), not most truthfully (*uerissime*), and wrote not to teach farmers but to delight readers. Even Hesiod had tempered didactic with descriptive as well as narrative set-pieces (e.g. winter and summer, *Works and days* 504–35, 582–96) and endowed it with moral import. In Lucretius the scientifically didactic had to be exhaustive to validate his message, but it is blended with descriptive and moral-philosophical elements to form a whole of cosmic imagination. In Virgil the technically didactic matter is eclectic, yet it forms too large a part of the poem for it to be taken as purely symbolic. Addison may supplement Seneca: 'this kind of poem addresses itself wholly to the

---

[1] See also *Ecl.* 6.33ff.; *Aen.* 6.724ff.
[2] On Virgil's sources, scientific and literary, see Büchner (1955) 305–9.

imagination... It raises in our minds a pleasing variety of Scenes and Landskips whilst it teaches us... We find our Imaginations more affected by the descriptions than they would have been by the very sight of what he describes.' Hellenistic writers had delighted in passages of description (*ekphrasis*), and Hellenistic landscape-painting was ubiquitous in Roman houses. The *Georgics* can be seen as the first poem in which the descriptive element (largely embodied in precept form) is the prime source of pleasure. Yet it is much more; for it uses teaching about husbandry to convey the essence of a way of life, hard and sometimes tragic, but regular and often rewarding. In the shameful darkness of contemporary Rome and Italy it shines a ray of hope and pride. But it is also representative of human life in general, with its rewards as well as its toil and with intimations of divine presences and paternal providence. Selective variety, another Hellenistic trait, and ingenious artistic structure sustain the whole.

4. STRUCTURE

In the case of a poem whose excellence depends on a variety of features the best, perhaps the only, way of doing justice to it is by a running commentary, in terms of structure. To several sensitive critics the *Georgics* has suggested a musical composition, a symphony with four movements and various themes enunciated and then harmoniously interwoven.[1] It falls into pairs of books, each pair having an 'external' proem. The first and third books emphasize the struggle against degeneration, disease and death and are generally sombre in tone; the second and fourth deal by contrast with work that is easier, are mainly cheerful, and end happily. But these are only crude generalizations: the modulations of mood are much subtler.

After a neatly economical summary of contents, addressed to Maecenas, the proem bursts into a breathless, grand-style invocation of agricultural deities (twelve, a canonical number), followed by a balancing invocation, in the exaggerated 'baroque' style of Hellenistic adulation, of the coming god Caesar (1–42). (Modern readers may find this distasteful; but ancient ones, familiar with the convention, and at that historical moment, will have taken it in their stride.) Then begins, with spring, a long section on field crops (43–203). At once the Hesiodic theme of hard work emerges. Ploughing slips insensibly into study of local differences of soil, thence to the picturesque variety of products of foreign lands, and so, by 'ring composition', a device as old as Hesiod, back again to ploughing in early spring (of rich land only – poorer must be ploughed in autumn: 63–70). So far, in twenty-eight lines since the proem, we have had four precepts only, but a vivid, pictorial impression of continual work. The

---

[1] The structure of the *Georgics* has been given a new dimension in the criticism of Burck (1929), Büchner (1955), Klingner (1963) and Otis (1963). See further Wilkinson (1969), Ch. IV.

mention of poorer soil leads into soil-improvement. The foreign lands theme is heard again, and two new ones emerge – religion (prayer for good weather and Ceres' help for him who helps himself) and the military metaphor of subduing the fields (71–117).

Injurious birds, weeds and shade, which impose a constant struggle, are the cue for an important and controversial philosophic passage (188–59), a theodicy. 'The Father himself did not want the path of husbandry to be easy, and introduced the skills of agriculture, sharpening the wits of mortals by cares.' The 'soft primitivism' of Golden Age mythology is rejected in favour of a Stoic solution of the problem of evil and justification of the ways of God to men. Rapidly Virgil reviews the consequent achievements of man's inventiveness, in a passage which ends with the famous words

labor omnia uicit
improbus, et duris urgens in rebus egestas.   (145–6)

Wicked toil has mastered everything, and the pressure of pinching poverty.

Improbus is always a pejorative epithet, and some critics take this conclusion to be wholly pessimistic.[1] But does it represent Virgil's reaction or that of the toiler? The recital of man's achievements is reminiscent of Prometheus' recital in Aeschylus (*Prom. Bound* 458–522) of the inventions he has taught man, but Virgil has boldly transferred Prometheus' role to Jupiter himself. One may feel that to him, as to Lucretius also (5.1361–78, 1448–57), the arts that give variety to life are worth the struggle involved. (*Varius* is a key-word that constantly recurs throughout the poem, see p. 27.) This passage, thus placed early, separates Jupiter from the conventional agricultural deities of the proem as the monotheistic Zeus of the Stoics, and sets the philosophical tone of the whole. With the passing of the easy Golden Age, the institution of ploughing, and more about the invasion of birds, weeds, and shade, the paragraph is rounded off – 'ring-composition' again.

The metaphorical warfare requires arms, which follow (160–75), some implements merely listed, some dignified with epithets recalling the mystic agricultural rites of Eleusis, with the making of a plough finally described in Hesiodic detail (*uariatio*). Divers detailed precepts follow (176–99), with a discernible train of thought-association, till the vivid simile (199–203) of a man rowing against the current and only just managing not to be swept away sums up a section whose theme has been relentless toil. It is a law of nature that everything tends to degenerate; but Virgil slips in at 168 a reminder of the reward for defeating the tendency – *diuini gloria ruris* 'the glory of a divine countryside'.

'Days' follow 'Works': a balancing section (204–350) deals with the

---

[1] E.g. Altevogt (1952).

farmer's calendar. Passages on the rising and setting of constellations as signals to him, and on the five zones of the earth, raise incidental thoughts (*idcirco* 231, *munere concessae diuum* 238) of the Providence that has ordered the universe for man with such signals and two habitable zones (204–58). Miscellaneous precepts follow for making good use of every moment, even winter nights and days of religious festival – though these give relaxation also (259–310). A spectacular descriptive passage of a storm at harvest-time is here introduced, ostensibly to remind the farmer to observe the signs and seasons and to propitiate the gods – a festival of Ceres (a synthetic one, it seems[1]) affords relief (311–50). The storm provides a natural lead into the next section, the Weather Signs, established by 'the Father himself'. Virgil draws freely on Aratus, though with much more picturesque detail; but he reverses his order so that the sun comes last as a sign-giver (351–463). He is thus able to lead, by way of the portents allegedly shown by it at the time of Julius Caesar's murder, into a tremendous rhetorical finale on other portents of that time, and an appeal to the old indigenous gods of Rome to allow the young Caesar to rescue an age careering to ruin (463–514).

Book 2 opens contrastingly with a short, cheering invocation to Bacchus, god of all trees but especially the vine (1–8). (The address to Maecenas, which every book contains, is deferred to 39–46.) The first main section (9–258) illustrates, and is sustained by, variety, with special reference to trees[2] – variety in methods (nine) of tree-propagation (9–82), variety of trees, and of vines in particular, which give occasion for a connoisseur's list of Greek and Italian wines (83–108). A passage on the different products of various lands (109–35) prepares for a rhetorical encomium of the all-producing land of Italy (136–76; cf. Varro 1.2.6), a famous passage in which pride in the (somewhat idealized) fertility, variety and beauty of the 'Saturnian' land (Saturn ruled in the Golden Age) mingles with pride in the men of Rome and their achievements. (This Romano-Italian patriotism, dating from the end of the Social War sixty years before, was to be an essential part of Augustanism, as in the latter part of the *Aeneid*.) The passage is in key with Book 2 by contrast with the finale of Book 1, where *squalent abductis arua colonis* 'the fields are unkempt, their tillers taken away' (508).

Abruptly, so as not to blur his climax, Virgil restarts at ground level, giving technical details about various soils and what they are suited for (177–258), with glimpses (surprisingly rare in the *Georgics*) of particular localities, notably ones familiar to him near Mantua, Naples or Tarentum, in the Italy just comprehensively praised. The next section (259–457) is on planting and care of trees, especially vines. The precepts, picturesque in themselves, are diversified

---

[1] Bayet (1955).

[2] The book can be seen as comprising three main parts, 9–258, 259–457, 458–542; alternatively, with Richter (1957), four: 9–126 variety in the production of trees; 177–345 nature and testing of soil, and planting; 346–457 work for the growth and protection of the plants; 458–542 finale.

by the simile of a legion drawn up for battle (279–85), the description of a great oak (291–7), and of a plantation fire (303–11), and the soaring paean on spring (322–45). The damage done by the goat, for which it is sacrificed to Bacchus, gives occasion for a description of the festival of Compitalia (380–96), corresponding to that of Ceres in Book 1 but in this case idealized by the introduction of Greek elements (for this is literature, not documentary).[1] It is important to realize that religion in the *Georgics* is more Greek than Italian.[2] (To see their life-scene in the light of their knowledge of Greek life and literature was peculiarly exciting to Romans, just as post-Renaissance Europeans loved to invest the present with classical trappings.) Other trees need less care than vines, and are treated in a light-hearted passage that ranges far and wide over the world (420–57).

The tone is thus set for the famous finale, the encomium of country life (458–542), which consummates the optimism of Book 2 by contrast with the finale that consummates the pessimism of Book 1. It is fine rhetoric on a conventional theme, even if the idyllic and Golden Age colouring belies the emphasis in Book 1, and particularly in the theodicy there, on the necessity for unremitting toil. Lines 495–512 are Lucretian-style satire on the hectic, immoral life of the metropolis, juxtaposed most effectively, through the sudden, asyndetic peace of the spondaic line, *agricola incuruo terram dimouit aratro* 'the farmer has gone on cleaving his land with the curved plough', to an enthusiastic description of the regular, moral life of the country, with its constant round of produce and pleasures, the life that in the past made Rome great.

Book 3 opens with a proem (1–48) in which Virgil speaks of his poetic intentions. The central portion (10–40) reveals a remarkable symbolic vision. Apparently with Pindar in mind, he imagines himself as both victor and master of ceremonies at games to be held at his native Mantua, whither he has led the Muses in triumph from Helicon. There he will build by the Mincius a temple to Caesar, with his cult-statue placed in the midst. (No doubt he was thinking of the temple of Divus Iulius which Caesar, who must here be Octavian, was shortly to dedicate, as well as the temple of Zeus by the Alpheus at Olympia and the Pindaric metaphor of building a temple of song.) Then, adopting another Pindaric metaphor, that of the chariot of song, already introduced at the close of the previous book, he says he will cause a hundred chariots to race by the river, and divert all Greece from Olympia and Nemea to these Mantuan competitions. He himself will lead the procession to sacrifice and also stage plays (a feature of Roman, not Greek, games). On the doors of the temple (here he may have had in mind another temple then rising, that of Palatine Apollo) he will have carvings descriptive or symbolic of Caesar's victories in the East, and there will be statues of the Trojan ancestors of Rome and Apollo the founder of

---

[1] Meuli (1955).   [2] Wissowa (1917) 98–9.

Troy. Caesar himself has now become the Triumphator, as he was shortly to be in reality. At 41, dropping the symbolism, Virgil intimates that he means to finish the *Georgics* and then soon gird himself to immortalize Caesar's battles. The most astonishing thing about this passage is the way in which the shy son of a Mantuan farmer, emboldened by Pindar, dares to represent himself as triumphant in poetry just as Caesar is in war, already the laureate of Augustanism. The quasi-deification of Caesar in the present is a feature of the enthusiasm of the first year or two after Actium (cf. 1.42; Horace, *Odes* 1.2 fin.): later Caesar himself was to enjoin more caution.

Seu quis Olympiacae – the train of thought from the proem to horses is clear in the opening of the first of two roughly-equal parts that constitute Book 3 – 49–283 on horses and cattle, the rest on sheep and goats. The pessimistic lines 66–8 on the swift fading of youth set the tone: as in Book 1, toil and trouble are again the burden. Sex and death emerge as dominant themes, with disease and age between (49–156). We read of the selection of breeding-stock in cattle and horses and the rearing of their young (157–208). There follows a passage on the power of sex, something that Virgil clearly regards as dangerous and debilitating, however necessary for procreation (209–83). The description of the battle between two bulls for a beautiful cow and the the come-back made by the defeated rival (215–41) moves us as Virgil's anthropomorphism so often does. Lust is indeed a madness (*furor*) common to all living things; and in a passage of headlong intensity (242–83) he instances its ravages, with humans represented by 'the youth' (Leander, but he is not named, thus seeming representative of all) who to come to his love set out even on a night of terrible storm to swim a strait, to his destruction and hers.

From the horror of this climax Virgil recalls himself to a new section, on the care of sheep and goats in winter and summer (284–338), humdrum matters which he resolves nevertheless, as a pioneer inspired by Lucretian enthusiasm, to dignify in verse (284–94). It is graced by an idyllic passage on pasturage at the first coming of spring (322–38), and a sketch of the nomad shepherds of Libya (339–48) and a longer one by way of contrast, on life in the frozen north (349–83). All this is descriptive poetry at its best. After further precepts (384–413) we come to the prevention and treatment of diseases (414–69), and hence to a great Lucretian-style finale (470–566), corresponding to the climactic passage on sex that ends the first part, and on a larger scale to the finale of Book 1 – a horrific description of a plague in the Nordic lands beneath the Alps which involved humans ultimately as well as animals in desolation and death. The horror is heightened by the fact that here, by contrast with other passages, the idea of providence is forgotten. Indeed the plague robs the gods of their rites. Once again, overall balance and poetic effectiveness seem to mean more to Virgil than consistency.

Book 4 transports us from this miasma to the 'heavenly gifts of airy honey' and the wonderful spectacle of the bees' world (1–7). A mock-heroic note is struck immediately with *magnanimosque duces* 'great-hearted leaders', and 'this play of great and small' is a feature of the first section of the book (8–115), especially in the battle-scene (67–85), which is brought to an end with the ironical curtain-lines, 'These upheavals of heart and these prodigious contests the throwing of a little handful of dust will reduce to quiescence.' The battle is between two kings (few ancients realized that the leader is queen, and also mother, of the hive) and their supporters, and the contrast between the superior and the inferior (88–102), both vividly described – the latter to be killed that the former may rule alone – is highly reminiscent of what was being said about Caesar and Antony by Caesarian propaganda at the time when the *Georgics* was being completed. Critics are divided as to whether any such application is intended.

In this section, dealing with settling, swarming, fighting, selection and swarming-fever, the bees are treated thus in an almost patronizing, half-humorous way. Apparently to mark off a change in approach Virgil here inserts a sketch for a garden Georgic he has no time to write, a description of a flourishing garden with apiary he once saw near Tarentum, made out of a small piece of unwanted land by an old immigrant from Corycus in Cilicia (166–48). The next section (149–227) deals with the peculiar *mores* of bees, a special gift to them from Jupiter – communism even as to children, loyalty to their homes and its laws, pooling of gains and division of labour, propagation without sexual intercourse (another vulgar error), readiness to sacrifice their life for the community, and finally, utter devotion to their ruler. It is clear that, to some extent, they are now being idealized. The passage is the obverse of those on anti-social behaviour at Rome in the finale of Book 1 and sexual lust in Book 3. It breathes the purer air of Augustan idealism. The section culminates (219–27) in a reference to a theory held by some, that bees have a share in divine intelligence, which merges into a wider theory, that of Platonic–Stoic pantheism Here Virgil only attributes this to 'certain people'; but that he was sympathetic to it himself is suggested by the fact that at *Aeneid* 6.729ff. he makes Anchises state it as fact.

Further precepts, about harvesting honey, are followed by short passages on pests, diseases and their remedies (239–80). This leads us on into the method of replacing an extinguished hive known as *bugonia*, a vulgar error countenanced by all ancient authorities known to us except Aristotle: from the carcase of an animal rightly treated, bees would appear by spontaneous generation. Virgil's version prescribes shutting up a bull-calf in a small specially constructed chamber amid aromatic branches and beating it to death without breaking the hide, then blocking up the natural orifices – presumably to keep in the life principle, which could thus pass into the emergent bees (281–314). Varro began his account of bees with *bugonia* (3.16.4); Virgil kept it till last, both logically and to prepare for the grand finale of the poem, an *aition* attributing its origin to the hero Aristaeus (315–558). The episode constitutes what we know as an epyllion (other extant examples in Latin are Catullus' 'Peleus and Thetis' and the pseudo-Virgilian *Ciris*), a short epic with a different, but in some sense relevant, story inset. Aristaeus, for the crime of causing Eurydice's death (she trod on a snake while fleeing from his embraces), lost all his bees. He had recourse to his divine mother Cyrene, who advised him to consult Proteus (315–414). Proteus when finally captured explained that he was being punished, and why, telling him also how Orpheus went down to the underworld and was retrieving Eurydice when he lost her again through disobediently looking back at her (415–527). Cyrene is then able to instruct him how to placate Eurydice's companions, the Nymphs, by sacrificing four bulls. He does so, and nine days later new bees are born from their carcases (528–58).

What function has this epyllion, a superb masterpiece in itself, in the poetic scheme of the poem (assuming that it was not a later substitute: see Excursus below)? Certainly the miracle of *bugonia* would have seemed a suitable climax to bee-lore. A finale was then needed, a set-piece to surpass even those that concluded the other books. *Aitia* (origins) were a favourite subject, and epyllia a favourite form of the Alexandrians in whose tradition Virgil was reared. Aristaeus, famous as pioneer of beekeeping, would be the obvious originator. It may be that there is no more to be said. But some modern critics are naturally loth to believe that Virgil, so careful over the structure of the rest of the poem, would have ended with a passage of some 244 lines that had little relevance to it. And what of the inset Orpheus story? So far as we know, Virgil was the first to connect Orpheus with Aristaeus, and the first to make him lose Eurydice through looking back because of overpowering love. He must have had some reason. These critics have therefore advanced symbolic interpretations of various kinds extending from the epyllion to the whole work (see Excursus). How convincing these are found, must depend on the individual reader's sense of probability in the context of what we know of ancient modes of thought. The propounders in turn may understandably be dissatisfied with the sceptic's explanation, or lack of one.

EXCURSUS

Servius twice indicates that the finale of Book 4 was, all or in part, a substitute: on *Eclogue* 10.1 he says that Book 4 from the middle to the end contained the praises of Gallus, which afterwards Virgil changed at the bidding of Augustus to the story of *Aristaeus*; while on *Georgics* 4.1 he says that the praises of Gallus stood in the place now occupied by the story of *Orpheus* (the inset portion ll. 453–527), which was inserted after the anger of Augustus led to Gallus' death. (Gallus, made first Prefect of Egypt in 30, was accused in 27 of treason and committed suicide.) 'Orpheus' here must surely be a slip for 'Aristaeus'; but Servius can often be convicted of fallacious concoction, and the story, mentioned by no one else, is dubious. For this is a public poem, and Gallus, though a close friend of Virgil, was less important than his patron Maecenas, let alone Caesar. How, with either political or poetic propriety, could it have ended with some 250 lines in his praise? The weight of scholarly opinion, despite some authoritative exceptions,[1] seems to have shifted towards accepting the original presence of the Aristaeus epyllion, and it has been assumed here. Nevertheless the origin of Servius' story remains a puzzle. Eight lines on Egypt (287–94) as the scene of bugonia occur in the transitional passage. Our text has been dislocated here, and a few lines about its new Prefect Gallus may have been removed through *damnatio memoriae*. Some tradition about this may have misled Servius or a predecessor to concoct the more drastic story.

As to possible applications of the Aristaeus epyllion to the poem as a whole, some have concentrated on the Orpheus episode. Orpheus figures as the enchanter of nature by his song, and also as centre of mystery cults of agrarian origin (Scazzoso, 1956, 5–28). The Mysteries *may* lie behind this episode, but the connexion of Orpheus with Aristaeus and of the epyllion with the rest of the poem is still not clearly explained. Some have suggested that Orpheus stood for Gallus, or that the epyllion was a substitute as a poem about tragic love of the kind he wrote, and so a veiled tribute to him (Coleman (1962) 55–71). But would this not have been seen as a reprehensible breach of *damnatio memoriae*?

J. Bayet (1930, 246–7) suggested that, whereas the theme of Book 3 was love and the Triumph of Death, that of 4 was chastity and the Triumph of Life; while Duckworth (1959, 225–37) characterized the ends of the four books as emphasizing respectively war, peace, death and rebirth. More comprehensive theories were put forward in 1963 by F. Klingner and B. Otis. Klingner (234ff.) interpreted the epyllion as a unity of opposites expressing Virgil's deepest intuitions, integrating two stories of newly granted and ever renewed life and of life passionately resought, almost regained, and then lost with utter finality. The life of the individual was fraught with pain, tragedy and death; but life is also the all-pervading and joyfully stirring spirit of life, which gives and takes back all individual life, so that, universally speaking, 'there is no room for death'. Klingner is, in fact, connecting the epyllion with the pantheistic views attributed to *quidam* (pl.) at 4.219–27. Disease and death for man and beast, represented in Book 3 without redemption, are redeemed and absorbed into a higher divine order (cf. Anchises' speech at *Aeneid* 6.724–51). Otis (186) also sees in ll. 219–27 'a theological idea to be set against the death-dealing nature of the second half of III'. To him the myth of the epyllion is the ultimate synthesis (in a different mode) of all the poet has been saying. 'We cannot understand the poem finally until we have understood the actual conclusion, its conception of the moral *cause* and *origin* of resurrection' (189). All the antitheses in the poem are resolved 'when man, exercising his full moral powers of control, work, self-sacrifice and devotion to his *patria*, finds himself sup-

---

[1] The case against Servius was revived in modern times notably by Anderson (1933) and independently Norden (1934). His more recent supporters include Büchner (1955) 294–7, de Saint-Denis (1956) and Richter (1957). Büchner suggests that Gallus was praised here as the elegiac poet of love. Richter (12–13) deduces that the *Georgics* cannot have been published until 26/5, after Gallus' death, so that the original Gallus passage was never published.

ported by the *logos* and indwelling spirit of the whole cosmos' (213). Otis well observes that the Orpheus section contrasts with the rest in that Virgil deals 'empathetically' with him, objectively with Aristaeus. C. Segal (1966), starting from this contrast, carried the symbolical interpretation to more complex depths. The Aristaeus episode is *necessary* to complete the *Georgics* because

> it ties together...the delicate and complicated relations between human activism and nature's resistance or acquiescence, between human destructiveness and nature's creativeness (or the reverse), between man's power over nature and nature's power over man. Human life, framed between the two figures (Aristaeus and Orpheus) is *essentially* tragic. And here emerges the significance of the first half of the Book, the bees: instead of collectivity selflessly devoted to the *genus immortale* we have in the second part individuals engaged in the personal emotions almost to the exclusion of anything else.

Explanation on these lines was persuasively reformulated by J. Griffin (1979). The bees' totalitarian kingdom, so admirable in its way, involves nevertheless tragic conflict in terms of human individuality, represented by juxtaposition in the story of Orpheus. This conflict was to permeate Virgil's treatment of the story of Rome and Aeneas.

Such interpretations are hard to summarize, let alone summarize fairly. Their diversity suggests that others will be produced. For a short summary of views on the Aristaeus epyllion down to 1969 see Wilkinson, 111–20 and Appendix IV of that publication.

5. OTHER POETIC FEATURES

A synopsis such as that given in the previous section may convey what the poem is *about*, but it can only begin to convey why it is *good*. Its merits are as multifarious as its subject matter. As to verse, the individual hexameter is that of the *Eclogues*, but much less often self-contained. Although, after the preliminary invocations (two headlong Lucretian periods of nineteen lines each), the sentences are rarely long, they have acquired impetus because the breaks within the line occur at such a variety of positions. The balanced 'Golden Line', overworked by Catullus, is reserved almost exclusively for rounding off a sentence, sometimes to great effect, as in

> impiaque aeternam timuerunt saecula noctem.   (1.468)

and an impious age feared that eternal night had come.

The rhetorical figures too are effectively but not obtrusively employed. Virgil's ear is faultless. In general he keeps his sound harmonious, with assonance and alliteration used discreetly; but he is still more distinguished for the expressiveness of sound and rhythm accommodated to sense, as can be observed particularly in the storm and the weather-signs in Book 1.[1] This greatly enhances the pictorial

---

[1] For expressiveness in *Georgics* 1.43–293 see Wilkinson (1963) 74–83.

quality so important in the poem. So does his habit of describing in terms of action. Thus where Varro says that a cow's tail should reach to her heels, Virgil says, 'and as she walks she sweeps her tracks with the tip of her tail' (3.59). Everything is seen in human terms. The plane-tree planted is 'destined to provide shade for drinkers'. The general tendency to anthropomorphize nature, especially animals, imparts vitality; and where men are concerned he shows that *humanitas*, sympathetic understanding, which is one of his chief characteristics.

6. TRANSITION TO THE AENEID

In the eight-line epilogue (4.559–66), as in the proem to Book 3, Virgil boldly presents himself alongside Caesar, this time by way of playfully ironical contrast: while Caesar has been thundering on the Euphrates, dealing laws to willing peoples and qualifying for immortality, he himself has been composing this kind of poetry at Naples, 'flourishing in the pursuits of inactive obscurity'. At the end of the proem to 3 he undertakes that, when he has finished the *Georgics*, he will sing of Caesar's battles. Though Rome's Trojan origins are emphasized by the statues of *Tros parens* and the line of Assaracus that are to stand in his imaginary temple, the idea of the *Aeneid* has not yet taken shape. He only knows that what he composes next will be epic of some kind inspired by the Caesarian revival of Rome's greatness.

4

THE *AENEID*

Virgil's *Aeneid* was conceived and shaped as a national and patriotic epic for the Romans of his day. Certainly the Romans hailed it as such, and it rapidly became both a set text in education and the natural successor to the *Annales* of Ennius as the great poetic exposition of Roman ideals and achievements. As will be seen later on, there are discordant elements in the patriotic theme, but it is essential to recognize that Virgil's primary intention was to sing of his country's glories past and present, and of the greatness yet to come. For all his universality he is a true Augustan.

For many years Virgil had been preparing himself for this crowning achievement of poetic ambition. The Romans regarded the epic poem as the highest form of literature, a form constantly refused by Horace and Propertius as too heavy for their frail shoulders. There is a passage in the *Eclogues* where Virgil himself says that his thoughts were beginning to turn towards epic, but he was rebuked by Apollo, god of poetry:

> cum canerem reges et proelia, Cynthius aurem
> uellit et admonuit: 'pastorem, Tityre, pinguis
> pascere oportet ouis, deductum dicere carmen.'   (*Ecl.* 6.3–5)

When I was going to sing of kings and battles, the god of Cynthus plucked my ear and chided me: 'Tityrus, a shepherd should feed his sheep to grow fat but sing a song that is slender.'

In his comment on the passage Servius tells us that this refers either to the *Aeneid*, or to the deeds of the kings of Alba Longa, which Virgil had begun to write about, but had abandoned the project because the names were unmanageable. Donatus (*Vita* 19) has the statement that Virgil began a Roman theme, but finding the material uncongenial went over to pastoral instead. We cannot be sure that these interpretations are correct, as the Virgilian passage may be a conventional 'refusal' (*recusatio*) of the Alexandrian type,[1] but it is quite certain that a few years later Virgil was indeed planning and preparing himself for the

---

[1] See Clausen (1964) 181ff. and above, p. 21.

heroic poem that would celebrate Rome's greatness. At the beginning of
Georgics 3 he speaks of his future poetic ambitions – he will not write on the
well-worn themes of Greek mythology, but will dedicate a special temple of
song in Mantua, his birthplace. In the midst of his temple will be Caesar
Augustus, with triumphal processions from all parts of the world offering their
tributes: Trojan ancestors of the race of Assaracus along with Apollo the patron
god of Troy will be present in the great concourse of Roman majesty. This is
a clear prolepsis of the *Aeneid*, with the Trojan connexion of the Romans in
general and the Julian *gens* in particular well to the fore. Evidently at this time
Virgil's ideas were already focused on the two extremes of the time-scale of the
Aeneid – the dramatic date which is the period immediately after the Trojan war,
and the symbolic date which is the Augustan age, of which so much in the
Aeneid is prototype and anticipation.

The eventual choice of Virgil's epic subject was becoming clearer in his mind
while he was writing the *Georgics*. He rejects the mythology of Greece; the
reason he gives is that it has become trite, but a deeper reason can clearly be
seen, namely that to satisfy him his subject had to be Roman. He did not wish
to write about the Argonauts (the theme of his later imitator Valerius Flaccus),
nor about the Seven against Thebes (on which Statius wrote a century later),
because his deepest poetic inclinations were rooted in Rome and Italy, the
country of which his own Cisalpine Gaul had only recently become a part,
which he already loved for the natural beauty of its farmlands and mountains
and was soon to love also for its imperial message of peace and civilization for
the world. But he decided too that direct historical writing or contemporary
panegyric would confine his sensitivity for the universal application, would clip
the wings of poetic symbolism; and so he left the panegyrics of Augustus to the
prose-writers, and the historical theme to the Silver Age poets Lucan and Silius
Italicus. He chose instead a subject which was national, yet shrouded in the mists
of legend; a subject capable of readjustment to suit his poetical purpose; a
theme which was well known but flexible, not unlike our King Arthur story
before it received its more definitive shape from Malory. The theme was the
foundation by the Trojan prince Aeneas of Lavinium in Latium: from here
Aeneas' son Ascanius (also called Iulus, as founder of the Julian *gens*) would
move to Alba Longa, and three hundred years later Romulus would transfer the
settlement to Rome. The voyage of Aeneas to Hesperia, the western land, was
destined by the gods so that a new city should replace the ruins of Troy; the
theme of destiny, the theme of the responsibility of Aeneas to fulfil the will of
the gods, is dominant throughout the whole poem, and is perhaps the major
point in which the *Aeneid* differs from its Homeric models. References to the
legend can be traced as far back as the sixth century B.C., but it was evidently in
the third century B.C. (as Rome began to expand into the Greek world) that the

story became well known and more fully developed (as for example in Lyco-
phron's *Alexandra*); by the time of Naevius and Ennius it had become a special
part of Rome's prehistory.[1]

The methods which Virgil used to connect this ancient legend with his
modern world were diverse and subtle: the double time-scale gave him many
opportunities both to universalize the particular, and to describe the past as an
essential ingredient in the present and the future. His love for the old Italian
virtues, prototypes of what he admired in his own times, is expressed very fully
in the catalogue of the warriors in 7.647f., prefixed as it is by an appeal to the
Muse to tell of the glories of the distant past:

> ...quibus Itala iam tum
> floruerit terra alma uiris, quibus arserit armis;
> et meministis enim, diuae, et memorare potestis;
> ad nos uix tenuis famae perlabitur aura. (7.643–6)

tell of the heroes by whose qualities the mother-land of Italy even then was glorious,
tell of the martial ardour she had; for, goddesses, you remember and can tell, but to us
barely does a faint breath of the story come through.

Aetiological allusions, so much a part of Alexandrian literature, are frequent:
sometimes these are based directly on place-names (Segesta, 5.718; Misenus,
6.234; Palinurus, 6.381; Caieta, 7.3); sometimes on family names (Iulus,
1.288; Mnestheus, 5.117; Atys, 5.568); sometimes on contemporary buildings
(6.69; 8.338) or contemporary institutions (3.278ff., 3.443ff., 5.59ff., 5.602).
By means of dreams and prophecies, and devices such as the description of
Aeneas' shield, later historical events enter the narrative (1.267ff., 6.756ff.,
8.626ff.). Above all the values of the Augustan world are foreshadowed as
Aeneas learns to leave the Trojan world of heroic and impetuous daring
and inaugurate the Roman world of forethought, duty, responsibility
(*pietas*).

Another method of allusion which links the past with the present is that of
allegory and symbolism. Virgil's allegory is beneath the surface, suggestive
rather than precise; the story of Dido is coloured by our thoughts of Cleopatra;
we may think of Augustus and Antony when Aeneas and Turnus come to their
final confrontation; but the method is always oblique and unexplicit. Similarly
symbolism is often present beneath the actual narrative: Hercules acts as an
exemplum of that endurance which must be shown by Aeneas and by Augustus
as they face their labours; the description of Atlas in 4.246ff. offers a symbol of
duritia; the contests in the funeral games in Book 5 illustrate some of the
characteristics which can prevail in the sterner context of real life. Again and
again the story of the events of long ago carries undertones, presents a kind of

---

[1] For further discussion and references see R. D. Williams (1962) Intro. 7ff.

penumbra of allusion which enriches and adds to the density and universality of the legend, so that Virgil could extend its significance from the heroic days of Troy to his own contemporary world.

What were the reasons which led Virgil to wish to extol Augustan Rome by symbolizing its trials and achievements in the person of its first founder? The ancient commentators were clear that this was his purpose, and, although it will be argued later that other purposes came more and more to the fore as the composition of the poem proceeded, their view was basically right. Servius says (at the beginning of his commentary on the *Aeneid*): 'Virgil's intention is to imitate Homer and to praise Augustus by means of his ancestors'; in Donatus (*Vita* 21) we are told that Virgil's special interest in the subject of the *Aeneid* was that it would contain the origin of the city of Rome and of Augustus; finally Tiberius Claudius Donatus (*Prooem. Aen.* 1) says 'his task was to depict Aeneas as a worthy first ancestor of Augustus, in whose honour the poem was written'. What reasons would Virgil have for regarding Rome under Augustus as the proper subject for his *magnum opus*?

First and foremost he had lived his life in a period of disastrous and appalling civil war, a period in which all that Rome had achieved through the long centuries of her history appeared likely to vanish in carnage and confusion. The wars of Marius and Sulla were succeeded by the struggle for power between Pompey and Caesar, culminating in the invasion of Italy by Caesar and his Gallic veterans. Pitched battles followed in which Roman fought Roman: the victory of Caesar was annulled by his assassination, and the power struggle broke out again, first with Antony and Octavian against Brutus and Cassius, and then with Antony and Octavian jockeying for power against each other, with the remnants of the Republican party of Pompey still threatening both of them. The sense of guilt felt by the Romans is powerfully expressed by Virgil himself at the end of the first *Georgic*:

> di patrii, Indigetes, et Romule Vestaque mater,
> quae Tuscum Tiberim et Romana Palatia seruas,
> hunc saltem euerso iuuenem succurrere saeclo
> ne prohibete. satis iam pridem sanguine nostro
> Laomedonteae luimus periuria Troiae;
> iam pridem nobis caeli te regia, Caesar,
> inuidet atque hominum queritur curare triumphos,
> quippe ubi fas uersum atque nefas; tot bella per orbem,
> tam multae scelerum facies, non ullus aratro
> dignus honos, squalent abductis arua colonis,
> et curuae rigidum falces conflantur in ensem.
> hinc mouet Euphrates, illinc Germania bellum;
> uicinae ruptis inter se legibus urbes
> arma ferunt; saeuit toto Mars impius orbe;

ut cum carceribus sese effudere quadrigae,
addunt in spatia, et frustra retinacula tendens
fertur equis auriga neque audit currus habenas. (*Geo.* 1.498–514)

Gods of our father-land, our native gods, and Romulus and mother Vesta, you who keep safe our Etruscan river Tiber and the Roman Palatine, do not forbid this young man at least from rescuing our ruined generation. Long ago now we have sufficiently atoned with our blood for the perjury of Laomedon's Troy; long ago now the palace of heaven has begrudged you to us on earth, Caesar, complaining that you are intent on mortal triumphs. For here right and wrong are interchanged: all these wars in the world, all these shapes of crime, no proper regard for the plough, the fields overgrown with their farmers taken away from them, the curved sickles beaten into steely swords. On one side Euphrates moves to war, on another Germany; neighbouring cities break their bonds of loyalty and bear weapons against each other: wicked Mars rages all over the world, just as when chariots stream forth from the starting-posts and speed on, lap after lap, while the charioteer vainly tugs at the reins but is carried on headlong by the horses and the chariot does not obey his control.

Two of Horace's *Epodes*, written at about the same time, convey the same sense of horror and guilt: *Epode* 7 and *Epode* 16.

Quo, quo scelesti ruitis? aut cur dexteris
   aptantur enses conditi?
parumne campis atque Neptuno super
   fusum est Latini sanguinis?

      . . .

furorne caecus, an rapit uis acrior?
   an culpa? responsum date!
tacent et albus ora pallor inficit
   mentesque perculsae stupent.
sic est: acerba fata Romanos agunt
   scelusque fraternae necis,
ut immerentis fluxit in terram Remi
   sacer nepotibus cruor. (*Epode* 7.1–4, 13–20)

Where are you rushing, where indeed are you rushing, men of crime? Or why are hidden swords ready in your hands? Has not enough Latin blood been shed on the land and the seas.. ? Is it blind madness or some wilder impulse that whirls you onwards, or is it sin? Answer! They give no answer, and a white pallor tinges their cheeks, and their hearts are smitten and astounded. Thus it is: bitter fate harasses the Romans, and the crime of a brother's murder, ever since the blood of guiltless Remus flowed on the ground, a curse on generations to come.

Altera iam teritur bellis ciuilibus aetas,
   suis et ipsa Roma uiribus ruit,
quam neque finitimi ualuerunt perdere Marsi,
   minacis aut Etrusca Porsenae manus,
aemula nec uirtus Capuae nec Spartacus acer
   nouisque rebus infidelis Allobrox,

nec fera caerulea domuit Germania pube
parentibusque abominatus Hannibal,
impia perdemus deuoti sanguinis aetas,
    ferisque rursus occupabitur solum.   (*Epode* 16.1–10)

Another generation is now being worn down by civil war, and Rome rushes to destruc-
tion by her own might. Her neighbours, the Marsians, could not destroy her, nor the
Etruscan forces of the threatening Porsena, nor the jealous power of Capua nor the
fierce Spartacus, nor the Allobrogians, disloyal and rebellious, nor fierce Germany
with her blue-eyed youths, nor Hannibal, a curse to our ancestors. But we, a wicked
generation of accursed blood, shall destroy her, and the ground will once again become
the habitation of wild beasts.

It is essential that these outcries should be properly understood in all their
sincerity and poignancy in order for us to appreciate properly the sense of relief
and hope which Augustus brought to a war-torn world. The outcries come from
poets who had no love for the military way of life, who wished only to gain
from war the hope that it would end war: the gentle Virgil played no part in
military activities, and Horace's role in the civil wars was undistinguished and a
subject for the poet's own mild depreciation (*Odes* 2.7). There is every reason
to suppose that many Romans felt as Virgil and Horace did, and that when they
express their gratitude to Augustus for what seemed to be a final end to this
madness they were themselves sincere and were expressing the sincere thoughts
of many of their compatriots.

For there was not only the negative achievement (the removal of violence
and bloodshed) to be greeted with joy, but also the positive prospect of a
return to what was seen as Rome's true self, a return to the *mos maiorum*, the
way of life of their ancestors. This concept was coloured by romance (as we see
very clearly from the stories in the early books of Livy) and idealized into an
idyllic vision of the simple virtues, virtues of *fides, pietas, religio, disciplina,*
constantia, grauitas. These virtues were not only embodied in the folk-lore and
early legends of Rome, but were considered to have been exemplified in the lives
of their historical heroes, men like Fabricius, Regulus, Fabius Maximus, Cato the
Censor and countless others. In addition to this they were the kind of virtues
valued most highly by contemporary Stoics,[1] and no doubt many Romans who
(like Horace) were not ardent adherents of Stoicism would have echoed the
admiration for Stoic qualities which he expresses in his Roman odes.

Upon this resurgence of hope and national pride Augustus set about building
his social and moral policy, and indeed his political stance of restoring the
Republic fitted into the scheme. He had been able to lead the Romans out of a
period of political confusion and instability into a new security, and all his
endeavours were directed to convincing the Romans that the new order was

---

[1] On Stoicism in the *Aeneid* see Bowra (1933–4) 8ff., Edwards (1960) 151ff.

nothing other than a restatement of the old order, nothing other than a restoration of the Roman state to what it had been and was by nature. He was removing alien elements which had been introduced and enabling the Romans to be their true selves again. How far this was true is another question – what seems very likely is that Augustus commanded the support of the majority of the Romans in this view of their contemporary situation, and it was to explore and to clarify these hopes that Virgil wrote the *Aeneid*. In it he presents his anticipations of history (the pageant at the end of Book 6, the description of the shield at the end of Book 8) in a fashion which accords with the Augustan view of the Roman achievement; and in his hero he exemplifies those virtues of *pietas, constantia, religio* which seemed so desirable in Romans of his day. In the last analysis Virgil found that these qualities fail, or seem to fail, to make complete order out of the world's chaos; but they were the qualities which his epic was designed to illustrate and exemplify, and the *Aeneid* in exploring what the Roman way of life had achieved and could achieve leaves the reader free to ponder on what it seemed in the last resort unable to achieve. And this surely is a primary virtue in a national epic.

2. THE 'AENEID' AND ITS LITERARY BACKGROUND

One of the fountains of the *Aeneid*'s inspiration was, as has been shown, the national aspiration of Rome in Virgil's time; another, of equal if not greater importance, was the epic poetry of Homer. The *Iliad* and the *Odyssey* represented in the classical world the highest achievement of Greek poetry, and the admiration universally felt by the Romans for Homer was for the great national poet of the Greek world whose literature they revered. His poetry was considered in Virgil's time to embody the perfect form of epic in its construction and organization, and to offer the reader moral lessons about life and how to live it as well as the excitement and intensity of dramatic action at its highest pitch and the aesthetic satisfaction of description and story-telling in a distant world which was half real and half supernatural. There can be no doubt that the poetry of Homer cast its spell over Virgil, and the idea of adapting and indeed continuing the Greek stories fascinated his poetic imagination. The comparison was immediately made by Propertius (2.34.65–6):

cedite, Romani scriptores, cedite Grai;
nescioquid maius nascitur Iliade.

Yield, you writers of Rome, yield, you Greeks; something is being born that is greater than the Iliad.

The idea was expressed in the Donatus life (21), where the *Aeneid* is described as a kind of equivalent of both Homer's poems – *quasi amborum Homeri*

43

carminum instar; and much later one of the characters in Macrobius' *Saturnalia* (5.2.13) speaks of the *Aeneid* as a 'mirrored reflection of Homer'.

All of this is true: the *Aeneid* is indeed a full-scale *aemulatio* of Homer, and in it Virgil uses again for his own purposes many aspects of the structure of the Homeric poems, their conventions (such as the similes, or the double action in Olympus and on earth), their episodes (like the catalogue, the visit to the underworld, the funeral games, the single combat), their characters (Aeneas and Turnus have strong relationship with Hector and Achilles, Pallas is like Patroclus, Palinurus like Elpenor), their very phraseology.[1] It has often been remarked that the first half of the *Aeneid* is Virgil's *Odyssey*, describing the wanderings of the hero, and the second half his *Iliad*, describing the battles; it is astonishing to find from a close investigation how very similar in structure and episode the first book of the *Aeneid* is to *Odyssey* 5–8; or how densely the last scenes of *Aeneid* 12 echo the events of *Iliad* 22.

But it is not only these similarities of epic structure and phraseology which constantly challenge comparison with Homer; the story itself is contemporary with, or a continuation of, the stories of Homer. Aeneas is an important character in the *Iliad*, the most important Trojan warrior after Hector, a man renowned for his religious observances as well as for his prowess in war. When he leaves Troy his voyage is contemporary (within a few months) with that of Odysseus, and several times in the *Aeneid* (for example with Achaemenides in Book 3, the Sirens in Book 5, Circe in Book 7) Aeneas is following in the footsteps of Odysseus very shortly afterwards. Virgil uses this Homeric time-scale to point the differences between Homer's heroes and his: Odysseus is one of the last heroes of the heroic world, attempting to re-establish his way of life in Ithaca as he knew it before the Trojan war; but Aeneas is the first hero of a new world, a proto-Roman world.

Similarly Aeneas' attitude towards battle can be contrasted with the Homeric attitude. In many ways his opponent Turnus has been built up as a new Achilles, and Aeneas – the new Hector – must confront his opponent as Hector had to confront Achilles. Yet he must confront him differently: he must show the valour and vigour of a Homeric warrior, but also the mercy and justice of a Roman ruler of empire. He does not wholly succeed, as all readers of the *Aeneid* know well; but it is by means of the Homeric comparison that Virgil tries to define the position and behaviour of the new hero, destined for an age no longer 'heroic'. More will be said later on this subject.

Virgil was deeply versed in post-Homeric classical Greek literature, and was especially influenced by Greek tragedy (see Macrobius, *Sat.* 5.18f.). There are individual echoes of the plays of Aeschylus, Sophocles and Euripides, and in particular *Aeneid* 2 shows marked signs of the influence of Euripides' *Troades*

---

[1] For a very full discussion of Virgil's use of Homer see Knauer (1964).

and *Hecuba*; elements that recall dramatic structure can be observed especially in this book and in *Aeneid* 4. But the real debt is one of concept rather than form: the concept of the whole development of Dido's love, leading to her ultimate self-destruction, is tragic in the fullest and most technical sense; similarly the events leading to the death of Turnus have the closest possible similarity to those in a Greek tragedy as the hero moves along his self-chosen path to destruction. And in a broader sense Virgil's whole attitude towards the human scene which he explores in his poem is similar to that often found in Greek tragedy: an intense sensitivity towards the suffering which human people bring upon themselves or have brought upon them by the pressure of hostile circumstances, coupled with a profound conviction that somehow in spite of all the catastrophes the world is not a senseless one, and that in some way hardly comprehensible to men these sufferings may form a necessary part in the ultimate fulfilment of the divine purpose for mankind.

Like the other literary figures of his time Virgil knew well the post-classical Greek literature of the Hellenistic age: the *Eclogues* with their fundamental debt to Theocritus, and the *Georgics* with their imitation and paraphrases of the didactic writers like Aratus and Nicander bear full witness to this. In the *Aeneid* it is Apollonius Rhodius whose story of Jason and Medea captured Virgil's imagination and contributed towards the construction of the story of Aeneas and Dido. Elsewhere in the *Aeneid* Apollonius is rarely recalled, and other parts of Apollonius' *Argonautica* than those about Medea hardly ever are used; but the second half of Book 1, which introduces the story of Dido, the whole of Book 4 which continues and finishes it, and the meeting of Aeneas with Dido's ghost in Book 6 use ideas and phraseology from Apollonius. Servius introduces his commentary on *Aeneid* 4 with the words: 'Apollonius wrote the *Argonautica* and in his third book brought in the love-story of Medea, from which all this book is taken.' This is a wild exaggeration, but it contains some seeds of truth: the marriage in the cave, the frivolous and selfish behaviour of the goddesses, the sleeplessness of Dido, her recourse to magic – these all find their origins in Apollonius. And in more general terms it is fair to say that the concept of using epic poetry to reveal the inner and intense emotions of the heroine (a feature far more normally associated with elegy) came from Apollonius. It is not to be found in Homer, nor in Ennius. But when this has been said, it needs to be said also that for all the material which Virgil took from Apollonius he did not make his Dido in the least like Apollonius' Medea. The queenly dignity, the resolution, the high tragic stature are Virgil's own, and quite alien from the gentle and confused young girl of Apollonius.

Of Roman poets Virgil knew and used especially Naevius, Ennius, some of the tragedians, Catullus and Lucretius. His debt to Lucretius was very great in the *Georgics*, and is considerable in phraseology and metrical movement in the

Aeneid (for example in the minstrel's song in *Aeneid* 1 and in Anchises' speech about the nature of life after death in *Aeneid* 6); but it is Ennius and Catullus who call for particular mention here. No two poets could be more unlike (Catullus' dislike for poetry of Ennius' type is well known), and it is one of the clearest indications of Virgil's many-sidedness that he deeply appreciated both, and used both in his epic.

Ennius stood in a special relationship to Virgil as being the father of Roman patriotic poetry, whom it was Virgil's aim to emulate. From the fragments of Ennius which survive a wide-ranging impression of Virgil's verbal debts can be gained.[1] Ennius is constantly quoted in Servius' commentary as a source of Virgil's phrases, and a substantial passage of Macrobius' *Saturnalia* (6.1–3) is taken up with citation and discussion of parallel passages. Virgil's debt to Ennius in structure and characterization is far less than to Homer, because Ennius' treatment of his theme was annalistic rather than dramatic, but in addition to verbal reminiscences there are two major ways in which Ennius influenced Virgil. One is that Ennius was the first Roman to adapt the Greek hexameter to the Latin language, so that all subsequent hexameter writers owed a debt to him as they set about modifying and smoothing the movement of the metre in Latin. By the time of Virgil such developments had taken place through the writings of poets like Lucretius, Catullus, Cicero that it was possible to recall the distinctive style of Ennius by deliberate metrical archaizing, and this Virgil quite often does in order to achieve an effect of antiquity. The second, and perhaps the most important aspect of Ennian influence, is in the national tone and spirit; the toughness and simplicity of the Romans of old is powerfully portrayed by Ennius, and this must have strengthened and enlarged Virgil's own sympathy for the ancestors of his race and his love of antiquity, especially that of his own country. It also helped him in the robust style of narrative in which much of the second half of the *Aeneid* is written. Consider for example the second half of Book 9. The first part has been taken up with the emotional story of Nisus and Euryalus, written in a style calling for the reader's personal involvement with the fate of these two young warriors. At the end of it the theme changes to the stern vigour of the narrative of the *aristeia*[2] of Turnus; this is more sinewy writing, more matter-of-fact in its presentation of events. It is introduced with a sentence immediately reminiscent of Ennius (*Aen.* 9.503–4 *at tuba terribilem sonitum procul aere canoro* | *increpuit* 'But the trumpet with ringing bronze uttered its dreadful sound in the distance', cf. Enn. *Ann.* 140), a reminiscence reinforced in the invocation (*Aen.* 9.528 *et mecum ingentes oras euoluite belli* 'and unroll with me the vast scroll of war', cf. Enn. *Ann.* 174) and immediately afterwards in the narrative (*Aen.* 9.532–3 *expugnare Itali summaque*

---

[1] See Bowra (1929) 65ff. and Norden (1915).
[2] *Aristeia*: an episode in which an individual warrior displays great prowess.

euertere opum ui | certabant 'The Italians strove to storm and overturn it with all their power and might', cf. Enn. *Ann.* 161). The mood of the narrative is active, vigorous, often reminiscent of Homer's *Iliad*, often of Ennius' *Annals*: the speech of Numanus (9.598ff.) expresses the values and ideals of archaic Rome; and the final scene of Turnus' exploits (*Aen.* 9.806ff.), when Turnus could at last hold out no longer, is very closely based on a passage of Ennius (*Ann.* 401–8), itself adapted from Homer (*Il.* 16.102ff.).

Virgil's debt to Catullus[1] is of a very different kind, virtually the opposite kind. Reminiscences of Catullan phrases are much rarer than reminiscences of Ennius, but where they do occur they are always memorable, always in passages of emotional sensitivity. There are the two flower similes, one for the death of Euryalus (9.435ff.) and one at the funeral of Pallas (11.68ff.), both reminiscent of flower similes in Catullus (11.22ff., 62.39ff.); there are Aeneas' last words to Pallas (11.97–8 *salue aeternum mihi, maxime Palla, | aeternumque uale* 'Hail and farewell for ever, great Pallas'; cf. Cat. 101.10 *atque in perpetuum, frater, aue atque uale* 'and for ever hail and farewell, my brother'); but above all there are the reminiscences in the story of the desertion of Dido, recalling the pathos of Ariadne's desertion in Catullus 64. Dido's pleading speech to Aeneas (4.305f.) begins as Ariadne's had with the reproach of broken faith (*perfide*) and she speaks of her hopes in Ariadne's phrases (4.316 *per conubia nostra, per inceptos hymenaeos* 'by our marriage and by the wedding on which we have begun'; Cat. 64.141 *sed conubia laeta, sed optatos hymenaeos* 'but (you promised me) a happy marriage and a longed-for wedding'); she uses a diminutive adjective in the style of Catullus – nowhere else in the *Aeneid* does Virgil use a diminutive adjective (4.328–9 *si quis mihi paruulus aula | luderet Aeneas* 'if a tiny Aeneas were playing in the palace'). At the end, just before she kills herself, she – like Ariadne – bitterly wishes that the ships that brought her lover had never touched her shores (4.657–8 *felix heu nimium felix si litora tantum | numquam Dardaniae tetigissent nostra carinae* 'blessed, o too much blessed, if only the Trojan keels had never touched our shores'; cf. Cat. 64.171–2 *Iuppiter omnipotens, utinam ne tempore primo | Cnosia Cecropiae tetigissent litora puppes* 'Almighty Jupiter, if only that first time the Athenian ships had never touched Cretan shores'). Of course Virgil's Dido is at most times very different from Catullus' Ariadne – but in her moments of pathos and desolation the impact of Virgil's description is increased by recollections of Catullus' tender heroine.

To survey the surviving literary sources of Virgil's *Aeneid* (and there were many other sources which have not come down to us) makes it very plain that as well as being moved by a commitment to contemporary Roman problems and aspirations he aimed at universalizing his exploration of human behaviour by relating the contemporary with the past through the medium of literature. In

[1] See Westendorp Boerma (1958) 55ff.

some sense the *Aeneid* is a synthesis of certain aspects of human experience as presented by writers of the past. Like Dante and Milton Virgil aims at including those things which had moved him in past literature as well as those which moved him in the contemporary scene. And what is especially remarkable in the *Aeneid*, and indeed perhaps unique, is the extent to which Virgil could sympathize with, and seek to incorporate, the attitudes and outlook of such totally different epochs as the Homeric and the Alexandrian and of such totally different poets as Ennius, sonorous and severe exponent of the national theme, and Catullus, the emotional and sensitive poet not concerned with the state at all but with the private world of the lonely individual.

3. THE COMPOSITION AND STRUCTURE OF THE 'AENEID'

The *Aeneid* as we have it is unrevised. We know on the authority of Servius and Donatus that at the time of his death in 19 B.C. Virgil planned to spend three more years revising the poem, and because he had not finished work on it he gave instructions on his deathbed that it should be burnt. These instructions were countermanded by Augustus, who ordered that it should be published by Varius and Tucca with the removal of unnecessary material (*superflua*) but without additions. There are a number of features in the poem, as we shall see, that testify to its lack of the poet's final revision, but there is no evidence whatever for thinking that any major alterations would have been made, and the poem as a whole should not be regarded in any important sense as unfinished. We can guess if we like that it might have been rewritten (to make it more Augustan or less Augustan) but if so it would have been another poem; our poem is finished in all but minor details of revision.

We have a good deal of ancient evidence about Virgil's method of composition,[1] and it agrees well with what we might deduce from the poem itself. Donatus tells us that Virgil first sketched the poem in prose and divided it into twelve books; then he composed the different sections as the mood took him, and so that the flow of his inspiration should not be checked he left some parts unfinished and in other parts he put in 'props' (*tibicines*) to hold up the structure till the permanent columns were ready. Instances of these *tibicines* have been collected and discussed by Mackail,[2] and the half-lines attest the method, as Servius saw: they indicate small gaps awaiting completion. Many of the fifty-odd instances of incomplete lines[3] are very effective as they stand, and give a haunting effect of pathos (e.g. 2.346, 623, 640): they would have been very difficult for Virgil to fill up to his satisfaction, but it should be regarded as certain that they are an indication of lack of revision and not a deliberate poetic

[1] See Mackail (1930) Intro. xlviiff.　　　　[2] Ibid. liiff.
[3] There is a full treatment in Sparrow (1931).

technique. None of his predecessors had used the technique, and – more significant – none of his imitators used it; there is a story in Donatus that Virgil completed certain half-lines *ex tempore* when giving a *recitatio*; it is also the case that quite a few of the half-lines (like *tum sic effatur*, 9.295) are clearly incomplete stop-gaps.

Servius has preserved for us what seems to be another instance of incomplete revision in the passage about Helen (2.567–88) – though there are still dissenting views about whether the passage is Virgilian or not.[1] This passage is not in any of the major MSS, but is quoted in Servius' introduction as an indication of lack of final revision. It reads like Virgil, but it contains certain awkwardnesses, and it is not completely dovetailed into the structure of the section. Evidently the last part of *Aeneid* 2 was undergoing revision, as the presence of six incomplete lines in the last two hundred suggests; and it is interesting to notice that here we have one of the finest parts of all the *Aeneid*, but still Virgil was not yet satisfied.

Other indications of the lack of final revision may be found in certain inconsistencies within the plot of the poem.[2] Too much should not be made of these – they are all minor, and a detailed scrutiny of any long work is likely to uncover a number of small inconsistencies or contradictions. Some of these are easily explicable: for example in 3.255 the Harpy Celaeno prophesies that Aeneas will not found his city until hunger has forced him to eat his tables, and when in 7.112f. the Trojans do in fact eat their tables, Aeneas joyfully recalls that this was the prophecy given to him by Anchises. He is wrong, but his error (or Virgil's) serves to remind us of the enormously important part played by Anchises in helping and advising his son during the voyage. Again, the chronology of the seven-years' voyage is difficult to fit into the events of Book 3, and the term '*septima aestas*' is used by Dido at the end of Book 1 and by Beroe, a year later, in 5.626. Certain shifts of emphasis centre on Book 3: Apollo is the guide there, not Venus as in the rest of the poem; there are difficulties about the progressive revelation of the Trojan goal; Helenus says that the Sibyl will tell of the wars to come, whereas in fact Anchises does. Book 3 is at a lower level of poetic intensity than the rest of the *Aeneid*, and there is only one simile. There was a tradition that originally Book 3 was written in third-person narrative (not in direct speech), and began the poem. This may suggest that when Virgil set out for Greece in 19 B.C. his intention was to gain local colour for the revision of Book 3, which is set in Greek waters; but it does not suggest any need for radical alteration.

The structure[3] of the poem is carefully and elaborately composed. This is to be expected from literary epic: the poet who undertakes this most ambitious and

[1] See for example Austin (1961) 185ff. and (1964) 217ff., and Goold (1970) 101ff.
[2] See Crump (1920).
[3] See Mackail (1930) Intro. xxxvii ff., Otis (1963) 217ff., Duckworth (1954) 1ff. and (1957) 1ff., Camps (1954) 214ff. and (1959) 53ff.

massive of genres proclaims his intention to be a builder, to undertake the architecture of symmetries and contrasts on a large scale. The most obvious way of looking at the *Aeneid*'s structure is to see two halves corresponding to Homer's two poems, the first six books being Virgil's *Odyssey* and the last six his *Iliad*. But an equally valid and significant division is into three parts, the tragedy of Turnus in 9–12 corresponding with that of Dido in 1–4, with the middle section taken up with material often closely related to Roman history and origins. There is also a balance round Book 7 so that 6 and 8 correspond as the great Roman books, 5 and 9 as episodic, 4 and 10 as the tragedies of Dido and Pallas, 11 and 3 as episodic, 12 and 2 as the triumph of Rome and the destruction of Troy. An alternative symmetry is seen by balancing 1 with 7, 2 with 8 (Troy and Rome), 3 with 9, 4 with 10, 5 with 11, 6 with 12. A particular kind of symmetry has been generally accepted since Conway elaborated it: the alternation of the Odyssean, more expansive books with the grave and Iliadic books, so that the even-numbered books which are intense are varied and relieved by the odd-numbered books. The function of Books 3 and 5, separating 2, 4, and 6, is very obvious in this connexion.

More elaborate schemes of structure have been proposed in recent times, including the large-scale use by Virgil of the mathematical ratio known as the Golden Section,[1] a ratio of 0.628 to 1. This ratio has played a most important part in the visual arts, but it seems impossible as well as inappropriate to apply it to a poem of the scale of the *Aeneid*. However important structural considerations are to an epic poet, we must remember that they constitute the supports to what he wants to say. In a cathedral the structure *is* what the architect wants to express, but in a poet it is the means to his end.

4. THE CHIEF CHARACTERS

Aeneas

The hero of the *Aeneid* has very often been a target for adverse criticism, even (somewhat paradoxically) from those who have regarded the *Aeneid* as among the greatest poems ever written. Charles James Fox's phrase is famous: 'always either insipid or odious'. Page, in often quoted words, says 'Virgil is unhappy in his hero. Compared with Achilles, Aeneas is but the shadow of a man', and Wight Duff conveys what has until recently been the general view: 'Aeneas is too often a puppet.' The key to a proper understanding of Aeneas is Leopardi's description of him as the opposite of a hero: in some senses this is exactly what he is. Virgil is trying to define the nature and behaviour of a hero in an age no longer heroic: not to produce a second-hand Achilles or Odysseus, but to investigate the qualities required in a complex civilization in which the straight-

[1] Duckworth (1962).

forward and simple individualism of an Achilles would be useless. Aeneas cannot cut a figure like Achilles because he must subordinate his individual wishes and desires to the requirements of others; he must be the group hero, and this is the quality which Virgil constantly stresses in him, his quality of *pietas*. This involves Aeneas in situation after situation where he must weigh up conflicting claims upon him, where he must ponder in anxious thought the proper course of action. He does not stride magnificently through life: on the contrary he is under constant emotional and intellectual pressure and only with extreme difficulty and often against all the odds does he succeed in keeping on going.

The most obvious and important way in which Aeneas differs from a Homeric hero is that he has devoted himself to a divine mission, he has accepted the will of heaven that he should be the agent of Jupiter's plan for the future happiness and prosperity of the human race under the civilizing rule of the Romans. This is abundantly clear through the *Aeneid*: in line 2 Aeneas is 'an exile because of fate' (*fato profugus*) and the poem is heavily laden with the concept of destiny throughout. The contrast between Aeneas' personal wishes and his divine duty is brought out especially clearly in his desertion of Dido (4.361 *Italiam non sponte sequor* 'it is not of my own free will that I go to seek Italy', 6.460 *inuitus, regina, tuo de litore cessi* 'unwillingly, o queen, did I leave your land'), but it is a perpetual theme throughout the whole action (e.g. 11.112 *nec ueni, nisi fata locum sedemque dedissent* 'and I should not be here, had not the fates allotted me an abiding-place').

Two principal criticisms have been levelled at Aeneas as man of destiny, two branches of the same objection: neither of them is true. One is that as man of destiny he is possessed of such supernatural strength and resolution that interest in him as an ordinary human being cannot be sustained: on the contrary, as we shall see, he is often frail and uncertain and barely able to continue. The other is that by accepting the divine destiny he sacrifices his free will. It would indeed be possible to present a man in Aeneas' situation in that way, but Virgil has certainly not done so. At each and every moment of the poem Aeneas is free to reject his mission – to say 'Thus far and no further.' When Mercury appears to him in Book 4 to tell him to leave Dido, he could refuse: he has to take the decision what to do, and he decides to return to his mission and sacrifice Dido. In one place the process of decision is presented to us in the most explicit terms – after the Trojan women have set fire to their own ships and Jupiter, in response to Aeneas' prayers, has quenched the fire Aeneas is so shaken by this turn of events that he wonders whether to give up the whole mission (5.700ff.):

> at pater Aeneas casu concussus acerbo
> nunc huc ingentis, nunc illuc pectore curas
> mutabat uersans, Siculisne resideret aruis
> oblitus fatorum, Italasne capesseret oras.

But father Aeneas, shattered by this bitter blow, turned and revolved his heavy anxieties one way and another in his heart: should he settle in the fields of Sicily and forget the fates, or press on to the shores of Italy.

Nothing could be more precise than this: he has two options, to give up his mission and forget the fates or to continue, and it is a long time before he decides. The Stoic platitudes of Nautes do not convince him, and it takes a vision of his father Anchises to make him realize that he must follow his duty and continue on to Italy.

The essential human frailty and fallibility of Aeneas, the courage with which he continues on a mission almost too much for his shoulders to bear, is revealed again and again in the poem. The hostility of Juno and the undeserved suffering she causes is presented in powerful terms at the beginning of Book 1, and the prelude to the poem ends with the famous and unforgettable line *tantae molis erat Romanam condere gentem* 'so great a task it was to found the Roman race' (1.33). Indeed it was, and one in which Aeneas succeeded by the narrowest of margins.

On Aeneas' first appearance in the poem, as he and his men are battered by the storm sent by Juno, we see him frightened and in despair –

> extemplo Aeneae soluuntur frigore membra;
> ingemit et duplicis tendens ad sidera palmas
> talia uoce refert... (1.92–4)

Straightway Aeneas' limbs were loosened in cold fear; he groaned, and holding out his two hands to the sky thus he spoke...

And the burden of his speech is that he wishes he had died along with his comrades at Troy.

After the storm has been calmed by Neptune Aeneas speaks to his men in heartening terms (1.198ff.), but immediately after the speech Virgil tells us that his confidence was feigned:

> talia uoce refert curisque ingentibus aeger
> spem uultu simulat, premit altum corde dolorem. (1.208–9)

So he spoke, and sick at heart with his terrible anxieties he feigned hope in his expression and suppressed his agony deep in his heart.

The scene of the poem shifts to Olympus where Venus indignantly complains to Jupiter of her son's apparently unending suffering, and Jupiter replies to her in the serene and glowing tones of his promise for Rome's future greatness. The reader is inspired with optimism, feeling that with such a reward the task must be and will be fulfilled. But the mortal Aeneas has not heard the speech in heaven, and must continue on darkly, helped only by vague knowledge of his destiny. His divine mother, in disguise, meets him as he explores the coast where his Trojans have been shipwrecked, and to her he complains bitterly (1.372ff., especially 385 *querentem*); as she leaves him she manifests her divinity, and again Aeneas complains of his hard fortune, deprived of normal maternal affection as he is (*crudelis tu quoque*, 407).

The hard and apparently almost hopeless quest continues. Aeneas gazes in envy at the walls of Carthage, already rising:

> 'o fortunati, quorum iam moenia surgunt!' (1.437)

> '*Lucky those whose city already is being built.*'

How far away seems his own city.

Throughout the first book the episodes and incidents have been closely modelled on *Odyssey* 5–8: the shipwreck, the landing on an unknown shore, the meeting with a disguised goddess, the friendly reception in a strange city, the banquet, the minstrel's song, the request for the story of the past.[1] We are invited to see Aeneas as a new Odysseus, and at the same time challenged to observe and ponder the difference. The difference is the decree of destiny, the requirement of future history as outlined in Jupiter's speech; and this means that Aeneas is not like Odysseus, a man seeking, if only he can, to return to the old way of life in his own home, but a man stepping out into the unknown future, leaving the ashes of Troy to found not merely a new city in a distant western land, but also a new way of life. From being the last Trojan he must become the first Roman. He is therefore involved, as Odysseus was not, in the needs of his followers; he must be the group hero, the social hero, bringing a new nation safely to a new country. Odysseus, the splendid individual, survived and reached home when his comrades, lesser men in resources and endurance, did not – but Aeneas must lead his Trojans safely to their Roman destiny. The pressure upon him is greater, a pressure only to be resolved by devotion to his divine mission, by what the Romans called *pietas*; and because this pressure is so much greater we see in him a figure who often seems frail and unequal to the task. And yet through toil and danger, through despair and agony, he keeps on going. This is the nature of the new heroism.

The remainder of the first half of the poem is filled with the trials, physical and psychological, which Aeneas must encounter. His account of his agonized sorrow at the fall of Troy (Book 2) reveals the human and impetuous side of him, not yet capable of accepting his divine destiny. The story of the long weary wanderings in the third book shows a gradual acceptance of fate, aided by the counsels of his father Anchises. In the fourth book, as will be seen later, the temptation of personal happiness comes near, very near, to causing Aeneas to abandon his mission altogether. The key to an understanding of this book is

---

[1] For details see R. D. Williams (1963) 266ff.

Aeneas could have given up the whole thing, personally wished to do so, yet – because of conscience, duty, *pietas* – did not.

The fifth book is a particularly poignant depiction of how Aeneas bears a burden almost too heavy for him. It begins with a last backward look at the events at Carthage, and the tragic outcome; it moves to a happier tone as the games are celebrated in honour of Anchises. Now for the first time the weight is for a few brief days off Aeneas. As he acts as president of the games he relaxes – but immediately comes another blow from Juno as she intervenes to cause the Trojan women to set fire to the fleet. Jupiter, in response to Aeneas' prayer, quenches the fire; but Aeneas is in deep distress, ponders whether to give up his mission, and is only persuaded to continue by the vision of his father's ghost, sent by Jupiter to urge him on with the divine task. Aeneas obeys, makes the necessary arrangements, and sails on the last lap to the western coast of Italy. One further disaster befalls him before arrival: the loss of his faithful helmsman Palinurus, who had guided the fleet thus far, through seven years of wanderings, but was fated not to survive until the final arrival to which he himself contributed so much.

Aeneas' visit to the underworld is for the most part full of gloom and sorrow: the ghosts of his past haunt him and he feels guilt and remorse at having failed to save them, or, worse, having caused their deaths. He meets the shade of Palinurus, so recently dead, of Dido – to whom he speaks in tones of deep remorse – , of Deiphobus, who died at Troy when Aeneas survived. These are traumatic personal experiences of events all brought upon Aeneas solely because of his acceptance of his mission: these are the prices he must pay for the Roman achievement.[1]

But at this moment when it seems that Aeneas' grief is unbearable (especially because of his personal responsibility for these tragedies) the light begins to shine in the underworld. He reaches Elysium, hears from his father of the nature of life after death, the rewards for the virtuous and the purification of sin, and then is shown a pageant of Roman heroes[2] waiting to be born if – and only if – he succeeds in his mission. They pass before his astonished eyes – the Alban kings, Romulus, and then (with the chronology broken) Augustus himself, a second Romulus who will re-found the city and bring back the golden age to Latium. The chronology is resumed with the kings of Rome, Brutus and the great heroes of the Republic, and the final summary by Anchises contrasts the artistic and intellectual achievements of the Greeks with the practical and political destiny of the Romans, namely to bring peace and civilization to the peoples of the world.

This is one of the great patriotic pieces in the poem, but it should not be regarded as a detachable purple passage: it is most closely integrated with the

---

[1] See Otis (1963) 290ff. and (1959) 165ff.   [2] See R. D. Williams (1972) 207ff.

development of Aeneas' character, and Virgil points this with emphasis. After the description of Augustus Anchises breaks off to ask his son

> et dubitamus adhuc uirtutem extendere factis,
> aut metus Ausonia prohibet consistere terra? (6.806–7)

And do we still hesitate to enlarge our prowess by deeds, or does fear prevent us from founding a settlement in the Ausonian land?

Aeneas does not answer – but we can answer for him; there can be no more hesitation now. And finally as Anchises escorts Aeneas along the way back to the upper world he has fired his heart with passion for the glory awaiting him: *incenditque animum famae uenientis amore* (6.889). This passion must overcome all other passions which Aeneas as an individual has felt and will feel again. His passive acceptance of duty now turns into a positive and dynamic urge.

In the second half of the poem the interest shifts from the question of whether Aeneas is strong enough and devoted enough to achieve his mission (his experiences in the underworld have ensured that he will be) to the question of how he is to achieve it. What does the man of *pietas*, the man of deep human sympathies, do when he is confronted by violent opposition? Virgil was too much a realist, and too much a child of his violent times, to pretend that opposition promptly melts away before righteousness; yet he was himself a gentle person with nothing of the soldier in him, and could take little pleasure in the ruthless triumph of power, however justly based it might seem to be. The second half of the poem explores this question, and this is one of the things which Virgil meant when he said in his new invocation (7.44–5):

> maior rerum mihi nascitur ordo,
> maius opus moueo

A greater series of events arises before me; I undertake a greater task.

For most of the time during the war in Latium Aeneas presents a picture of a just and merciful general, caring for his own men, and generous to the enemy. When Lausus intervenes in the battle to try to save his father Mezentius, and Aeneas is forced to kill him, he is filled with remorse and sorrow and himself lifts up the dead body with words of compassion (10.821ff.). When the Latin envoys ask for a truce to bury the dead, Aeneas willingly grants it and wishes there could have been a truce for the living too (11.106ff.). When the arrangements for a single combat between himself and Turnus are violated and general fighting breaks out again, Aeneas rushes into the midst, unarmed and unhelmeted, urging his men to control their anger (12.311ff.). It is on the whole true to say that Aeneas hates war and fights because it is his bitter duty, in contrast with Turnus who is most himself on the battlefield.

But there are very strong qualifications which must immediately be made. Quite apart from the fact that Turnus for all his violence is often presented sympathetically there are three places in particular in this part of the poem where Virgil goes out of his way to emphasize Aeneas' own lapses into the violence which is a characteristic of his opponent. The first of these is after the death of Pallas (10.510ff.), where Aeneas' behaviour is wild and savage in the extreme, including the capture of eight of the enemy for human sacrifice at Pallas' tomb (a horrible piece of barbarism which is fulfilled at 11.81ff.). The second is when Aeneas is wounded (12.441ff.), and his fierce deeds in battle are in every way similar to those of Turnus. The third, and perhaps the most significant of all, is at the very end of the poem. This is a passage on which we must pause.

During the single combat between Aeneas and Turnus (12.697ff.) we have been constantly reminded of the duel between Achilles and Hector in *Iliad* 22. Many of the famous passages have been recalled (*Il.* 22.304–5 ~ *Aen.* 12.645–9; *Il.* 22.209ff. ~ *Aen.* 12.725ff.; *Il.* 22.158ff. ~ *Aen.* 12.763ff.; *Il.* 22.199ff. ~ *Aen.* 12.908ff.) and we are aware that the second Achilles (Turnus, cf. 6.89) is fighting now against the second Hector (Aeneas), but that the outcome will be the opposite from Homer's story. We recall that Aeneas is fighting to avenge Pallas as Achilles was fighting to avenge Patroclus, but we know that the character of Aeneas is different, more civilized, more just than that of Achilles. Consequently we are confident that in the moment of victory he will show mercy; he will not display the arrogant joy of Achilles (*Il.* 22.344ff.); he will surely spare the conquered.

This parallelism with Homer makes it all the more shattering when Aeneas does not in fact spare his victim, but rejects his pleas precisely as Achilles had rejected Hector's. After a thousand years it is exactly the same in the end; the victor, in his wild anger (is it 'righteous' anger?), takes vengeance by killing his victim. Much has been written on these final scenes, sometimes in defence of Aeneas (he can do no other than remove from the scene a barbarous opponent whose way of life cannot be accepted in the new order of things), sometimes against him (he yields to wild fury, he gives in to the very kind of behaviour which throughout the poem he has been combating in himself and others). But two things are evident from Virgil's text: the first is that there is no other motive for Aeneas' action than the desire to exact vengeance (940–1, 945, 948–9) even although Turnus has been brought low and is no longer one of the proud (930). We are perhaps invited to think of Augustus' temple to *Mars Vltor* and of his vengeance on the assassins of Julius Caesar. The second is that this action is taken by the hero of the poem with whose behaviour and destiny all Romans are closely identified: it is certainly not the case that the hero has turned villain at the last (as some recent writers[1] have argued), but rather that in an imperfect

---

[1] For example Putnam (1965) chapter 4.

world the best of us (like the worst) take actions which in a perfect world would be unacceptable. The poem ends with confusion, with paradox; the poet would have us ponder. This is the measure of the greatness of the poem – it shirks no issues, it aims at no specious falsifications. Nothing could have been easier than to avoid this dilemma: Aeneas' spear-cast could have killed Turnus instead of wounding him, and the final situation would not have arisen. But it was Virgil's intention, here as elsewhere in the poem, to involve his readers in a dilemma concerned with real human issues as he saw them in the Roman world.

Dido

From the *Aeneid*'s publication up to the present day the story of Dido has always been the most popular part of Virgil's epic (Ov. *Trist.* 2.535–6) in spite of, or sometimes because of, the fact that we are here further away than else-where in the poem from the Roman theme. Here we have the strongest possible protest against the apparently senseless suffering of the world, and many readers who have been unmoved by the Roman ideals and values of the poem have, like St Augustine, shed tears for Dido. Here Virgil shows how the private world of the individual is violated by the march of Roman destiny, and he leaves his readers profoundly unhappy that it should be so. There are of course many undertones in the story – the defeat of Carthage by Rome, the triumph of Stoic ideals over Epicurean (4.379–80), the threat of Cleopatra in Virgil's own times – but basically and essentially the presentation is concerned with the personal suffering and tragedy of its heroine. It is Catullan in its deep sympathy and sensitivity, and there are many echoes of the phraseology and episodes of Catullus' poem about Theseus' desertion of Ariadne. No poet was more inter-ested in people and less in affairs of state than Catullus, and here in the midst of his state poem Virgil speaks with a voice often reminiscent of the pathos of Catullus' desertion poems.

The whole of the second half of *Aeneid* 1 is about Dido, and in it Virgil builds up a picture of a totally admirable and enviable queen. Dido is beautiful, like Diana; she is kind and hospitable to the Trojans; she is highly efficient as a ruler and beloved by her people; she has been through hardship and exile and is now triumphantly achieving what Aeneas seeks to achieve in the future – the foundation of a new city for her people. In the joyful scenes of the banquet which she gives in honour of the Trojans the notes of disaster to come are not absent, yet it is hard to imagine that a person of such qualities could destroy herself as Dido does.

The first half of the fourth book depicts how she yields completely to a love which she must have known was impossible; she allows it to annihilate all her other qualities and Carthage comes to a halt (4.86–9). Her situation is presented with strong pathos, culminating in her plea to Aeneas (305–30) not to leave her when she has given her whole self to her love for him. Aeneas replies that he is not free to stay, and at this Dido changes from a pathetically deserted woman to a personification of hatred and vengeance. In a highly rhetorical speech (365–87) she distances herself from her lover, ceases to be a human individual with whom communication is possible, and becomes instead a kind of avenging Fury, an archetypal and terrifying symbol of slighted pride and bitter anger. In her long curse against her lover (590–629) she revolves thoughts of the horrors she could have inflicted (600–2) and ends by invoking the long years of history to achieve her vengeance, calling on every Carthaginian to hate and destroy the Romans at every possible opportunity. In her last speech of all, just before she kills herself, she unites both aspects of her tragic character, first re-invoking (651–8) the pathos which was the dominant feature of the first part of the book, and finally returning to her passionate hatred for the lover who has scorned her, upon whom she must have vengeance (661–2).

As so often with a Greek tragedy the reader is astonished and horrified not merely at the actual events of the disaster, but at the total disintegration of what had once been a strong, noble and virtuous character.[1] He seeks explanations, he seeks to apportion blame. There are clearly contributory causes, things that might have been done otherwise: Aeneas should have perceived that he was allowing a situation to develop from which he might escape but Dido would not; Dido should not have broken her vow of chastity to her dead husband Sychaeus, and she should have fought against a passion which she must have known could lead her nowhere. But in essence what we have is a tragic and moving study of a wholly sympathetic character broken and destroyed by the pressure of circumstances which she could not in fact resist. She might have done, it was not impossible to try, but they were in the event too strong for her. To a large extent this is symbolized in the scheming of the goddesses Venus and Juno – they enmeshed Dido in a net from which she was not in the end able to break out. She had to measure her own character and her own will against the force of hostile circumstances. The tragedy of her story is that she allowed herself to be defeated.

The last word should be on the significance of the tragedy of Dido within the structure of the poem (far too often it has been treated as if it were detachable). Above all it introduces a note alien to the serene prophecy of Jupiter in Book 1: it becomes apparent that the Roman mission is not to be achieved without tragic events which cast doubts on the whole concept (it has indeed been a common view that Book 4 'breaks the back of the whole poem'). Nothing could have been easier than for Virgil to depict Dido as an obstacle to the Roman destiny whose removal we could all applaud, a sort of Circe, a Calypso, a Siren.

---

[1] See Quinn (1963) 29ff., and (1965) 16ff.

But that was exactly what Virgil was not prepared to do, whatever the cost to the credibility of Rome's heaven-sent mission. We are left deeply unhappy at the close of the book, but it is important to end with the thought that while Dido rejected all her obligations to her people and destroyed herself for reasons entirely personal to her, Aeneas was able to dismiss the promptings of self and return to the duty which he owed to others.

Turnus

The role of Turnus[1] in the *Aeneid* is in broad ways very like that of Dido: in brief he is an obstacle to the Roman mission, yet often arouses our sympathy. He does this in two ways: like Dido (but much less poignantly) he is an individual who does not belong to the cosmic plan – he must suffer because his hopes and aspirations are contrary to those of destiny. But unlike Dido he also wins sympathy because he represents a people even more important to the greatness of Rome than Aeneas' Trojans, namely the ancestors of the Italians.

But for all this there are aspects of Turnus which alienate us. He represents personal prowess, irresponsible individuality, barbaric energy in contrast with the public and social virtues which Aeneas shows or tries to show. He is fierce and violent (the word *uiolentia* is used of him only in the *Aeneid*) in contrast with Aeneas' attempts to show control; he represents, in Horace's phrase (*Odes* 3.4.65–6) *uis consili expers* in contrast with *uis temperata*. Words applied to Turnus and not to Aeneas are *uiolentia, fiducia, audax, superbus, turbidus, insania*; words applied to Turnus more often than to Aeneas include *amens, ardere, furor, ira*. Turnus fights for his own glory and reputation: Aeneas fights because he must, in order to establish peace and bring civilization. Aeneas fights a *bellum iustum*, Turnus does not. Examples of Turnus' violence and arrogance may be found at 7.413ff.; 7.461–2 *saeuit amor ferri et scelerata insania belli,* | *ira super* 'passion for steel rages in him, and the accursed madness of war, and anger above all'; 7.785ff.; 9.126 (= 10.276); 9.760–1 *sed furor ardentem caedisque insana cupido* | *egit in aduersos* 'but his frenzy and his mad lust for slaughter drove him all ablaze against the enemy'; 10.443; 10.492; 12.9–11; 12.101ff. (a description of his delight as he arms for battle). No less than fifteen similes are used to describe him, almost all conveying energy and ferocity: he is compared three times with a lion, twice with a bull, twice with a wolf, once each with an eagle, a tiger, a war horse, Mars, the north wind, fire and torrent, a land-slide, and finally, when all is lost, with the helplessness of the dream world.

The treatment of Turnus' story is deepened and made more intense (like that of Dido) by similarities with the progression of a hero of the Greek tragic stage towards a disaster which he himself makes more and more inevitable. His proud

[1] On Turnus see Otis (1963) 345ff., Small (1959) 243ff.

self-confidence leads him to arrogant behaviour such as the gods do not love. The outstanding instance of this is when he kills Pallas in circumstances of cruelty and brutality (reminiscent of Pyrrhus killing Polites before Priam's eyes), wishing that Pallas' father were there to see (*aspere et amare dictum*, comments Servius), and after his victory in the unequal fight returning Pallas as Evander 'deserved to have him' (*qualem meruit Pallanta remitto*). Virgil intervenes here into his narrative to reflect on the tragic outcome that must await these deeds:

> nescia mens hominum fati sortisque futurae
> et seruare modum rebus sublata secundis!
> Turno tempus erit... (10.501–3)

How ignorant are men's hearts of fate and destiny to come, and of how to keep within bounds when exalted by success! A time will come for Turnus...

At the moment when defeat and disaster surround him he is seen reduced to total perplexity – the tragic hero, under the too heavy pressure of adverse forces, no longer is master of himself:

> obstipuit uaria confusus imagine rerum
> Turnus et obtutu tacito stetit: aestuat ingens
> uno in corde pudor mixtoque insania luctu
> et furiis agitatus amor et conscia uirtus. (12.665–8)

Turnus stood amazed, confounded by the shifting picture of events, and he halted, gazing and not speaking: in one human heart there seethed deep shame, madness mingled with grief, love driven on by frenzy, and the knowledge of his prowess.

Just before the final scene, Jupiter sends a Fury in the shape of an owl to beat its wings in Turnus' face, and we are reminded of the lonely and terrified Dido whose nightmare visions and torments of conscience were accompanied by the long-drawn hooting of an owl (4.462ff.). This reminiscence of the events of Book 4 is immediately reinforced as Juturna bids farewell to her doomed brother in phrases and terms reminiscent of Anna's farewell to her sister (12.871 ~ 4.673; 12.880–1 ~ 4.677–8). The last scenes of the tragedy of Turnus are thus linked with the tragedy of Dido.

These aspects of Turnus' bravery in battle (cf. also 12.894–5, 931–2), coupled with his native Italian qualities, have led Voltaire and some since to take his side against Aeneas: Scaliger had said of him 'dignus profecto qui aut vinceret aut divinis tantum armis neque aliis vinceretur' 'Turnus indeed deserved to conquer or at least to be conquered only by heavenly arms and no other'. We think of Blake's statement that in *Paradise Lost* Milton was 'of the Devil's party without knowing it', and it is interesting that a number of Milton's descriptions of Satan are based on Turnus.[1] But in the end it is the Homeric

[1] See Harding (1962).

aspects of Turnus' behaviour which mean that he cannot survive in the proto-Roman world which Aeneas is founding. In the Sibyl's prophecy (*Aen.* 6.89) Turnus is said to be another Achilles; he is equated, or equates himself, with the Greeks in 7.371–2, 9.136–9, 9.742; in the final scenes he is the Achilles figure placed now in the loser's position. We have already seen that Aeneas has by no means succeeded fully in replacing Homeric violence by a new and more civilized attitude towards the defeated – by no means; but he has made a start in that direction, he wishes to find a new way however imperfect his efforts to find it. Turnus on the other hand is wholly devoted to the old Homeric way, and however much our sympathies may sometimes be with him, our judgement must be in favour of the new way.

5. DESTINY AND RELIGION IN THE 'AENEID'

Above everything else, the *Aeneid* is a religious poem. It is based on the un-questioned assumption that there exist powers outside the world of men, and that these powers direct and influence mortal actions in accordance with a far-reaching plan of their own, extending over the centuries as far as history can reach, and concerned with the long destiny of nations.

The nature of this divine plan and the part which Rome is to play in it is outlined in Jupiter's speech to his daughter Venus in 1.257ff. In it he reveals to her the fates of the future as he will bring them to pass, especially with regard to the Roman mission. He has given the Romans rule without end (*imperium sine fine dedi*) and he stresses two aspects of their destiny. The first is by means of conquest to establish universal peace:

> aspera tum positis mitescent saecula bellis...
>   dirae ferro et compagibus artis
>   claudentur Belli portae...   (1.291–4)

Then the harsh generations will be softened with wars laid aside...the gates of War, terrifying with their tight bands of steel, will be closed...

The second is to establish law (*iura dabunt*, 293; cf. 4.231 *totum sub leges mitteret orbem*). This concept of the mission is broadened in the famous words of Anchises at the end of the pageant of the ghosts of Roman heroes (6.851–3):

> tu regere imperio populos, Romane, memento
> (hae tibi erunt artes), pacique imponere morem,
> parcere subiectis et debellare superbos.

But you, Roman, must remember to rule the peoples with your government – this will be your art – to add to peace a civilized way of life, to spare the conquered and crush the proud.

Here again we see both aspects of the mission: first peace after crushing the proud, and mercy to the conquered; then government, i.e. settled laws, administrative order (*regere imperio*). This last concept is enlarged by the use of the word *mos* in its sense of a moral way of life, a civilized way of behaving (the word is more common in the plural in this sense, but cf. 8.316 *quis neque mos neque cultus erat* 'who had no code of morals and no civilization').

Another passage in which the destined history of Rome is given full and vivid expression is the description of Aeneas' shield (8.626.). Amidst the famous scenes around the outside the most striking is the one at the top, a picture of the delivery of Rome from the Gauls by the sacred geese, with religious orders such as the Salii and the Luperci included in the description; the gods have saved the righteous Romans from destruction. In the centre is the Battle of Actium with Augustus leading his Italians to battle 'with the Senate and the people, the gods of the hearth and the great gods'. And at the end Aeneas picks up the shield, lifting on to his shoulder the fame and destiny of his descendants – *attollens umero famamque et fata nepotum*.

Thus the part played in the poem by fate, and by Jupiter as its agent, is clear and unequivocal: the Romans, as a god-fearing people, will rule the world (cf. Cic. *Nat. D.* 3.5, Prop. 3.22.21ff.) and guide all the nations in the way that providence decrees; in the words of Horace, addressed to the Roman people (*Odes* 3.6.5) *dis te minorem quod geris imperas* 'because you are servants of the gods, you rule on earth'. But the situation in heaven is more complex than this: the Olympian deities, major and minor, constantly influence the human action, and are crucial to the poetic concept of the poem. This was a feature of epic technique which Virgil took from Homer and adapted in various ways. In Homer the anthropomorphic aspect of the Olympian deities was real in religious thought; the Homeric warrior might indeed believe that Apollo or Athene in person could intervene to save him from death. In Virgil's time a more sophisticated concept of deity prevented this belief except in a very symbolic sense. Yet Virgil decided to accept the Homeric convention in a poem written in a different religious environment – Why?

First and foremost Virgil uses the Olympian deities so as to enlarge the range of his poetic imagination. The visualization of shapes not seen by mortal eyes fascinated him, and he could paint pictures of the world beyond the clouds as if with brush on canvas. Consider the majestic figure of Juno moving with regal majesty in the halls of Olympus (1.46); the radiant brilliance of Iris descending by her rainbow (4.700–2); the strange splendour of Neptune and his sea-deities (1.144–7); the swooping figure of Mercury (4.252–8); the supernatural beauty of Venus as she re-assumes her divinity (1.402–5). These were magical shapes which captured Virgil's visual imagination, imbued as he was with the Greek art and literature which had so constantly portrayed them. With them he could transport his readers into another world of fancy and beauty, and achieve for them what Venus achieved for her son when she showed him what the gods could see, but mortals not:

> aspice (namque omnem, quae nunc obducta tuenti
> mortalis hebetat uisus tibi, et umida circum
> caligat, nubem eripiam...)   (2.604–6)

Look, for I will remove from you all the cloud which now veils and dims your mortal sight, and casts a damp shadow around you...

The Olympian deities enabled Virgil to enter in description the mythological world which delighted Ovid in his *Metamorphoses*.

But the Olympian deities do more than provide another world of visual imagination: they also symbolize the relationship between man and the divine. We have seen how Jupiter (interpreting fate) is a symbol of the benevolence of providence towards the righteous: the lesser Olympians symbolize different aspects of man's total environment and experience. Juno represents the hostility of fortune towards the Trojans, and more will be said about her shortly; Venus is a strange mixture of the protecting mother-goddess (*alma Venus*) caring for her children, for Aeneas and for all his Romans, and the reckless Greek goddess Aphrodite, rejoicing in her power over mortals (cf. 1.657–94, 4.105–28); Apollo is the guardian god of Troy and also the god who helps those who set out on difficult and dangerous expeditions (this aspect of him is especially seen in Book 3) – he is also the special patron of Augustus (8.704–6); Neptune is the saviour by sea (1.124–56, 5.779–826). In some cases the deities may be seen as symbolizing an aspect of personality of the human actors: the torch which Allecto at Juno's instigation hurls at Turnus (7.456–66) easily fires an already inflammable character; the intervention of Mercury on Jupiter's orders to instruct Aeneas to leave Carthage (4.265–78) may well be seen as a manifestation of Aeneas' guilty conscience: he has allowed himself to become out of touch with the divine, but now he listens to Jupiter's instructions, being the kind of man who can and does respond to a message from heaven.

But it is of course Juno of all the Olympians who plays the major part in the poem. Visually she is strikingly portrayed, and as a character in her own right she is formidable, relentless, brilliantly rhetorical in expressing her anger or her guile (1.37–49, 4.93–104, 7.293–322); but above all she is symbolic of opposition to the Trojans. Some reasons for her opposition are given by Virgil in mythological and personal terms, reminiscent of the motivation of Homeric divinities; she was angry because of her support for the Greeks whom the Trojans had opposed for ten years, because of the judgement of Paris, because of Ganymede (1.23–32). But other reasons also are given, with strong emphasis, in historical terms: Juno is the guardian deity of Carthage

(1.12–22) and therefore opposes the Trojans by whose descendants her favourite city would be destroyed. This historical opposition is an undertone throughout the story of Dido, as Juno schemes to divert the kingdom of Italy to the shores of Libya (4.106). And in addition to both these aspects of her, Juno symbolizes in the broadest possible way the hostile environment, the apparently senseless disasters that befall the virtuous, the 'slings and arrows of outrageous fortune'. Everywhere and implacably she attempts to bring disaster upon the Trojans (1.36ff., 5.606ff., 7.286ff., 9.2 ff., 12.134ff.), and she is directly responsible for much of the suffering in the poem. Her relationship with the fates is a paradox which Virgil sensitively explores; she cannot change the immutable purposes of destiny, but in all kinds of ways she can delay its fulfilment, cause such difficulty that the fulfilment may be less glorious, less complete. She does not in fact seriously impair the purpose of the fates, but she does – again paradoxically – modify it to the great benefit of the Romans.

In the final reconciliation scene between Jupiter and Juno (12.791–842) Juno makes specific requests which are fully granted. She asks that the Latins should keep their name, their language, and their habit of dress; Jupiter accepts all these conditions for the Roman people who are to spring from Trojan–Italian stock, with the significant enlargement of 'habits of dress' into 'way of life' (*mores*). He continues by saying that he himself will give them religious rites and customs (thus superseding the Trojan deities which Aeneas had brought with him), and promising that the Roman race will in its *pietas* surpass all other mortals and indeed the gods themselves. Thus Juno is wholly successful in her pleas against the Trojans, and we see that her hostility has in fact achieved for the Romans what was essential to their greatness – that a large Italian element should combine with the exiles from Troy. Under these conditions (*sit Romana potens Itala uirtute propago* 'let the Roman stock be mighty because of Italian qualities' 12.827) Juno is prepared to be accepted as a Roman deity, to be one of the Capitoline Triad, to defend the Romans and Italians with her help (as she certainly would not have defended the Trojans, cf. Hor. *Odes* 3.3). Ironically and paradoxically her opposition to Aeneas turns out to be beneficial for the Romans, not only because they had been hardened through suffering (*tantae molis erat Romanam condere gentem* 'so great a task it was to found the Roman race' 1.33; cf. Donatus' comment *magna enim sine magno labore condi non possunt* 'great things cannot be achieved without great toil'), but also because it was Juno who secured for the Italians, the enemies of Aeneas, their dominance in the Roman race whose achievements Virgil anticipates in his poem.

The Olympians, then, apart from forming part of the machinery of the poem and offering Virgil opportunity for pictorial imagery in a supernatural world, also enabled the poet to symbolize his thoughts and feelings about the relationship of human beings to the powers above them, about the nature of their individual free will within the framework of a divine purpose, about the problems of evil and suffering in a world guided by benevolent providence. His preoccupations are those to which Christianity was so shortly to give its answers; his own answers are very halting and uncertain. In his invocation to the Muse (1.8–11) he asks to be told the causes for Juno's hostility towards a man outstanding for his devotion to his gods and his fellow men (*insignem pietate uirum*), and he concludes with the question *tantaene animis caelestibus irae?* 'Can there be such anger in the minds of the gods?' For all the final success of Jupiter's purpose, for all the final reconciliation of Juno, the note of suffering and pathos is very often dominant in the poem. Unlike Milton, Virgil does not profess to be able to 'justify the ways of God to men', but this is the theme which he explores in countless situations in the poem, as he sets different aspects of human experience, human aspiration, human suffering in the context of a story laden with destiny.

The religious content of the poem is (naturally enough) largely concentrated in the narrative as the Olympian deities scheme and counter-scheme and Jupiter guides events towards the way which destiny demands, and as the human actors pay their worship, make their prayers and fulfil their religious ceremonies (the *Aeneid* is remarkably full of religious ritual, partly because of Virgil's love of ceremony and antique customs, and partly because of the essentially religious nature of Aeneas' destiny). But there is one place in the poem where an exposition of theological doctrine is set forth in a didactic fashion; this is where the ghost of Anchises explains to his son when they meet in Elysium the nature of the life after death (6.724–51). The exposition does indeed serve the plot, because it is needed to explain the presence of the ghosts at the river of Lethe, but it is primarily a religious message to the Roman reader, several times reminiscent in style of the didactic method of Lucretius and strongly coloured with the Stoic ideas which Virgil had come to find more acceptable than the Epicureanism which he followed in his youth. The message is the more striking because of its total contrast with the afterlife in Homer, whose *Nekyia* in *Odyssey* 11 had suggested some of the structure of *Aeneid* 6. The essence of the speech[1] is based on Orphic and Pythagorean ideas as purified by Plato: this life is merely a preparation for a richer life to come, and in proportion as we concentrate on the spirit and not on the body during this life our soul will be the more easily purified of its stains and made fit to dwell for ever with the divine essence from which it came. Upon death we all undergo purification – only a few can be purified sufficiently to stay in Elysium, while the rest must be reborn for a new life on earth. But the gates of Elysium are open wide (6.660–4), not only for those who died for their country, or were priests and poets, or enriched life by their discoveries, but also for those who

---

[1] See Bailey (1935) 275ff.

made people remember them by their service. Thus in some way only dimly seen virtue in this world is rewarded in the next; the confusion and suffering and sorrow of our life will be compensated for after death. It is a vague picture, and not presented with any kind of certainty – the whole of *Aeneid* 6 is really a vision personal to Aeneas rather than a confident statement about the hereafter. It is presented in groping hope, not in the sureness of faith; but it prevents a poem which is not always serenely confident about the potential perfection of Rome's Golden Age and which is so deeply preoccupied with suffering from becoming a poem of pessimism.

6. STYLE AND METRE

It is only possible here to make a few brief remarks about Virgil's style and metre. His narrative method can be contrasted with that of Homer in a number of ways: it has less directness and immediacy, but rather aims at density and elaborate balance[1] in a way appropriate for literary epic, and it is more concerned with foreshadowing and interweaving: it looks backwards and forwards. It is essentially a subjective style of narrative[2] in which the author involves himself and the reader empathetically in the action. This is done in many different ways: e.g. by elaborating the state of mind or the viewpoint of the character concerned rather than of the observer (e.g. 4.465ff., 12.665ff.); by the use of apostrophe in moments of particular intensity (e.g. 4.408ff., 10.507ff.); by 'editorial' intrusion into the narrative (4.412, 10.501ff.). The use of imagery[3] is highly sophisticated, containing correspondences with other parts of the narrative of such a kind as to illuminate the particular situation or character involved; this can be seen especially in a study of the similes,[4] where the imagery often serves not merely to illustrate and strengthen the immediate narrative but also to make thematic links with the mood and tone of the wider context (e.g. *Aen.* 1.498ff., 4.69ff., 4.441ff., 12.4ff., 12.908ff.).

The movement of Virgil's narrative is indeed much less rapid than that of Homer (Ovid is much nearer to Homer in speed and directness), and a slow, descriptive and reflective mood is generally thought of as especially characteristic of Virgil (e.g. 2.624ff., 5.833ff., 6.450ff., 11.816ff.). This is basically true, but what is really remarkable about Virgil's style is its extraordinary variety; this is what maintains the impetus throughout the length of the poem. He can be ornate and baroque (1.81ff., 3.570ff., 5.426ff.) or plain and matter-of-fact (as often in Book 3 or in the ship-race, 5.151ff.); he can be sonorous and sublime (1.257ff., 6.756ff.) or exuberantly mock-heroic (6.385–416). And he

[1] See the analysis of Virgil's adaptation of Homer's games in R. D. Williams (1960) Intro. xiii ff.
[2] See Otis (1963) *passim*.
[3] See Pöschl (1950) *passim*, Putnam (1965) *passim*. [4] See Hornsby (1970).

can on occasion use the crisp and rapid narrative of Homer (e.g. the disguised Trojans in 2.370ff., the hunt in 4.129ff., the Rutulian attack in 9.33–46, the episode of Nisus and Euryalus in 9.314–445 and much of the second half of Book 9). But generally Virgil aims at and achieves a denser style by extending and enlarging the conventional vocabulary of epic, not perhaps so much by neologisms (though there are some) as by unusual combinations of words, by the *callida iunctura* of Horace (*A.P.* 47–8). Epithets are transferred, the constructions of verbs altered, the attention arrested by unusual phrases which seem to hover around several meanings rather than pinpoint one in the Ovidian manner. This penumbra, this evocative indistinctness may be what Agrippa meant when he accused Virgil of a new kind of stylistic affectation (*cacoʒelia*: *Vita Don.* 44). Some outstanding examples of this dense and evocatively pictorial style may be studied at 1.159ff., 2.230ff., 7.177ff., 11.59ff., 12.587ff.

The arrangement of the words, while nothing like as intricate as that of Horace's *Odes*, nevertheless differs greatly from that of normal Latin prose. Nouns and their adjectives are often separated so as to make a patterned line, though extreme patterning such as that in a Golden Line is rarer than in the *Eclogues*. With this expectation of style set up in his readers Virgil can make a great impact by abandoning it in favour of the simple order of noun and adjective placed adjacently, as for example the famous lines beginning *ibant obscuri* (6.268–70) or the description of Elysium (6.638–9).

Words and constructions with a prosaic ring are avoided (for example *cum* with the pluperfect subjunctive is never found), and the normal Latin method of subordinating clauses within a long period is much rarer than in Virgil's predecessors (Lucretius was fond of clauses with subordinating conjunctions and Catullus of participial clauses). The effect of this is to produce what is perhaps the most striking of all the stylistic features of the *Aeneid* – its very high proportion of main verbs, that is to say its paratactic style. Examples of this directness may be found easily and frequently, e.g. 1.208–13, 2.407–12, 3.561–9, 4.579–83, 5.673–9. All this is not to say that Virgil does not use the slower, more conventional Latin sentence where he needs it, e.g. the description of Iris at 4.693–702, the speech of old Neptune at 5.804–11, the picture of the Tiber at 8.86–9, the description of Pallas' funeral at 11.39–41.

A large proportion of the *Aeneid* is taken up with speeches,[1] and here Virgil commands a vivid rhetorical and oratorical skill, as is attested by the speakers in Macrobius' *Saturnalia* (5.1) where they discuss whether a student of oratory would learn more from Cicero or Virgil, and Eusebius suggests that Virgil has more variety of oratory than Cicero – *facundia Mantuani multiplex et multiformis est et dicendi genus omne complectitur* 'His eloquence is manifold and diverse, embracing every style of speaking'. Examples of particularly

---

[1] See Highet (1972).

powerful rhetoric are found especially in the speeches of Juno and Venus (1.37–49, 1.229–53, especially 10.18–62, 63–95), and of Sinon (2.108–44), Dido (4.365–87, 590–629) and Drances and Turnus (11.342–75, 378–444). Often the nature of the situation requires that the rhetoric should be less over-powering, e.g. 1.257–96, 1.562–78, 2.776–89, 3.154–71, and here Virgil demon-strates that he can use his art to conceal art as well as to flaunt it.

A final word must be said about epic dignity. It was conventional to use heightened phrases to describe ordinary events (as Virgil does everywhere in the *Georgics*, a form of convention which the English eighteenth century fully accepted); examples are the servants and kitchenmaids in 1.701–6, the pigs of Circe in 7.15–20, the simile of the top in 7.378–84, the sow and its piglets in 8.81–5. Virgil does not attempt to imitate the 'low' style (*humilis*) which Homer achieved so outstandingly when describing ordinary or homely situa-tions: Quintilian recognized this when he said that no one could possibly surpass Homer's propriety in small things (*proprietas in paruis rebus*). Virgil's sublimity and grandeur, never or very rarely broken by un-epic situations or phraseology, is sustained and strengthened by a fondness for poetic Grecisms and for archaisms in appropriate places to match the antiquity of his subject (Quintilian called him *amantissimus uetustatis* 'deeply enamoured of what was old'); echoes of the phraseology of Ennius and of archaic forms used by Ennius and Lucretius often occur, enhancing the dignity and conventional remoteness of the epic form by means of which Virgil was able to express concepts and ideas which are intimately connected with the real life of real people.

Metre

Virgil's command of the rhythm of the hexameter has always been acclaimed: Dryden spoke of 'the sweetness of the sound' and Tennyson's line is well known: 'Wielder of the stateliest measure ever moulded by the lips of man'. Virgil was fortunate in receiving from Ennius the heritage of a metre of extra-ordinary flexibility, both in regard to the speed of the line as regulated by the interchange of dactyls and spondees, and especially because the system of quantity taken over from the Greek hexameter could be used as a metrical base (ictus) against which the word-accent of Latin with its stressed syllables could be used as a second rhythm in the line. This potentiality had been barely explored by Virgil's predecessors, Ennius, Lucretius, Catullus, Cicero; in Virgil's hands it became a highly sophisticated method for conveying conflict and struggle (when the two rhythms are opposed) or serenity and peace (when they coincide). This aspect of Virgil's hexameter has been studied widely in recent times[1] and figures largely in modern commentaries on the *Aeneid*, and

---

[1] See Knight (1939) and (1966) 292ff., Wilkinson (1963) 90ff.

more cannot be said here than to indicate that this is one of the most fruitful methods of appreciating the infinite variety of Virgil's verse.

A second area in which Virgil greatly developed the work of his predecessors was in the relationship of sentence structure to verse pattern. Ennius, Lucretius and Catullus had for the most part (with exceptions, of course) preferred a metrical movement where the sentence structure corresponded with the verse ending: for example in Catullus 64 the proportion of run-on verses (or mid-line stops) is very small. Virgil, like Milton, experimented with an enjambment involving a frequent tension between verse structure and sentence structure. The variety of the position of his sense-pauses is very great, and the effect achieved by (for example) the verb run on to the end of the first foot of the following line (e.g. 2.327, 467) or by a series of lines where the clauses stop in different places in the line (e.g. 5.670–3, 9.390–401) can be very great indeed. As there is a tension between ictus and accent, so there is a tension between verse and sentence.

Virgil's employment of unusual metrical features (hiatus, spondaic fifth foot, monosyllabic ending, absence of caesura and so on) is highly selective and used generally for special effect. In Ennius, Lucretius and Catullus these features often indicate either an insufficient mastery of technique, or a special idiosyncrasy (like Catullus' fifth-foot spondees); in Ovid and his successors they are used much more rarely. Virgil succeeds in departing from the expected norm sufficiently often, but only sufficiently often, to arrest the reader's attention.

Finally Virgil used the devices of alliteration and assonance, of lightness or heaviness in metre, in such a way as not to cloy. It was traditional in Latin poetry to use these effects, and Virgil follows in the tradition, but in a fashion sufficiently sophisticated almost to escape notice until detailed analysis is made. In poetry these effects are generally significant potentially rather than in themselves: that is to say that if other methods are being employed to raise the reader's interest in particular directions the use of alliteration and assonance can reinforce the impact. This is the essence of Virgil's ability to suit the sound to the sense; we are aroused by the context to expect and respond to a particular effect before the effect is presented to us. Consider for example the angry speech of Iarbas to Jupiter (4.206–18) where he complains of how Aeneas the intruder is preferred in Dido's eyes to himself; we are involved in his indignation and when he ends:

> nos munera templis
> quippe tuis ferimus famamque fouemus inanem   (217–18)

we are reinforced in our feeling by the unusual and violent alliteration of *f*.

Consider as an example some of the stylistic and metrical effects in Dido's last long speech:

'pro Iuppiter! ibit   590
hic,' ait 'et nostris inluserit aduena regnis?
non arma expedient totaque ex urbe sequentur,
deripientque rates alii naualibus? ite,
ferte citi flammas, date tela, impellite remos!
quid loquor? aut ubi sum? quae mentem insania mutat?   595
infelix Dido, nunc te facta impia tangunt?
tum decuit, cum sceptra dabas. en dextra fidesque,
quem secum patrios aiunt portare penatis,
quem subiisse umeris confectum aetate parentem!
non potui abreptum diuellere corpus et undis   600
spargere? non socios, non ipsum absumere ferro
Ascanium patriisque epulandum ponere mensis?
uerum anceps pugnae fuerat fortuna. – fuisset:
quem metui moritura? faces in castra tulissem
implessemque foros flammis natumque patremque   605
cum genere exstinxem, memet super ipsa dedissem.
Sol, qui terrarum flammis opera omnia lustras,
tuque harum interpres curarum et conscia Iuno,
nocturnisque Hecate triviis ululata per urbes
et Dirae ultrices et di morientis Elissae,   610
accipite haec, meritumque malis aduertite numen
et nostras audite preces. si tangere portus
infandum caput ac terris adnare necesse est,
et sic fata Iouis poscunt, hic terminus haeret,
at bello audacis populi uexatus et armis,   615
finibus extorris, complexu auulsus Iuli
auxilium imploret uideatque indigna suorum
funera; nec, cum se sub leges pacis iniquae
tradiderit, regno aut optata luce fruatur,
sed cadat ante diem mediaque inhumatus harena.   620
haec precor, hanc uocem extremam cum sanguine fundo.
tum uos, o Tyrii, stirpem et genus omne futurum
exercete odiis, cinerique haec mittite nostro
munera. nullus amor populis nec foedera sunto.
exoriare aliquis nostris ex ossibus ultor   625
qui face Dardanios ferroque sequare colonos,
nunc, olim, quocumque dabunt se tempore uires.
litora litoribus contraria, fluctibus undas
imprecor, arma armis: pugnent ipsique nepotesque.'   (4.590–629)

The speech begins in mid-line with staccato phrases, with unusual sense pauses after the fifth foot of 590 and after the first syllable of 591: emphasis is given to the bitter words *inluserit aduena* enclosed within the rhyme from caesura to line ending (*nostris...regnis*). The staccato impression is continued with a very strong sense pause after *naualibus* (echoing that in 590) and the series of short clauses in 594 with violent alliteration of *t*. Then as Dido realizes that there is no one to hear her agitated commands the metre slows totally and the simple words of 596 produce an entirely spondaic rhythm; the question she asks herself is answered in equally simple words, in an even shorter sentence of absolute finality (*tum...dabas*).

Now Dido's anger rises again as she passes from self-blame to emotional resentment of her lover's actions: alliteration of *p* in 598–9 reinforces her dis-belief in the traditional stories of Aeneas' virtues and the impersonal *aiunt* is strongly contemptuous. Had she not heard it all from his own lips? The gruesome imagery of 600 is allowed to run on to the next line; and again empha-sis is put on the intervening words *epulandum ponere* by the rhyme from caesura to line ending (602). As she reflects on the doubtful issue of the horrifying deeds she has suggested to herself her words are given impetus by two very rare trochaic sense pauses (603, 604); and the certainty that all the actions she might have taken are now for ever unfulfilled is reflected by the remarkable rhyming effect of the pluperfect subjunctives (*tulissem, implessem, exstinxem, dedissem*).

Now the trend of her thoughts changes direction entirely from the agony of the unfulfilled past to her passion for vengeance in the future. The rhythm slows entirely, with a high proportion of spondees and two monosyllables to commence her invocation (607), with rhyme of *harum...curarum* (echoing *terrarum*), with lines that are complete in themselves with pauses at the end of each, and with the strange sound-repetition of *et Dirae...et di*. After the solemnity of the invocation the prayer itself is given in three short clauses involving sense pauses in the second foot, at the line ending, and in the fourth foot (611–12). Thus the invocation itself has a sonorous majesty as each verse, complete in itself, reinforces the previous one; while the actual prayer reflects metrically the urgent call for action.

The subject matter of the prayer begins with a long sweeping sentence with end-stopped lines, given vehemence by places of marked conflict of accent and ictus (613, 615) and coming to a pause abruptly and powerfully on the word *funera*: death is her desire for others as well as for herself and there is no more emphatic way of stressing the word than by placing it last in its sentence and first in the line. The next phrase begins very slowly with monosyllables (618) and comes to its violent climax with the conflict of accent against ictus on the word *cadat*.

In the resumption of her curse, as she extends it from Aeneas personally to the long vista of the years to come she uses the same technique as in 618 to give emphasis to the intense irony of *munera* (624). Her invocation of the unknown avenger has hissing *s*'s to reinforce the syntactical strangeness of the third person *aliquis* with the second person verb *exoriare*, and rhyme of *Dardanios*...*colonos* as well as of *exoriare*...*sequare*. After the three self-contained lines (625–7) the speech concludes with lines containing mid-line stops (after the fourth foot in 628, after the first and in the third of 629), and ends with the very rare device of hypermetric elision, a device which is in fact impossible here because the speech is over and Dido's last word *nepotesque* cannot be elided. She is unable at the end to fit the torrent of her words to the metrical scheme.

A brief and very selective analysis of this kind gives perhaps some idea of the complexity and variety of Virgil's rhythm, a variety sufficient to sustain the interest over many thousands of lines. More than any other Roman poet Virgil was able to make the movement of his words and the sound of his verse match and therefore reinforce the content and mood of the subject matter.

7. CONCLUSION

The *Aeneid* is above all a poem of the exploration of conflicting attitudes, an attempt to harmonize the different and often discordant facets of human experience. Its relationship with the poems of Homer sets up a double time-scale in which the qualities and ideals of Homeric life can be compared and contrasted with the needs of a new type of civilization. Its parallel narrative on two planes, divine in Olympus and human in the mortal world, perpetually compels our attention to the interrelationship of the everlasting divine laws and transient human action. But above all the poem explores the relationship between the strong vigorous national world of Roman organization and empire and the quiet private world of the lonely individual who is not interested in, or is excluded from, or is destroyed by the cosmic march of Roman destiny.

We may distinguish these two elements by speaking of Virgil's public voice (patriotic, national, concerned with the march of a people) and his private voice (sorrowful, sensitive, personal). There need be no doubt that the *Aeneid* is intended primarily to celebrate the public aspect of optimism, of power, of organized government. But side by side with this, and perhaps increasingly as the poem progressed, Virgil was preoccupied with the suffering of those who fall by the way, or are trampled underfoot as the march of destiny proceeds forward. The outstanding examples of this are of course Dido and Turnus, but instances of tragic and unhappy death occur throughout the poem: Orontes drowned by Juno's storm (1.113ff.), Priam and Laocoon and many others in Book 2, like Coroebus, Rhipeus, Polites; there is the pathos of Andromache and Achaemenides in Book 3; the sudden and inexplicable loss of Palinurus in Book 5; the plight of the ghosts in Book 6, especially Palinurus, Dido and

Deiphobus; the deaths of Galaesus in 7, of Nisus and Euryalus in 9, of Pallas and Lausus in 10, of Camilla in 11, of Aeolus in 12:

> hic tibi mortis erant metae, domus alta sub Ida,
> Lyrnesi domus alta, solo Laurente sepulcrum.   (12.546–7)

Here was your end of death; your lofty house was beneath Mt Ida, at Lyrnesus your lofty house, but your tomb is in Laurentian soil.

All of these and many more mark Virgil out as the poet of *lacrimae rerum* (1.462), of sympathy for the world's suffering; this has been the aspect of his poetry which has been most strongly stressed and most widely appreciated during the last hundred years. Sainte-Beuve spoke of *tendresse profonde*, Matthew Arnold of 'the haunting, the irresistible self-dissatisfaction of his heart', Myers of 'that accent of brooding sorrow'.

We may move this conflict between Virgil's public voice and his private voice into a literary setting. His public voice is set firmly in the tradition of Ennius, national poet of Rome's history and the greatness of her people; it would have been approved by Cicero, and it is echoed in Livy's history and Horace's Roman odes (3.1–6). It is stern, severe, detached, epic in the full sense in that it deals with the large-scale movement of great events. His private voice is in the tradition of Catullus, the poet of the individual's hopes and fears and joys and sorrows. There is a lyric quality, even an elegiac quality in many passages in the *Aeneid*, as for example the funeral of Pallas with its reminiscences of Catullus (11.59–99). Virgil has combined two modes, the hard and the soft, because he could sympathize with both. He has a foot in both camps; no other Roman poet was less dogmatic, more able to appreciate the viewpoint of contrasting personalities. It is because of his many-sidedness that in every generation since his own Virgil has been the most widely read of the Roman poets.

5

HORACE

I. A CRITIQUE OF THE TRADITIONAL STEREOTYPE

Horace is commonly thought of as a comfortable cheerful figure, well adjusted to society and loyally supporting the Augustan regime; a man without any strong beliefs or emotions, who smiled gently at human foibles, wrote and behaved with unfailing tact and good taste, and was in all respects the personification of *mediocritas*. As this picture has been remarkably consistent over the years and has not varied with the poet's popularity (but rather explains such variations) one would expect it to contain a good deal of truth. And so indeed it does; but on closer inspection we find that the colours have faded, contrasts of light and texture have disappeared, much of the detail has been lost, and the result is like a fresco damaged by time and neglect.

To recover a more vivid sense of the original we have to remind ourselves of a few fundamental points. First, it is misleading to classify Horace as an Augustan poet *tout court*. His life was more than half over when the Augustan age began, and the Emperor survived him by more than twenty years. Most of the satires and epodes belong to the period before Actium (31 B.C.). Few of these touch on politics, and those that do convey attitudes of disgust (*Epod.* 4), disillusion (*Sat.* 1.6), or despair (*Epod.* 7 and 16). Only five poems mention Octavian. They were all written at the time of Actium or shortly after, and except in the case of *Epod.* 9 the lines in question are of minor importance.

Secondly, although his imagination normally operated in the central areas of human experience, Horace was far from being average or typical. Even in an age of social ferment it was extraordinary for a freedman's son to go to school with the aristocracy, to study at the Academy in Athens, to serve as a military tribune under Brutus, and later to become accepted and esteemed by the imperial court. Success of this kind was not achieved without cost. In an early satire (written about 36 B.C.) Horace complains that everyone runs him down for being a freedman's son – *libertino patre natum* (*Sat.* 1.6.45–6). Elsewhere, especially in the first book of *Epistles* (about 20 B.C.), he shows a keen, almost anxious, awareness of social nuances, and even at the height of his fame he speaks as if he can still detect traces of resentment (*Odes* 4.3.16, about 13 B.C.).

Thirdly, in the late fifties, when Horace was in his teens, life in Rome was disrupted by riots and gang warfare. The political atmosphere grew steadily more oppressive until the storm of civil war broke in 49 B.C. After Caesar's assassination Horace joined Brutus and saw the carnage at Philippi 'when bravery was smashed' (*Odes* 2.7.11). He returned to Italy under a general amnesty to find that his father had died and the family home had been confiscated. Peace was still dreadfully precarious. In 37 B.C., as described in *Sat.* 1.5, Horace accompanied Maecenas to the conference at Tarentum, where Octavian met Antony. Later he was on the point of going to Actium (*Epod.* 1), though it is doubtful if he was actually present at the battle. We do know, however, that on another occasion (perhaps earlier, in 36 B.C.) he narrowly escaped drowning (*Odes* 3.4.28). If in middle age he opted for a quiet life, most people would feel he had earned it. In any case we must beware of the notion fostered by the older source criticism that Horace absorbed all his experience at second hand by reading Greek texts.

Again, when the doctrine of the mean is applied too rigidly to Horace's work, we get the impression of a rather dull and insipid personality. It is true, of course, that he often affirms the traditional belief (most fully developed by Aristotle) that virtue lies between two extremes. But in many cases he is primarily concerned to ridicule the extremes. Thus in *Epist.* 1.18 he states the doctrine succinctly in l. 9 – *uirtus est medium uitiorum* – and then immediately goes on to describe the sycophant and the boor. When he does speak of the mean itself he usually brings out its elusive nature – it varies according to a man's character, circumstances, and situation. Above all, it involves movement; for however stable the right condition may be in theory, we do not live in a stable world. We are always adjusting our position in order to maintain equilibrium:

> rebus angustis animosus atque
> fortis appare: sapienter idem
> contrahes uento nimium secundo
> turgida uela.   (*Odes* 2.10.21–4)

When in the straits of fortune show yourself spirited and brave. You will also do well to reef your sails when they are swollen by too strong a following wind.

The mean, then, is not easy to achieve; and it is certainly not attained, or even sought, in all Horace's poetry. Granted, he did not write about his sexual emotions with the intensity of Catullus, or goad himself into long rhetorical tirades in the manner of Juvenal; yet there were times when he deliberately flouted the accepted standards of good taste:

> rogare longo putidam te saeculo
> uiris quid eneruet meas,
> cum sit tibi dens ater et rugis uetus
> frontem senectus exaret

hietque turpis inter aridas natis
podex uelut crudae bouis.   (*Epod.* 8.1–6)

To think that you, who are rotten with decrepitude, should ask what is unstringing my virility, when your one tooth is black, and extreme old age ploughs furrows across your forehead, and your disgusting anus gapes between your shrivelled buttocks like that of a cow with diarrhoea.

Whether the victim of this foul attack existed or not we cannot say. If she did, Horace was not concerned to tell us who she was. On the other hand, we have no right to assume that because the poem contains no name and clearly belongs to the abusive tradition of Archilochus the woman must therefore be fictitious. Better to admit ignorance and pass on to a more important question, viz. what effect had the poet in mind? When we discover that the woman is aristocratic (the masks of her ancestors will attend her funeral), wealthy (she is weighed down with big round jewels), pseudo-intellectual (volumes of Stoicism lie on her silk cushions), and adulterous (she is eager for extra-marital thrills), the only plausible interpretation is that the whole thing is a horrible kind of joke, based on deliberate outrage. The poem is exceptional but not unique – *Epod.* 12 shows the same scabrous ingenuity, and two later odes, though less offensive, exploit a similar theme (1.25 and 4.13). Needless to say, the unpleasant epodes, and also most of *Sat.* 1.2 (which is bawdy, but clean in comparison) were omitted by the Victorian commentators; and as those admirable scholars have not yet been superseded it still has to be pointed out that Horace was not invariably polite.

Nor was he always happy. The struggle for tranquillity is well illustrated in *Odes* 2.3, which begins by affirming the importance of keeping a level head when things are steep (*aequam memento rebus in arduis | seruare mentem*). The next two stanzas speak of enjoying a bottle of Falernian in a secluded field with trees overhead and a stream running by. 'Bring wine, perfume, and roses', says the poet; but already there are darker overtones, for the lovely rose-blossoms are 'all too brief' and we can only enjoy ourselves 'while circumstances and youth and the black threads of the three sisters allow us'. The prince will have to leave his castle (17–20); like the poor man he is a victim of pitiless Orcus (21–4). Continuing the image of the victim (i.e. a sheep or a goat), the final stanza begins *omnes eodem cogimur* 'we are all being herded to the same place'; then the picture changes:

omnium
uersatur urna serius ocius
sors exitura et nos in aeternum
exilium impositura cumbae.   (25–8)

Everyone's pebble is being shaken in the jar. Sooner or later it will come out and put us on the boat for unending exile.

The choice of image whereby the shaken pebble conveys both the randomness and the inevitability of death, the compression of thought in which a lot-pebble puts someone on board a boat, and the sonorities of the whole stanza with its sequence of -er-, ur-, -er-, -or-, -ur-, -er-, -ur- and its two final elisions – these features produce a powerful effect; but it is hardly one of cheerful serenity.

On other occasions we find Horace in a state of high excitement. *Odes* 3.19 begins in a tone of good-humoured exasperation, saying in effect 'You keep talking about the dates and genealogies of the early Greek kings, but you say nothing about the cost of a party and who will act as host' (one notes the balance of dates/how much, genealogies/who). We then move forward in time; the party is under way, and Horace, now in exalted mood, calls for a series of toasts in honour of Murena the new Augur. As a thunderstruck (i.e. inspired) bard he can demand an especially potent mixture. 'Let's go mad!' he cries; 'Why is there no music? Start it at once! Throw roses! Let old Lycus and the girl who lives next door hear the wild uproar.' Wine, poetry, music, roses, and finally love: Rhode wants the romantically good-looking Telephus; Horace longs for his Glycera.

There Bacchic inspiration is loosely, and humorously, connected with a symposium. In *Odes* 3.25 it is directly related to the praises of Augustus. This is a more ambitious poem in that it attempts to convey the actual nature of a mystical experience:

> quo me, Bacche, rapis tui
>   plenum? quae nemora aut quos agor in specus
> uelox mente noua? (1–4)

Where are you rushing me, Bacchus, after filling me with yourself? To what woods and caves am I being hurried away in this strange condition?

It is not surprising that this dithyramb, with its exciting rhythm and fluid structure, should also contain one of the most striking pictures in Horace:

> non secus in iugis
> exsomnis stupet Euhias
>   Hebrum prospiciens et niue candidam
> Thracen ac pede barbaro
>   lustratam Rhodopen, ut mihi deuio
> ripas et uacuum nemus
>   mirari libet. (8–14)

On the mountain ridge the sleepless Bacchanal gazes out in astonishment at the river Hebrus and Thrace white with snow and at Mt Rhodope traversed by barbarian feet; so too, away from the paths of men, I love to marvel at the lonely riverbanks and woods.

Such passages must be given full weight if we are to appreciate the poet's richness and diversity.

A similar point can be made about Horace's ideas. If we compare what he says in different places on any particular subject we find that his opinions are usually reconcilable; but there are exceptions, and these sometimes occur in quite important odes. As an illustration let us consider what he says about the course of history. Some passages speak of man as having emerged from barbarism guided by rational self-interest (*Sat.* 1.3.99ff.) or a divine bard (Orpheus in *A.P.* 391f.) or a god (Mercury in *Odes* 1.10). But this process is never regarded as steady or assured, and at times, within the narrower context of Roman history, we are faced with a decline. In *Odes* 3.6, written about 28 B.C. before the Augustan recovery had got under way, the decline is supposed to date from the early part of the second century; and it will continue, says the poet, until the old religion is revived. In *Epod.* 7, where a curse is said to have pursued the Roman people ever since Romulus murdered his brother, we have a different kind of assertion. The vague chronological reference, located at a point before history emerged from legend, provides rhetorical force, but we are not meant to examine the statement's literal accuracy. After all, the Rome which became mistress of Italy and then went on to conquer Hannibal and Antiochus could hardly be thought of as accursed. So too, when Horace calls on his fellow-citizens to sail away to the isles of the blest where the golden age still survives (*Epod.* 16), he is not appealing to anything historically verifiable, but is using a myth (which is exploited for rather different ends by Virgil in the fourth *Eclogue*) to condemn the mad world in which he is living. Allowing for differences of perspective and idiom, there is no basic contradiction between these passages.

In *Odes* 1.3, however, there *is* a contradiction. The hardiness of the first sailor is seen as an arrogant defiance of god's will; and that sailor was typical of mankind as a whole which 'has the audacity to endure all, and goes hurtling through what is wrong and forbidden'. Examples follow: Prometheus stole fire and gave it to men – all kinds of sickness ensued; Daedalus invaded the air, Hercules the underworld. 'Nothing is too steep for mortals. We make for heaven itself in our folly, and by our wickedness we do not allow Jove to lay aside his angry thunderbolts.' This is not a manifesto of heroic humanism. Admittedly by using the word *audacia* Horace may acknowledge the other tradition in which Prometheus, Daedalus, and Hercules were admired for their courageous services to mankind, but he explicitly repudiates that tradition by giving *audacia* an unfavourable sense. Human inventiveness has led only to disaster. Such a view is, of course, naive and one-sided (though no more so than the belief in progress which has recently withered). And the uncompromising statement which it receives in *Odes* 1.3 is indeed untypical. But Horace was not always typically Horatian, and *Odes* 1.3 is a very good poem.

Finally, perhaps the most serious point forgotten in the popular conception of Horace is the fact that he was a great innovator. In the rest of the present section this will be illustrated by observations on his poetic career.

The seventeen epodes, which Horace referred to as *iambi*, were something quite new in Roman literature. One could amplify this by saying that no one had yet written a collection of Latin poems modelled on the work of Archilochus. Yet that would be misleading, not only because Horace differed in many ways from the seventh-century Greek, but because the whole vocabulary of modelling, copying, and imitating is apt to suggest something external and even mechanical. It is better to suppose that Horace found in Archilochus a poet with whom he had an instinctive affinity, and then used him as an aid to realizing and expressing what was in himself.

Keeping that in mind, we may turn to *Epist.* 1.19.23ff. where Horace says that he followed the *numeri* (metres) and *animi* (vehemence or spirit) of Archilochus, but not his *res* (subject matter) or *uerba* (words). Of the epodes nos. 1–10 consist of iambic couplets in which trimeters are followed by dimeters, nos. 11–16 contain various combinations of iambic and dactylic rhythms, and no. 17 is in trimeters throughout. Here there is a direct debt to Archilochus, for most of the schemes are found in his fragments; yet the technical achievement of producing these rhythms in Latin should not be underrated.

By *res* and *uerba* Horace means the subject matter of Archilochus' personal life and the language in which it was presented. Such features could only have been reproduced in a translation. In a more general sense, of course, Horace does use the same material as Archilochus (love, wine, war etc.), and his diction ranges from noble to foul as the situation requires. But the setting and characters are in most cases unmistakably Roman, and there are several poems, e.g. the melodramatic mimes about the witch Canidia (5 and 17) and the two poems addressed to Maecenas at the time of Actium (1 and 9), where the contribution of Archilochus is negligible.

As for the *animi*, if Horace means 'vehemence' then nos. 4, 6, 8, and 12 would be the most obvious examples, though the force of the attack is weakened by the victims' anonymity and by the lack of any explicit account of their relation to Horace. If *animi* has the vaguer meaning of 'spirit' then more pieces could be included, but we should not press this comparison too far, for the epodes were also influenced by more recent literature, such as Hellenistic mimes (as in 5 and 17) and perhaps even Latin elegies (as in 11 and 15). And in one case at least Archilochus' spirit is taken over only to be transformed into something utterly different. This is in no. 10, where Horace prays that the voyage of

Mevius may end in disaster. Similar imprecations are found in the so-called Strasbourg epode, usually attributed to Archilochus,[1] which Horace almost certainly knew. The difference between the two poems is not between the real and the imaginary (for Mevius was a real person, whether or not he was making a journey), but between the deadly seriousness of Archilochus and Horace's playful malice. *Epod.* 10, in fact, is a literary joke, in which the kindly form of the *propemptikon* (or send-off poem) is filled with grandiloquent invective so as to annihilate a fellow poet.

In satire Horace's role was rather different. Here the pioneer work had been done by a Latin poet, Gaius Lucilius, a hundred years earlier. That ebullient and wide-ranging man had taken over the idea of verse miscellanies (*saturae*) from Ennius. Then, by settling on the hexameter and using it to project a lively critical spirit, he had succeeded in creating a new and specifically Roman genre. It was, however, undeniably rough and sprawling, and Horace's contribution was to reduce and refine it so as to meet his own, more purely classical, standards. This meant concentrating mainly on a few central topics – in particular man's enslavement to money, glory, gluttony, and sex; narrowing the linguistic range by restricting the use of vulgarisms, archaisms, Greek importations, and comic coinages; cutting down on elisions and end-stopped lines so as to ease the rhythmic flow; and modifying Lucilius' buffoonery, coarseness, and abuse. Yet Horace greatly admired the older satirist, and he carried on the Lucilian tradition not just by ridiculing vice and folly but by writing in an informal and amusing way about himself.

The main differences between the two books of satires are as follows: Book 1 (published in 35 B.C. or soon after) includes a few pieces where the ethical element is small (as in 8 and 9) or negligible (as in 5 and 7) and the main purpose is to entertain; the attacks on moral and literary faults are conducted by the poet himself (sometimes with the aid of an anonymous opponent), and they are made specific and interesting by the frequent use of proper names. In Book 2 (30 B.C.) fewer figures are attacked, and new techniques are employed for communicating the ideas. Thus Horace sometimes delivers the homily himself, sometimes reports it, sometimes listens to it, sometimes appears as a person being warned or rebuked, and sometimes withdraws completely. Dramatic presentations are more frequent, and there is an extensive use of parody.

Perhaps the most notable feature of the *Satires* as a whole is their pervasive reasonableness. Horace assumes at the outset that we are living in a civilized society where there is no need to handle such monstrous aberrations as sadism, cannibalism, and incest. He also assumes that within our social and moral

[1] See Kirkwood (1961) 267–82, van Sickle (1975).

framework we have the power to discriminate between different degrees of wickedness, that we have a sense of proportion to which he can appeal, and that in however faltering a way we can bring thought to bear upon our attitudes and conduct. He therefore pays us the compliment of addressing our intellect. In most pieces the satirical attack is carried out through an argument or disquisition which moves in an orderly though subtle way from one point to another. The poet's tone is rarely abusive. He does not seek to establish too much; he hears objections; makes concessions. And so at the end of the poem the reader feels not only that he has been listening to a sensible man but also that the ethical point has been made progressively clearer and more precise. Such an impression would, of course, be ruined if Horace appeared self-righteous or superior. He avoids this danger by laughing at himself and adopting a manner which, though basically serious, never asks for a heavily emotional response. Horace is not, in fact, primarily concerned to influence the reader's morals. He invites him, rather, to contemplate human folly as a subject of perennial interest. The contemplation is made enjoyable by the satirist's art. And then, as Persius observes (1.116–18), the moral insights emerge from the enjoyment.

After the publication of the *Epodes* and *Satires* 2 in 30 B.C. Horace confined himself to lyric, and in the next seven years produced what is normally regarded as his greatest work – viz. the first three books of *Odes*. Thirty years earlier Catullus had written two poems in sapphics, four in combinations of glyconics and pherecrateans, and one in asclepiads, but there was as yet no body of verse that could be called Roman lyric, and in fact the idea of a *Latinus fidicen* ('Latin minstrel') would have sounded paradoxical. In *Odes* 3.30 Horace claims to be 'the first to have adapted Aeolian verse to Italian tunes' – i.e. to have written Latin poetry in Greek verse-forms.[1] To have taken over these metres, modified them, and employed them for larger poetic ends was a significant part of Horace's originality. But only a part. Horace was a different kind of poet from any of his Greek predecessors. He was closest to Alcaeus and worked with many of the same lyric types, such as hymns, love-poems, and drinking songs. But Alcaeus was an aristocrat, an important figure in the political struggles of a small city state, a poet who sang to the accompaniment of a lyre poems which were often immediately related to the occasion of their performance. None of this was true of Horace. Moreover, the Roman poet also drew on such different writers as Pindar (fifth century), Callimachus (third century), and Meleager (first century); on Greek sermons and panegy-

---

[1] The main systems which he employed – viz. the four-line alcaic and sapphic stanzas and various combinations of asclepiads, glyconics, and pherecrateans – are set out in every edition and are analysed in detail by Nisbet–Hubbard.

rics; and on Latin literature from Ennius to Virgil. He was therefore a sophisticated writer, availing himself of a long cultural tradition. To a lesser poet such
a position could have been stifling, but Horace was able to assimilate these
influences and use them to create something of his own.

In interpreting the *Odes* it is hard to maintain the conventional distinction
between Greek and Roman. The two are blended in various proportions. We
might, for instance, want to say that for Horace national affairs meant the
traditions, values, and welfare of Rome; but for over a century Rome had been
the capital of an empire which included Greece, and the city itself had a sizeable
Greek population. Again, love in the *Odes* is love as Horace observed and
knew it; but his attitude and treatment must have been coloured by his reading
of Anacreon and poets of the Greek Anthology. His friends were (of course)
living contemporaries, but they were also bilingual, and when one of them died,
like Quintilius, it was natural to cast the Latin lament in the form of an epicedion
(1.24). Conversely an ode like the hymn to Mercury (1.10), which had no Roman
features except the god's name, would not have seemed foreign to Horace's
readers, because from childhood they were as familiar with Greek mythology
as with the stories of early Roman history. So too, in the prophecy of Nereus
(1.15) they would all have picked up the allusions to the *Iliad* and some would
have caught the flavour of Bacchylides. In the symposium odes the mixture is
especially hard to analyse. Undoubtedly Horace had read many Greek poems
set in the context of a party with its wine, music, and girls. But as a Hellenistic
city Rome had absorbed countless Greek customs, including that of the symposium, and parties were a regular feature of Horace's life. So it is best to assume
that he drew on both kinds of experience. How many elements of a given party
were historically authentic is another question, and one which is usually
unanswerable. In such matters we must follow logic and common sense as far
as they take us and then stop. The same applies in other areas too. Thus we
disbelieve the story that doves covered Horace with leaves (3.4), accept that
he was narrowly missed by a falling tree (2.13), and keep an open mind about
what he did with his shield at Philippi (2.7).

All this is a rather crude summary of a complex question, but it may serve
to show that the *Odes* were a new phenomenon in ancient literature. One should
add that as well as marking the beginning of Roman lyric they also represent
its highest point. Here the closest parallel comes from pastoral, in which
Virgil's *Eclogues* hold a similar position.

On finishing *Odes* 1–3 Horace returned to *sermones* (conversational hexameters)
using them as a vehicle for moral comment of a more general and less satirical
kind. The epistles of Book 1 (published in 19 B.C. or slightly earlier) had no
direct antecedents in Greek literature, though scholars have suggested various

sources of influence, including Epicurus, Theocritus, and Menippus. In Latin, leaving aside the correspondence of Cicero, which is only marginally relevant, one can point to a verse-epistle of Lucilius in which he complained that a friend had failed to visit him when sick,[1] and to certain 'humorous letters in verse' written by Lucilius' contemporary Sp. Mummius in 146 B.C.[2] But the idea of composing a whole book of verse-epistles was something quite novel.

The nature of the epistles was also distinctively Horatian. They were addressed to real people; they contained real information about the poet's opinions and way of life; and although not inspired by anything like reforming zeal they were surely meant, like the *Satires*, to have *some* effect on the reader's moral outlook. (It is an aberration of our own century to believe that Horace made ethical assertions without any ethical purpose.) At the same time the *Epistles* should not be thought of as just ordinary letters versified. They are primarily poems, and they vary considerably in their relation to actuality. In *Epist.* 1.3 the relation is very close – Horace asks Julius Florus various questions about himself and his friends and looks forward to receiving an answer. In *Epist.* 1.9 we are at one remove from a real letter; presumably Horace had in some way recommended Septimius to Tiberius, but the epistle itself does not constitute the original recommendation. At the other end of the scale *Epist.* 1.6 is a set of reflections on peace of mind (*nil admirari*); its epistolary status is purely nominal.

Epist. 2.2 (19 or 18 B.C.) takes the form of an excuse for not writing lyrics: 'I was always lazy and never pretended to be anything else; Rome is impossible – the noise is appalling and I've no patience with the literary set; poetry is hard work, and anyhow at my age one has more serious concerns – like philosophy.' Within this framework there are passages of great vividness and diversity, including autobiography, complaints about urban life, a fine statement of classical poetic theory, and amusing stories like those about Lucullus' soldier and the lunatic of Argos.

Epist. 2.3, referred to by Quintilian (8.3.60) as the *Ars poetica*, may also belong to the period 23–17 B.C.; if not, it must have been written after *Odes* 4, near the end of the poet's life; for in l. 306 he implies that he has given up lyric. Unfortunately the addressees – Piso and his two sons – cannot be identified with any confidence. In the case of the *Ars poetica* the problem of originality passes into one of structure; for while the individual precepts are easily apprehended, difficulties begin when we try to group them under larger headings and to discern some overall plan in the work. Is there, as many have thought, a division between *ars* (1–294) and *artifex* (295–476)? Should we go further

---

[1] Lucilius, ed. Warmington (1957) frs. 186–93. Lucilius may well have written some other epistles too. He refers to the epistle as a form in fr. 404.

[2] Cicero, *Ad Atticum* 13.6a.

and subdivide *ars* into style (*poema*) and content (*poesis*)? Advocates of this view point out that the same three terms were used by Neoptolemus of Parium (a scholar-poet of the third century B.C.) and that according to Porphyrio (a commentator of the third century A.D.) Horace 'gathered together the precepts of Neoptolemus of Parium on the art of poetry, admittedly not all, but the most significant'. But can we be sure that *poema* and *poesis* had these functions in Neoptolemus, and what degree of precision can be attributed to the statement of Porphyrio? These and other problems surrounding the *A.P.* 'have resulted in a neurotic confusion unexcelled even in classical studies'.[1] We need not add to that confusion here, but it is fair to observe that if Horace took over this tripartite scheme (as he may have done) he put such varied material into each section, and so blurred the lines of demarcation, that the separate parts would not have been readily apprehended by his readers. From which one infers that the scheme as such was not meant to be of central importance.

The question of the *A.P.*'s relevance is also disputed, and it may well be that no neat answer can be given for the poem as a whole. Some of the precepts – e.g. those on how to revivify the language (46–72) and on the need for disinterested criticism (419–51) – are applicable to all Roman poetry; others – e.g. those regarding structural unity (1–22 and 136–52) – are equally general in principle, though Horace is mainly concerned with epic and tragedy; others again – e.g. those about characterization (99–127, 153–78) – apply almost entirely to tragedy and comedy. This last point raises the question: 'How vital was new dramatic writing in the age of Augustus?' As none has survived and the evidence is very meagre, we may infer that tragedy and comedy were almost extinct; or that performances still went on, though we don't happen to know about them. As for Horace's intentions, we may believe that he was hoping to revive the old theatrical traditions in opposition to the increasingly popular mimes and pantomimes; or that he was not really addressing himself directly to the contemporary situation at all.

The same question arises in a more acute form in connexion with the passage on satyr-plays (220–50); for this was a genre which no Roman had attempted. The same range of answers is available. If we maintain that here too Horace was trying to encourage young playwrights, we cannot be refuted and the poem remains homogeneous in its relevance. But many would find it uncomfortable to hold a view for which there was so little evidence. If we take the other line, we can suggest that the long section on drama was included partly for its intrinsic interest, partly because drama held a dominant position in the most important Greek criticism, viz. that of Aristotle and his successors, and partly because it offered various topics which could be exploited for satire, moral affirmation, or simply general reflections on life. This may be the right

[1] D. A. Russell in Costa (ed.) (1973) 116.

approach, but if so it fails to preserve the poem's unity of intent, for, as we have seen, a good deal of the *A.P.* refers directly to the Roman literary situation. But whatever view we adopt, there can be no doubt that the *A.P.* covers an immense historical scope; it handles a variety of topics with lightness, humour and good sense; and as no one had ever previously written a poem on poetics it remains a work of impressive originality.

Epist. 2.1, addressed to Augustus about 15 B.C., deals with the role of poetry in society, and again there is quite a lot of general discussion about drama. But the spirited defence of contemporary poetry and the complaints about conservative taste (1–92) are certainly coloured by Horace's own experience:

> indignor quicquam reprehendi, non quia crasse
> compositum illepideue putetur, sed quia nuper;
> nec ueniam antiquis, sed honorem et praemia posci. (76–8)

I find it deplorable that a thing should be criticized not because it's considered coarse or clumsy in style but because it's modern, and that instead of excusing the poets of the past [e.g. Plautus, Naevius, and Ennius] *we should be expected to honour and reward them.*

Those words *crasse* and *illepide* (cf. *tenui* in l. 225) recall how Catullus and the moderns of an earlier generation used to talk about poetry. Horace had never been totally opposed to them. He accepted the ideals of neatness and crafts-manship which they had derived from Callimachus, and like them he avoided the larger genres. But his more extrovert temperament, and perhaps his social background, led him to choose forms which had less room for affectionate diminutives, mellifluous Greek words, 'aesthetic' effects of sound and metre, and the romantic and sentimental use of mythology. More important, Horace always enjoyed making poetry out of human behaviour and the ideas which were meant to regulate it. This interest eventually enabled him to respond to the achievement of Augustus by writing on political themes. Finally, although he felt incapable of undertaking epic and tragedy himself, he never regarded these genres as outmoded or impossible; the work of Varius and Virgil proved the contrary. When all due respect had been paid to Callimachus' dictum (*Hymn to Apollo* 108ff.), a large river was not *invariably* dirty (*Epist.* 2.2.120f.)

Before *Epist.* 2.1 Horace had already written the *Carmen saeculare* to be sung at the celebrations of 17 B.C., which, as they were supposed to mark the end of an epoch, were called the *Ludi Saeculares*. This choral hymn (the only ode composed for musical performance) was specially commissioned by Augustus. As a result of its success and of further encouragement from the Emperor, Horace went back to lyric and eventually in 13 B.C., or perhaps later, published

a fourth book of odes. Three or four of the pieces (2, 3, 7, and perhaps 5)
show him at his very best; all the others contain memorable stanzas; and even
the smallest (10) makes a positive impression. If we take the book as a whole it
is interesting to see how the magnificence of the laureate, addressing the
Emperor and his family in lofty Pindaric style and confident of his ability to
confer lasting fame, is tempered by personal feelings of melancholy and
nostalgia. The poet is close on fifty (1); Cinara is dead (13); Ligurinus is young
and heartless (10); Lyce is a sad reminder of the past (13); Phyllis will surely
be his last love (11). If Virgil in no. 12 is the dead poet and not some unknown
contemporary, then that ode too evokes memories of earlier days. Like the
other collections, *Odes* 4 shows signs of deliberate arrangement; 4 and 5 (on
Augustus' step-sons and Augustus himself) correspond to 14 and 15, and the
opening poem includes several themes which occur later, viz. love, ageing,
poetry, and the praise of a distinguished contemporary. For the rest, it is hard
to observe anything sufficiently bold and regular to be called an architectural
pattern, but this view is disputed.[1]

Adapting and promoting new poetic forms naturally entailed the development
of an individual style, or range of styles. No modern critic would dare to
describe such an achievement in a few words, but Quintilian made a brave
attempt. Writing of the lyric Horace in the first century A.D. he said: *insurgit
aliquando et plenus est iucunditatis et gratiae et uarius figuris et uerbis felicissime
audax* 'He rises every now and then to grandeur; he is full of delight and
charm; he shows variety in his figures of speech, and in his language he is
triumphantly adventurous' (10.1.96). Here are a few examples of the sort of
thing that Quintilian had in mind:

1.
> parcus deorum cultor et infrequens,
> insanientis dum sapientiae
> consultus erro nunc retrorsum
> uela dare atque iterare cursus
> cogor relictos.   (1.34.1-5)

*I was a niggardly and infrequent devotee of the gods; expert in a senseless philosophy
I strayed from the truth. Now I am forced to sail back and resume the course I had
abandoned.*

The whole poem is made up of antitheses, some so sharp as to be paradoxical,
and they dramatize the central paradox of thunder from a clear sky – an event
which brought two philosophies into collision. It is unusual for the meaning
of an ode to be enacted so fully by the form (another example is the teasing
repartee of 3.9); but the ingenious placing of semantic blocks so as to build a

---

[1] See Ludwig (1961) 1–10.

poetic structure is entirely typical. One should perhaps add that Horace was not really an Epicurean before this ode or a Stoic after it.

2.   eheu fugaces, Postume, Postume,
                         labuntur anni, nec pietas moram
                            rugis et instanti senectae
                               adferet indomitaeque morti.   (2.14.1–4)

Alas, Postumus, Postumus, the years are slipping swiftly by, nor will devotion succeed in checking wrinkles, the onset of old age, and invincible death.

The repetition of a proper name is without parallel in Horace (and how apt a name it is!). By putting it here he delays the completion of the sentence, thus linking the key word *fugaces* to the emotional *eheu*. The beginning almost certainly suggests a river (cf. *lympha fugax* in 2.3.12), but the second sentence brings a change of metaphor – viz. the hopeless fight against age and death. One notes the climax *rugis, senectae, morti*, and the Homeric phrase *indomitae morti* ('Ἀΐδης ἀδάμαστος) which contributes to the stanza's sombre dignity.

3.   gelidos inficiet tibi
                         rubro sanguine riuos
                            lasciui suboles gregis.   (3.13.5–8)

The offspring of the frisky herd will stain your cool streams with his red blood.

Here we have a chiastic pattern of adjective...adjective noun noun – 'cool... red blood streams'. At the same time two other adjectives are implied, for the red blood is warm and the cool streams are clear. The result is a strong sensuous effect. The ode offers a subtle blend of realism and pathos. To call it callous is unnecessarily squeamish, unless one happens to be a vegetarian.

4.   urit me Glycerae nitor.   (1.19.5)

I am burned by Sweetie's brilliance

– a triple assault on the senses.

5.   post equitem sedet atra Cura.   (3.1.40)

Behind the horseman sits Angst dressed in black

– a picture worthy of Dürer.

6.   nauis, quae tibi creditum
                            debes Vergilium finibus Atticis
                         reddas incolumem, precor,
                            et serues animae dimidium meae.   (1.3.5–8)

O ship, you to whom Virgil has been entrusted and who owe him to the soil of Attica, discharge him there intact, I pray you, and save fifty per cent of my soul.

I have overtranslated to bring out the extended commercial metaphor.

7.
> pallida Mors aequo pulsat pede pauperum tabernas
> regumque turris. o beate Sesti,
> uitae summa breuis spem nos uetat incohare longam.
> iam te premet nox fabulaeque Manes
> et domus exilis Plutonia.   (1.4.13–17)

Pale Death kicks with impartial foot the poor man's cottage and the prince's castle. My well-off Sestius, the short span of life forbids us to initiate long hopes. Soon night and the storied spirits and the meagre Rich house will hem you in. [Pluto, like Dis, means 'rich'.]

Note the plosives and dentals in the first sentence, the contrast of *summa breuis* with *spem longam*, and the juxtaposition of *exilis* and *Plutonia*, which gives an added reminder to the *beatus Sestius*. (The meaning of *exilis* is guaranteed by *Epist.* 1.6.45f.)

8.
>   'o sol
> pulcher! o laudande!' canam, recepto
> Caesare felix.   (4.2.46–8)

I shall sing 'Day of beauty, day of glory!' in my happiness at having Caesar back.

Here the trochaic rhythm of a popular song of triumph has been cleverly incorporated in a sapphic stanza.

9.
> illic omne malum uino cantuque leuato,
> deformis aegrimoniae dulcibus alloquiis.   (*Epod.* 13.17–18)

There lighten every misfortune with wine and song, those sweet assuagers of ugly depression.

Chiron is advising the young Achilles on how to face the miseries of the Trojan war, from which he will never return. This is the first recorded instance of *alloquium*; and it is used in the extended sense of 'assuager'. Bentley, who noticed the peculiarity, took it to indicate textual corruption instead of poetic originality; but he was probably right in thinking that Horace had in mind the Greek παραμύθιον. The expression *deformis aegrimoniae* looks back to 'scowling moroseness' (5) and to the glowering storm of l. 1.[1]

10.
> parcius iunctas quatiunt fenestras
> iactibus crebris iuuenes proterui,
> nec tibi somnos adimunt, amatque
> ianua limen.   (1.25.1–4)

Not so relentlessly do wild young men shake your closed shutters with volleys of stones; they do not rob you of your sleep, and the door hugs the threshold.

The sarcasm derives its force from the implication that to any respectable woman the cessation of these disturbances would be a welcome relief; whereas

---

[1] See Rudd (1960) 383–6.

for Lydia it marks the beginning of the end. Later in the ode, women past their prime are spoken of as *aridae frondes* 'dry leaves'. In another place (4.13.12) Horace talks of *capitis niues* 'head snow', when he means 'white hair'. This may not strike us as very daring, but no parallel is recorded and Quintilian (8.6.17) thought it a harsh metaphor (*dura translatio*). What, one wonders, did he think of 2.11.6–8 where sexual pleasure is driven away by 'dry whiteness' – *arida canitie* – an expression combining the two ideas of dry leaves and white hair?

T. S. Eliot once spoke of 'that perpetual slight alteration of language, words perpetually juxtaposed in new and sudden combinations'. He can hardly have been thinking of Horace's dictum in *A.P.* 46ff., yet the resemblance is remarkably close:

> in uerbis etiam tenuis cautusque serendis
> dixeris egregie notum si callida uerbum
> reddiderit iunctura nouum.

You should also be subtle and careful in weaving words together. If a clever combination makes a familiar word new, that is distinguished writing.

2. A CRITIQUE OF THE ACADEMIC DICHOTOMY

Whereas the traditional stereotype is popular and superficial, the two divergent views which we shall shortly consider are represented (in various degrees) by several important works of scholarship. Before coming to them, however, let us grant that Horace's poetry offers a number of contrasting features, e.g. public/private, urban/rural, Stoic/Epicurean, grand/plain. How should these be interpreted? Certain answers may be set aside at once. One might say, for instance, that consistency was not to be expected – Horace wrote as the mood took him. There is something in this, for the poet refuses to be tidied up. Yet to distinguish two sides of his poetic character and then to leave the matter there is not satisfactory. (A similar procedure has failed with Catullus and Juvenal.[1]) Or we could say that the whole question was irrelevant – Horace simply dons different masks, which must, presumably, be taken at their face value. But this only moves the question one step back, for we still want to know whether the *personae* are themselves related. Or we might try to see a chronological development in which Horace gradually moved from one side to the other. But this doesn't work, because both sets of concerns are visible at every period.

Of the two serious approaches which we have to discuss, one maintains that most of what is lasting and important in Horace is to be found in the public column, whereas the private column contains engaging but essentially ephemeral *nugae*. According to the other view the true Horace only reveals himself

[1] See Frank (1928) and Ribbeck (1865).

in the private column; the public compositions show signs of strain and arti-
ficiality; and the natural explanation is that they were written to order. Instead
of adopting either of these approaches it seems better to ask how clear the
dichotomy really is. Are there not ways in which the two sets of characteristics
may be related?

First of all, form. Let us take a poem which belongs very clearly to the right-
hand column, viz. the little ode to Pyrrha (1.5). Boy and girl are together in
a grotto; the boy will weep when he discovers Pyrrha's fickle nature; now
unsuspectingly he enjoys her charms; Horace has discovered what she is like.
Within this scheme of present, future, present, past, the characters and their
relationships are presented. The boy – slim, perfumed, trusting – is in for a
shock. The girl is bright and alluring; her appearance smart yet uncontrived
(*simplex munditiis*); but her simplicity will prove deceptive. Now comes a metaphorical substitution: the boy will gaze at 'the rough sea with its black winds',
i.e. the new, hostile, Pyrrha (not 'the sea of love' or 'the couple's relationship').
Another substitution follows: the boy is 'unaware of the treacherous breeze'.
Then the two terms of the metaphor (Pyrrha and the sea) are brought explicitly
together: *miseri, quibus intemptata nites* 'poor devils who, not having embarked
on you, are fascinated by your shimmer'. Finally another substitution: Horace
has hung up his wet clothes as a thank-offering to Neptune for his escape.

The grotto-scene is part of a wistful reverie and represents a single imagined
occasion. The second vignette – that of Pyrrha binding back her hair – is
probably of the same kind; for the two pictures appear to be companion
pieces (boy embracing girl, girl setting out to attract boy). No background is
supplied for the second; so we can, if we wish, imagine Pyrrha finishing off
her hair-do in her bedroom – but not in the grotto, where she is otherwise
engaged. The pictures are cleverly brought together in l. 9 where *qui nunc te
fruitur* 'who now enjoys you' recalls the grotto-scene and *aurea* 'golden'
glances back to Pyrrha's hair.

For the movement of the poem across the stanzas, the enfolding word-order
of l. 1, the novelty of *emirabitur insolens* 'he will gaze in astonishment', the
verbal play of *aurea/aurae*, and various other features, reference must be made
to Nisbet–Hubbard.[1] But perhaps enough has been said to show that what
looks like a piece of dainty porcelain is as strongly made as many of the large
Alcaic odes. Its feeling is correspondingly complex: for the boy an amused,
slightly patronizing pity, mixed with envy; and on Horace's own part relief,
with a touch of nostalgia. It is all conveyed very lightly (much more lightly
than in *Epod.* 15), but it is still there.

Odes 1.5 revolves around Pyrrha, and the tone and style remain fairly constant. In many other cases, however, there is a discernible movement. *Odes* 2.13,

---

[1] Nisbet and Hubbard (1970) 72–80.

for instance, opens with a series of imprecations directed at a rotten tree which had nearly killed the poet. The tone is one of mock horror, rather as in the epode on garlic (no. 3). Then, in stanzas four and five, Horace goes on to reflect in a calmer mood on the unpredictability of fate – death comes from the most unexpected quarter. This leads into the second half of the poem – a vision of the underworld in which Sappho and Alcaeus give joy and comfort by singing to the dead. So the lyric poet's narrow escape from death, which is treated comically, paves the way for a profoundly serious affirmation: even death cannot prevail against the powers of lyric poetry.

Before leaving this ode it is perhaps worth noting that of the two Greek poets Alcaeus has the keener audience, and *his* story is of battles and the expulsion of tyrants – i.e. political events. If Horace's chief model could write of politics as well as of love and wine (cf. *Odes* 1.32) we may be sure that Horace saw nothing anomalous in doing the same.

The kind of tonal variety described above is also claimed for satire:

> et sermone opus est modo tristi, saepe iocoso,
> defendente uicem modo rhetoris atque poetae,
> interdum urbani... *(Sat.* 1.10.11–13)

You also need a style that is sometimes severe, sometimes gay, now suiting the role of an orator or poet now that of a sophisticated talker...

Often an elevated tone is used for comic contrast, as in *Sat.* 1.5.9ff. where the beautiful description of night is a prelude to the backchat of bargees, or for purposes of burlesque, as in *Sat.* 1.7 where a vulgar altercation is reported in Homeric style. But there are passages in both the *Satires* and the *Epistles* where the level rises because the theme is noble. One thinks of the prayer to Mercury (*Sat.* 2.6.1ff.), the portrait of the Stoic sage (*Sat.* 2.7.83ff.), the encomium of Augustus (*Epist.* 2.1.1ff.) and the lines on the mortality of man and his words (*A.P.* 6off.).

In the *Odes* the spectrum is wider, for they include adaptations of various types of Greek lyric ranging from the stately choruses of Pindar to Anacreon's little songs about love and wine. Again, the divisions are not always clear-cut. In the opening of *Odes* 3.11 the invocation of Mercury, the explanatory *nam* clause, the myth of Amphion, and the reference to the seven-stringed lyre and its welcome presence at banquets and religious ceremonies – all this prepares the reader for a dignified Pindaric ode. It then transpires that the god is being asked to provide a song which will sway the affections of Lyde – a skittish young filly who is refusing to think of marriage. The filly comes from Anacreon. The serious style is resumed as we hear of the marvellous achievements of the lyre in the hands of Orpheus. But Lyde is still in the background, for if song can charm tigers and the savage Cerberus surely it can tame a filly. As the

poet's imagination moves through Hades it comes to rest on the daughters of
Danaus. These girls had rejected marriage in the most violent way by murder-
ing their bridegrooms, and are now paying the penalty by filling a leaky barrel.
Here is a story Lyde ought to hear; so Horace tells it, very economically, ending
with the words of the noble Hypermnestra who alone deceived her father
(*splendide mendax*) and allowed her husband to escape. Although the ode may
be in some way related to an actual situation, Lyde should not on that account
receive too much attention. It is equally wrong, however, to assert that she is
there simply to introduce the story of Hypermnestra. The two girls come from
different poetic neighbourhoods. It was Horace's clever idea to bring them
together and let them interact.

Another hymn begins with a solemn address to a deity, recalling the circumstances of her birth and the various ways in which she controls the life of
men. Horace then begs her to come down and join her devotees; he rehearses
the numerous blessings she confers, and promises that she will be the centre
of a joyful celebration. The diction is reverent and ceremonious, but it is also
shot through with double meanings, because the deity in question is a wine-jar.
The whole piece (3.21) is a delightful parody of a cletic hymn.[1]

High and low are brought together for a rather different purpose towards
the end of *Epist.* 2.1. Horace is addressing the Emperor: poets, he says, like
artists and sculptors, can commemorate a ruler by portraying his achievements;
Virgil and Varius have performed this service for you. I too, instead of composing 'conversation-pieces that crawl on the ground' (*sermones...repentis
per humum*), would prefer 'to tell of your exploits, of distant lands and rivers,
of castles on mountain-tops, and barbaric kingdoms, of warfare concluded
under your inspired leadership throughout the world, of the bars that enclose
Janus the guardian of peace, and of the terror brought to the Parthians by your
imperial Rome'. Hardly a specimen of the low style. Horace then continues:
'...if only my desires were matched by my abilities. But a small poem is not
appropriate to your exalted state, and I in my diffidence am not so rash as to
attempt a task too heavy for my strength.' Thus, with a neat manoeuvre, the
poet is back again on his usual level.

The most interesting example of *recusatio* (a refusal to write a more ambitious
type of poem) is found in the first half of *Odes* 4.2. There Horace states in the
sapphic metre that he cannot hope to write a Pindaric ode; he fashions his poems
in the painstaking manner of a bee; not for him the swan's flight or the rushing
torrent of Pindar's eloquence. But as that great periodic sentence sweeps
through five stanzas displacing caesuras and submerging line-divisions, and as
Pindar's lyric forms come past us one by one from dithyramb to dirge, celebrat-
ing gods, heroes, and men, we become aware that Horace has achieved some-

[1] I.e. a hymn in which the god is called on to appear: see Norden (1913) 143ff.

thing very like the effect which he has disclaimed. So here again, in the ironic structure of the *recusatio*, two contrasting styles co-exist. It only remains to add that the event which the poet was so superbly unfit to celebrate was the return of Augustus from Gaul.

Finally, the two styles may be related by placing two contrasting poems side by side. *Odes* 1.37 is an ode of triumph on the destruction of Cleopatra. Nearly six centuries earlier Alcaeus had cried exultantly νῦν χρῆ μεθύσθην 'Now's the time to get drunk...for Myrsilus is dead.' So when Horace begins with *nunc est bibendum* he is not only 'acknowledging a shared culture' (to use Nisbet–Hubbard's excellent phrase) but also asserting a kindred political experience: a tyrant is dead. Lines 5–21 present the dissolute, drunken, power-mad queen of Octavian's propaganda. As we read about her, however, we should not use our historical sources to censure Horace's inaccuracy; for he was not reporting the battle of Actium as it actually took place, but rather reflecting the general mood of triumph and delirious relief. Then, as in *Odes* 2.1, the poet's initial and spontaneous reaction gives way to something altogether deeper and more humane, and in ll. 21–32 we are shown the defeated Cleopatra, determined to avoid humiliation, calmly taking her own life like a Roman Stoic. Both moods are accommodated in the grand style with its glorious effects of sound and diction.

Some of Horace's most dignified 'public' compositions end on a quiet note, e.g. 3.5 and 4.2; once or twice he checks an ode apparently in mid flight and brings it back to the level on which he normally meets the reader, e.g. 2.1 and 3.3. An analogous effect is produced by placing the very short ode *Persicos odi* after 1.37 and using it to round off the book. Though not strictly a sympotic poem it is related to 1.37 by the theme of drinking and by the anti-oriental sentiment. Also, in its own way, it is artfully contrived. For example, the first stanza deprecates Persian elaborateness, garlands woven on *philyra* (a Greek word, meaning lime bast), and the search for late roses; but it contains no negative words. The second affirms the sufficiency of myrtle (*simplici myrto*) and the pleasure of sheltered relaxation, but it is couched entirely in negatives. Yet the contrasts with 1.37 are more obvious and important. Instead of complex periods we have two sapphic stanzas with short asyndetic sentences; the literary ancestry is found in Anacreon and Hellenistic epigram, not in Alcaeus or Pindar; and after the jubilant celebration of Cleopatra's defeat we are brought back to the Horatian norm by the picture of the poet enjoying a quiet drink in his summerhouse.

In this section we have noted how small light poems can be structurally complex, how within a given ode the style may shift from one level to another, how parodies use solemnity for comic effect, how in a *recusatio* the grand style can be disavowed and employed at the same time, and how a contrast can be exploited by juxtaposition.

After style, theme. One theme, recurrent at all periods, is that of simplicity. Here perhaps the best example of a public ode is 2.15 (*iam pauca aratro*). The abuse in question (viz. uncontrolled building) is a civic abuse affecting the country's economy. No one is addressed, except the community at large, and at no point does the poet speak in the first person. An appeal is made to the traditions of Romulus, Cato, and the Romans of an earlier day who spent their money on public rather than private buildings, and these old traditions were, we are told, enforced by law. Several of the same features are found in 3.24; there too the poet asserts that no change of heart can come about without the aid of laws.

When we turn to 3.1, however, the situation is less straightforward. For although *odi profanum* is the first of the so-called 'Roman odes', its argumentation comes from the world of private ethics. Acquisitiveness and extravagance are criticized not for their social or national effects but for what they do to the individual. The greedy man is reminded that money does not guarantee happiness and that it usually brings worry and resentment. Such reasoning is familiar from the *Satires* and *Epistles*. Again, though the poet appears initially as the Muses' priest (*Musarum sacerdos*), at the end of the ode we hear the familiar Horace talking about his Sabine farm. So apart from the first two stanzas the ode is essentially a lyrical diatribe.

Although the theme of simplicity connects both sides of Horace's work, his treatment of the matter is not simple. First, Horace had no objection to wealth in itself, as long as it was used in a generous and enlightened way (*Sat.* 2.2.101–5, 2.8; *Odes* 2.2). His main target was acquisitiveness; for the man who thought only of making money harmed both himself and society. Secondly, Horace was not so hypocritical as to maintain that extreme poverty was in some way beneficial. His *aurea mediocritas* ruled out 'the squalor of a tumbledown house' just as firmly as 'the mansion that excites envy' (*Odes* 2.10.5–8; cf. *Epist.* 2.2.199). He does, however, occasionally express the view that since life is precarious any man may find himself in poverty, and that he should be able to survive the experience without being shattered (*Odes* 3.29.53ff.; cf. 4.9.49). In particular, young men in military training should learn to rough it (*Odes* 3.2.1).

Thirdly, it is sometimes helpful to distinguish between what Horace admired and what he liked. We cannot doubt, for instance, that he admired the toughness of the early Romans, but he would hardly have chosen to sit beside Regulus at a dinner party. If pressed hard, this distinction could leave him open to the charge of insincerity, and he knew it. 'You praise the good fortune and character of the men of old', says Davus (*Sat.* 2.7.22ff.), 'but if a god urged you to go back you'd strenuously refuse.' But we must be careful here, for some of the warmest praise of the hardy peasant is uttered by characters other than Horace himself. The homily in *Sat.* 2.2 is delivered by Ofellus, Cervius tells the story of the two mice (*Sat.* 2.6) and the rustic idyll in *Epod.* 2 turns out to be a money-lender's day-dream. While Horace admired certain (idealized) features of country life, he never yearned to be a farmer. Anyone careless enough to identify him with the speaker in *Epod.* 2 deserves to fall into the trap at the end.

Certain inconsistencies remain. They are amusingly described in the letter to Numonius Vala (*Epist.* 1.15). There Horace compares himself to Maenius, a parasite, who if he failed to cadge a dinner used to inveigh against the luxury of the rich, but who when given the chance would devour every delicacy in sight. As far as Horace is concerned the picture is, of course, a caricature (cf. *Sat.* 2.7.29ff.); and when he says that 'the only people who know anything about the good life are those whose money is solidly and conspicuously based on splendid villas' he is obviously pulling his friend's leg. The nucleus of truth consists in the idea of alternation. For while Horace respected the monolithic type of character who was always predictable because always the same, and may indeed have acknowledged that ideal as a steadying influence, the pattern of his own life was less monotonous. He needed change, and occasionally this led to restlessness and depression (*Sat.* 2.7.28–9; *Epist.* 1.8.12); but normally the poet's sense and good taste enabled him to control his temperament, and so he was in a position to laugh at the wild oscillations of men like Priscus and Tigellius (*Sat.* 2.7 and 1.3). We need not doubt, for instance, that he enjoyed the hospitality of Maecenas and could look after himself very well when on holiday (*Epist.* 1.15), but his usual style of living was much simpler. And although with eight farmhands to run his estate he may seem well enough off to us, there was no comparison at all between him and the great men to whom he addressed his poetry.

This adaptability, which has an obvious analogy in the poet's style, cannot be confined within the doctrines of any philosophy (*Epist.* 1.1.14–19). And yet it does represent a kind of principle: to live a life of civilized hedonism as far as one's nature and circumstances allow, but to retain a tough core for withstanding hardship. Correspondingly, in national affairs, we find Horace rejoicing in Rome's prosperity (*Epist.* 1.12.28–9; *Carm. Saec.* 53–60) and sharing in her various celebrations (*Odes* 3.14, 4.2), but employing Stoic ideas of virtue when handling ideas more closely concerned with her well-being and survival (*Odes* 3.2, 3, 5).

We now come to a number of odes connected in one way or another with hospitality. At first sight they seem to show that Horace was a thoroughgoing escapist, too sensitive or too indolent to contemplate the world of affairs: 'Have the good sense to put an end to your sadness and the troubles of life with mellow wine', 'Fill the gleaming cups with Massic wine that brings forgetfulness', 'Why not lie at ease beneath this tall plane or pine and drink while we may?' 'Gladly accept the gifts of the present moment and forget all that's grim.' It is tempting to compare such advice with Omar's:

> Ah fill the cup; what boots it to repeat
> how time is slipping underneath our feet?
> Unborn tomorrow and dead yesterday –
> Why fret about them if today be sweet?

Tempting, but misleading; for the passages must be read in context. The first is from 1.7, addressed to the consular L. Munatius Plancus, who in 41 B.C. joined Antony but went over to Octavian in 32 and retained his influence in the years that followed. Velleius called him 'a pathological traitor' (*morbo proditor*), but no one with any historical sense will accept that as a final verdict on his character.[1] The point we are concerned with here is that, whether or not he held a military command at the time of the ode's composition, he was certainly engaged in public life. At the end of the poem the heroic Teucer concludes his speech with the words: *nunc uino pellite curas | cras ingens iterabimus aequor* 'now drive away your troubles with wine, tomorrow we renew our journey over the vast ocean'. So too, Plancus is being urged to relax when he can. The second passage is addressed to Horace's old comrade Pompeius, who has just returned to Italy after fighting for over twelve years on the side of Octavian's enemies (2.7). The third quotation is from the ode to Quinctius Hirpinus, who is worrying overmuch about foreign affairs (2.11). To judge from *Epist.* 1.16 he was a man of considerable wealth and importance. We may be sure that when Horace sent him this invitation he was not urging him to abandon his political career. The same is true *a fortiori* of 3.8, which is addressed to Maecenas. As a final illustration we may take 1.20 (*uile potabis*) – a very slight and informal piece. But the central stanza recalls the ovation given to Maecenas when he reappeared after a serious illness. That public dimension is entirely lacking in the epigram of Philodemus (*Anth. Pal.* 11.44) which Horace is thought to have used.

These hospitality poems are therefore set against a background of busy public life. What did Horace know about this kind of world? Perhaps more than one sometimes assumes. As schoolboy and student he must have mixed on reasonably free terms with upper-class people – see, e.g., the end of *Sat.* 1.10 and *Sat.* 2.1.75–6. He obtained a post in the treasury about 40 B.C. and ten years later he talks as if he still had to attend meetings (*Sat.* 2.6.36–7). On the strength of *Sat.* 1.6 some commentators believe he was encouraged to stand for the quaestorship. What we do know is that later Augustus tried to make him his private secretary. Horace managed to get out of it (his health was so

---

[1] See Tyrrell and Purser (1933) lxxvi–lxxxiv.

terribly unreliable...), but the offer shows that his competence and discretion were recognized in the highest quarters. It is amusing to reflect that Q. Horatius Flaccus might have been the first of those imperial secretaries who later acquired such immense power and dislike. As it was, he kept out of public affairs, but socially he was much in demand (see *Odes* 2.18.10–11; 3.11.5–6); great men, including Augustus, were eager to be mentioned in his poems; and we may be sure that at the dinner tables on the Esquiline he heard a good deal of political conversation.

Another unifying thread is the poet's love of the Italian countryside. An early example is the second epode, where the idealized picture is qualified but not cancelled by the final twist. A smaller, but not dissimilar, picture is painted at the end of the last Roman ode (3.6). Or again, the delightful hymn to Faunus (*Odes* 3.18) contains the stanza:

> ludit herboso pecus omne campo,
> cum tibi Nonae redeunt Decembres;
> festus in pratis uacat otioso
> cum boue pagus.

The whole herd plays over the grassy fields when the Nones of December come round again to do you honour; the villagers keep the festival, taking it easy in the meadows with the oxen which are also on holiday.

A shorter scene occurs in *Odes* 4.5:

> tutus bos etenim rura perambulat,
> nutrit rura Ceres almaque Faustitas.

The ox safely wanders through the land. Ceres and benign Prosperity nourish the land.

The second picture, however, has a political frame: rural Italy is flourishing under the Augustan peace. To recall the importance of this idea in imperial ideology one has only to think of Virgil's *Georgics* and the figure of Tellus (or Venus) on the Ara Pacis.

In several odes the countryside is related to Horace's vocation as a writer. In 1.17 (a very private piece) Faunus is said to protect the Sabine farm because the poet and his muse are dear to the gods. 3.13 has a wider scope and shows a new awareness of power; for while the *fons Bandusiae* with its bright water and shady trees inspires a lyric poem, the poem in turn makes Bandusia as famous as the legendary springs of Greece. Later again, the streams and foliage of Tibur are said to have made Melpomene's favourite known for Aeolian song (*Odes* 4.3); this fame is then defined: Horace is 'the minstrel of the Roman lyre'. So there was no real boundary between the national and the local. Horace was aware of this when, at the end of his first collection of odes, he wrote: 'I shall grow for ever renewed by the praises of posterity, as long as the priest climbs the Capitol with the silent Vestal' – and then immediately added: 'I shall be spoken of where the wild Aufidus roars and where Daunus, poor in water, ruled over rustic folk' – i.e. in the remote country district where he was born.

On a personal level Horace's love of the countryside, like his love of simplicity, involved a tension between rural and urban values. At first sight this is not obvious because he spends so much time praising the country and grumbling about the city (e.g. *Sat.* 2.6; *Epist.* 1.10 and 14). Yet Rome was more than smoke and noise. It also represented vitality, excitement, and the pleasures of a cultivated society. In due course it became the centre of his national recognition (*Odes* 4.3.13–15), but even in earlier days the city had other, humbler, attractions: 'I wander off by myself wherever I wish, asking the price of greens and flour. In the evenings I often stroll around the Circus and Forum, those haunts of trickery; I loiter beside the fortune-tellers; then I make my way home to a plate of minestrone with leeks and peas' (*Sat.* 1.6.111–15). As a student of the human comedy Horace could never be wholly satisfied with rural seclusion. His personality had room for the town- as well as the country-mouse.

When one comes to talk about Horace's conception of nature it is useful to distinguish the area over which man has some control (e.g. fruit, crops, animals) from that which is beyond him (e.g. the weather and seasons). In the first case the poet assumes the presence of a natural power which has to be tended and trained and brought to full growth. That is the farmer's work. It demands skill and labour, and it is sometimes frustrated (*Odes* 3.1.29–32; *Epist.* 1.7.86–7); but when it succeeds, the result not only sustains the community but gives delight too (*Epist.* 1.16.1–16). The writer has a similar task, for his natural powers produce a crop of words which have to be disciplined by art:

> luxuriantia compescet, nimis aspera sano
> leuabit cultu, uirtute carentia tollet.   (*Epist.* 2.2.122f.)

He will check excessive growth, smooth what is too rough by beneficial care and take out whatever lacks strength.

Similar metaphors are applied to human nature – temper is like a horse which has to be bridled (*Epist.* 1.2.63); a wild young girl is not yet broken in (*Odes* 2.5.1); sin has to be cut back (*Odes* 3.24.34). A particularly interesting example is *Odes* 4.4.29–34:

> fortes creantur fortibus et bonis;
> est in iuuencis, est in equis patrum
> uirtus...
> doctrina sed uim promouet insitam,
> rectique cultus pectora roborant.

The valiant are born from the valiant and the good. Steers and steeds have their fathers' quality...but training develops inborn power and the right kind of care strengthens the heart.

Here the principle has a special application, because Horace is talking of the young princes Tiberius and Drusus. Education is related to imperial power by the fostering of authority.

Since we cannot control the weather and seasons, there is naturally no direct connexion between the official odes and poems like *Odes* 1.4, 9, 11, 4.7, and *Epod.* 13. But these poems command attention in their own right because they contain some of Horace's most memorable writing. *Odes* 1.11 (*tu ne quaesieris*) urges Leuconoe to stop trying to foretell her death and the poet's by means of astrology:

> ut melius, quidquid erit, pati
> seu pluris hiemes seu tribuit Iuppiter ultimam,
> quae nunc oppositis debilitat pumicibus mare
> Tyrrhenum.

How much better to endure whatever comes, whether Jupiter has allotted us more winters or this be our last which is now exhausting the Tuscan sea on cliffs of volcanic rock.

What is the function of the storm? Why is it at the centre of the poem? Wouldn't a bright summer day have done just as well? One has only to put these questions to realize that the sea must not be calm, because the girl herself is not calm. The tossing waves suit her thoughts. Furthermore, the most striking line is that which describes winter as wearing out the sea by pounding it against a barrier of rock. In those three choriambic words *oppositis debilitat pumicibus*, with the metrical ictus pulling against the accent, we hear 'the tired waves vainly breaking'; and this reminds us that Leuconoe's attempts at precognition are a futile waste of effort. The curtain between present and future is just as impenetrable as the rock.

Another winter scene is used in a rather similar way in *Odes* 1.9:

> uides ut alta stet niue candidum
> Soracte, nec iam sustineant onus
> siluae laborantes, geluque
> flumina constiterint acuto?

Do you see how Soracte stands white with deep snow, how the straining trees no longer bear their burden and the streams are halted by sharp ice?

Although dazzlingly vivid, it is a harsh scene, and Horace at once turns away from it, calling on his host to make merry indoors with wine and a good fire. The second part of the poem contains a similar set of ideas – don't worry about the future, enjoy life to the full while you're still young and 'while from you being green hoariness cantankerous is absent'. (That is a literal translation of *donec uirenti canities abest morosa*.) In other words, the lapse of time and the onset of old age are, like the snowy day, part of a natural process over which we have no control. But we do have some control over our friendships and our own state of mind. That is where happiness and serenity must be sought.

As one reads through the ode the initial image of Soracte acquires symbolic overtones. This does *not* mean that the snow-covered mountain is a poetic fiction or that the stanza really represents something else. In Hemingway's famous story 'The Snows of Kilimanjaro' the mountain is put into our minds at the outset; we then hear nothing more about it until the end, when the dying writer dreams that he is being taken there in an aeroplane. Hemingway provided an introductory note: 'Its western summit is called by the Masai "Ngàje Ngài", the House of God.' But we hardly need that information any more than we need Servius' note on Soracte: *dis manibus consecratus est* 'It is sacred to the gods of the dead.'[1]

The same simple yet profound ideas lie behind *Odes* 1.4 and 4.7. Here the warning is given by spring, not winter; but since the year is a circle one can start from any point on its circumference. From one aspect spring is a season of pure happiness. That is the view presented by a number of delightful poems in the Greek Anthology – notably 9.363 (Meleager) and the opening pieces in 10 (Leonidas, Antipater, and others). Yet there is also something poignant about it, for while the seasons return men do not. This perennial theme is capable of endless variations – 'When lilacs last in the dooryard bloomed', 'Loveliest of trees the cherry now', 'April is the cruellest month'; the two odes themselves present striking differences. 1.4 is more intricate. It has two panels: spring (1–12) and death (13–20), but in ll. 1–4 spring is seen as the departure of winter, and in 18ff. death is described as lacking certain joys of life. Antithetical images of warm/cold and liberation/confinement are found in both panels, and the ambivalence of certain phrases contributes to the poem's complex unity. For example, in the joyful panel the words *imminente luna* 'beneath the overhanging moon' have a faint undertone of uneasiness,[2] and the expression *caput impedire myrto* 'to bind one's head with myrtle' foreshadows the prisonhouse of death (16–17), because *impedire* nearly always implies *unwelcome* constraint. The poem is also less sombre. The joy of the first part is reflected in various occupations – shipping, pastoral farming, ploughing, and (on the mythological level) industry. This gives the section a solid vitality. Death, on the other hand, means farewell to wine-parties and rather fragile young men. So at the end of the ode the balance remains tilted towards life.

[1] Servius on Virgil, *Aen.* 11.785.
[2] The moon is associated with change in *Odes* 2.11.10–11; 2.18.16; 4.7.13.

A CRITIQUE OF THE ACADEMIC DICHOTOMY

In 4.7, however, death begins to intrude as early as l. 7 – *immortalia ne speres* – and in l. 15 he asserts his dominion over great figures of Roman legend and history – Aeneas, Tullus, and Ancus. As Manlius Torquatus, the addressee, is an important barrister (*Epist.* 1.5) and belongs to a noble family with traditions of loyalty (Livy 7.5), he embodies the old values of *genus* (birth), *facundia* (eloquence) and *pietas* (devotion); but even those qualities cannot prolong life. This Roman *grauitas* helps to give the poem a deeper and more impersonal despair. In the opening scene there are no human figures; and (apart from Gratia) all the mythological names are found in Hades, where they testify to the power of death. The opposite is the case in *Odes* 1.4. Finally the language of 4.7 is simple and forceful, with few of the ambiguities which we noticed in the earlier piece.

In these odes the pattern of nature is used as the basis for recommending some kind of behaviour. The propriety of this behaviour is sometimes stated (e.g. *nunc decet* in *Odes* 1.4.9 and 11, *decet* in *Epod.* 13.5), elsewhere implied (e.g. *Odes* 2.9, 10, 11). In other places the standard of decorum is supplied by the human cycle of youth, maturity, and decay. This is sometimes linked with the cycle of plants and animals – e.g. Lalage is like a young heifer or an unripe grape, so Horace advises his friend to be patient (*Odes* 2.5); Chloe behaves like a young fawn, though she is really old enough for a man – *tempestiua uiro* (*Odes* 1.23). At other times the human cycle functions by itself: Ibycus' wife is too old to frolic with teenagers; her behaviour is not becoming – *non decet* (*Odes* 3.15.8 and 14; cf. 4.13.2–3). Frivolous amusements, like lyric poetry, are suitable for youngsters; the same is true of riotous parties (*Epist.* 2.2.142 and 216). Here, as elsewhere, Horace at times ruefully admits that he has failed by his own standards. His interest in love-poetry at the age of fifty is hardly proper (*Odes* 4.1.9 and 35).

In a famous passage of the *A.P.* words, like men, are said to have a life-cycle (60–72). At one point it looks as if usage (*usus*) is what determines the vitality of any given word (71–2); but there is more to it than that, for a good poet will *modify* usage, by reviving old words, producing novel combinations, and admitting new words. All these procedures are governed by propriety. This concept, which was elaborated by the Peripatetics, is also important in other passages of the *A.P.* Thus theme should be appropriate to ability (38ff.) and style to subject matter (73ff.). A speaker's language ought to suit his emotion (99ff.) and also his rank, age, occupation, and nationality (114ff. and 156ff.). An understanding of these matters is obtainable from moral philosophy (309ff.). From here we can move across to *Epist.* 1, where one of the main philosophical strands is the question of 'what is right and proper' – *quid uerum atque decens* (*Epist.* 1.1.11). The emphasis lies on individual behaviour; when the context is supplied it is that of social relations, whether with friend, patron, or slave. A further dimension is added in some of the official odes, which present a picture of benign protection and supervision descending from Jupiter to Augustus, and from him to the Senate and people of Rome. Rising upwards in return are feelings of gratitude and devotion which find expression in religious observances and acts of patriotism. Hence in times of danger 'it is sweet and fitting to die for one's country' – *dulce et decorum est pro patria mori* (*Odes* 3.2.13). Now there are, of course, obvious differences between these situations – differences which could be used to draw a more detailed map of the poet's ideas. The common factor, however, is the belief that it is prudent to acknowledge and adapt oneself to some given pattern whether of nature, language, or morals.

With the theme of *pax* we can be more specific. I use the Latin term because it admits the two ideas of 'peacefulness' and 'pacification' and so enables us to take account of Horace's attitude to imperialism. In the decade after Philippi there was no stability in the country at large. As firm government had broken down, happiness and peace of mind could only be attained within the circle of one's friends; and so comradeship, contentment, and inner serenity were all-important. The various kinds of folly that interfered with these private values were ridiculed in the *Satires*. In *Epod*. 13 wine, music, and good fellowship were seen as the only answer to the *horrida tempestas* in the world outside, while nos. 7 and 16 cried out in despair against the madness and chaos of civil war. These last two poems, however, contained another significant idea in that they deplored civil war not only as crime and impiety but also as a betrayal of Rome's imperial tradition (7.5–10, 16.3–10). In this respect they foreshadowed certain odes in the first collection. Pondering on the guilt of civil war in 1.2, Horace thinks how much better it would have been for the Romans to turn their weapons against the Parthians (l. 22; cf. 51–2); similar sentiments are found in 1.21.13ff. and, at greater length, in the Fortuna ode (1.35). In 3.6 Rome's civil wars, which are seen as a symptom of moral corruption, are said to have left her open to foreign attack:

> paene occupatam seditionibus
> deleuit urbem Dacus et Aethiops.   (13–14)

The Dacian and Egyptian almost destroyed the city, occupied as it was with internal strife.

(The Egyptian menace was, of course, the combined strength of Antony and Cleopatra.) But the most elaborate treatment of this dual theme is presented in 3.3, where Juno promises world dominion, provided there is no revival of the corruption and discord of the late Republic.

Juno's speech is also interesting for another reason. It is one of the very few references to territorial expansion. The other passages are 2.9.18–24 and 3.5.1–4, neither of which is comparable in rhetorical grandeur. But this rhetoric draws attention to a further point, viz. that the emphasis falls heavily on the proviso noted above: 'You may conquer every corner of the globe *provided* you check internal disunity and decay.' Those might be the words of a man who was passionately keen on the spread of Roman power, but they might not. If we turn to 3.5 we see that there Horace is less interested in the conquest of Britain and Parthia than in the character of Regulus; the first stanza is a kind of starting mechanism to get the poem under way. Instead of dwelling on the acquisition of new territory Horace more often speaks in terms of defence: the Medes must not be allowed to raid unpunished (1.2.51), the kings defeated by Caesar were once a menace (2.12.12), the Parthians are a threat to Latium (1.12.53). This does not mean that Augustus' foreign wars were always defensive; in fact there is a good case for believing that the Emperor's policy was one of continuous, though deliberate, expansion until the disaster of the Teutoburg forest in A.D. 9.[1] I am only pointing out that in the passages cited above Horace chose to present the campaigns in that light.

Other passages again present quite a different view. Because he is in love (1.19) or inspired (1.26) Horace professes an airy indifference to frontier battles; and he urges Quinctius Hirpinus (2.11) and Maecenas (3.29) not to be obsessed with foreign affairs. But (at the risk of stressing the obvious) this does not mean that in the poet's total scheme of things such issues were unimportant. There is only one ode which is ostensibly anti-imperialist, and that is 1.29 which jokingly remonstrates with Iccius for joining in the campaign against Arabia.

In *Odes* 4, where the laureate is more in evidence, two ideas are developed from the earlier collection. The first is that the Romans have already *achieved* world domination. The germ of this is found in 3.8.17–24, but it becomes a feature of the later lyrics in *Carm. Saec.* 53–6, 4.14.41–52 and 4.15.21–4. The second, which is closely related, is that since Augustus is in charge of the empire, the men and women of Italy can go about their business in safety. This is foreshadowed in 3.14.14–16 and recurs with greater emphasis in 4.5.17–20 and 25–8 and in 4.15.17–20.

To sum up: with the victory at Actium chaos was pushed back to the borders of the empire, and this allowed Horace's private ethic (seen in the *Satires* and *Epodes* and in many of the informal odes) to expand into a Roman ethic. The state now assumed a position analogous to that held by the individual. Happiness still depended on inner peace, but this could now be seen to include peace within the empire. As the individual's well-being demanded a careful discipline of the emotions, so Rome's health depended on the control of destructive

[1] See Brunt (1963) 170–6.

social forces like extravagance, lawlessness, and domestic immorality. And, as in times of trouble the individual had to build spiritual defences against the outside world, so Rome's security required a strong policy against the hostile and unruly peoples beyond her frontiers. It is a commonplace of history that the heirs of an imperial tradition are usually in favour of maintaining it, as long as they can assert their superiority without an unacceptably heavy cost. Horace was no exception. He was proud to be a Roman and could on occasion rise to the imperial theme. But his work as a whole suggests that he valued the empire not so much for its power and prestige but rather because it enabled him and others to enjoy in peace the pleasures of friendship and poetry and the amenities of civilized life:

> quis Parthum paueat, quis gelidum Scythen
> quis Germania quos horrida parturit
> fetus, incolumi Caesare? quis ferae
>   bellum curet Hiberiae?   (*Odes* 4.5.25–8)

Who would fear the Parthian or the icy Scythian or the young brought forth in the forests of Germany as long as Caesar is unharmed? Who would care about the war in wild Spain?

The poet's private *otium* is guaranteed by the *pax Augusta*.

Another approach, which will take us closer to Augustus, is through religion. In an early ode, written in the form of a Pindaric paean, Horace reflects on the disasters which have shaken Rome. Only divine intervention can save her; Apollo, Venus, and Mars are invoked in turn; but perhaps there is already a god on earth; is the young Octavian really Mercury in human form (*Odes* 1.2.41ff.)? To explain why Octavian is associated with Mercury scholars have referred to the Emperor's youthfulness, beauty, and eloquence. But surely the main clue is supplied by *Odes* 1.10: 'Mercury, eloquent grandson of Atlas, who didst shape the savage ways of new-born men.' Was it not the god's benign, civilizing, spirit that made him a possible model for the young ruler? As the inventor of the lyre, Mercury had also a special significance for Horace. It was Mercury who rescued him at Philippi (*Odes* 2.7.13), and because the poet was one of Mercury's men he escaped being killed by a falling tree (*Odes* 2.17.27ff.).

Naturally Horace also owes allegiance to the Muses, who preside over both his formal and his informal poetry (*Musarum sacerdos* in *Odes* 3.1.3 and *imbellisque lyrae Musa potens* in 1.6.10). In *Odes* 3.4 he tells how as a small child he strayed from his nurse and fell asleep, and how he escaped harm thanks to the protection of heaven. Then addressing the Muses, he says: 'As long as you are with me I will gladly sail into the raging Bosphorus or walk into the scorching desert of Syria.' Half the poem is taken up with this intimate spiritual relationship, then suddenly we come upon this surprising stanza:

> uos Caesarem altum, militia simul
> fessas cohortes abdidit oppidis,
> finire quaerentem labores
> Pierio recreatis antro.   (37–40)

You refresh great Caesar in a Pierian cave as he longs to bring his labours to an end after settling his battle-weary troops quietly in the towns.

So the Emperor too is under the Muses' care. They refresh his spirit (i.e. he takes pleasure in poetry), but more important they advise him to act with gentleness and good sense:

> uos lene consilium et datis et dato
> gaudetis almae.   (41–2)

It is significant that Horace should have given a central position among the Roman odes to a poem which expressly connects his own activity with that of Augustus and ascribes both poetic and political power to the same divine source.

A similar point can be made with reference to Bacchus. On the one hand we have passages like *Epist.* 2.2.77–8, where Horace protests that as a servant of Bacchus (i.e. a poet) his proper milieu is the countryside, or *Odes* 3.8 where he offers a goat to Bacchus to celebrate his escape from death. On the other hand Bacchus is also associated with Augustus. As a hero who has benefited mankind, Bacchus achieved divinity; the same will be true of Augustus (*Odes* 3.3.11–15). Only after becoming a god did Bacchus receive due praise from men; Augustus receives it already (*Epist.* 2.1.5ff.). The triangular relationship becomes closer in *Odes* 2.19, a hymn to Bacchus which testifies to Horace's inspiration and then goes on to record some of the god's achievements. One of these was his defence of Jupiter against the Giants. That same battle, which symbolized the triumph of civilization over barbarism and was known to Horace's readers from Pindar and Greek sculpture, is used again in *Odes* 3.4.49ff. as a means of glorifying Augustus. Finally, in *Odes* 3.25 Bacchus' inspiration is specifically connected with Horace's new political lyrics in honour of the Emperor.

The deity most closely associated with Augustus, however, was Apollo. In the Republican period Vediovis, the god of the Julian gens, became assimilated to Apollo; Apollo was the son of Jupiter, and Augustus was the (adopted) son of Julius, who in his lifetime had assumed the attributes of the king of the gods; Apollo had helped Rome's Trojan ancestors against the Greeks, and as the god of sanity and order he had been a powerful psychological ally in the struggle against Antony/Dionysus. These and other affinities were attested in the magnificent temple of Apollo on the Palatine, dedicated in 28 B.C. It is

HORACE

interesting to hear that within the temple a prominent place was occupied by
a statue of Apollo the lyre-player, which is said to have borne the features of
Augustus himself.[1]

At the end of an amusing satire (1.9) Apollo intervenes to rescue Horace
from the clutches of a pest who has been trying to wangle an introduction to
Maecenas. In *Odes* 1.32 Horace addresses the lyre as the 'glory of Phoebus'
(*o decus Phoebi*) and asks it to inspire his alcaic verse. On the official side we
have the *Carmen saeculare*, which was written to be sung by a choir of boys and
girls at the celebrations of 17 B.C. The performance took place before the temple
of Apollo, and several stanzas are addressed to him. Augustus also figures in the
hymn as 'the illustrious descendant of Anchises and Venus'. Elsewhere public
and private coalesce. The occasion envisaged in *Odes* 1.31 is the vintage festival
of the Meditrinalia, which in 28 B.C. took place just after the dedication of
Apollo's temple. In the opening stanza the *uates* wonders what he should
pray for; the answer is given in the last stanza by Horace the private individual:
it is health of body and mind, and continued inspiration. *Odes* 4.6 is a hymn to
Apollo, prompted by the success of the *Carmen saeculare*. It recalls how the
god slew Achilles and preserved Aeneas to found Rome. Apollo the minstrel
is asked to protect 'the glory of the Daunian Muse' – which could mean either
Italian or Horatian poetry. Then in the remaining stanzas Horace speaks of his
personal debt to the god:

> spiritum Phoebus mihi, Phoebus artem
> carminis nomenque dedit poetae. (29–30)

Phoebus granted me inspiration, the art of song, and the name of poet.

Apollo's dual aspect was represented by the lyre and the bow (see *Odes*
1.21.11–12; 2.10.18–20). Another Apolline symbol which linked poet and
Emperor was the laurel. In *Odes* 3.4.19 the infant Horace is said to have been
covered with laurel leaves; later, at the end of his first collection of odes Horace
asks Melpomene to place a crown of Delphic laurel on his hair (3.30.15–16).
In other passages the laurel is that worn by a triumphant general – viz. *Odes*
2.1.15 and 4.3.6–7. As early as 36 B.C., following his victory over Sextus
Pompeius, Octavian was voted a laurel crown. Later, in 27 B.C., the doors of
his house were decorated with laurel, and the same symbol appeared on coins
and reliefs.

Last of all, we should bear in mind certain words which describe the processes
and powers of lyric composition. Orpheus 'led' forests and checked rivers
(*ducere* and *morari* in *Odes* 1.12.12 and 9, cf. 3.11.14); Cerberus 'surrendered'
to the lyre (*cedere* in 3.11.15); Amphion 'led' the stones of Thebes (*ducere* in
A.P. 396). The word for tune or rhythm is *modus*, and the verbs *moderari* and

[1] Servius on Virgil, *Ecl.* 4.10; ps.-Acro on Horace, *Epist.* 1.3.17.

modulari are both used of playing the lyre (1.24.14; 1.32.5; *Epist.* 2.2.143). But as the central idea in *modus* is that of limit or proportion, the management of the lyre is seen as a kind of organization. The same idea lies behind *temperare*. In *Odes* 1.12.16 and 3.4.45 the earth, sea, and sky, and the affairs of men, are said to be 'tempered' or 'controlled' by Jupiter. In *Odes* 4.3.18 the Muse 'tempers' the sweet din of the golden lyre. Or again, in *Odes* 2.12.4 themes are 'adjusted' (*aptare*) to the strains of the lyre (cf. *Epist.* 1.3.13); in *Odes* 3.30.14 aeolian verse is 'set to' or 'settled amongst' Italian tunes (*deducere*); and in *Odes* 4.9.4 an 'alliance' has to be made between strings and words (*sociare*). Like the creator in the old myths the poet imposes order and harmony on already existing material. This material, which is shapeless, discordant, and meaningless, is sometimes seen as the lyre, sometimes as language, and some-times as theme; but whatever it may be, it must eventually yield to the poet's authority.

Horace's attitude to Augustus was complex, and it is hard to see it in per-spective. One can appreciate the poet's independent spirit by recalling that he did not speak about Octavian until the time of Actium; that he remained loyal to old Republican friends; that only a small proportion of *Odes* 1-3 was written in praise of Augustus and those odes were notably restrained in comparison with the usual type of Hellenistic panegyric;[1] and that although the Emperor took a more direct interest in Horace and his work after 17 B.C. no very close friendship ever existed between the two men. Nevertheless, Horace acknow-ledged and admired the colossal achievements of Augustus; he saw that the Princeps had a power and status which set him apart from ordinary men, and that this power had on the whole been used to promote harmony throughout the empire. Finally, he recognized that after a century of civil war Rome stood in desperate need of regeneration, and that this involved *religious* regeneration too. Such feelings, which were shared by the vast majority of his countrymen, allowed Horace at certain times to adopt the role of *uates* ('priest' or 'bard') and to speak about Roman affairs in traditional religious language. It is quite true that all this did not add up to theological conviction and that Horace's normal attitude to the state religion was one of indifference. Yet this area of expression is notoriously imprecise. A patriotic feeling for the past, the sense of a great occasion, a close familiarity with the age-old symbols of one's culture – such factors combine to blur definitions and blunt charges of hypo-crisy. Housman's '1887' (commemorating Victoria's golden jubilee) concludes thus:

> Oh, God will save her, fear you not:
> Be you the men you've been,
> Get you the sons your fathers got,
> And God will save the Queen.

[1] See Doblhofer (1966).

Housman, of course, was an unbeliever; but he fiercely repudiated the suggestion that '1887' was not seriously intended.[1]

If this account is in any way correct it means that, when allowance has been made for untypical passages and for a range of inconsistency to which anyone is entitled, there remains a large central area in Horace's work where the main strands criss-cross. The dichotomy outlined above is therefore artificial and gives little help towards a just appreciation of his work. When we take the lyrics as a whole we can point to a memorable ode about Horace's poetic achievement (3.30) and a poor one (2.20), a great Roman ode (3.4) and an inferior one (3.2), a strong attack on an ageing beauty (1.25) and a weaker one (4.13), an impressive tribute to Augustus' step-sons (4.4) and a less attractive one (4.14), a substantial invitation-poem to Maecenas (3.8) and a slight one (1.20). Horace would have cheerfully accepted this attitude, for he did not look for indiscriminate adulation either as a poet or as a man (*Epist.* 1.4.1; *Sat.* 1.3.69–72). He might, however, have added that if we wanted to study one ode which more than any other contained the essence of his spirit we should turn to *Tyrrhena regum* (3.29). In that magnificent poem we find the Greek past alive in the Roman present, an inimitable blend of grandeur and intimacy, solemnity and humour; and a sad awareness of transience and insecurity combined with a tough-minded intention to survive. No translation can hope to do it justice, but two stanzas in Dryden's paraphrase give a measure of its quality:

> Happy the Man, and happy he alone,
> He who can call to day his own:
> He, who secure within, can say
> To morrow do thy worst, for I have liv'd to day.
> Be fair, or foul, or rain, or shine,
> The joys I have possest, in spight of fate are mine,
> Not Heav'n it self upon the past has pow'r;
> But what has been, has been, and I have had my hour.

[1] See C. Brooks in Ricks (ed.) (1968) 76.

6

LOVE ELEGY

I. GENERAL INTRODUCTION

The elegiac distich appears as a fully developed poetic form in Greece in the seventh century B.C. It is used, as far as we know, for inscriptions, but also in long poems which were sung or chanted to the music of the *aulos* (Latin *tibia*), a pipe with a reedy tone something like the modern oboe. There seems to be a linguistic connexion between the Armenian word *elegn* 'reed' and the Greek term ἐλεγεῖον (*sc.* μέτρον). The derivation from ἒ ἒ λέγειν 'to say woe! woe!' offered as an etymology by Alexandrian scholars is fanciful, to say the least. For Propertius (2.30B.13–16; 3.10.23) the sound of the *tibia* is somehow associated with drinking wine, making love and, possibly, reciting love poetry. On the other hand, both Horace (*A.P.* 75–8) and Ovid (*Amores* 3.9.1ff.) seem to think that the elegiac metre is ideally suited for laments. This probably means that they knew Greek funeral elegies of the archaic or classical period which we no longer have. Horace limits the elegiac distich to votive inscriptions (*uoti sententia compos*) and laments (*querimonia*), i.e. epigrams of the kind which we have in Books 6 and 7 of the Greek Anthology. He ignores the erotic epigrams of Meleager's Garland which now form Books 5 and 12 of the Greek Anthology, though he must have known some of them. Incidentally, the satiric epigram was not yet a popular genre in the Augustan age.

In the earliest period, Greek poets of such different temperaments and tastes as Callinus, Tyrtaeus and Mimnermus (all seventh century B.C.) wrote elegiac poems on a variety of themes, but of the three only Mimnermus seems to have dealt with love. *Nanno*, the title traditionally given to Mimnermus' collection of elegies (of which we have only fragments), might be the name of a woman he loved (a flute-player, it is sometimes said). Propertius 1.9.11 *plus in amore ualet Mimnermi uersus Homero* 'In love Mimnermus' verse is more powerful than Homer' contrasts light erotic poetry in the elegiac manner with the heroic epic; for him Mimnermus is the poet of love, just as Homer is the great epic poet.

We hear about late classical and Hellenistic collections of elegies which had a woman's name as a title, perhaps following Mimnermus' example: Antimachus'

Lyde, Philitas' *Bittis* (or *Battis*), Hermesianax' *Leontion*. They may have dealt with love-tales of mythological heroes and heroines, and yet they were related, it seems, to a real woman. Antimachus is said to have comforted his grief by putting mythological tales (tragic love-stories, no doubt) into elegiac verse when his wife or mistress, Lyde, had died. Hermesianax gave a long catalogue of poets in love, presumably because he was a poet in love himself; but then he must have said so in at least one poem of the collection. Similarly, Antimachus must have said that he loved Lyde, Philitas that he loved Bittis (cf. Ovid, *Tristia* 1.6.1–4). Still this does not tell us anything about the character of a whole elegiac *Gedichtbuch* in the Hellenistic period.

Among the many papyrus fragments which have contributed so much to our knowledge of Callimachus not one elegy has been found that might be compared to, e.g., one by Propertius. But perhaps such texts will be discovered. Recently two elegiac fragments have been published in the series of the *Oxyrhynchus Papyri* (vol. 39, 1972): nos. 2884 and 2885. The first one is the lament of a woman who confesses her 'passionate love', θαλυκρὸς ἔρως, to the goddess Artemis and complains about the cruelty of the man she loves. The other one lists some mythological heroines who hurt close relatives because they were in love with a man; this is addressed to all women in love as a warning. We also have the Sorbonne Papyrus 2254, a curious curse-poem not unlike Ovid's *Ibis*, but not related to anything we read in the *Amores*.[1] Perhaps the Hellenistic poets did prefer the format of the epigram when they talked about their own love experiences. It is true that some Latin elegies could be interpreted as expanded Greek epigrams (cf. Prop. 2.12 and *Anth. Pal.* 5.176 and 177 or Ovid, *Amores* 1.13 and *Anth. Pal.* 5.172). Or a fairly close translation of a Greek epigram may be woven into the context of a Latin elegy (e.g. Leonidas, *Anth. Pal.* 9.337 (= XXIX Gow–Page) in Prop. 3.13.43–6). But it would be wrong to derive one genre from the other; both seem to have coexisted from the earliest times.

In a broader sense all Roman elegiac poets were influenced by the great Hellenistic poets, for instance Callimachus, because they mention him frequently as a model, but probably more as a model of style. Others, such as Euphorion, may have furnished obscure myths to serve as *exempla*. When Virgil, *Ecl.* 10.50f. makes Gallus say *ibo et Chalcidico quae sunt mihi condita uersu | carmina, pastoris Siculi modulabor auena* this simply means that Gallus will now write pastoral poems in the style of Theocritus (like Virgil himself) rather than epic or elegiac poems in the style of Euphorion.[2] In the Ἐρωτικὰ παθήματα, 'Stories of passionate love', Gallus' friend and literary adviser Parthenius gives, among other things, prose versions of Euphorion's *Thrax* and his *Apollodorus*. The Roman poets probably did not find it too difficult to

---

[1] Barnes and Lloyd-Jones (1963) 205–27.   [2] Schöpsdau (1974) 268ff.

transform Greek narrative elegies into their own preferred 'subjective' form: Propertius 1.18 is a good example.[1] But the Romans did not commit the elegy to one specific theme or genre: they wrote elegiac *epicedia* (Prop. 3.18; Ovid, *Amores* 3.9) which differ in metre only from such lyric epicedia as Horace, *Odes* 1.24.

This chapter will concentrate on the four famous Augustan love-poets. For our purposes the love elegy or the book of love elegies may be considered a creation of the Augustan age, though Catullus is sometimes included. His poem 68 would seem to represent the prototype of the Augustan love elegy though love is only one theme among many; it is interwoven most skilfully with the themes of friendship, the loss of his brother, the Trojan War. Their interrelationship is the following: Catullus' friend Allius offered him a house for secret meetings with Lesbia; hence the poem is a token of gratitude. The death of Catullus' brother had a serious impact on his life: it ended abruptly the happy, playful period of his life (*multa satis lusi*, l. 17). Now that his brother is dead, it would be time for Catullus to marry and settle down. Catullus, as his curious wedding poems prove, understands the middle-class morality of Verona.[2] But marriage is out of the question, for in the meantime he has met Lesbia and fallen in love with her. Brief, superficial love affairs are no longer possible, but neither is a conventional marriage. Finally, his brother's death in the Troad reminds him of the Trojan War; the place has been cursed ever since then. These are the themes, and this is the way in which they are interwoven; no later elegist has achieved such a degree of complexity.

2. CHARACTERISTICS OF THE AUGUSTAN LOVE ELEGY

(*a*) The elegy does not claim to be one of the elevated genres of literature; it places itself below epic and tragedy though, it would seem, above the mime and the satire. The elegists (Tibullus excepted) like to call their verse *nugae* 'trifles' or *lusus* 'playthings'. All the same they are proud of their work; they look down on the *profanum uulgus* just like the greatest lyric poet of the age (cf. Propertius 2.23.1ff.; Lygd. 3.20) and they count on immortality. This is the attitude of the Alexandrian literary coterie: enough to be admired by a small group of connoisseurs which hardly included the typical Roman businessmen and politicians, Catullus' 'rather rigid old men' (*senes seueriores* 5.2; cf. Prop. 2.30.13ff.; Ovid, *Amores* 1.15.1ff.).

(*b*) The elegiac poets of the Augustan age, beginning with Gallus, write whole books of elegies. The collection sometimes bears the name of a woman, following the Greek tradition mentioned above. Propertius probably published Book 1, the *Monobiblos*, under the title *Cynthia*. Tibullus' two books of elegies

---

[1] Cairns (1969) 131–4.   [2] Luck (1974) 23ff.

may have been known as *Delia* and *Nemesis* respectively, for Ovid (*Amores* 3.9.31ff.) in his vision of the two women at the poet's funeral seems to be speaking of the two books as well: *altera cura recens, altera primus amor* 'one a recent interest, the other his first love', where *cura recens* can mean 'a new book' as well as 'a new love'. *Neaera* was almost certainly the title of Lygdamus' small book of six poems (*Corp. Tib.* 3.1–6), and the first (lost) edition of Ovid's *Amores* may have been published under the title *Corinna*.[1]

(*c*) We still know too little about the status of women in Rome during the first century B.C., and we ought to be careful not to interpret love poetry as if it were historical evidence. But roughly speaking we can distinguish three types of 'elegiac women':[2]

(i) the *matrona*, the married woman who enjoys a certain independence. She may have many affairs, like Clodia (Catullus' Lesbia), or she may be faithful to her husband like Cornelia (Prop. 4.11).

(ii) the *femme entretenue* who may be married but is more likely to be single or divorced and who has firm attachments that last for months or years.[3]

(iii) the *meretrix*, the prostitute with whom men have brief, casual encounters.

It is essential to keep these three classes apart; Cynthia, for instance, is not a *meretrix*. Propertius (2.23) and Ovid (*Amores* 1.10.21ff.) make the distinction quite plain, though, of course, there are transitions from one class to the other. Contrary to general opinion today,[4] affairs with married ladies were not the rule. Propertius, in theory at least (loc. cit.), is against such involvements; he uses the arguments of the Hellenistic diatribe which are best known from Horace, *Sat.* 1.2. Such affairs were risky, for anyone caught *in flagranti delicto* could be whipped or even killed by the angry husband. Sex was a natural and necessary activity, and marriage was not always conducive to intellectual and artistic pursuits; hence some philosophers recommended using prostitutes, and even snobs like Propertius (loc. cit.) did not always despise the cheap and simple pleasures found on the Via Sacra. The women of the second class, as well as those of the first, may belong to the high aristocracy; this could be true for Cynthia, if Prop. 1.16 refers to her (the lady of 3.20 is certainly not Cynthia). Tibullus' Delia seems to belong to the lower middle class, a pretty girl who becomes for a while the mistress of a rich and well-bred gentleman before marrying someone of her own class, a phenomenon not entirely unknown today. To complete the picture, Gallus' Lycoris was an ex-slave, a music-hall artist of great fame and beauty, and a formidable courtesan who attracted not only the poet but such political figures as Mark Antony and Brutus.

---

[1] Luck (1959) 174ff. [2] Luck (1974) 15ff.
[3] Maurois (1957) 188–9 amusingly describes the *demi-monde* in nineteenth-century Paris, and what he says about the *aristocratie de la galanterie* and the fact that even the *hautes coquines*, under the influence of romantic literature, dreamt of pure love may serve as an illustration.
[4] G. W. Williams (1968) 542.

(*d*) Homosexual love no longer plays the important role it played in Hellenistic poetry. All of Callimachus' love poems were addressed to boys: *Anth. Pal.* 12.43 (= II Gow–Page) and 12.73 (= IV Gow–Page) may be considered classics of the genre; the latter was translated into Latin by the consul of 102 B.C., Q. Lutatius Catulus. This shows, perhaps, a taste not only for this kind of poetry but also for this kind of love, among the Roman aristocracy of the late second century B.C. In Catullus' book, four love poems (24; 48; 81; 99), the last two in elegiac distichs, are addressed to a young man whom Catullus calls 'dear flower of the Juventii', *flosculus Iuuentiorum* (24.1). In their intensity they are comparable to the Lesbia poems; if the wish to give Lesbia thousands of kisses is sincere in poem 5, the same wish in a Iuventius poem (poem 48) is probably not mere rhetoric. These are highly emotional affairs, and it should surprise no one that we find here exactly the same *topoi* (e.g. the cruelty of the beloved, 99.6) as in the other poems.

The Marathus elegies in Tibullus' Book I seem to form a cycle within a cycle. The god Priapus, in his role as 'love counsellor', *praeceptor amoris*, lectures in 1.4 about the technique of seducing handsome boys, and Priapus' reputation would suggest that physical love, not just a romantic attachment, is meant. Another poem of the cycle, 1.8, presents a curious set of relationships: Tibullus, in love with the boy Marathus, urges the girl Pholoe whom Marathus happens to desire, to be kind to the boy; but Pholoe is apparently in love with a third man who, in turn, longs for another woman. Tibullus pleads on the boy's behalf (1.8.17ff.) and even arranges secret meetings with Pholoe for him (1.9.41ff.). Because of this rather unusual constellation the poems have never been clearly understood; but that seems to be the rather complicated relationship they imply, and if anything could stimulate the jaded tastes of the Augustan gilded set, this is it.

Homosexual love is practically absent in Propertius and Ovid, though Ovid's friend Proculus (*Pont.* 4.16.32) still writes in the Callimachean manner. Propertius' comparison (2.4.17ff.; cf. 9.31–6; 3.19.1–10) is more theoretical and mainly designed to show that woman is the more emotional, irrational, intractable creature. Ovid (*Ars Am.* 2.683f.) makes another point: 'I dislike any kind of sex that does not relax both partners; this is why making love to a boy appeals to me less' *odi concubitus qui non utrumque resoluunt:* | *hoc est cur pueri tangar amore minus.*

(*e*) Much of elegiac poetry is persuasive, directed towards a very practical, very simple aim: to conquer the woman. Some poems are written to please her, some promise to make her immortal. This is especially true in the case of Propertius, less so for Catullus.[1]

(*f*) The elegiac poets vary in their attitude towards politics. Catullus attacks

---

[1] Stroh (1971) *passim.*

several political figures of his time, Caesar among them, but this type of pole-
mic disappears from the Augustan love elegy, and the poets, with the exception
of Tibullus, are paying lip service to Augustus. Tibullus never even mentions
him, but his silence may not mean anything. Propertius' family seems to have
been on the wrong side in the civil war (cf. 1.21; 4.1), but his friendship with
Maecenas opens to him the house of the Emperor, and he dutifully celebrates
Roman victories (4.6), echoes the themes of official propaganda (3.11.29ff.),
and inclines himself before the ruler (3.3.1; 11.66; 4.6.14; 11.60).[1] But he
refuses to write an epic in honour of Augustus (2.1.17) and, like Tibullus, is
more impressed by Rome's past (see the Roman Elegies of Book 4) than by its
present. Ovid's poetry expresses his loyalty to the Emperor, and the tragic
incident which brought about his exile was clearly not a political crime.

(g) Cornelius Gallus, like Virgil and Horace, was born of humble parents
but given a first-rate education. He worked his way up as a protégé of his
former class-mate Octavian. Tibullus was a Roman knight from a wealthy
family (the complaints about his poverty seem to be a literary *topos*) and served
on Messalla's staff in several military campaigns. When in Italy he preferred
country-life to life in the city. Propertius was born in Umbria, the son of
impoverished land-owners. After the publication of Book 1 Maecenas became
his patron, and in later years he lived in a fashionable neighbourhood in Rome,
as a man-about-town. Ovid, also a Roman knight, had an excellent education
in Rome and later travelled in Greece and Asia Minor. For a short time he was,
like Tibullus, a member of Messalla's circle. He held minor political offices
but preferred a writer's independence and lived comfortably at the foot of the
Capitol, keeping the old family estate in Sulmo in the Abruzzi and cultivating
his gardens outside of Rome. To sum up: most of these poets belong to fairly
prosperous (or just recently impoverished) families. Two are known to have
been Roman knights. All seem to have enjoyed the best education that was to
be had at the time. All of them had, at least for a time, a powerful patron. At
least Propertius and Ovid seem to have been celebrated writers in their lifetime; whether they had any income from the sale of their works we do not
know.[2] The careers of Gallus and Ovid were cut short by disgrace which led
the one to suicide, the other to permanent exile.

3. CORNELIUS GALLUS

Since Virgil's *Ecl.* 10 in which Gallus is made to speak of his unhappy love
was probably not written before 40 B.C. we may assume that the elegies which
made him famous appeared between 50 and 40 B.C. when Gallus was in his

[1] With Prop. 2.16.41f. cf. Virg. *Aen.* 6.847ff.; Livy 30.42.17; Aug. *Res Gest.* 2.42.
[2] Luck (1959) 173ff.

twenties. Of the four books only one line is preserved. He calls his mistress Lycoris; her real name was Volumnia, her stage name Cytheris.

We have only a few clues as to the character of Gallus' poetry, but since he was Virgil's friend he may have influenced the *Eclogues*, and *Ecl.* 10.31ff. especially is said to be an imitation of Gallus' elegiac themes. Gallus himself was influenced by Callimachus and Euphorion; he also used a collection of thirty-six love stories in prose compiled for him by a late Hellenistic poet, Parthenius of Nicaea: they were to be inserted as *exempla* in Gallus' epyllia and elegies. Gallus is called *durior* 'harsher' than both Tibullus and Propertius by Quintilian, *Inst.* 10.1.93; according to the same critic, Ovid is *lasciuior* 'more frivolous' than the others. Horace's *Epod.* 11 may be a parody of Gallus' themes and manner. He was certainly an important link between the Neoterics and the later Augustans.

4. ALBIUS TIBULLUS AND THE 'CORPUS TIBULLIANUM'

Tibullus' friendship with the great statesman M. Valerius Messalla Corvinus is one of the main themes of his poetry. He accompanied Messalla, probably between 31 and 27 B.C., on various campaigns, notably in Gaul and in the Near East. Messalla may have known Horace, either as a student in Athens or as an officer in Brutus' army. He fought in the battle of Philippi (42 B.C.) with distinction, later served under Antony and finally made his peace with Augustus without ever forsaking his Republican ideals. He became a patron of the arts and encouraged young poets. Messalla's 'circle' seems to have included, at one time or another, his niece Sulpicia, the young Ovid (cf. *Tristia* 4.4.27f.; *Pont.* 1.7.27f.) and others. The *Corpus Tibullianum*, as we have it today, may be considered an anthology of poems written by members of that circle, probably published after Messalla's death. It is reasonable to assume that all these authors had some connexion with Messalla, even if we did not know this in the case of Tibullus and Sulpicia. We do not have to discuss the *Panegyricus Messallae* here, since it is not an elegy. It is not great poetry, but it is more than an exercise in rhetoric, and given the character of ancient *encomia* and the difference between the genres it may well be a work of the young Tibullus.

'Lygdamus' is perhaps the most professional or at least the most ambitious of these other poets. He describes the year of his birth (3.5.17f.) in the same words Ovid uses (*Tristia* 4.10.5f.): it is the year 43 B.C. when both consuls, Hirtius and Pansa, died of wounds received in the War of Mutina. There are many other striking parallels between the six relatively short elegies of 'Lygdamus' and Ovid's works from all periods of his life. One short passage, Lygd. 5.15–20, shows similarities to Ovid's *Amores* 2.14.23f.; *Ars Am.* 2.670 and *Tristia* 4.10.6. One tends to assume that Lygdamus imitates Ovid (just as he imitates Tibullus, especially in his second and fifth elegies), but there is a difficulty: he calls himself *iuuenis* (in 3.2.2) which seems impossible considering that this contemporary of Ovid's is old enough to read Ovid's exile poetry. Could he be the young Ovid who imitates himself later on? No satisfactory solution has been found.[1] The poetry itself is competent and not without a certain grace, but definitely sentimental.

The poems dealing with the love of Sulpicia and Cerinthus (here the man has a pseudonym, just like the women in Catullus, Propertius and Tibullus) are probably identical with the *epistulae amatoriae* mentioned in the ancient *Vita*. The first group (3.8–12 = 4.2–6) consists of poems ostensibly not written by Sulpicia herself, but by a sympathetic observer of her love affair, perhaps Tibullus. They form a poetic commentary on the affair by a third person, which is rather unusual (but cf. Prop. 1.10). The second group (3.13–18 = 4.7–12) consists of poems written by Sulpicia herself. Messalla's niece is an independent young woman who insists on her right to love; she is educated (she must have read at least some of the authors prescribed by Ovid, *Ars Am.* 3.329ff.) and handles language and metre well.

Tibullus' favourite themes are romantic love and the pleasures of country life. His pastoral passages show the influence of Virgil's *Eclogues* and *Georgics*. Though he is the only elegiac poet known to have spent years of his life in military service, he hates war and denounces the greed for power and wealth which leads to it. Money also corrupts love; this is something Tibullus claims to have experienced in all the affairs he tells about. A woman he calls Delia dominates Book 1 (above, p. 112); her real name was Plania; she seems to have lived with her old mother, and apparently she was a devotee of Isis. Nemesis, the mistress of Book 2, looks more like an experienced courtesan who may have been under the control of a 'go-between' (*lena*). Marathus, also mentioned in Book 2 (above, p. 113) is a handsome boy who attracted, at least for a short time, Tibullus as well as other men.

As a poet, Tibullus is, perhaps, more self-centred than the other elegists. He seems to live in a dream-world of his own. His nostalgia for a distant Golden Age may have obscured, for him, the grandeur of the Roman Empire and the blessings of the *Pax Augusta*. The only poem with 'national' themes (2.5) shows, perhaps, the influence of the *Aeneid*; it is important as a forerunner of Propertius' Roman Elegies (Book 4) and Ovid's *Fasti*.

From his poetry Tibullus appears to have been a great Roman gentleman. There is a delicacy of feeling in his elegies that is, perhaps, only found in Virgil, but Mackail was perhaps less than fair when he called Tibullus a 'Virgil without the genius'. There is genius as well as good breeding and good taste. Though he never mentions other poets and avoids any ostentation of learning,

---

[1] On the efforts to make him a contemporary of Statius and Martial see Luck (1959) 207ff.

mythological or otherwise, he is very well read, especially in Alexandrian authors.[1] Of course he knows Virgil and Horace, and his Book 2 may already reflect Propertius' Books 1 and 2. He has a charming sense of humour (not the biting kind which is Propertius' speciality), and the glimpses of real life which he gives us are welcome: the farmer's tipsy return, on his cart, with wife and children, after a country festival (1.10.51–2); the old grandfather playing with the baby (2.6.93–4); the invitation to the god Apollo to attend Messallinus' inauguration in his best attire (2.5.7–10).

Often, it seems as though he lets his mind, his imagination, wander from theme to theme; thus 1.1 begins with the praise of the simple but secure life of a poor farmer (ll. 1–44), continues with the theme of happy love (45–58), followed by a vision of the poet's death and funeral (59–68), recalls the enjoyment of life and love (69–74) and ends with the contrast of war and peace, wealth and poverty (75–8). There is a unity of mood and feeling; and the last two sections clearly echo the first two, but in a more concentrated form. Scholars have attempted to transpose couplets and whole passages, especially at the beginning of Book 1, to establish a more 'logical' order; but none of these transpositions is convincing, and careful interpretation usually reveals the poet's intention and his art.

5. SEXTUS PROPERTIUS

Propertius is, perhaps, the most difficult of the Roman elegiac poets, but also the one who appeals most to the modern taste. His tempestuous love affair with a woman he calls Cynthia (her real name was Hostia) fills most of the four books of elegies he wrote. The affair itself seems to have lasted five years (3.25.30) but whether a period of separation (3.16.9) was counted or not, is unknown. We may assume that the earliest poems of Book 1 were written in 29 B.C., and Book 3 with its emphatic farewell to Cynthia (3.24 and 25) was probably published in or shortly after 23 B.C. This would allow us to fit the five (or six) years conveniently between 29 and 23, but fact and fiction are so closely intertwined that no straight answer can be given. It should be said, however, that 3.20 tells of a new liaison with an unknown woman whom Propertius may have married; this elegy gives us no further information about Cynthia.

In Book 1 we meet some of the poet's friends in Rome: Tullus, a wealthy young man about to embark on a political career, the poets Ponticus and Bassus. He does not mention Ovid, though we know from *Tristia* 4.10.45–8 that they were all friends, *sodales*, and that Propertius used to read his love poems to Ovid. These might be some of the elegies now included in Book 2; Ovid was probably too young to have heard those of Book 1.

[1] Bulloch (1973) 85ff.

After a brief but not unhappy affair with a woman whom he calls Lycinna (3.15) Propertius fell in love with Cynthia. He speaks of her flaming eyes (2.13.14), her auburn hair (2.2.5–6), her long fingers and her striking figure (2.2.5–6). She was well read, musical, wrote verse herself and danced. Later, Propertius admits that he exaggerated her beauty (3.24 and 25), and after Cynthia's death her ghost gives a cruel assessment of Propertius, the lover, in a magnificent poem (4.7) which represents a supreme effort at self-criticism and self-irony by the poet; the result is a gentle but gripping evocation of the real Cynthia, nostalgic and without bitterness on his part.

His own image, as Propertius projects it, is that of a pale, intense young man (1.5.21), something of a dandy with perfumed hair and a slightly affected walk (2.4.5–6), who enjoys parties (3.5.19–22) and all the other pleasures of city life; the country does not attract him as much as it does Tibullus (but cf. 2.19). In later years, he seems to have become 'respectable' without losing his ability to view himself with irony (4.1).

The poems of Book 1 made him famous (a *succès de scandale*; cf. 2.24A.1ff.), and after Maecenas became his patron, the house of the Emperor was open to him. He wrote funeral elegies for two persons close to Augustus: 3.18 for his nephew Marcellus, and 4.11 for Cornelia. It speaks for Maecenas that he was capable of friendship with men as different as Virgil, Horace and Propertius (we know too little about the other members of his circle, such as L. Varius or Valgius Rufus). Propertius himself had the greatest admiration for Virgil, and around 25 B.C. he hails (2.34) the great new Roman epic in progress, though he probably knew little of the shape into which it grew. He never mentions Horace, though the influence of the *Odes* is fairly obvious, especially in the elegies of Book 3;[1] and Horace never mentions him by name, unless the slightly foppish elegist caricatured in *Epist.* 2.2.90ff. happens to be Propertius. Neither he nor Tibullus mention each other, but it is difficult to imagine that they ignored each other's work. Propertius 1 and Tibullus 1 may, in fact, be independent of each other, but Propertius 2 and 3 seem to show the influence of Tibullus 1, and his Roman Elegies (in Book 4) owe something to Tibullus 2.5.

Propertius sees himself as the great romantic lover. Like Byron, like D'Annunzio, he flies or wants to fly from woman to woman, always ready to offer, though not always giving, all of himself. To play this role (for it is a role) it is not enough to be passionate and tender: one needs a kind of contemptuous pride, an air of mystery; and behind the lover the reading public must feel the hero always engaged in fighting against the jealousy of the gods, the man who is greater than his destiny. Love, to him, is a transcendental power, and all accepted values – nobility, power, wealth – are revalued by love. Three lines,

[1] Cf., for example, 3.9.1 with Horace, *Odes* 1.1.1; 3.2.17 with *Odes* 3.30.2; 3.9.17 with *Odes* 1.1.2; 3.13.60 with *Epod.* 16.2 and on the whole question Wili (1947) 181ff.; Solmsen (1948) 105ff.

taken from his earlier poems, are characteristic: 1.5.24 *nescit amor priscis cedere imaginibus* 'love cannot yield to ancestral portrait busts'; 1.14.8 *nescit amor magnis cedere diuitiis* 'love cannot yield to great wealth'; 2.7.6 *deuictae gentes nil in amore ualent* 'conquered nations mean nothing if you are in love'. Here the three traditional Roman values are summed up and matched against the irrational force of love. But *amor* is also close to *pietas*; Propertius says to Cynthia (1.11.23–4) *tu mihi sola domus, tu, Cynthia, sola parentes: | omnia tu nostrae tempora laetitiae* 'you alone, Cynthia, are my house; you alone my parents; you are, for me, every moment of joy'. This love takes the place of all the emotional, religious attachments within the house, the family, and it becomes the ruling passion of one's life.

Propertius is not a philosophical poet. He wishes to keep more serious thoughts and studies for his old age, when he is no longer in love.[1] A clear line leads from the Alexandrian manner of Book 1 to the new realism of Book 4 with its awareness of Roman history. A great empire has come to be and is in danger of falling. Rome, too, will fall some day (*frangitur ipsa suis Roma superba bonis*, 3.13.60), just as the great kingdom of the Etruscans is a thing of the past: *heu Veii ueteres! et uos tum regna fuistis, | et uestro posita est aurea sella foro* 'alas, ancient Veii! once you were a kingdom, and the golden throne was placed on your market place' (4.10.27–8). The idea that Rome has become too powerful for her own good returns in Lucan and was perhaps a theme in Livy's preface to his famous account of the Civil War.

Invited by Maecenas to write an epic on Roman history Propertius refuses time and again (2.1; 3.3; 3.9) but finally offers a sort of compromise in the Roman Elegies of Book 4. Here he has found a congenial new theme and a fresh style. It is not true that he lost his poetic genius along with Cynthia – on the contrary: he continues to be creative in a different genre. The witty portrait of the astrologer in 4.1, the powerful caricature of the bawd in 4.5, the very funny description of the private orgy to which he treats himself in Cynthia's absence (4.8) reveal a gift of satire, a sardonic humour reminiscent of Horace in his best pieces. And 4.11, the 'queen of the elegies', is one of the most beautiful and moving poems written in Latin.

Propertius' early style is best described as *blandus* 'smooth and winning'. He is fond of this adjective,[2] and his friend Ovid applies it to him (*Tristia* 2.465; 5.1.17). It characterizes well the verbal melodies, the sometimes luxuriant use of lovely Greek names (1.3.1–4), the subtle technique of alliteration (1.1.1–2).

---

[1] 3.5.23–46 is a catalogue of philosophical (or scientific) themes. Cf. Lucr. 1.102ff.; 3.977ff.; Virg. *Geo.* 2.477ff.

[2] Propertius calls himself *blandus amator* (2.3.16); he speaks of the appeal of his verse as *blandi carminis obsequium*. The nameless lover in 1.16 who is suppliant (l. 14) and full of misery (l. 45) may be Propertius himself, because of the *arguta...blanditia*, the 'eloquent flattery' of his songs (l. 16).

6. PUBLIUS OVIDIUS NASO

Ovid is the last in the series of the Augustan elegists; and it seems the genre itself was dead long before Ovid's death in exile. His earliest elegies were collected in five books, the books probably coming out in chronological sequence, and then published as a whole, it would seem, under the title *Corinna*.[1] This edition is lost; Ovid replaced it by another in three books which is preserved under the title *Amores*. In the prefatory epigram the poet says that two books (i.e. a corresponding number of elegies) were suppressed to make the work more agreeable to read. Most scholars agree that he added some poems, and attempts have been made to identify them, but the whole problem of the revision may be more complicated. Thus 2.18 with its clear reference to the finished tragedy *Medea* (ll. 13–14), the *Ars amatoria* (ll. 19–20) and the *Epistulae Heroidum* (ll. 21–38) must belong to the second edition. Some of the elegies can be dated, e.g. 3.9 on the death of Tibullus (shortly after 19 B.C.), but a poem like this could have been written 'between editions' and then included in the second one.

Perhaps we can postulate that none of the poems that show the influence of Propertius' Book 4 (and *Amores* 3.9 is one of them) was part of the first edition. This hypothesis is based on two assumptions: (1) Propertius influenced Ovid, not vice versa; (2) his Book 4 represents a new style, a new artistic achievement, and therefore a challenge to his younger friend. It has often been observed that Ovid likes to treat the same theme in two poems, usually separated by other elegies. The most striking pair is 1.5 and 2.11, both describing the first time the poet made love to Corinna. This shows how futile any biographical interpretation of these poems would be. In such a case, one poem may very well have been kept from the first edition, while the other was written some years later. Ovid may want to show how he treats the same theme ten or fifteen years later, as a more experienced craftsman, possible under the influence of Propertius' late style. To determine which of the two belongs to the second edition we would have to search for passages that show the influence of Propertius' later poems. This is not so simple in this case, since neither poem has striking parallels to the elegies of Propertius' Book 4; only the imagery of 2.12 (the conquest of a beautiful woman is like a military victory) is close to Propertius 3.8.29–36, whereas no possible Propertian reminiscence in 1.5 seems to lead beyond Book 2. This would make 2.12 a poem of the second edition, treating the theme of the earlier 1.5 in Ovid's mature manner. But this is just a hypothesis which will have to be tested in other cases.

Rome with its streets, its colonnades, its temples and theatres, is the background of the *Amores*; only a few poems, e.g. 3.13, take us out of the city, to

---

[1] Luck (1959) 172ff.

the countryside (here, incidentally, the influence of Propertius Book 4 is strong). Rome is the capital of the world, a beautiful city full of life, but also the city of constant temptation; it is difficult not to fall in love or to have an affair: *illic Hippolytum pone: Priapus erit* 'put Hippolytus here, and he will be Priapus' (2.4.32). Ovid is the amused chronicler of a society for which pleasure was everything and which treated a love-affair as a work of art. Many poems are built around the stock characters of this society; some of them are familiar from New Comedy.

Ovid is skilful at developing a theme in the rhetorical manner, showing his early training. He argues, e.g., against abortion in 2.14, as a lawyer might in court. Or he describes scenes that might be taken from Comedy, e.g. the sequence 2.7 and 8. In the first poem he denies Corinna's accusation of having been unfaithful to her with her maid. Apparently she believes him, for in the next piece he boasts to the maid: 'See how cleverly I lied; haven't I earned a reward? You refuse? I shall tell her everything.'

Ovid's *Medicamina faciei femineae*, a fragmentary collection of cosmetic recipes for ladies in verse, is usually counted among his erotic poetry. It really celebrates beauty, love and the kind of sophistication which improves upon nature. The introduction is a lecture on the theme *culta placent* (ll. 3–50), the appeal of 'culture' in the broadest sense of the word, including bodily care. It is difficult to judge the effectiveness of the cosmetic preparations which Ovid lists; but he seems to have done a good deal of research. He himself calls this work *paruus, sed cura grande, libellus, opus* 'a book, small in size but great in care' (*Ars Am.* 3.206).

The *Ars amatoria* is more an 'Art of pleasing' or a 'Technique of seduction' than an 'Art of love'. It is not comparable to one of the sex manuals which are so popular today; it reads more (at least in parts) like one of the essays on women and love produced in such abundance, with infinite variations on the same few themes, by the French moralists of the seventeenth and eighteenth centuries. They studied the same kind of society for which Ovid wrote, and they considered love a fascinating game of enticement and temporary involvement. Love-making, to them, is a legitimate artistic pursuit; everything has to be done with a certain style. Though Ovid claims that his work is based on his own experience (*usus opus mouet hoc*, 1.29) he insists later on, in exile (*Tristia* 2.349–60), that 'a large part of my works are invented and fictitious and took more liberties than their author' (*magna...pars mendax operum est et ficta meorum:|plus sibi permisit compositore suo*); hence, it would be wrong to judge his morals on the basis of his works. He probably used some Greek sources, possibly Philaenis' 'Art of love' which is known to us now from papyrus fragments.[1] Some didactic themes he found in Tibullus 1.4 and Propertius 4.5.

---

[1] P. Oxy. 2891 (2nd century A.D.) contains parts of the 'Technique of seduction' and the section 'On kissing'.

The tone is debonair and occasionally borders on the frivolous, but the work as a whole can hardly be called immoral or corrupting. There are passages that must have annoyed Augustus; for example, Ovid's comment on religion (1.637–8): *expedit esse deos et, ut expedit, esse putemus:* | *dentur in antiquos tura merumque focos* 'it is useful that gods should exist, and since it is useful, let us believe that they exist, and let incense and wine be offered on ancient altars.' At least Ovid fully believed in equal opportunities for women, for Book 3 (perhaps added in a later edition) is addressed to them.

As a sequel to the *Ars* Ovid wrote a few years later the *Remedia amoris*, a guide for those who wish to fall out of love. The idea itself is amusing, but it has a serious background, and it almost looks as though Ovid had found a new role: that of helper and adviser to those who are troubled and unhappy. Stoics and Epicureans agreed that love was a form of madness, a mental disease; they only disagreed about the therapy. In this work, Ovid seems to have borrowed from both Stoic and Epicurean sources, and in a sense the *Remedia* represent a playful version of the ψυχαγωγία theme which was so popular in Hellenistic philosophy; it is a spiritual guidebook for the soul towards a better, saner, more rational life. Though many themes are taken from the elegiac tradition, Ovid's concern, his desire to help, are real, and his psychological insight and understanding are admirable.

7. OTHER ELEGISTS

There were other elegiac poets in Rome during this period but very little is known about them. Ovid (*Tristia* 2.423–66) gives a list of poets of the late Republic who dealt with the theme of love, some of them in elegies: Catullus, Calvus, Cinna, Valerius Cato, Anser, Cornificius, Ticida, etc. Another list (*Pont.* 5.16) contains mainly names of younger contemporaries; the only elegists identified as such are Montanus and Sabinus; the only love poets described as such are Tuscus and Proculus; of the latter Ovid says (ll. 31–2) *cum... Callimachi Proculus molle teneret iter* 'while Proculus kept to the soft path of Callimachus'; which must refer to homoerotic epigrams or elegies in Callimachus' style. Horace seems to have written elegies, too; but Suetonius (*Vita Horatii*) who claims to have seen them finds them 'trivial' (*uulgares*); perhaps they were never published.

In the *Appendix Vergiliana* several elegiac poems are preserved, but since this collection is dealt with elsewhere we shall only mention here the charming piece *De rosis nascentibus* which seems to show the influence of Ovid's exile poetry. Though this would exclude Virgil's authorship the poem cannot be dated with certainty; some scholars have placed it in the fourth or fifth century; others have attributed it to Ausonius.

The Latin love elegy thus appears to be the rather short-lived creation of the late Republic and the early Empire. Ovid's younger friends no doubt imitated him, as Passennus Paulus, a direct descendant of Propertius, imitated his ancestor (Pliny the Younger, *Epist.* 6.15; 9.22) in the second half of the first century A.D. But there is no evidence of a fresh creative impulse. The genre was revived by Maximian, in the middle of the sixth century A.D.; his five elegies seem to deal with erotic experiences of his distant youth and his advanced years; but idiom and imagery are still those of the Augustan elegists, especially Ovid.

7

OVID

1. 'FAME IS THE SPUR'

There had been nothing diffident or tentative about Ovid's literary début. In the very first of his surviving works, the *Amores* (Loves), he manifests astonishing confidence in himself and in his professional future. The three opening poems of Book 1, read as they are clearly intended to be read, that is as a connected sequence, sketch a poetic programme which is then carried through with masterful assurance until it achieves its ordained end in the double renunciation, of 'elegiac' love and of love-elegy, in the last poem of Book 3. The design and execution of the *Amores* can be properly understood only in relation to Ovid's predecessors. He had taken a genre already exploited, after Gallus, its inventor, by Tibullus and Propertius, and exploited it in his turn, originally but with a deadly efficiency that left no room for a successor. (The work of 'Lygdamus' shows how barren a mere recombination of the conventional motifs of love-elegy was bound to be.) As a demonstration of technical virtuosity the *Amores* verges on insolence; it was a remarkable, and tactically profitable, feat of literary originality, as originality was understood by the ancients, to impart to a well-established form with the inherent limitations of love elegy this new semblance of vitality. More than a semblance it cannot be accounted, but for Ovid's purpose that was enough. In the *Amores* he had put himself on the map; he had measured himself against his elegiac precursors, implicitly criticized them and some of the literary values accepted by them, and shown himself at the very least their technical equal. Having established his claim to consideration he began to look around for fresh worlds to conquer. In his farewell to Elegy (by which he means elegiac poetry of the Gallan-Tibullan-Propertian type) he speaks of the more important tasks awaiting him:

> corniger increpuit thyrso maiore Lyaeus:
> pulsanda est magnis area maior equis.   (*Am.* 3.15.17–18)

Horned Bacchus has struck me with a weightier thyrsus: a greater plain is to be smitten by greater horses.

The symbols are old and conventional; the poet's passion for fame is vital and sincere. One genre has served its turn; in retrospect it will be seen chiefly as having been a stepping-stone to higher things.

The phrase *area maior* suggests the major genres of tragedy and epic. Of Ovid's only tragedy, *Medea*, nothing remains but a tiny handful of fragments, and the praises of Quintilian and Tacitus reveal nothing of its quality.[1] Some notion of his treatment of the heroine may perhaps be inferred from her other appearances in the surviving works, in *Heroides* 12 and *Metamorphoses* 7; and it seems hardly possible that Seneca's play on the same theme was not influenced by Ovid. Already in Book 3 of the *Ars Amatoria* he had displayed an unusual – one might say, Euripidean – ability to see things from a woman's point of view. The new direction taken by his genius, which was to culminate in the *Metamorphoses*, allowed this ability full play. We meet the new Ovid for the first time in his extant works in the *Heroides*, which he himself went out of his way to claim as an original literary creation:

> ignotum hoc aliis ille nouauit opus.   (*Ars Am.* 3.345)

This kind of poetry was unknown until he invented it.

The chronology of Ovid's early poetry is perplexed and obscure, so that the composition of the *Heroides* cannot be exactly placed in a sequence with the two editions of the *Amores* and with the *Ars amatoria* (Art of love). It appears that Ovid had already embarked on the single letters, and probably the *Ars amatoria* as well, before completing the final revision of the *Amores*.[2] Thus, before the ink was dry on his initial *tour de force*, he was already carrying the congenial theme of love into one new literary field after another. Under the cool wit of 1.1–3 and the other programmatic poems of the *Amores* burned a flame of ambition and creative enterprise for which Ovid's limitless fertility of invention and technical resource was to provide abundant fuel.

In the proem to Book 3 of the *Georgics* Virgil had dismissed mythological subjects as too hackneyed for poetry; in later poets the idea became something of a cliché.[3] Ovid's whole poetic career constituted an implicit rejection of this position. From the beginning his imagination had nourished itself on mythology and legend. Even in the *Amores* an interest in mythological themes begins to make itself evident in Book 3, where it plays a part in the gradually developing and carefully stage-managed reaction against the inherited *leitmotiv* of devotion to a wilful mistress and the sort of poetry associated with such devotion.[4] In the *Ars amatoria* and *Remedia amoris* (Cure for love) a major part in the power of the poems to entertain is played by the narrative illustrations, in which Ovid

---

[1] Quint. *Inst.* 10.1.98, Tac. *Dial.* 12.   [2] *Am.* 2.18.19–34; cf. Appendix.
[3] Virg. *Geo.* 3.3–8; cf. Manil. 2.49–52, Nemes. *Cyn.* 15–47, *Aetna* 17–23, Juv. 1.7–13.
[4] Cf. *Am.* 3.6 (ll. 45–82), 10, 12, 13.

drew freely on myth and legend. In the *Heroides* the material is taken entirely from this sphere; and in this sense they may be seen, not only as important poetry in their own right, but also as foreshadowing Ovid's *chef d'œuvre*, the *Metamorphoses*.

2. THE 'HEROIDES'

The first series of *Heroides* consists of letters from famous women of Greek legend to absent husbands or lovers. For this new genre there was no single Greek or Roman model. Its originality, however, as with love-elegy itself, consisted in the blending of existing elements from the literary and rhetorical tradition. Catullus, Propertius and Ovid himself had already handled erotic themes from Greek mythology in the new 'subjective' style. Separation from the beloved, and attendant ideas of infidelity and betrayal, played a prominent role in love-elegy. Several of the *Amores* are essentially semi-dramatic monologues; and Ovid's early training in declamation was calculated to foster his predilection for this type of composition. Monologues by wronged or abandoned or suffering women were to be found in more than one existing genre, but the monologue as such was not a recognized literary form or *genus*; it required a setting such as that provided by a play or epyllion (e.g. Ariadne in Catullus' *Peleus and Thetis*). Ovid legitimated, so to say, his heroines' soliloquies by couching them in the form of letters. Strictly speaking the letter was not a genre in the full sense, but as a literary form it was as old as Plato, and it had been naturalized in Latin poetry by Lucilius and Horace. The convention could be, and by Ovid was, handled with considerable freedom. Unlike real letters the *Heroides* are self-contained works of art, neither needing nor indeed leaving room for an answer. The idea of the letter-form seems to have come to Ovid from Propertius' epistle of 'Arethusa' to 'Lycotas' (4.3); the scale on which he exploited this modest hint strikingly illustrates his powers of reception and re-creation.

The material of the *Heroides* comes principally from Greek epic and tragedy; the exceptions are the epistles of Dido (7), where his only source was the *Aeneid*, and Ariadne (10), where he drew extensively on Catullus. Given the fundamental identity of theme, monotony could be avoided only by the greatest possible variety of treatment and tone. About this undertaking there is an obvious whiff of the *tour de force*: to write no fewer than fourteen substantial poems of this sort in itself smacks of bravado. One limitation which at best could only be palliated was inherent in the letter-form itself, its basically static and undramatic character. Apart from the perhaps doubtful case of Deianira,[1] Ovid respects the rule that nothing affecting the course of events is allowed to happen during the writing of the letter. The heroine's situation is given; the

---

[1] *Her.* 9.143; see Appendix.

resultant action is entirely in her mind and heart. Relief is provided by brilliant rhetoric and by narrative retrospects, which include some very lively writing (e.g. Ariadne on her awakening, 10.7–50; Hypermnestra on her wedding night, 14.21–84), but it is on their merits as psychological drama that these poems must stand or fall.

To exemplify Ovid's treatment of his material two epistles which invite comparison with known originals may be briefly examined. Euripides had handled the story of Phaedra and Hippolytus in two plays, the first of which, now lost, had given offence by presenting Phaedra as totally shameless. It appears to have been this lost play on which Ovid principally drew for his Phaedra (*Her.* 4).[1] The implausibility (not to mention the anachronism, which is common to all the epistles) of her writing to Hippolytus is simply brazened out. Love-letters were part of the apparatus of contemporary intrigue (*Ars Am.* 1.455–86, 3.469–98, 619–30), and Ovid's Phaedra is envisaged very much as a contemporary elegiac figure. The hunting motif which in Euripides formed part of her delirium (*Hipp.* 215–22) is transmuted by Ovid into the typical *obsequium* (devotion to the wishes of the beloved) of elegy (37–50).[2] The logic of her pleading is elegiac and declamatory: Theseus' treacherous abandonment of her sister Ariadne (a cross-reference, as it were, to *Her.* 10) becomes the basis of her appeal to Hippolytus to betray his father with herself. The grim message of Euripides is trivialized and 'elegized' into a snippet of proverbial wisdom:

> quid iuuat incinctae studia exercere Dianae
> et Veneri numeros eripuisse suos?
> quod caret alterna requie, durabile non est;
> haec reparat uires fessaque membra nouat.　　　　(4.87–90)

How does it profit to cultivate the pursuits of the huntress Diana and rob Venus of her function? Nothing lasts if it is not allowed occasional rest; this is what restores strength and refreshes the weary body.

Without Venus the countryside is – countrified (102); the thought is straight from the world of the *Amores* and *Ars amatoria*. In the elegiac triangle Theseus is cast for the role of deceived husband, and it is elegiac logic that he deserves no better; he has his consolation in the arms of Pirithous (110–11). Equally elegiac is Phaedra's defence of her 'new' morality (129–46). Here too *rusticus* is used as a term of contempt for what is old and unfashionable; her remarks on family honour take the reader straight into the Rome of Augustus (131–2). In general in the *Heroides* Ovid can be seen reverting to a traditional pre-elegiac view of love as a passion felt in its full intensity only by women; but his

---

[1] In some places, however, he is clearly indebted to the extant *Hippolytus*. Whether these were passages retained by Euripides from the earlier version or whether Ovid laid both plays under contribution we cannot tell.

[2] Cf. Prop. 1.1.9–16, Tib. 1.4.49–50, [Tib.] 4.3.11–18, Ov. *Ars Am.* 2.185–96.

Phaedra expresses herself in the style of the bawd Dipsas (*Amores* 1.8). What she proposes is a clandestine affair in the palace itself, and she uses the very clichés of *furtiuus amor*:

> non tibi per tenebras duri reseranda mariti
> ianua, non custos decipiendus erit.   (4.141–2)

There will be no stern husband's door to unbar at dead of night, no guard to trick.

Her final appeal crystallizes the matter in a single phrase: *quid deceat non uidet ullus amans* 'a lover does not know the meaning of shame' (154).

This epistle is the closest in spirit of the single *Heroides* to the *Ars amatoria*; in it Ovid seems to have deliberately modernized and degraded his heroic and tragic material. It was not part of his plan to reinterpet in this way all the stories that he took in hand: in the epistles of Canace (11) and Hypermnestra (14) equally bizarre situations are handled so as to bring out tragic or noble qualities in the protagonists. His treatment of Phaedra may have been intended to suggest that her love was indeed essentially squalid, if not actually comic; possibly he was simply showing off. The same light-hearted devaluation of mythical and heroic love recurs in his great apologia in *Tristia* Book 2, a line of defence from which prudence perhaps ought to have restrained him (*Trist.* 2.259–62, 289–300). Devaluation of a rather different kind is at work in his treatment of Dido (*Her.* 7); this makes sense only if it is read as a challenge to Virgil's justification of Aeneas' behaviour towards her.

The contrast with Virgil and a hint of Ovid's aim emerge in the first line of the epistle with the word *abiectus* 'cast away'. Dido is attempting what she already knows to be hopeless, but when all else is lost, what does the loss of a few words signify (5–6)? This is a different Dido from Virgil's stormy and imperious queen. From time to time a bitter epithet or reflection escapes her, but in the main her tone is one of gentle pleading or reproach, and her logic is woman's logic. Ovid's Dido has no conception of her lover's divine mission; to her his wanderings are merely a judgement on him (37–8). His orders from heaven are the special and specious pleading of the eternal predatory male, who gratifies his desire and passes on; she is equally the eternal female, whose instinct is to tame, to settle, to domesticate (15–22). She calls herself Aeneas' wife, using a word which belongs to elegy, *uxor*, rather than the epic *coniunx*. The famous disclaimer put by Virgil into the mouth of Aeneas (*Aen.* 4.172) and allowed by his Dido (4.431) is by Ovid implicitly treated as an evasion of the truth. His Dido's love for Aeneas is elegiac in its quality: her hope that he may at least suffer her to love him even if he cannot return her love is straight from the *Amores* (*Her.* 7.33–4 ~ *Am.* 1.3.3–4). As with his Phaedra, Ovid has transposed a theme from elegy, here the conventional subjection of the poet-lover, the *servitium amoris*, into his new feminine mode. Nowhere does his

Dido threaten; the destinies of Rome and Carthage are nothing to her. All she asks is that Aeneas should be a little kind to her.

In this portrait of a highly un-Virgilian Dido Ovid deliberately draws heavily on the *Aeneid*. By doing so he directs attention to what he is doing and challenges his readers to compare the two interpretations of the story. It was the essence of school declamation to devise *colores* 'colours', new and ingenious (often perversely so) interpretations of the given data; but there is more than declamatory ingenuity here. In presenting Dido as a woman pure and simple rather than a queen Ovid declares himself. He instinctively rejected the Augustan myth, whatever lip-service he might on occasion pay it, and with it much of the literature in which the myth found expression. He did not much believe in divine missions, excepting that of the poet; for a man to betray a woman was inhuman and wrong. Virgil had pleaded for the worse cause, even if he had shown some, perhaps involuntary, sympathy for the better. Compared with the subtle ambivalence of Virgil's treatment Ovid's is bound to appear simplistic, even crude; but the case that he argues is not an ignoble one. Faced with the choice of deserting his country or his beloved, is it beyond question which a man should choose? A critic should be very sure of his own position before he ventures to say that Ovid's was untenable.

The more carefully the *Heroides* are read, the more differences of intention and treatment between the different epistles will be found to emerge. Nevertheless the single letters cannot be altogether rescued from a charge of monotony. But Ovid had by no means finished with the genre. Some years later, stimulated we may guess by the action of his friend Sabinus in equipping some of the single letters with answers (*Am.* 2.18), he published three pairs of epistles in which a man wrote first and a woman answered him. These are considerably more ambitious compositions; the combined total of lines in each pair (646, 428, 490; average length of *Her.* 1–14 c. 150) amounts to that of a short *libellus*.[1] In each case the situation and the poetic treatment are carefully differentiated. The correspondence of Paris and Helen (16–17) is a highly entertaining *jeu d'esprit* in the spirit of the *Ars amatoria*. That of Acontius and Cydippe (20–1) is a study in obsession. For Paris and Helen he drew on several sources, the background to the Trojan War being common mythological property. For Acontius and Cydippe he used Callimachus' *Aetia*, but altogether transformed the story by endowing the protagonists, especially Cydippe, with new personalities and presenting the situation as a clash of wills, male against female, strong against weak.[2] The story of Hero and Leander (18–19) cannot have been long familiar when Ovid decided to use it. Its first appearance is in the *Georgics*, by way of passing allusion (3.257–63). Evidently the legend had come to notice

---

[1] See *The Early Republic*, p. 18.
[2] Kenney (1970). Callimachus' story had already inspired Propertius (1.18) and possibly Gallus (Ross (1975a) 89).

in the latter part of the first century B.C., probably in a lost Hellenistic poem.[1]
It was Ovid who gave it the literary form which has proved definitive. Comparison with the *Hero and Leander* of the late fifth-century A.D. Greek poet
Musaeus, who in certain respects followed the original source quite closely,
shows the freedom with which Ovid treated it. An obscure story originally
connected with a local landmark, the 'Tower of Hero', was immortalized in
one of the most romantic poems in all ancient literature.

The epistle of Leander (*Her.* 18) begins *in mediis rebus*: a storm is brewing
and he cannot cross the straits to Hero. This emphasis on separation and the
emotions which it engenders in the two lovers dominates Ovid's handling of
the story; with the mechanics of the plot he scarcely concerns himself. In
Musaeus' poem the social status of Hero and the circumstances of their first
meeting bulk large; Ovid does not mention them, and we are left to surmise
why Leander's parents must be kept in the dark (13). As in a Savoy Opera, the
situation is given, what interests the poet is the consequences. In Musaeus the
crossing of the straits is dealt with briefly and drily, in Ovid the narrative of
Leander's visits to Hero and their romantic concomitants form the centrepiece
of his letter (53–124). The actual descriptive touches are not many, but they are
sketched in surely and delicately; this is what Macaulay called 'sweet writing':

> unda repercussae radiabat imagine lunae
>   et nitor in tacita nocte diurnus erat;
> nullaque uox usquam, nullum ueniebat ad aures
>   praeter dimotae corpore murmur aquae.
> Alcyones solae, memores Ceycis amati,
>   nescioquid uisae sunt mihi dulce queri.   (18.77–82)

The water shone with the reflected radiance of the moon, and the silent night was
bright as day. No voice, no sound came to my ears but for the murmur of the water
as I swam. Only it seemed to me that I heard the halcyons singing some sweet lament
in memory of the beloved Ceyx.

Similarly the lovemaking of the pair is suggested rather than described (105–
10). With a brief account of his departure and return Leander comes back to
Abydos and the present (124), but the poem is not yet half over. There follows
a long expostulation, liberally embellished with verbal and mythological
conceits, against his situation. Like Narcissus in his celebrated soliloquy in the
Metamorphoses (3.446–53), he dwells on the paradoxes of his position, and like
Narcissus he resorts to elegiac cliché:

> quo propior nunc es, flamma propiore calesco,
>   et res non semper, spes mihi semper adest.   (177–8)

As it is, the closer you are, the hotter I burn; but it is only the hope of you, not the
reality, that is always with me.

[1] Cf. Page (1950) 512–13, Kost (1971) 20–1.

Finally his impatience breaks out into a vow that, come what may, he will try his luck again; if he is drowned he prays to be washed up dead at Hero's feet (193–200). This shallow and heartless posturing, like the manic persistence of Acontius, is essential to Ovid's portrayal of Leander's character. Though he immediately retracts and promises that he will not be rash (a promise not kept), his restless attitudinizing contrasts painfully with the passive and anxious role for which Hero is cast.

Her reply (*Her.* 19) begins with extraordinary address and delicacy. From her impatience to see Leander again, which equals his own, she passes to the disparity between their positions. Men can find distractions in manly pursuits (9–14); her only resource is her love (15–16). Here are epitomized the opposing roles of the protagonists – his to take risks, hers to endure and think of him:

> quod superest, facio, teque, o mea sola uoluptas,
> plus quoque quam reddi quod mihi possit amo. (19.17–18)

All there is for me to do, I do – I love you, my only joy, more even than you can ever love me.

It is the tragedy of a love such as Hero's that she should think more of her lover than he of her; her words are an implied reproach to the selfish boasting of his letter (18.195–200). Throughout the long day and the longer night that follows her thoughts are all of him. In the picture of Hero spinning with her nurse Ovid exploits a familiar image of a peculiarly Roman type of domesticity[1] to illustrate both the quality of her love and the contrast between the calm lamplit sanctuary which is his goal and the storm through which he must pass (and in which he will perish) to reach it. From conversation with the nurse Hero passes (55–6) to a soliloquy, occupying most of the letter, in which she reviews her doubts and fears and hopes. Whereas heroines such as Byblis (*Met.* 9.474–520) and Myrrha (10.320–55) argue with themselves about, and must in the end reach, a decision, Hero's part – and this, as has already been said, is the essence of her position – is purely passive. Thus her letter presented Ovid with a more demanding technical challenge than even that of Cydippe, who had in the end to say yes or no to her suitor. Hero's only resource is self-torment:

> omnia sed uereor: quis enim securus amauit?
> cogit et absentes plura timere locus. (19.109–10)

I fear everything – a lover knows no peace, and distance and separation increase one's fear.

[1] Virg. *Aen.* 8.407–15, Prop. 4.3.41–2 (Arethusa), Tib. 1.3.83–8 (Delia), Ov. *Fast.* 2.741–58, Livy 1.57.9 (Lucretia); cf. Ogilvie (1965) 222.

Eager as she is for him to come, she urges caution in words which reflect her conflicting feelings:

> me miseram, cupio non persuadere quod hortor,
>   sisque precor monitis fortior ipse meis,
> dummodo peruenias excussaque saepe per undas
>   inicias umeris bracchia lassa meis.   (19.187–90)

Alas, I find myself wishing that my words shall not carry conviction and praying that your valour will outrun the discretion which I urge – just so long as you come safely across and throw about my neck those arms tired from long swimming.

With her account of an ominous dream (193–204) she returns to the long vigil that began at l. 33 and that has provided the setting for her soliloquy. Her vision of the dying dolphin, which even she can scarcely misread (203), held no mystery for Ovid's readers,[1] and her parting injunction reminds us again of the deep and unselfish quality of her love:

> si tibi non parcis, dilectae parce puellae,
>   quae numquam nisi te sospite sospes ero.   (19.205–6)

If you will not spare yourself, spare the girl you love, for without you I shall not be able to live.

In the double *Heroides* Ovid achieved a substantial technical advance. Viewing relationships from opposite sides in this way undoubtedly added depth and interest to the psychological portrayal. Yet the possibilities were still restricted by both the form and the verse medium. Even in the double letters very little in the way of real interaction occurs between the characters; the drama is still, as it were, frozen, though at two points rather than one. Moreover, for large-scale poetry the elegiac couplet, though handled in virtuoso fashion, has serious limitations. That these, in a particular genre, might be to some extent transcended, is shown by the *Fasti*; but the peculiar turn of Ovid's genius for exploring the vagaries of the human heart needed, for the full realization of its capabilities, the broader canvas of the epic.

3. THE 'FASTI'

At the end of the *Amores* Ovid had announced that a 'greater room' (*area maior*) awaited him. In his apologia for his life and work he listed as his three great voyages on the sea of poetry the lost tragedy *Medea*, the *Fasti*, and the *Metamorphoses* (*Trist.* 2.547–56). The two latter poems complement each other in more than one way. The obvious progenitors of the *Fasti* (Calendar) were Callimachus and Propertius. In Ovid's early work, apart from *Heroides* 20–1

[1] Cf. *Anth. Pal.* 7.215 (Anyte), 216 (Antipater of Thessalonica), 214 (Archias).

THE *FASTI*

(Acontius and Cydippe), Callimachus figures only by way of sporadic allusion.[1]
This is in contrast to Propertius, who had pledged formal allegiance to
Callimachus (2.1.39–41, 3.1.1–2); who, indeed, in announcing the new kind
of antiquarian elegy to which he had turned after the rupture with Cynthia
(3.24, 25), had actually styled himself the Roman Callimachus (4.1.64). Now
Ovid, as he had done with the *Heroides*, moved in to annex and consolidate
the new genre. Whereas Propertius had experimented in a rather tentative
fashion with a mixed collection of erotic and aetiological elegies, Ovid, as was
his habit, went the whole hog and projected a single homogeneous poem of epic
scale; the *Fasti* if completed would have been almost exactly the same length
as the *Aeneid*. The break with love and love-elegy announced at the end of the
Amores was now apparently complete.

Ovid's plan was to describe the Roman calendar and the various observances and festivals of the Roman year, and to explain their origins:

> tempora cum causis Latium digesta per annum
> lapsaque sub terras ortaque signa canam.   (*Fast.* 1.1–2)

*The seasons of the Roman calendar in due order, their origins, and the risings and
settings of the constellations – these shall be my theme.*

His chief models were Hellenistic, Callimachus' *Aetia* and Aratus' *Phaenomena*,
and the ostensible impulse for the poem came from Propertius. However, the
Aeneid must also be taken into account. The originality of Ovid's undertaking,
as usual in Latin literature, consists in the combination of hitherto disparate
elements: learning of a distinctively Hellenistic type is used to adorn themes
from Roman history and antiquities, with a gloss of contemporary allusion
which frequently shades into outright propaganda for the *Pax Augusta*. In
crude terms this would also serve as a description of the *Aeneid*. That the two
poems are in fact vastly different from each other is due in the first place to their
different literary forms: the epic is impersonal, whereas Ovid's Callimachean
model was didactic and anecdotal. More important still is the difference in
temperament between the two poets, with their respective preference for the
suggestive and the explicit. Most important of all, however, is the fact that the
Aeneid represents a deeply meditated *credo*, whereas the *Fasti* is a purely literary
exercise.

This was Ovid's first and only attempt at an Augustan poem, in the sense
that, whatever derogations from high solemnity he might permit himself,
his ostensible aim was to celebrate the idea of Rome, the *res Romana*.
The original proem, displaced in revision, not only stresses the literary

[1] E.g. *Ars Am.* 1.619–20 ~ Callim. *Epigr.* 44.3–4. The same is generally true of Augustan poetry:
Ross (1975a) 6–7.

133

importance of the work (2.3–8) but also claims it as a contribution to the public service:

> haec mea militia est: ferimus quae possumus arma,
> dextraque non omni munere nostra uacat. (2.9–10)

Here is my service: I bear such arms as I can, and my right hand is not totally exempt from duty.

In the light of the general tone of the poem and what has been called the 'eroticization' of his Roman material this must be regarded as window-dressing. It is precisely the discrepancy between matter and manner – the *res Romana* served up *à la grecque* – that constitutes the attraction of the *Fasti*. Much of the material is indeed Roman only by courtesy and contrivance, for Ovid introduced a good deal of Greek legend, including the occasional episode also incorporated in the *Metamorphoses* (e.g. Proserpine, *Fast.* 4.417–620 ~ *Met.* 5.341–661; Callisto, 2.155–92 ~ 2.401–530). The patriotic flourishes and the flattery of the Princeps and his family serve only to accentuate the fundamental frivolity of the work. But Ovid was not simply writing a comic history of Rome, Livy *travesti*; he was challenging Alexandrian *doctrina* on its own ground. Writing the *Fasti* necessitated much research, and Ovid drew on many sources, Greek and Roman. The astronomical, antiquarian and religious learning of the poem is an essential element in it, bulking almost as large as the illustrative narratives. As literature the result is not entirely satisfying. In the narratives Ovid was free to be himself, and they contain much brilliant and effective (though little affecting) writing. In the rest of the poem he was constrained to play the part of *Romanus uates*, and the sly wit with which he performs his role merely draws attention to its inappropriateness. Like nearly everything else he wrote the *Fasti* is a *tour de force*, but the fact is more obtrusive even than in the *Ibis*. Comparison with the contemporary *Metamorphoses* again emphasizes the inferiority of the elegiac couplet, however adroitly handled, to the hexameter as a medium for sustained narrative. Students of Roman religion must (perforce and with caution) use the *Fasti* as an important source of information, and generations of schoolboys have first met Ovid in its more (ostensibly) edifying pages. From the literary critic it tends to elicit admiration tempered with apology.

4. THE 'METAMORPHOSES'

In the *Ars amatoria* and *Remedia amoris* Ovid had illustrated and diversified his precepts by narrative excursuses. These vary in tone and elaboration, ranging from the mildly lubricious (Achilles on Scyros, *Ars Am.* 1.681–704; Mars and Venus, 2.561–92) through the marvellous-aetiological (Ariadne, 1.527–64; Daedalus and Icarus, 2.21–96) and the grotesque (Pasiphae, 1.289–326) to the tragic (Cephalus and Procris, 3.685–746; Phyllis, *Rem.* 591–606). Retrospective narratives also contribute to the effectiveness of *Heroides* 10–14, 16–21. The *Fasti* was the first of his works in which narrative played a quantitatively significant, if not a preponderant, part. However, the *Fasti* was more than an exercise in story-telling; in it Ovid applied to the creation of a specifically Roman poem a formula already used (with profoundly different results) by Virgil in the *Aeneid*. Considered as a bid for the highest poetic honours the *Fasti* suffered from the fundamental handicap of not being an epic. Ovid saw himself as the Virgil of Roman elegy:

> tantum se nobis elegi debere fatentur,
> quantum Vergilio nobile debet epos.　　　　(*Rem.* 395–6)

Elegy acknowledges that it owes as much to me as the epic owes to Virgil.

The claim bears examination, indeed what Ovid made of elegy is in some ways even more surprising than what Virgil had made of epic. The fact, however, remained that the epic, deriving from Homer, the source of all poetry and eloquence,[1] was the *genus nobile*, the genre of genres. If Ovid wished to assert a serious claim to a place in the muster-roll of the greatest Roman poets he had to write an epos. To this ambition the greatest single obstacle, given that Ovid suffered from no doubts about his talents, was the existence of the *Aeneid*.

Ovid was far too genuinely respectful of Virgil and far too shrewd to think of emulating him on his own ground. Neither Dido's epistle to Aeneas nor the later, 'Aenean', books of the *Metamorphoses* constitute such a challenge; and the form and character of the *Fasti* show Ovid to have been well aware of the imprudence of a direct confrontation. It was one thing to offer to displace Propertius as the Roman Callimachus; the position of the Roman Homer was secure. Virgil had revitalized the genre by a unique and unpredictable fusion of Greek and Roman elements, but by the same token he had killed traditional epic stone dead. After the *Aeneid* a reversion to historical epic *à la* Ennius or mythological epic *à la* Apollonius ought to have been unthinkable. Ovid and the best of the epic poets of the Silver Age understood and acted on this essential premiss. The problem was to find a formula for a poem that in scale and originality could stand alongside the *Aeneid*. Ovid's solution was an even more brilliant feat of creative adaptation than those which produced the *Ars amatoria*, the *Heroides*, and the *Fasti*. The *Metamorphoses* (Transformations) is a long poem of some 12,000 lines in 15 books which in effect presents an anthology of Greek and Roman, but predominantly Greek, myth and legend. The length and elaboration of the individual episodes vary enormously, from passing allusions in a single verse to almost-autonomous epyllia occupying

---

[1] Cf. Ov. *Am.* 3.9.25–6, Dion. Hal. *De comp. verb.* 24, Quint. *Inst.* 10.1.46.

several hundred lines. Formally a semblance of unity is given in several ways. Most obviously the theme of metamorphosis, change of shape, plays a part, though with marked variations of emphasis, in nearly every story. Since however Ovid's ingenuity was equal to inventing a connexion or even a metamorphosis whenever it suited him, whether the tradition offered one or not, this ostensible *leitmotiv* imposed very little restriction on his choice of material. The narrative follows a chronological pattern from the Creation to the murder and apotheosis of Julius Caesar. Here too, since mythical chronology has never been an exact science, he might permit himself considerable latitude in the ordering of his material. Continuity between episodes is provided by hugely ingenious transitional and framing devices which earned the poet a magisterial rebuke from the humourless Quintilian (*Inst.* 4.1.77).

No single model for such a poem as this existed in Greek or Latin. In its character as what some critics have called a 'collective' poem (*Kollektivgedicht*) it is Hesiodic; and to the extent that Ovid had enrolled himself under the banner of Hesiod it might be claimed that the *Metamorphoses* implicitly claimed different but equal status with the *Aeneid*. More than one Hellenistic poet had exploited the theme of transformation. Callimachus in the *Aetia* had used the format of discrete and disparate episodes strung on a thread of 'editorial' association.[1] In scale and scope, however, the *Metamorphoses* is unique. By drawing on the last syllable of recorded time (as known to his sources) Ovid allowed himself *carte blanche* to include whatever stories appealed to him and to develop them in what seemed to him the appropriate style. Thus the poem includes samples of all the important genres, though transposed, so to say, into the peculiar idiom of the *Metamorphoses*: comedy, elegy, pastoral, tragedy, oratory, didactic, hymn – not forgetting the epic itself.

The impression received from a continuous reading of the poem is thus one of incessant variety, of change (metamorphosis, in fact), and of pleasure springing from the unexpected. The surprises range all the way from the light play of linguistic wit, as when the length of the seasons is figured in the words and metre used to describe them –

$$\cup\cup - \,-\,- \,-\,- \,-$$
et inaequales autumnos

$$-\,\cup\cup -$$
et breue uer

(1.117–18)

unequal autumns and brief spring

– to the inclusion of a complete episode by way of a *tour de force*, as with the long monologue of Pythagoras (15.12–478). Ovid indeed begins the poem by playing a little trick on the reader. The opening words: *in noua fert animus* seem to be a self-contained sentence meaning 'my inspiration carries (me) on

---

[1] For his technique see fr. 178 Pf.

to new things' – a proclamation of the novelty of his literary undertaking. In what follows the reader is undeceived:

> in noua fert animus mutatas dicere formas
> corpora,

my inspiration carries me to tell of shapes changed into new bodies;

yet the ambiguity remains and must be deliberate. In a declaratory proem of only four verses every phrase and every word must have been carefully weighed; by allowing himself this verbal sleight of hand at the outset Ovid was showing his readers something of what was in store for them, as well as emphasizing two points: that nothing like the *Metamorphoses* had ever been attempted before and that he was coming before the public in a totally new guise. The very obliquity and allusiveness of the communication is an implicit act of homage to Callimachus.

In what follows the innuendo becomes more specifically Callimachean. Ovid continues

> di, coeptis (nam uos mutastis et illa)[1]
> adspirate meis primaque ab origine mundi
> ad mea perpetuum deducite tempora carmen.

Gods, favour my undertaking – for it was you who changed that too – and bring down from the beginning of the world to my own times a continuous song.

First, the conventional plea for divine assistance is manipulated so as to represent the poem itself, the *Metamorphoses*, as the product of a metamorphosis. As with the opening words this can be understood on two levels. The obvious sense is that Ovid has been metamorphosed from elegist into epicist. But if the original sense of *coepta* as 'beginnings' is pressed, the phrase reflects on the character of the poem as well. Just as Apollo had intervened to turn Callimachus and Virgil from epic (Virg. *Ecl.* 6.3–5, Callim. fr. 1.21–8 Pf.), so the gods have saved Ovid from setting his hand to some less auspicious plan.[2] Still with Callimachus in mind he asks the gods to further his intention of writing a *perpetuum carmen*, a 'continuous song'. This is precisely what Callimachus had disavowed and had been criticized for not producing.[3] So a wilful paradox is propounded. Though metamorphosis was a specifically Alexandrian subject (Nicander's *Heteroeumena*, 'Things changed', must have been quite well known), Ovid's treatment is not to be Callimachean but conventionally epic, for this is the obvious implication of *perpetuum*.[4] The paradox is underlined discreetly by the use of the word *deducite*. In the context this seems to mean no more than 'bring down', 'carry through'; but its use with the gods rather than

---

[1] *illa* P. Lejay: *illas* MSS. Cf. Kenney (1976) 47–9.
[2] Cf. Galinsky (1975) 103–7; *contra* Wilkinson (1955) 214–18.
[3] Callim. fr. 1.3 Pf. ἐν ἄεισμα διηνεκές 'one continuous song'.
[4] Cf. Hor. *Odes* 1.7.6 and Nisbet–Hubbard (1970) ad loc.

the poet as subject is unusual and may be intended to draw attention to a further implication. The result, if the gods cooperate, will in literal terms be a *deductum carmen*, the 'fine-spun song' enjoined by the Virgilian-Callimachean Apollo – a contradiction in terms. Ovid's language, however, implies that the *Metamorphoses* will manage to be both Callimachean and un-Callimachean at once.

This brief scenario, closely read, excites both attention and a measure of surprise. Its effect is to redirect the reader to the opening words of the poem: *in noua*...no question but that the *Metamorphoses* is to be something unexampled in the annals of poetry. The reader soon finds, however, if his previous acquaintance with Ovid has not already taught him, that it will not do to take all this quite literally. There is continuity, of a kind, in the poem, but it is very different from the continuity of the *Annales* or the *Aeneid*; and continuity, after all, is not the same thing as unity. What the *Metamorphoses* is supposed to be about, apart from metamorphosis, does not readily emerge. The *Aeneid* had a clear message, well summarized in Donatus' Life of Virgil, to present *Romanae simul urbis et Augusti origo*, the origins of Rome and of Augustus – in other words, to justify the present and the future in terms of the legendary past. It might indeed be held that in one way or another this had been the purpose of all the specifically 'Augustan' poetry of Virgil and Horace. What, if anything, was Ovid trying to prove in the *Metamorphoses*? The question is intimately bound up with that of the poem's unity. If it is simply a collection of good stories written to entertain, the quest for unity and a message is a wild-goose chase. The scale and the tone of the coda, at all events (15.871–9), suggest higher pretensions.

Attempts have been made to detect a unity and hence a message in such aspects of the poem as its structure or its symbolism – even (perhaps a counsel of despair) in its very diversity. As to structure, critics have generally agreed in identifying three main divisions of approximately equal length in which the protagonists of the stories are, respectively, the gods (1.452–6.420), heroes (6.421–11.193), and what (on the premiss that ancient history began with the Trojan War) may broadly speaking be termed historical figures (11.194–15.744). The main body of the poem is framed by what may be called a Prologue (1.5–450: Creation–Deluge–Repeopling of Earth) and an Epilogue (15.745–870: Apotheosis of Julius Caesar), the latter being introduced by what is perhaps the most blatantly contrived transition of all, bridging a chasm into which six centuries of Roman history disappear without trace. The fleshing of this simple skeleton is complex and has given rise to much disputable interpretation. Within the overall chronological scheme, which is not followed rigidly, the stories are arranged in groups of varying size and complexity, the stories within a particular group and the groups themselves being linked and related in varying ways – thematic, geographical, genealogical – now by association, now by contrast, now by ingenious and unscrupulous legerdemain. Though flexible the structure is far from anarchic; but it is not easy to reduce to system. Attempts have been made to show that under this informal, though not formless, arrangement of the material there may be detected a more strictly ordered architecture of proportion and symmetry. It seems *a priori* unlikely that Ovid, who is sometimes elusive but almost never obscure, should have expected readers of the *Metamorphoses* to detect structural subtleties on which modern critics disagree so sharply; and difficult to see what emphases he intended them, when detected, or subliminally apprehended, to convey. Moreover he has incorporated in the structure of the poem one hint which seems to point the other way. In the *Aeneid* the division into books, originally a matter of practical convenience,[1] is made to play an essential literary role in the economy of the poem. Ovid's narratives are deliberately contrived to overrun these divisions, which in consequence have a merely local effect, by way of surprise or creation of suspense; and the individual books have a unity only in so far as the poet takes care that the literary texture of each one should in its variety reflect the texture of the poem as a whole. This can be read as a tacit declaration that balance and symmetry of the Virgilian type, with such emphases as they may connote, are not to be looked for in this quite un-Virgilian epic.

Little or nothing, therefore, of the poet's intention appears to emerge from the structure of his poem except for an evident intention to surprise, divert and amuse. A clue to deeper meaning has been sought in the symbolism of, for instance, his descriptions of landscape. There can certainly be no question of the symbolic significance of the setting of some of the stories, notably the pool of Narcissus (3.407–12). These landscapes, it is suggested, are places where anything can happen; and that accords with the sense of otherness (so to call it) with which Ovid has invested this world of his own creation. This is an autonomous universe in which for the most part it is divine caprice that reigns unchecked. But such symbols as these seem to possess no more than a, so to say, local validity when compared with the pervasive symbolism of the *Aeneid* or the imagery on which Lucretius relies to enforce his argument, and they cannot be seen as a strongly unifying element in the *Metamorphoses*. At most they provide immediate but limited emphasis.

If the *Metamorphoses* is in some important sense significant – if, that is, it ought to be regarded as something better than a graceful florilegium of ancient mythology – it can only be on the strength of Ovid's treatment of his material, the myths themselves. Outside a purely factual handbook myth cannot be treated 'straight'. Literary treatment of myth inescapably entails interpretation, and it would have been impossible for Ovid to avoid imparting an individual colouring to the stories that he chose to tell, even had he wished to. Of course

---

[1] Cf. *The Early Republic*, p. 18.

he had no such wish. *In noua fert animus*: the whole scope of his poem demanded that he reshape and reinterpret the myths. Critics differ as to whether the reshaping was purely in the interests of entertainment value, the imparting of a modern verve and piquancy to the traditional tales through the free play of Ovid's iconoclastic wit, or whether the treatment did in truth deepen their significance. This question has a bearing on that of unity, if it can be shown that Ovid's treatment of his mythical material was guided by some principle which in this sense informed the poem.

That these are not straightforward questions is shown by the difficulty experienced by critics when they try to define the *Metamorphoses*. Clearly it is a special kind of epic, an epos *sui generis*, but of what kind? What most interested Ovid and provided him with a limitless field for exploration (in the end, most tragically, in his own case) was human behaviour under stress. The *Metamorphoses* is above all an epic of the emotions. Given both Ovid's own predilections and the basic facts of human nature the predominant emotion is, predictably, love. By taking his plots from traditional mythology and creating a special world for his characters to inhabit Ovid released himself from the need to respect certain aspects of probability. The premisses of the situations in which his characters found themselves could, as in the *Heroides*, be taken for granted; what mattered was their reactions. Of these premisses the most fundamental is the almost absolute power of the gods and their lack of moral scruple in its use. Like the human actors in the drama the gods are the slaves, though less frequently the victims, of their passions. Granted all this, however improbable or even outrageous the particular circumstances, the interest lay in following out the consequences. As a literary formula this was not new: it had been brilliantly used by Aristophanes and it was of the essence of the declamatory exercises on which Ovid and his generation cut their literary teeth. But by contrast with this attitude to the given premisses, in Ovid's development of the story therefrom probability, or at all events conviction, was paramount; all the poet's art was applied to achieve credibility (*fides*) and to persuade the reader that in the circumstances described people must have behaved so. Callimachus had put the matter in a nutshell: 'let me so lie as to convince my hearer'.[1] In reading the story of Pygmalion (10.242–97) we forget that in the real world statues do not come to life; we know only that if they did this is how it would be. In principle no situation was too bizarre or morally reprehensible (incest is the subject of two episodes) to qualify for this poetical analysis.

The formula in itself carries no guarantee of the success which it achieves in Ovid's hands. Simply to ring rhetorical and emotional changes on traditional material was not enough. The *Metamorphoses* might have emerged as yet

---

[1] *Hymn* 1.65 ψευδοίμην ἀίοντος ἅ κεν πεπίθοιεν ἀκουήν.

another catalogue of suffering heroines and star-crossed lovers; that it did not is due to Ovid's prodigious fertility of invention, his wit, and his masterful way with the Latin language. In treating the original stories freely he availed himself of a traditional licence, but being Ovid used the licence to the full. As he found it the story of Pygmalion was a smoking-room anecdote; its charming and innocently sensuous character as one of the great stories of wish-fulfilment is entirely his achievement. Just as he had transformed Acontius from a love-sick youth into a man with an obsession bordering on the psychopathic, so the credibly middle-class Erysichthon of Callimachus' Hymn to Demeter becomes in the *Metamorphoses* (8.738–878) a fairy-tale monster. Conversely the Iliadic Odysseus is downgraded in the wrangle over the arms of Achilles (13.1–398) into a contemporary committee-man, public relations expert, and smart-aleck lawyer. Ingenious combination brings familiar or less familiar figures into new and piquant situations. In the story of Cyclops and Galatea (13.735–897) the pastoral setting of the Alexandrian treatment (Theoc. 6, 11) is retained, but Theocritus' rustic booby is reinvested with the horrendous attributes of the original Homeric Cyclops; and the theme of Beauty and the Beast is accentuated by the introduction of Acis in the character of the successful rival. But the episode has something of a pantomime quality; Acis is crushed under a rock hurled, in Homeric fashion, by the monster, but all ends happily with a transformation scene and tableau in which he emerges as a river-god, equipped with the typical attributes of his new status, the whole being rounded off with an *aition* (13.887–97). By skilful assimilation of elements from several literary sources (including Virgil, who had also drawn on the story in the *Eclogues*) Ovid constructs a grotesque-idyllic episode of a unique kind, burlesque of a high poetic order, which was to bear its full fruit only after some seventeen centuries in the collaboration of Gay and Handel:

> Galatea, dry your tears!
> Acis now a god appears.

This example, which could be multiplied a hundredfold, of the reception and exploitation of the *Metamorphoses* by later European writers and artists, is the strongest possible testimony to Ovid's importance, already referred to apropos of the story of Hero and Leander, as mediator between the old world and the new.

Even in his moments of inspired nonsense Ovid's preoccupation with abnormal psychological states is not forgotten. In his version of the story Galatea hears the lament of the Cyclops with her lover lying in her arms. This is characteristically Ovidian, a touch of sexual cruelty to emphasize the unbridgeable gulf between Beauty and the Beast; and the passion of the Cyclops, like that of Acontius, is a type of the love that will destroy if it cannot possess. The fact that the Middle Ages found in the *Metamorphoses* an endless store of symbol and allegory shows that in reshaping the myths to provide varied and piquant entertainment Ovid certainly did not – to put it no higher – divest them of their inherent validity. A particularly striking case is that of Narcissus and Echo (3.339–510). The story as Ovid tells it can be made to yield more than one moral. It is a lesson against the desire and pursuit of the unattainable. More specifically it illustrates the destructive quality of self-love seen in its effects on both self (Narcissus) and others (Echo). But the length and elaboration of Ovid's treatment cannot be attributed to a wish to underscore any moral that the story may offer; still less (as a rule) does he draw attention overtly to such implications. His interest is in exploiting to the full the paradox, indeed the absurdity, of the situation. By emphasizing at the outset the oddity of Narcissus' passion and its outcome (3.350 *letique genus nouitasque furoris*) he shows what is in his mind. Echo, with the incidental comedy that her disability entails and the wistful ghost of her voice, is a foil to bring out the lengths to which Narcissus' own emotional disability ends by taking him. On the way to the dénouement the poet of the *Amores* diverts himself and us by standing all the elegiac clichés of the thwarted lover on their heads:

> uror amore mei, flammas moueoque feroque:
> quid faciam? roger anne rogem? quid deinde rogabo?
> quod cupio, mecum est; inopem me copia fecit.
> o utinam a nostro secedere corpore possem!
> uotum in amante nouum: uellem quod amamus abesset.   (3.464–8)

It is myself for whom I burn, I both inflict and suffer this fire. What am I to do? Court or be courted? But what will courting effect? What I desire is mine already; it is riches that make me a pauper. If only I could quit my own body – a novel thing this for a lover to wish, that the beloved were elsewhere!

The mixture of sentiment and humour in such an episode is a challenge to the reader, who must react with a corresponding mixture of emotional participation and intellectually detached amusement. So in the story of Ceyx and Alcyone, one of the longest and most elaborately constructed episodes in the poem (11.410–748), the truly tragic treatment of Alcyone's selfless love for her husband and of the fate of the pair is offset by the extravagance of the two contrasting descriptive excursuses, the storm (which verges on a parody of a stock epic theme) and the Cave of Sleep. It is not always easy to know where to have Ovid or how to respond to these astonishing stories.

The culminating metamorphosis of the body of the dead Narcissus to the flower that bears his name sits very loosely to the story of his passion. Similarly the metamorphosis of Ajax into a hyacinth is a very slender excuse for the inclusion and extended treatment of the *Iudicium armorum*, the debate between Ajax and Ulysses as to who should inherit the arms of the dead Achilles

(13.1–398). This is a brilliant demonstration of how to argue on both sides of a question. That the Unjust Argument wins the day is not stated in so many words, but an attentive reader is left in no real doubt of it. However, the outcome might also be construed as demonstrating the superiority of intelligence (*consilium*) over brute force (*uis*). It is not surprising that the passage enjoyed an independent circulation in the Middle Ages and was esteemed by Macaulay. Here too Ovid shows great skill in transforming his sources. In the main he drew on the *Iliad*, but the gloss that he places on the exploits of the heroes is heavily influenced by the post-Homeric tradition in which Ulysses became a type of unscrupulous cunning. In general the choice of episodes and the scale of the treatment were suggested by the content of the stories and what might be made of them rather than by the metamorphoses with which they were (or might be) associated. It is unusual when, as with Pygmalion, a metamorphosis is integral to the story. Sometimes it provides a purely mechanical release from an intolerable situation: Daphne is changed into a laurel as an alternative to being raped (1.548–56). True 'happy endings' are not very common in the *Metamorphoses*; the story of Ceyx and Alcyone achieves its dénouement in a rare mood of tranquil beauty:

> fatis obnoxius isdem
> tum quoque mansit amor, nec coniugiale solutum est
> foedus in alitibus: coeunt fiuntque parentes,
> perque dies placidos hiberno tempore septem
> incubat Alcyone pendentibus aequore nidis.
> tum iacet unda maris; uentos custodit et arcet
> Aeolus egressu praestatque nepotibus aequor. (11.742–8)

Their love survived in their new guise, and even after they became birds the marriage-bond was not severed. They mate and rear young, and through seven calm days each winter Alcyone hatches her brood in a nest floating on the water. Then the sea is smooth: Aeolus shuts up the winds in their prison and grants his grandchildren a level ocean.

Even this pretty conceit is an *aition* thinly disguised; and similarly Baucis and Philemon, though happy in the manner and occasion of their death, serve in the end chiefly to point a moral and launch an epigram:

> cura deum di sunt et qui coluere coluntur. (8.724)

Those who guarded the gods have become gods and the worshippers are themselves worshipped.

In general Ovid is not concerned to find solutions to the predicaments of his characters. It is of course broadly true that all good poets avoid simplistic 'explanations' of the great myths, preferring to accept, even to compound, their uncertainties. That is not quite Ovid's position, which is one of calculated detachment. It is rare for him to involve himself (his narrative *persona*, that is), except for apostrophes of a conventionally pathetic kind, with the fates of his actors. Sometimes indeed this detachment rises to a degree that repels the modern reader, as in the gruesome details of the Battle of the Centaurs and Lapiths (12.245–458) or the flaying of Marsyas by Apollo, where the victim in the midst of his agonies is made to utter a punning comment on what is happening to him (6.385–91). In such passages detachment seems to pass over into open relish of suffering. They are not, however, so numerous as to dominate or fundamentally colour the poem as a whole, and no doubt represent an unfortunate concession to a certain kind of contemporary taste for the sado-masochistic. Essentially they represent an excess of a quality which continually pervades and informs the *Metamorphoses*: what the Romans called *ingenium* and the English Augustans wit. Ovid's approach to the stories he tells is intellectual rather than emotional; the subject is the passions, but the object is less to excite sympathy in the reader in any profoundly moving way (let alone attempt any sort of catharsis) than to stimulate and feed a well-informed interest in the illimitable variations of human experience. Life and people being what they are, experience mostly takes the form of inflicting or enduring suffering; a fact which one need not be hard-hearted in order to contemplate with amusement. 'Life is a comedy to those that think, a tragedy to those that feel.' The *Metamorphoses* is written for those that think. Moreover profound emotion is bound up with morality, and the world of the *Metamorphoses* is conspicuously amoral. Ovid's gods are beings emotionally human but invested with supernatural powers and free from all moral constraint because not subject to any sanctions from above – they are what most men and women, if absolutely free to choose, would be if they could. Ovid was certainly in the conventional sense an unbeliever, but his treatment of the Olympian pantheon is not a sneer at traditional religion so much as a sardonic comment on human nature. In spirit he is much nearer to Lucretius than to Virgil, though he did not believe in prophets either.

In certain respects it can be suggested that the *Metamorphoses*, which in spite of the great surface disparities persistently invites comparison with the *Aeneid*, is the more universal poem of the two. Certainly it is more difficult to evaluate its message or even to be sure if it has one. Ovid shows humanity to itself in a great distorting mirror of its own creation, the myths that formed the staple of both popular and literary culture. The great Virgilian commentator James Henry found Ovid 'a more natural, more genial, more cordial, more imaginative, more playful poet...than [Virgil], or any other Latin poet'[1] – in a word, more human; and the essential unity, or, better, harmony of the *Metamorphoses* is to be sought in its humanity. In spite of the intellectual distance

[1] Henry (1873–89) 1 618.

maintained by the poet between himself and his creations, in spite of the excesses and lapses of taste into which his wit was apt to lead him, in spite of the relentless pursuit of point and paradox, in spite even of the apparent heartlessness of some episodes, this remains the distinctive quality of the poem. Its unclassical characteristics, which also emerge from the comparison with the *Aeneid*, should offer no obstacle to appreciation in an age which appears to have broken definitively with classicism in literature, art and music. Balance and proportion are not necessarily and self-evidently the most important of the artistic virtues. Ovid's vision of the world was not one of order and uniformity but of diversity and change. For him the Augustan settlement was not, as it had been for Virgil, the start of a new world, *nouus saeclorum ordo*, but another sandbank in the shifting stream of eternity. The *Aeneid* stops where it does because of the logic of a situation: there is a knot which can be cut only by the sacrifice of Turnus. Blood must be shed so that reconciliation may follow. The *Metamorphoses* stops where it does because this is where history has got to. In the coda to the poem Ovid foretells his own metamorphosis and apotheosis:

> iamque opus exegi, quod nec Iouis ira nec ignis
> nec poterit ferrum nec edax abolere uetustas.
> cum uolet, illa dies, quae nil nisi corporis huius
> ius habet, incerti spatium mihi finiat aeui;
> parte tamen meliore mei super alta perennis
> astra ferar, nomenque erit indelebile nostrum,
> quaque patet domitis Romana potentia terris,
> ore legar populi perque omnia saecula fama,
> siquid habent ueri uatum praesagia, uiuam.   (15.871–9)

And now I have finished a work which neither Jove's anger nor fire nor iron nor gnawing age shall have power to destroy. That day which has authority only over my body may when it pleases put an end to the uncertain span of my life; with the better part of me I shall soar immortal high above the stars and my name shall not be extinguished. Wherever the sway of Rome shall extend over the conquered lands, I shall be read by the tongues of men and for all time to come, if the prophecies of bards have any truth in them, by and in my fame shall I live.

In a perilous and uncertain universe the only created thing that can hope for survival is poetry, for it comes from and lives through the spirit. In the mind of a rationalist and a humanist this is the only kind of immortality that there is. Only so can man's unconquerable soul ensure its own survival.

5. THE POEMS OF EXILE

The *Metamorphoses* was, so far as can be seen, substantially complete, if not formally published, in the shape in which we now have it by A.D. 8. Ovid then stood on the pinnacle of success; none could challenge his position as Rome's most eminent living poet. That he was himself acutely conscious of this fact is an essential key to the understanding of much of his later poetry. The *Metamorphoses* had concluded with a group of transformations that might be seen as the climax of all those that had preceded: the apotheoses of Julius Caesar (accomplished) and of Augustus (awaited) and, linked with them, the last great metamorphosis of history, begun by Caesar and to be completed by his successor (Jupiter on earth: 15.858–60), of an age of war and confusion into one of peace and stability (15.832–9). It was therefore supremely ironical that Augustus should have chosen the moment when the *Metamorphoses* was about to appear before the world to visit its author with disgrace and ruin. It was also ironical that one of the reasons for his downfall was a poem, the *Ars amatoria*. The other reason remains unknown; Ovid calls it an indiscretion (*error*). On the evidence available it cannot be categorically said that Augustus' resentment was unjustified; Ovid indeed, for what that is worth, acknowledges that it was not. The form that it took, on the other hand, was severe to the point of calculated cruelty. Ovid was exiled, or rather relegated (for he was not deprived of citizenship or property), not to one of the usual Mediterranean islands customarily used for this purpose, but to a place on the very edge of the civilized world, where he was cut off from everything that for a man of his temperament made life worth living: friends, the society of the capital, books, the Latin language itself – and above all peace of mind. Spiritually it was a death sentence.

Ovid refused to die. More than once in the poems of exile he alludes to his peculiar gifts, his *ingenium*, as the cause of his destruction;[1] but by the same token they were his only resource in his hour of need:

> indignata malis mens est succumbere seque
>   praestitit inuictam uiribus usa suis...
> ergo quod uiuo durisque laboribus obsto
>   nec me sollicitae taedia lucis habent,
> gratia, Musa, tibi: nam tu solacia praebes,
>   tu curae requies, tu medicina uenis,
> tu dux et comes es, tu nos abducis ab Histro
>   in medioque mihi das Helicone locum,
> tu mihi, quod rarum est, uiuo sublime dedisti
>   nomen, ab exequiis quod dare fama solet.
>
> (Trist. 4.10.103–4, 115–22)

My mind disdained to sink beneath misfortune and by its own strength showed itself unconquerable...And so the fact that I still live and hold out against affliction, the fact that for all its vexations I am not yet weary of life, this, o Muse, I owe to you. It is you who offer me consolation, you come as rest and medicine to my unhappiness; you are my guide and companion, you carry me away from the Danube and bring me to an honourable seat on Helicon. You have given me what is rarely given, a lofty name while I still live, something that fame is apt to confer only after death.

[1] *Trist.* 2.1–2, 3.3.73–7, *Pont.* 3.5.4.

Ovid was not a philosopher and he did not endure his fate philosophically. His reply to the good advice of his friend Rufinus is, for all its ostensible submission to the lesson of patience, perceptibly ironical (*Pont.* 1.3). So far as he could, he protested, using the one means open to him, his poetry. Augustus was an autocrat, accountable, whatever constitutional fictions might suggest, to none, and his later years were embittered by a series of misfortunes[1] which rendered him increasingly touchy and suspicious and therefore the more prone to arbitrary exercise of his enormous power. It behoved Ovid to be careful; but he had some room for manoeuvre. Augustus clearly wanted him out of the way, but had stopped short of putting him to death, which (as Ovid himself repeatedly insists) he might well have done. If Augustus baulked at the extreme measure, it can only have been through respect for public opinion; in Tomis he must have hoped that Ovid, out of sight, would also be out of mind. To the extent, however, that Ovid had access through his poetry to Roman public opinion, the Princeps might be amenable to pressure. If it was too much to hope for pardon, at least a more tolerable place of exile might be conceded.

Some such reasoning must underlie what may be called the grand strategy of the first and most important part of Ovid's production in exile, the five books of the *Tristia* ('Sorrows'). Form and style were a matter of tactics, but the elegiac form in a manner imposed itself. For Ovid's contemporaries the elegiac couplet was still the vehicle *par excellence* of love-poetry, but it had reputedly originated as a metre of lament. In terms of tone and situation an Ovidian model was to hand in the *Heroides*. But whereas the *Heroides*, like all Ovid's earlier work, dealt in impersonation, in the *Tristia* he was now writing *in propria persona* and with a strictly practical end in view: to keep his name before the public, to ensure that he was not (from Augustus' point of view) conveniently forgotten, and above all to indicate with all the emphasis possible short of outright statement that in consigning, on his own authority, the greatest poet of Rome to a living tomb[2] Augustus had gone too far; that he had indeed, in so far as it was merely temporal, exceeded his authority.

That this was from the first the main aim of the *Tristia* is evident from Book 1, composed on the voyage to Tomis and sent to Rome on arrival. The introductory poem sets the tone. Formally it is a valediction addressed to the book, a device used by Horace in the epilogue (20) to his first book of Epistles. A number of important motifs are broached. The book is an ambassador, sent where the writer may not venture (1–2, 57–8). It is to be discreet, and its appearance must be unkempt, as befits the representative of an exile (3–14). It must not force itself on people (21–6). Above all it must not intrude incontinently upon Augustus (69–86) but must be satisfied for the present to find readers in the public at large (87–8). Later a friend may introduce it at Court

---

[1] Plin. *N.H.* 7.149–50. [2] *Trist.* 3.3.53–4, 1.3 *passim*, 1.7.38, 3.14.20, *al.*

(91–8), for there are still some who wish Ovid well (27–34). He has no illusions about the quality of his work, produced in physical and mental distress, but it is not fame that he now seeks (35–56). What he does seek is clear, reconsideration of his case; and the real addressee of the poem, and hence of the book, is Augustus. These are the opening shots in a campaign which Ovid waged with more of both finesse and courage than he has usually been given credit for. His attempt to work on Augustus' feelings relies less on his frequent invocation of the Princeps' famed clemency, celebrated by himself in his *Res gestae* (chh. 3, 34), than on the constantly reiterated implicit appeal over Augustus' head to contemporary public opinion and the verdict of posterity. The appeal harps on two ideas, both illustrated by *Tristia* 1.1: the irresponsible, indeed tyrannical, character of Augustus' authority; and its ultimate inferiority to the power of mind and spirit. This is the ground on which poet and Princeps meet in the *Tristia*, and the moral victory is with the poet.

In warning his book to steer clear of the Palatine Ovid introduces an image that is to become familiar. He dreads the spot because from it was launched the thunderbolt that destroyed him:

> ignoscant augusta mihi loca dique locorum:
>   uenit in hoc illa fulmen ab arce caput.
> esse quidem memini mitissima sedibus illis
>   numina, sed timui qui nocuere deos...
> uitaret caelum Phaethon, si uiueret, et quos
>   optarat stulte, tangere nollet equos.
> me quoque, quae sensi, fateor Iouis arma timere,
>   me reor infesto, cum tonat, igne peti.   (*Trist.* 1.1.71–4, 79–82)

Without offence to that august place and its gods, it was from that citadel that there fell the bolt on my head. I remember that the Beings who live there are most merciful, but I fear the gods who have done me harm...If Phaethon had lived he would have stayed clear of heaven and would have shrunk from meddling with the team that he had foolishly asked to drive. I admit that I too fear the weapon of Jupiter, having felt it, and whenever it thunders I think that I am the target of the threatening flame.

A reader fresh from the *Metamorphoses* might recall that Phaethon had been in Ovid's version of the story an innocent victim of the thunderbolt, which is described as 'unjustly launched' (*Met.* 2.377–8).[1] The identification of Augustus with Jupiter, often in association with the thunderbolt image, occurs in over thirty of the fifty poems that make up *Tristia* Books 1 and 3–5. The cumulative effect of these allusions is unflattering. In his lifetime the *numen* and *genius* of Augustus received divine honours, but he was not yet officially a god; the

---

[1] It is possible that our text of the *Metamorphoses* goes back to a copy revised (like the *Fasti*) by Ovid in exile, and that one or two apparently 'prophetic' touches such as this were introduced by him during revision. They are certainly striking, but hardly numerous enough for coincidence to be ruled out.

distinction is carefully observed by the punctilious Horace (*Odes* 3.5.1–4, *Epist.* 2.1.15). In ascribing actual divinity to Augustus, as he had already done more than once in the *Fasti*, Ovid was no doubt voicing a common sentiment. In the *Tristia*, however, the reiteration of the idea, given the writer's situation, was bound to be tinged with bitterness, more especially when it is remembered how often in the *Metamorphoses* divine anger is the prelude to an act of cruelty or injustice. This repeated equation of Augustus with the traditional Jupiter and of his power with the thunderbolt is more critical than complimentary. Ovid's reflections on the character of 'divine' justice are indeed not always merely implicit: in his apologia he observes that the gods punish mistakes just as savagely as crimes:

> scilicet in superis etiam fortuna luenda est,
> nec ueniam laeso numine casus habet.   (*Trist.* 2.107–8)

Apparently when one is dealing with the gods even ill-luck must be expiated, and when a deity is offended misfortune is not accepted as an excuse.

Recurring variations on these ideas and catalogues of *exempla* illustrating them leave no room for doubt as to what Ovid thought of the way in which he had been treated. The message is clear: he was a victim of tyranny and injustice.

It is not, however, primarily as a citizen wronged before the law or at all events in equity that Ovid presents his case, but in his special quality of poet. This is clearly evident in the elaborate apologia that forms the whole of the second book of the *Tristia*; it is also implicit in the poetry itself, often unjustly belittled by critics, and in the very fact that it was through the public medium of poetry that he chose to appeal. The existence of the *Tristia* was a demonstration that Ovid still counted; that his hat, so to say, was still in the ring. Even a poem that begins by apologizing for the technical deficiencies of his work (*Trist.* 4.1.1–2) will modulate into a more positive strain:

> utque suum Bacche non sentit saucia uulnus,
>   dum stupet Idaeis exululata modis,
> sic ubi mota calent uiridi mea pectora thyrso,
>   altior humano spiritus ille malo est;
> ille nec exilium Scythici nec litora ponti,
>   ille nec iratos sentit habere deos.   (*Trist.* 4.1.41–6)

And as a Bacchante though wounded does not know it, so rapt is she while she shrieks in orgiastic strains, so when my spirit has taken fire, struck with the burgeoning thyrsus, it rises above human ills; it does not feel exile or the Scythian shore or the anger of the gods.

A similar apology ushers in Book 5 (5.1.3–4); the promise that follows, to write in a better and happier vein if Augustus will relent (35–46), is another way of bringing moral pressure to bear. It is a fresh reminder that Ovid, as a poet, has been destroyed by what has been done to him. This emphasis on his status as poet is evident from the first: *Tristia* 1.1 ends with what amounts to a reminder of his achievement, in the shape of an enumeration of the books that stand on the shelf ready to welcome the newcomer (105–18). Even in deprecating the *Ars amatoria* he manages to convey a suggestion that there is really nothing to deprecate:

> tres procul obscura latitantes parte uidebis:
>   sic quoque, *quod nemo nescit*, amare docent.
> hos tu uel fugias uel, *si satis oris habebis*,
>   Oedipodas facito Telegonosque uoces.   (*Trist.* 1.1.111–14)

Three volumes you will see skulking in a dark corner; even there they continue to teach – not that anyone needs the lesson – how to love. Them you should avoid or, if you have the face, make a point of calling them Oedipus or Telegonus [i.e. parricides].

The subsequent reference to the *Metamorphoses* is also glossed: the fate of its author may itself rank as a metamorphosis (119–22). The wit of the paradox – the creator of the poem now part of his own subject matter – reads like a bitter echo of the proem of the *Metamorphoses*; in the context it is sharp and, in the light of the previous characterization of Augustus' power, suggestive. Not only is Ovid's fate cruel, but the writer of such a poem might have expected some better recognition of his achievement than himself to be numbered among the victims of divine anger.

Thus the first poem of the first book of poetry sent home by Ovid after his sentence is, for the most part implicitly but still unambiguously, programmatic. If *Tristia* 1 consists of a series of sighting shots, Book 2 is a full-scale barrage. Ovid here comes as near as anywhere in the *Tristia* to defiance; when he turns from pleading to refutation the tone is almost overtly satirical.[1] He addresses himself to the sense of his cultivated readers, appealing over the head of the powers that be to enlightened public opinion. 'His reply...is a riotous *reductio ad absurdum*, and what is meant to seem absurd is the attitude of the Emperor.'[2] But though the manner of presenting his case may be flippant or sarcastic, his fundamental premiss is absolutely serious. He is saying that the world of poetry is autonomous, a spiritual domain where the writ of temporal rulers does not run. In Book 3 he was to restate this thesis in lines in which Macaulay hailed 'a Miltonic loftiness of sentiment':

> singula ne referam, nil non mortale tenemus
>   pectoris exceptis ingeniique bonis.
> en ego cum caream patria uobisque domoque
>   raptaque sint, adimi quae potuere mihi,

---

[1] Wilkinson (1955) 310; cf. Wiedemann (1975) 268–71.   [2] Wilkinson, ibid. 310–11.

ingenio tamen ipse meo comitorque fruorque:
　　Caesar in hoc potuit iuris habere nihil.
quilibet hanc saeuo uitam mihi finiat ense,
　　me tamen extincto fama superstes erit,
dumque suis uictrix omnem de montibus orbem
　　prospiciet domitum Martia Roma, legar. 　　(*Trist.* 3.7.43–52)

In short, all that we possess is mortal except for what mind and spirit confer. Even to me, who have lost my country, my family and my home, from whom has been snatched all that there was to take, my mind is company and pleasure: over that Caesar could have no power. Anyone may put an end to my life by the edge of the sword, but my fame will survive my death, and so long as warlike Rome shall survey the whole world victorious from her hills, I shall be read.

And he was to conclude Book 4 with a pronouncement in the same vein:

siue fauore tuli, siue hanc ego carmine famam,
　　iure tibi grates, candide lector, ago. 　　(*Trist.* 4.10.131–2)

Whether it is partiality or merit that has earned me my fame, to you, kind reader, are rightly due the thanks.

To his readers *and to no one else* – so runs the implication – is he beholden. Supposing that Augustus read these poems and took the point, he is unlikely to have been much mollified. The *Tristia* have been criticized as abject; in some respects they show Ovid as bold to the point of foolhardiness.

The individual books of the *Tristia*, like those of the *Amores*, are constructed so as to throw their main themes into relief.[1] Books 3 and 4 begin and end with poems that in one way or another are about Ovid's poetry. *Trist.* 3.1 again uses the book-as-ambassador motif, this time with the book personified and speaking; 3.14 commends his poetry to a friend and apologizes for its quality. *Trist.* 4.1 begins on the same note of apology, to which, after the more positive development previously noted, it returns. A phrase in this concluding section looks forward to the last poem in the book: Ovid records his frustration at the contrast between what he now was and what he had been – *qui sim fuerimque recordor* (99); and what he had been is precisely the theme of 4.10: *qui fuerim . . . ut noris, accipe, posteritas* (1–2). This latter poem is usually referred to as an autobiography, but it is rather what would now be called a personal statement: what Ovid wished to go on record to allow posterity to judge between him and Augustus. It is therefore highly selective. Ovid attempts to show that, though he had done his duty as best he could by the state and by his family, his first loyalty was to poetry, and that this was not merely a matter of personal preference but an imperative vocation. In a famous (and frequently misinterpreted)[2]

---

[1] Martini (1933) 52, Froesch (1968) 61–2, Dickinson (1973) 160–1, 175, 180, 183–4.
[2] Stroh (1968).

OVID

passage he recalls that he had tried to repudiate the Muses but that their claims were too strong to be denied:

> motus eram dictis totoque Helicone relicto
> scribere temptabam uerba soluta modis.
> sponte sua carmen numeros ueniebat ad aptos,
> et quod temptabam scribere uersus erat. (*Trist.* 4.10.23–6)

In obedience to my father I abandoned Helicon completely and tried to write prose. Willy-nilly a poem would come in correct metre, and all my attempts to write were verse.

That was the faith by which he had lived and now must die: the word *ergo* ('therefore', 'and so') at l. 115 introduces a final apostrophe to the Muse which culminates in words clearly designed to recall the epilogue to the *Metamorphoses*:

> siquid habent igitur uatum praesagia ueri,
> protinus ut moriar, non ero, terra, tuus. (129–30)

So if the prophecies of bards have any truth in them, though I die tomorrow, earth will not claim me as her own.

The traditional symbols and the repeated prediction of posthumous survival enshrine a real certainty that the poet is a channel between the rest of humanity and something greater than himself:

> est deus in nobis et sunt commercia caeli;
> sedibus aetheriis spiritus ille uenit. (*Ars Am.* 3.549–50)

There is godhead in poets and we enjoy communion with heaven. Our inspiration comes from on high.

It is inspiration or genius or whatever it is to be called that entitles a poet to honour and consideration. In this he partakes of the immortality otherwise reserved for the gods. So Ovid proclaims his independence of temporal authority and his citizenship of a polity of letters in which it is the judgement of posterity and not the arbitrary sentence of a monarch that determines the fate of a writer.

Such affirmations, placed in commanding positions in their collections, are reinforced by the implications of the other poems. The technique is essentially that of the *Amores*, but now applied in deadly earnest. Ovid must have been deeply aware of the need to avoid monotony in poetry which was designed to keep the public well disposed towards him; now of all times he could not afford to bore his readers. Under the superficial sameness for which he apologizes there is in *Tristia* 1 and 3–5 a considerable diversity of subject matter. Critics have tended to single out the obvious anthology pieces, the poems in which he describes the incidents of his journey (1.2, 10), the place of his exile (3.10, 5.7,

10), or his personal sufferings (1.3, 3.3). These are indeed attractive because immediately appealing, but they do not give a complete or adequate idea of the purpose and nature of Ovid's poetry in exile. In particular the anthologizing approach disguises the extent to which Ovid was, as he himself says, identified with his poetry: *carmina maior imago | sunt mea* (*Trist.* 1.7.11–12). Everything he wrote was in some sense a declaration and made a point: thus the well-known poem on the fate of Absyrtus (*Trist.* 3.9) is a demonstration that something could be made poetically out of even dismal Tomis and a reminder, since in form it is an aetiology, of the literary heritage of Greece and of Ovid's role in its transmission. The storm described in *Trist.* 1.2 no doubt really occurred; but it is in its details the conventional epic storm as Ovid had previously described it in the *Metamorphoses* (11.490–569) and as Ulysses and Aeneas had experienced it in the *Odyssey* and *Aeneid.* Ovid compares himself in this poem (7–12) to these heroes and more than once reverts to the comparison: again the implied paradox that he is now at the mercy of forces which as a poet he had controlled.

To diversity of subject matter is allied diversity of literary artifice. A good example of the allusive and ingenious way in which Ovid manipulates his material, in particular through the exploitation of earlier poetry so as to awaken echoes in the reader's mind, is given by *Trist.* 4.8. It opens with an apparently innocent remark; Ovid is showing the first signs of age:

> iam mea cycneas imitantur tempora plumas,
> inficit et nigras alba senecta comas. (1–2)

Now my temples imitate the plumage of the swan and the whiteness of old age dyes my black hair.

The image in *cycneas* is especially appropriate to a poet. Swans were associated with Apollo and figure prominently in programmatic contexts.[1] There is here too the suggestion of the swan-song (cf. *Trist.* 5.1.11–14): the poetry Ovid is writing now may be his last. Our reader fresh from the *Metamorphoses* might also recollect that the first of the three persons called Cycnus who are there changed into swans met his fate as a consequence of Phaethon's death by the thunderbolt and that it was in fear of the fire described by Ovid as 'unjustly launched' that the newly-fledged bird flew low. Besides these possible associations, a contemporary reader could hardly fail to be reminded of Horace's symbolical metamorphosis into a swan (*Odes* 2.20). That Ode is a proud boast, Ovid's elegy is a gentle complaint. He too contemplates (perforce) a metamorphosis, but a less romantic one: not a whole suit of feathers but a touch of white plumage at the temples. The image is ironically devalued by the follow-

---

[1] Callim. *Hymn* 4.252, Theoc. 5.137, Lucret. 3.6–7, 4.180–2, Virg, *Ecl.* 8.56, 9.36.

ing paraphrase;[1] and so far from thinking of flying, Ovid has trouble in walking: *iamque parum firmo me mihi ferre graue est* (4).

There follows (5–12) a conventional description of the pleasures of a peaceful retirement, a generalized image of the settled contentment to which a man may aspire when his life's work is done. For this Ovid had hoped and believed he had earned: the equation of his deserts with his hopes is suggested by the parallel phrasing of the verses (13–14). But though he proposed, the gods disposed:

> non ita dis uisum est, qui me terraque marique
> actum Sarmaticis exposuere locis. (15–16)

The gods decided otherwise; they have driven me over land and sea and cast me away on the Sarmatian shore.

The reminiscence here is unmistakeable; but the famous half-line of Virgil which Ovid has adapted must be recalled in its context for the innuendo to be clear:

> cadit et Rhipeus, iustissimus unus
> qui fuit in Teucris et seruantissimus aequi
> (dis aliter uisum)... (*Aen.* 2.426–8)

There fell too Rhipeus, who in justice and respect for the right was without peer among the Trojans – but the gods thought otherwise.

'The comment...may show resignation, it may be accusing...it is hard not to hear the accusing note.'[2] Ovid clearly intended to accuse. The adapted tag follows on the words *dignus eram* 'I was worthy' (14), exactly as the original in Virgil followed on the statement of Rhipeus' merits, and the allusion to Virgil deepens the bitterness. This was not the first time that the gods had oppressed a just man. So an English writer steeped in the Bible might allude to Job. The rest of the couplet also glances at Virgil: Ovid's fate is compared to that of Aeneas, who was 'harried by land and sea' (*Aen.* 1.3) – but whereas Aeneas in the end attained a peaceful haven, Ovid is a castaway (*exposuere*).

Next the reflection that to all things comes a time of superannuation, illustrated by a cluster of images (17–24) adapted from Ovid's own earlier treatment of the same commonplace at *Am.* 2.9.19–22:[3] ships, horses, soldiers, gladiators As often in the poems of exile Ovid turns to serious ends imagery that had previously embellished a *jeu d'esprit*. Here the earlier arrangement is changed so as to bring the gladiator into the apodosis of the comparison:

> ...sic igitur, tarda uires minuente senecta,
> me quoque donari iam rude tempus erat. (23–4)

Just so, now that old age is slowing and diminishing my force, it is high time that I was presented with my wooden sword.

---

[1] The words of l. 2 are borrowed from Propertius (3.5.24).
[2] Austin (1964) 173–4.
[3] Cf. Prop. 2.25.5–8.

The language and the application of the idea to the case of a poet again recall Horace: at the beginning of his first book of *Epistles* he had written of having earned his congé: *spectatum satis et donatum iam rude* (*Epist.* 1.1.2), and had gone on to apply the image of the ageing gladiator quite explicitly to himself. Delicately Ovid is hinting that he, no less than (for instance) Horace, had done honour to poetry and had deserved the sort of retirement that Horace – whether in earnest or jest is no matter – had laid claim to for himself. He rounds off the argument by restating the two themes of retirement, now with specific reference to himself ($25-8 \sim 5-12$, $29-30 \sim 13-14$), and of ruin ($35-6 \sim 15-16$). With mention of old age as the moment when he might reasonably have expected to be granted his *otium cum dignitate* ($29-36$) the poem returns to its point of departure.

An emphatic *ergo* ('so then') introduces the final section. These hopes were shattered because Ovid in his folly had offended the man who was the very personification of clemency ($37-9$). True, he was allowed to live – but at Tomis ($40-2$). If Delphi and Dodona had foretold his fate he would have disbelieved them, but the moral is clear:

> nil adeo ualidum est, adamas licet alliget illud,
>   ut maneat rapido firmius igne Iouis;
> nil ita sublime est supraque pericula tendit,
>   non sit ut inferius suppositumque deo.
> nam quamquam uitio pars est contracta malorum,
>   plus tamen exitii numinis ira dedit.
> at uos admoniti nostris quoque casibus este
>   aequantem superos emeruisse uirum.   ($45-52$)

Nothing is so strong, though adamant bind it, that it can resist the swift fire of Jove; nothing is so high or reaches so far above danger that it is not lower than and subject to god. For although some part of our misfortunes are brought on us by wrong-doing, more destruction is caused by the anger of godhead. But do you be warned by my fate to deserve well of the man who is the equal of those above.

From Jupiter to Augustus the argument moves through a series of variations: from *Iouis* (46), the king of the conventional pantheon, through *deo* (48), 'god', and *numinis* (50), 'godhead', to (52) the man with all the attributes of divinity. Lines 45–8 are bound to recall yet once more the proud affirmation at the end of the *Metamorphoses*:

> iamque opus exegi quod nec Iouis ira nec ignis
>   nec poterit ferrum nec edax abolere uetustas.   (*Met.* 15.871–2)

In an earlier poem (*Trist.* 1.7) Ovid had implied that in condemning him Augustus had condemned his creation, the *Metamorphoses*, or tried to.[1] Now it seems to be suggested that the condemnation had been effective: that here is

---

[1] Grisart (1959).

a power before which nothing – not even the traditional immortality of the poet through his works – is secure. There is an especial bitterness in the wording of the final couplet: *emeruisse* connotes time-serving. It is not enough, Ovid is saying, to write good poetry; the poet who wishes himself and his work to survive must keep on the right side of the man who combines the power with the irresponsibility (for such, after the *Metamorphoses*, is the implication of *numinis ira*) of deity.

This is irony and not to be taken literally. The very next poem shows that Ovid had not given up. *Trist.* 4.9 breathes anger and defiance; in it he claims the power, through his poetry, of blasting his correspondent's name for all time to come. The man addressed is not identifiable, and may be a fiction; the message is in effect a retractation of 4.8.45–52, and the cap, were it not for the (detachable) parenthesis of ll. 11–14, fits Augustus better than anyone else. Only here does Ovid attribute to himself (3) the *clementia* which elsewhere in the *Tristia* (cf. especially 4.8.39) is the prerogative of the Emperor. This is not the only poem in which his words can be construed as a threat against Augustus. In his prayer to Bacchus at *Trist.* 5.3.35–46 the references to the mythical figures of Lycurgus and Pentheus are pointed. These were kings who offended the god who protects poets and were in consequence destroyed. What Ovid dwells on, however, is not their deaths but their posthumous infamy, which is contrasted with the eternal glory reserved for those who deserve well of Bacchus. The corollary is the unspoken question: is Augustus to figure in their company?

It has proved unfortunate for Ovid's reputation that his fight to rehabilitate himself and his poetry had on his side to be conducted with the gloves on. The stakes were enormous, indeed incalculable: not merely his own existence and poetical identity, but the freedom of the artist to express what the gods have given him to express. Such momentous ideas could only be suggested through the techniques of literary allusion[1] and the significant placing of poems intended to be read in contrast or complement to each other: *Trist.* 4.8–10 is a striking example of such a group. This is to demand a good deal of the reader, and even Ovid's more sympathetic critics have preferred to dwell on the human interest – great but essentially incidental – of the *Tristia* to the neglect of the qualities which are fundamental to their message. In writing these poems Ovid's aim was not to crystallize personal experience or communicate a sense of suffering, though it may on occasion suit him to represent his poetry as a mere reflex, a cry of pain. His will to write and the nature of what he chose to write are the index of a moral strength in him for which self-respect is too weak a term. It is bound up with his consciousness of identity as a poet. Seen in this

---

[1] A particularly poignant instance at *Trist.* 1.3: Ovid's description of his last night in Rome is presented in terms intended to recall Aeneas' last night in Troy as narrated by Virgil in *Aeneid* 2.

light the *Tristia* are as characteristic of him as anything he ever wrote, and do him as much credit.

The criticisms which have been directed against Ovid's exile poetry as 'abject' or the like[1] apply with much more force to the *Epistulae ex Ponto* ('Letters from the Black Sea') than to the *Tristia*. Formally they differ from the *Tristia* only in being called letters and in naming the addressees (*Pont.* 1.1.17–18); and they do not suggest that his poetical powers had completely deserted him. There is probably less artifice in the arrangement of the poems in their books,[2] but literary associations are still, as in the *Tristia*, exploited in new and ingenious ways to reinforce the continual appeal.[3] A poem such as *Pont.* 3.1 shows Ovid consciously using the poetical implications of his situation: his own case ranks as an *exemplum* in the canonical lists (49–56). Such passages, however, are rarer than they are in the *Tristia*, and in general the *Epistulae ex Ponto* are less forceful; indignation is succeeded by resignation, even apathy. The allusions lack the edge of irony and the tone is predominantly pathetic. At his best in these poems Ovid is moving because simple and dignified; a poem such as *Pont.* 3.7 depends for its effect on directness of acceptance and statement. He has nothing more to say, and will cease to pester his friends and his wife for help. He will bow to the inevitable and resign himself, if Augustus allows (here, however, a note of rather tired irony is allowed to intrude), to dying stead-fastly as an exile:

> dummodo non nobis hoc Caesaris ira negarit,
> fortiter Euxinis immoriemur aquis.   (*Pont.* 3.7.39–40)

In this poem Ovid has finally arrived, it would appear, at that philosophy of fortitude in adversity which some of his critics, such as Macaulay, would have had him robustly profess from the start. The lesson went against the grain and was in the end forced upon him by sickness, age, and despair. These are the accents of a broken man, as we hear them again at the end of the poem which the unknown redactor of the posthumous Book 4 chose to place last in that book:

> omnia perdidimus: tantummodo uita relicta est,
> praebeat ut sensum materiamque mali.
> quid iuuat extinctos ferrum demittere in artus?
> non habet in nobis iam noua plaga locum.   (*Pont.* 4.16.49–52)

I have lost everything; only life itself remains to provide material for and consciousness of suffering. What is the use of plunging a sword into a body already dead? There is no longer any room in me for a fresh wound.

---

[1] Cf. Wilkinson (1955) 347, Otis (1966) 339. Before assenting to such judgements a critic would do well to ponder the words of Johnson: 'Those are no proper judges of his conduct who have slumbered away their time on the down of plenty, nor will any wise man presume to say, "Had I been in Savage's condition, I should have lived or written better than Savage."'

[2] But cf. Froesch (1968).

[3] E.g. *Pont.* 3.3; cf. Kenney (1965) 44–8.

The choice was apt in more ways than one, for the body of the poem consists of a catalogue of contemporary poets; and it is in this context that Ovid, for the last time, assesses his own achievements:

> dicere si fas est, claro mea nomine Musa
> atque inter tantos quae legeretur erat.   (*Pont.* 4.16.45–6)

If it is allowable to say so, my poetry was of good repute and worthy to be read in this company.

It is these dignified and restrained lines, rather than the final despairing outburst which may best serve as epigraph for the *Tristia* and *Epistulae ex Ponto*. As a modern English poet has said: 'The only effective answer that a poet can make to barbarism is poetry, for the only answer to death is the life of the spirit.'[1]

During his first years at Tomis Ovid had written one poem in something like his old vein, though novelly motivated, the *Ibis*. This is a curse, imprecating on an unidentified enemy some scores of gruesome and mutually incompatible fates as suffered by various mythical and historical characters. His motives for writing the work were literary rather than personal. Callimachus had written an attack on Apollonius of Rhodes and called it *Ibis*; but Ovid probably took little from Callimachus except the original idea, the metre, and the riddling language. Invective was almost a minor genre in its own right, and Ovid's misfortunes must have given him the idea of showing what he could do in this department, if only – supposing, as seems most likely, that 'Ibis' was not a real person[2] – by way of notifying the world that with a pen in his hand he was still to be reckoned with. It is almost impossible to take the *Ibis* at its face value. The undertaking was in any case out of character for Ovid, as he begins by stressing: hitherto his poetry had harmed nobody but himself (1–8). For his catalogue of unenviable deaths, which occupies nearly 400 of a total of 642 verses, he had combed the highways and byways of the learned tradition, and the expression is often as obscure as the sources. Everything suggests that the *Ibis* is intended as a practical demonstration of the *doctus poeta* in action. Ovid had few books at Tomis; the material was probably for the most part in his head or his notebooks at the time of his exile. He must have read enormously in preparation for the *Metamorphoses* and the *Fasti*; here was an opportunity to turn to account a surplus that would otherwise have been wasted. As a technical *tour de force* the *Ibis* has a limited appeal to the modern reader, but for the contemporary public it was another reminder of Ovid's poetic status. Augustan literary history can be viewed (in part at all events) as a process of coming to terms with Callimachus and what he was thought to stand for. In comparison with Callimachus' *Ibis*, which Ovid calls a little book (*Ibis* 447),

---

[1] Sassoon (1945) 193.   [2] Housman (1972) 1040.

Ovid's was a much more ambitious undertaking. Here was exemplified in yet another genre the prodigious fertility, exuberance and versatility of his genius. In a sense the *Ibis* rather than the *Epistulae ex Ponto* should be reckoned as his swan-song.

6. ACHIEVEMENT AND CHARACTERISTICS

For an epitome of Ovid's poetical career one need look no further than to the opening words of the *Metamorphoses* previously discussed: *In noua fert animus*. Every one of his surviving works represents a new literary departure, an unpredictable and individual variation on inherited themes and techniques. Originality in this sense was of course what the Roman public expected of its poets, and it was not peculiar to Ovid; none exemplifies it with greater brilliance and versatility. In the technical sphere he left a mark on the Latin poetic tradition that still endures: for the modern composer of elegiac couplets is normally expected to abide by the Ovidian 'rules'. The Augustan rejection of the metrical freedoms enjoyed by Catullus was not arbitrarily motivated but dictated by the phonetic realities of the Latin language; however, Ovid seems almost to have gone out of his way to accentuate the inherent limitations of the couplet form. Thus he not only avoids enjambment between couplets,[1] but in securing the obligatory disyllable at the end of the pentameter[2] he often resorts to the use of colourless words in this position.[3] The effect, by throwing the verbal interest back into the body of the verse, is to make each couplet even more autonomous than its metrical nature already dictates: and Ovid further accentuates this tendency by his distinctively antiphonal treatment of hexameter and pentameter. For the crisp epigrammatic strokes of wit appropriate to the *Amores* and *Ars amatoria* this was an ideal medium; only Pope, using a broadly comparable type of verse, has excelled him in such writing. For the more ample effects aimed at in the *Heroides* elegiacs are less satisfactory; the double epistles especially, for all their undoubted merits, are often diffuse, and the fact has something to do with the verse medium. It was in the management of the hexameter that Ovid's dexterity in the manipulation of language enjoyed full play. Epic called for a kind of expressiveness inappropriate in elegy, and Ovid's ingenuity in coining words and varying diction and syntax, tempo and stylistic coloration to suit the demands of his narrative came into its own in the *Metamorphoses*.

The influence of his technical achievements may be clearly traced in subsequent Latin poetry. Of later composers in elegiacs one only is a major artist, Martial. If anything he is even more accomplished than Ovid, but that verdict

---

[1] True enjambment is very rare in Ovid's elegiacs: Platnauer (1951) 33 finds two examples in the entire corpus.

[2] Breaches of this 'rule', nearly all in the poems of exile, are few: Platnauer (1951) 15–17.

[3] Axelson (1958).

must be heavily qualified. The epigrammatist's square of ivory is a very small one, and technical perfection is correspondingly easier to compass; and after all the trail had already been blazed by Ovid. In epic the debt to Ovid's hexameter is less obvious but quite pervasive and extremely important. In the verse of the *Metamorphoses* he had perfected what may be called a poetic *koine*, an omnicompetent dialect of literary Latin. His verse, like Virgil's, was carefully tailored for the work in hand;[1] unlike Virgil's, however, his style is (to a degree) imitable. This is because his linguistic manipulations are of a kind that can be classified and even learned. He takes liberties with Latin, but they are, as Virgil's are not, the sort of liberties that any poet might take once he had thought of them for himself. He is very much a craftsman, *poeta* in the full sense of the original ποιητής, a maker. The technical differences between Ovid and Virgil are a function of both temperament and aims. Virgil is ambiguous and ambivalent where Ovid is definite; Ovid said only what he had the means of expressing, whereas for Virgil the resources of language – the prose of Henry James being as yet in the womb of time – were clearly insufficient to convey all that he felt of the conflicts and uncertainties of the human condition. The strain shows: Virgil's commentators inconclusively dispute the meaning of a word or phrase as Ovid's hardly ever need to do. Thus the only epic poet of the Silver Age who aspired to close stylistic imitation of Virgil, Valerius Flaccus, merely succeeded in being obscure. Into this trap Lucan and Statius, even (to some extent) Silius Italicus, were too prudent to fall. Statius professed to follow Virgil, but his style owes much more to Ovid.[2] Lucan and Silius are fundamentally more Virgilian than Statius: Silius simply and avowedly so, Lucan as the poet of an epic that is, so to say, programmatically anti-Virgilian and that must be read as in a sense an answer to the *Aeneid*. Both write hexameters that resemble Ovid's much more than Virgil's. Neither could possibly be mistaken for Ovid: but whereas Lucan's verse atones in weight and dignity for what it lacks in speed and variety, Silius' is at best drearily efficient. Outside the epic tradition Ovid also left his mark on Juvenal, the best poetic craftsman (at his best) of the Silver Age.

Both in spirit and execution the most Ovidian of later Latin poets is Claudian, whose native tongue was Greek. The fact invites remark, since so much of Ovid's best work, above all the *Metamorphoses*, is Greek in matter, in manner, and even in versification.[3] For the Romans the legacy of Greek culture was a persistent problem with which in the end they never really came to terms. Virgil and Horace took the process of assimilation begun (essentially) by Ennius a stage further; Ovid, if he did not actually deflect the current, struck out a course of his own. In the *Aeneid* Greek and Roman elements were blended

---

[1] Kenney (1973).   [2] Vessey (1973) 11.
[3] Duckworth (1969) 73.

in a new and timeless synthesis; in the *Metamorphoses* Greek myth is translated and transposed into a contemporary idiom. The two poems demand from the reader a fundamentally different response. Without firsthand knowledge of (at least) Homer innumerable and essential resonances and implications in the *Aeneid* will simply be missed. The reader of the *Metamorphoses*, though he may relish in passing the contrast between Ovid's sources (if he chance to recognize them) and what Ovid made of them, does not depend on such recognition for the understanding and enjoyment of the poem. In this sense the *Metamorphoses* is more autonomous and more universal than the *Aeneid*; Ovid has rendered his models (almost) expendable. It is here that Ovid stands in truth between two worlds: his response to the riches of the Greek poetic imagination bore fruit, paradoxically, in a self-sufficient work of art that could serve, and in the Middle Ages perforce did serve, as a substitute for direct access.

This is the most important respect in which Ovid is 'un-Augustan'. A man of his sceptical and rationalist disposition growing up in the generation after Actium was bound, it might be surmised, to react against the Augustan 'myth' which was developing at this time and which depended heavily on an implicit and of course highly selective appeal to the authority of the past. Overt resistance is hardly to be detected in his work on any significant scale before the *Tristia*; the pin-pricks administered to official pomposity in the *Ars amatoria*[1] are hardly sufficient to identify its author as a dissident. So far as his poetry is concerned his reaction took the form of simply going his own way, which was the way of a poet to whom what mattered were individual human beings. It is this confidence in his fellow creatures, expressed with an exuberance and gaiety to which extant Latin literature offers no counterpart, that has chiefly recommended Ovid to the posterity on the ultimate rightness of whose judgement he has told us that he relied.

[1] Rudd (1976) 13–29; but cf. Holleman (1971).

8

LIVY

Internal evidence suggests that Livy began to write his History of Rome in or shortly before 29 B.C. by which time Octavian, the later Augustus, had restored peace and a measure of stability to the Roman world. A note in the *periocha* of Book 121 records that that book (and presumably those which followed) was published (*editus*) after Augustus' death in A.D. 14. The implication is that the last twenty books dealing with the events after the death of Cicero until 9 B.C. were an afterthought to the original plan and may also have been too politically controversial to be published in Augustus' lifetime.

The sheer scope of the undertaking is formidable, presupposing, as it does, the composition of three books a year on average. The introductions, especially to Books 6, 21 and 31, show that Livy began by composing and publishing in units of five books, the length of which was determined by the size of the ancient papyrus roll. As his material became more complex, this symmetrical pattern is less self-evident but it is likely that he maintained it. So far as can be reconstructed, the shape of the history was as follows (the lost books being in brackets).

   1–5 From the foundation of the city until the sack of Rome by the Gauls (386 B.C.)
   6–10 The Samnite Wars
[11–15 The conquest of Italy
 16–20 The First Carthaginian War]
 21–30 The Second Carthaginian War (until 201 B.C.)
 31–45 Events until the end of the war with Perseus (167 B.C.)
[46–50 The final subjugation of Greece and Asia
 51–60 Internal affairs from the fall of Carthage to the legislation of C. Gracchus
 61–70 The thirty years between Gracchus and M. Livius Drusus
 71–80 Civil Wars until the death of Marius (86 B.C.)
 81–90 Civil Wars until the death of Sulla (78 B.C.)
 91–100 The rise of Pompey to 66 B.C.
101–110 The dominance of Pompey
111–120 Civil War: from the death of Pompey to the death of Cicero (43 B.C.)

The final 22 books (perhaps unfinished on his death) comprised an appendix on contemporary events which was presumably not planned when he embarked on the main history.]

Historical activity had flourished at Rome for 200 years before Livy and the project of writing the complete history of the state was not a new one. But unlike his predecessors Livy was not a public figure. Whereas Q. Fabius Pictor, the elder Cato, L. Calpurnius Piso, C. Licinius Macer or Sallust himself had all been active in politics, Livy, so far as we know, held no office and took no part in affairs. This had certain consequences. His exclusion from the Senate and the magistracies meant that he had no personal experience of how the Roman government worked and this ignorance shows itself from time to time in his work (as at 1.32.12, or 3.40.5). It also deprived him of first-hand access to much material (minutes of Senate-meetings, texts of treaties, laws, the records of the priestly colleges, etc.) which was preserved in official quarters. But the chief effect is that Livy did not seek historical explanations in political terms. For others history was a political study, through which one might hope to explain or excuse the past and the present, but Livy saw history in personal and moral terms. The purpose is clearly set out in his Preface:

I invite the reader's attention to the much more serious consideration of the kind of lives our ancestors lived, who were the men and what the means, both in politics and war, by which Rome's power was first acquired and subsequently expanded: I would then have him trace the process of our moral decline, to watch first the sinking of the foundations of morality as the old teaching was allowed to lapse, then the final collapse of the whole edifice, and the dark dawning of our modern day when we can neither endure our vices nor face the remedies needed to cure them. The study of history is a fruitful medicine; for in history you have a record of the infinite variety of human experience plainly set out for all to see: and in that record you can find for yourself and your country both examples and warnings.

Livy was, indeed, acquainted with Augustus (Tacitus, *Annals* 4.34), who called him a Pompeian, which implied a conservative independence of outlook (Seneca, *Contr.* 10 *praef.* 5), and he acted as literary adviser to the future emperor Claudius (Suetonius, *Claudius* 41.1), but it is impossible to trace political motives in his writing. There is no sign of his attempting to justify, or to attack, the policies and aims of Augustus, although like any other creative writer, he does reflect to some extent contemporary preoccupations, such as the desire for peace, stability and liberty.

Although Sallust and earlier historians had also adopted the outlook that morality was in steady decline and had argued that people do the sort of things that they do because they are the sort of people that they are, that is, have the moral character that they have, for Livy these beliefs were a matter of passionate concern. He saw history in terms of human personalities and representative individuals rather than of partisan politics. And his own experience, going back perhaps to his youth in Padua, made him feel the moral evils of his time with peculiar intensity; for, like most Roman men of letters, he was a provincial and retained something of a provincial austerity in his attitude to life. He punctuates his history with such revealing comments as 'fortunately in those days authority, both religious and secular, was still a guide to conduct and there was as yet no sign of our modern scepticism which interprets solemn compacts to suit its own convenience' (3.20.5). Yet his attitude to religion is ambivalent. On the one hand he stresses, as in the history of Camillus, the importance of *pietas* and attributes disasters, such as the defeat of the Fabii at Cremera, to religious neglect. On the other, he frequently rationalizes miracles (e.g. the apotheosis of Romulus) and is sceptical about divine intervention in human affairs. Such a contradiction was not uncommon among educated Romans of his day: Caesar and Cicero showed it. But certainly, for Livy, human nature, not divinity, determines the course of human events.

In interpreting history in terms of individuals, Livy was following very much in the Hellenistic tradition. It goes back at least to Theopompus who, in his *Philippika*, organized his account of contemporary events round the person of Philip of Macedon. This was the approach even of Aristotle who defined history as being concerned with 'what Achilles did or suffered' (*Poet.* 1451b10), that is, with the particular doings of individuals, and we can presume that this was the character of the lost works by historians such as Ephorus and, later, Duris and Phylarchus. Interest in human character was predominant, as much in works such as Aristotle's *Nicomachean Ethics* or Theophrastus' *Characters* as in the biographies or biographical encomia which were a feature of the fourth and third centuries. But although Aristotle sharply differentiated drama from history, it was inevitable that some of his dramatic theory should be applicable to more general literary composition. There is no evidence that his successors developed a special Peripatetic or 'tragic' mode of writing history any more than they 'invented' biography, but Hellenistic historians do seem increasingly to have reworked their material in order to dramatize the individual.

Such an approach inevitably conditioned his historical technique. There was a wide range of source material at his disposal: the antiquarian researches of Atticus, Cicero's friend and correspondent, or M. Terentius Varro, whose *Human and divine antiquities* had been published perhaps in 46 B.C. And even if he did not have access to some documents, there were many manuscripts and inscriptions in Rome for all to see. Livy, by his own confession, did not explore such resources. His mission, as he saw it, was not to collect material – that was for the composer of *commentarii* – but to produce creative writing. So it should be no surprise that he shows no knowledge of Atticus or Varro, that he did not inspect the surviving inscriptions in the temples of Jupiter Feretrius (4.20) or Diana on the Aventine (1.45) or in the Comitium (4.17.2). Nor, if the careful analysis of scholars can be trusted, did he critically assess the historical accounts which were already at his disposal. He was content to have as a basis a narrative which he could elaborate and write up. What his practice was when dealing with contemporary history we are sadly unable to know, but with earlier history, certainly down to 100 B.C., he selected the more recent historians and simply reshaped and rewrote their material. For the very early period he seems to have relied on two main authors, Valerius Antias and C. Licinius Macer, who wrote in the aftermath of the Civil Wars of the 80s and interpreted earlier history in the light of their conflicting standpoints at the time. Antias was a political supporter of Sulla, Macer of Marius: both wrote history to justify and explain the present. Despite the fact that our knowledge derives only from fortuitous fragments, we can reconstruct the scale and character of their works. In the period of the mid-Republic he had Polybius to consult and, although for an educated Roman, who might be expected to be bilingual, he was demonstrably deficient in his knowledge of Greek, he made the fullest use of Polybius and we can in several passages make a detailed assessment of how he adapted and transformed him. This is of incalculable value in trying to view his own contribution to the composition of history. Polybius, as a Greek, was primarily interested in Graeco-Roman relations but Livy was able to turn to Antias and to two other Latin historians, L. Coelius Antipater and Q. Claudius Quadrigarius, for the raw material of Italian and western events.

His method was to follow one historian for a section, largely working from memory, and to switch to another when a particular theme had been exhausted. As an intelligent man he was indeed aware of the conflicts between his sources, and also of their individual prejudices, but he did not regard it as necessary or possible to unravel such discrepancies. A typical comment is (4.23.3): 'When so much is veiled in antiquity this fact also may remain uncertain.'

Given, therefore, the assumption that the most important thing about history is that people have a certain inherited personality (*ingenium*, cf. 3.36.1; Ap. Claudius) which determines their actions and that a historian can, even when the specific evidence is lacking, infer how someone of a certain character would have behaved in any given set of circumstances, Livy's aim was to construct a meaningful series of scenes. To understand how he does this it is necessary to remember that he, like his contemporaries, had been educated along almost exclusively rhetorical lines. That education involved learning how to compose a speech (whether forensic or merely ceremonial) and a major stage in any such speech was the essential business of expounding in the simplest possible terms the basic facts that led up to the present situation. The *narratio*, as it was called, is analysed by all the leading exponents of rhetorical training (e.g. *De inventione* 1.28; Cicero, *Orator* 122) and is perfected in such speeches as Cicero's *Pro Archia* (4–7). The requirements were three. A *narratio* should be brief (*breuis*), that is, it should not go into unnecessary preliminaries or diversions. It should be lucid (*aperta*), that is, it should be factually and chronologically coherent, even if this entailed the suppression or revision of some of the evidence. Above all, it should be plausible (*probabilis*), that is in particular the facts should be adjusted to the natures of the actors involved (*ad naturam eorum qui agent accommodabitur*). The whole technique, as has been indicated above, stems from the observations which Aristotle made in the *Poetics* about the necessary and sufficient qualities of a good plot in tragedy. Indeed Aristotle even went so far as to say that 'one could praise someone for doing something, even if there were no evidence, if he were the kind of person who might have done it' (*Rhet.* 1367).

It was this rhetorical background which enabled Livy, both on a practical level, to cope with the great undifferentiated mass of Roman historical happenings and, philosophically speaking, to make sense of it. The genre required of him that he should preserve to a large extent the annalistic framework, according to which, as in a chronicle, the events of every year were recorded, even down to the trivialities of prodigies and minor elections, but from these he selected certain topics which were inherently significant. In early Republican history this was relatively easy. Events were of a sufficiently short compass to form self-contained units in themselves. But even here Livy displayed his art of creating coherent episodes that revealed the character of the participants. Coriolanus, for instance, conducted his campaign against Rome over a number of years and led at least two separate expeditions against the walls of the city. In Livy's account two complete consular years are simply omitted and the two distinct expeditions are combined with an arbitrariness that makes as much geographical nonsense of the whole resulting narrative (2.33–40) as the two quite different routes combined for Hannibal's crossing of the Alps (21.31–7). But that narrative is, for the reader, brief, lucid and plausible, and, therefore, as a work of art, carries its own conviction. When Livy came on to deal with more extended episodes, such as the Hannibalic and Macedonian wars, the problem was on a very much greater scale. Yet, even so, one can see his instinct at work in shaping the material into manageable units, such as the siege of Abydus in 200 B.C. (31.17–18). One unifying factor in this process was to single out the special quality of the protagonist. Thus his account of the reign of Tullus Hostilius centres on the king' *ferocia* (a word which, with its derivatives, occurs nine times in as many chapters) and the events are tailored to bring out that characteristic. So Camillus is built up as an example of *pietas*; an undistinguished soldier, Tempanius, as an example as much of moderation as of bravery (4.40–1); Hannibal, as a model of perfidy and impetuosity; or Flamininus, as Polybius' very different picture of him makes very clear, as a sympathetic and philhellene man of action. On a less personal scale, the siege of Abydus is told in terms of madness (*rabies*, a word which occurs three times in Livy's account and for which there is no prompting in his source, Polybius). History was, for Livy, a psychological record.

One extended example will illustrate the technique. Livy 3.1–8 deals with a series of minor wars against the Aequi and Volsci, spread over five years. In themselves they are of no great significance. They are typical of the aimless happenings (γενόμενα) which Aristotle scorned as the raw material of history: they do not comprise an action, they are not a plot, they have no coherence, no end. Dionysius of Halicarnassus (9.58–71) relates the same facts from the same, or very similar, sources and a comparison between the two authors shows how Livy has handled the problem. In the first place he has concentrated on two basic themes – Rome's external relations both with the Aequi and Volsci and with her allies, and Rome's internal difficulties (e.g. plague, unrest) which affect those relations. As a result he omits a number of irrelevant details to be found in Dionysius: Aemilius' abortive invasion of Sabine land, Servilius' activities in 466 B.C., the dedication of the temple of Semo Sancus Dius Fidius, the fighting on the ramparts, the description of the walls of Rome, the abortive proposals of Sex. Titius. Secondly he tries to secure a natural and logical flow in the narrative so that each event seems to be motivated by its predecessor. One way of achieving this was to make one individual, Q. Fabius, responsible for much of the initiative. In Dionysius it is the Senate, in Livy Fabius who proposes the colony at Antium: in Dionysius it is the Senate, in Livy Fabius who offers peace-negotiations to the Aequi. In Dionysius the unrest at Antium in 464 B.C. is quite unmotivated: Livy attributes it to the Aequi and Volsci stirring up feeling among the former inhabitants who have been dispossessed by the colony. Unlike Dionysius, Livy makes the plague the direct cause of the Roman inability to help their allies, and transfers the account of the combined attack by Aequi and Volsci on Tusculum from 462 to 463 B.C. in order to simplify and smooth the chain of events in 462 B.C. These are all small points: collectively they bring order out of chaos. But even in the details Livy is at pains to make the narrative coherent. Dionysius made the Romans retreat in 465 B.C. because their swords were blunt – a charming detail, but improbable, and omitted by Livy. Dionysius asserts that in 463 B.C., when the plague was at its height, the allies arrived to ask for help from the Senate on the very day that the consul died and the senators were carried into the senate-house on stretchers. That is too melodramatic for Livy's purpose. Finally Livy unites all the events of these five years by a common thread – the clemency (*clementia*) and good faith (*fides*) of the Romans (3.2.5, 6.5, 7.4, 7.5) against the treachery (*perfidia*) and vindictiveness (*odium*) of the Aequi and Volsci (3.2.4, 2.6, 2.12, 7.1). These moral overtones are not in Dionysius and they serve to give the whole section unity and significance. Livy pays the highest attention to the literary structure of each episode and this determines his selection and emphasis of the details.

But the enormous field of history which he had set himself to cover raised further problems. How was the interest of the reader to be sustained over all 142 books? Quintilian characterized his style as possessing a 'milky richness' (10.1.32, *lactea ubertas*) which might be thought to imply the measured pace of a Gibbon, but, in fact, Livy is remarkable for the extreme range of styles which he uses in his narrative in order to achieve variety. At one moment, when recounting essentially perfunctory details he will use a matter-of-fact style, with stock vocabulary and the minimum of syntactical subordination. A major episode, such as the battle of Cannae, Trasimene or Cynoscephalae, will have its own unity. There will be the indication of a temporal break (e.g. *sub idem forte tempus* 'about the same time') and a summary of the scene and the actors (e.g. 2.31.5 *erat tum inter castra iuuenis Cn. Marcius nomine* 'there was in the camp at the time a young man called Cn. Marcius'). Then will follow a series of complicated sentences which set out the preliminary dispositions, often with participial clauses explaining the motives and thoughts of the chief figures. The action will be described in the stereotyped language of a military communiqué (especially the use of the impersonal passive) or short, staccato sentences, employing the historic infinitive or historic present. Finally, in describing the climax or its aftermath, Livy will allow his language to be coloured with words which (such was the particularity of the Latin stylistic tradition) could normally only have been used in heroic poetry. A terse comment – *haec eo anno acta* 'this happened that year' – will round off the episode. By this variation Livy was able to convey an impression not only of the military facts but also of the emotional experience of the participants.

Livy's language has been much studied and the publication of a complete *Concordance*[1] has opened new doors for the appreciation of his verbal sensitivity, such as, for example, the realization that he uses the exclamation '*o*' only once in the surviving books, in the solemn reply of the Delphic oracle to Brutus and the Tarquins (1.56.10). If Livy's concern was to see history as the literary embodiment of individuals, then his success depended to a very large extent on making those historical characters come alive and sound authentic. Earlier historians – Thucydides, Xenophon, Philistus – had been criticized for putting speeches into the mouths of their leading characters which did not truly bring out their individuality (Dionysius of Halicarnassus, *ad Pomp.* 3.20 *et al.*), but Livy, as he himself says, was able to enter into the spirit of his characters (43.13.2 *mihi uetustas res scribenti nescio quo pacto antiquus fit animus*). The climax of any episode is often a passage of direct or indirect speech, which characterizes the chief actor. In the passage analysed above (Livy 3.1–8) one of the high-

---

[1] Packard (1968).

lights occurs when the Aequi taunt the Romans with being cowards. The speaker uses *ne* with the imperative for a prohibition (*ne timete* 'be not a-feared'), an archaic and poetical usage. He also strengthens a common taunt (*ostendere bellum* 'to make a show of fighting') by substituting the much rarer and more forceful frequentative *ostentare*. The effect is subtle and suggestive. Sometimes the idiom will be coarse and colloquial if the speakers are lower-class. Again, a rough citizen from Aricia, Turnus Herdonius, who was described by Livy as a seditious criminal (1.50.7 *seditiosus facinerosusque homo*) inveighs against Tarquinius Superbus in a bitter repartee which includes the word *infortunium* 'hard luck', not found elsewhere in classical prose authors but common in the slave-talk of Plautus and Terence. Or some embittered tribunes of the people complain that the patricians thwart their ambitions at every turn (4.35.5–11) using several expressions found also only in colloquial context (e.g. *sugillari* 'to rebuff', *praebere os* 'to expose oneself to'). Sometimes when the occasion is one of high drama Livy will allow his speakers to use language more associated with poetry than prose. Thus the climax of the story of Coriolanus is the great scene with his mother at the gates of Rome. She speaks to him, as Jocasta to her sons in Greek tragedy, and her speech contains several unique features which stamp it as tragic (2.40.5–7): *sino* 'I allow' with the subjunctive rather than the accusative and infinitive, *quamuis* 'although' with the indicative (only here in Livy), the rare *senecta* for *senectus* 'old age', the phrase *ira cecidit* 'anger subsided' found elsewhere only in the poets.

As he moved on to history of more recent times, Livy, inevitably, did not characterize his speakers quite so graphically. In consequence there has been thought to be a development away from the highly coloured vocabulary of the speeches of Books 1–10. But this does not reflect any fundamental change of style. It is simply that the protagonists of the late third century were nearer in time to Livy and he made them speak more like orators of his own day. Indeed some of their actual speeches, such as Cato's *On the Rhodians*, survived and were on hand to be utilized. Nevertheless Livy, at least in the surviving books, maintained his practice of using speeches to bring out the character of the actors. A good example of this is the interchange between Philip and M. Aemilius over the siege of Abydus (31.18.2–3). Polybius preserves a version of their conversation but Livy rewrites it in more powerful language, which gives a grandeur to Philip that was lacking in the original, and makes it the turning-point of the episode. Philip's brief words contain a striking *tricolon*, two notable clausulae (*ferociorem facit, sentietis*), two effective alliterations (*ferociorem facit, nomen...nobile*) and a dramatic use of the present tense instead of the future in a future conditional clause. One can *hear* him speak. In fact detailed research into Livy's latinity in recent years makes it evident that, as far as we can tell from the surviving portions of his work, he continued both to pay special attention to the language of speeches and to employ more generally a vocabulary that was appropriate to the genre of historical writing, as Coelius Antipater and Sallust had sophisticated it. Such a vocabulary was bound, from the nature of the subject matter, to contain its fair share of archaic or unusual words.

Livy was criticized stylistically by a contemporary for his 'Patauinitas' (Paduanness: Quint. *Inst.* 1.5.56, 8.1.3). The point of the criticism eludes us, but perhaps it did concern his use of such wide-ranging vocabulary in his speeches. Certainly no other Roman historian was so inventive.

9

MINOR FIGURES

1. POETRY

The poetic output of Augustan times was prolific. Sadly, however, we have lost the works of several important figures – Varius, Aemilius Macer, Valgius Rufus, Domitius Marsus. Our evidence for them is poor, their fragments scanty or lacking. Nonetheless we can see that the genres were well subscribed, and of some we have considerable remains. In didactic, we have the works of Grattius and Manilius; for the minor Alexandrian forms, we can point to the *Appendix Vergiliana*. Horace, especially in his hexameter works, tells us a certain amount about the literary scene – about Fundanius, Titius and Iullus Antonius for instance – and Virgil's *Eclogues* help to reconstruct the literary atmosphere of the triumviral period, when the work of Calvus and Cinna was still in vogue, and new poets like Varius and Pollio were emerging. For later times, when the flush of enthusiasm for experiment had died away, leaving openings for reversion, or else a pale and standardized reflection of the poetics of Callimachus, our evidence is the poetry of Ovid's exile, which often gives us little more than names, but at least serves to show that verse was not in short supply at Rome. Several writers attempted more than one literary form; but in what follows, the attempt has been made as far as possible to group authors according to genre. First of all, the *Appendix Vergiliana* and other minor forms are discussed, especially epigram and elegy; then didactic, mythological epic and tragedy, other drama, and finally historical epic.

First then, the minor poems attributed to Virgil, the so-called *Appendix Vergiliana*. Donatus, probably drawing on Suetonius, attributed a *Dirae*, Servius and Charisius, a *Copa*: but we have to wait until the ninth century before we hear of a *Moretum*. All three works (four in fact; the *Dirae*, a series of curses, is succeeded at line 103 by an independent love lament, the *Lydia*) look like productions of the Augustan age: none of them pretends to be by Virgil. A realistic vignette of country life, the *Moretum*, like most of the poems in the collection, is an example of later Roman Alexandrianism. Its subject allies it to compositions such as Callimachus' *Hecale*, where the poet recounted Theseus' humble entertainment in the house of an old woman; Ovid's Philemon and Baucis episode in *Metamorphoses* Book 8 is of the same type.[1] Its style is patchwork, but accomplished, sometimes self-consciously prosaic and circumstantial, sometimes mock-heroic and poetic: above all, it has movement. The main affinity is with pastoral, but not that of Virgil, even given his brief description of the preparation of a salad at *Ecl.* 2.10–11. Theocritus, with his realistic bucolics and mimes, provides a better parallel. In the earlier first century, probably the seventies, Sueius had written a *Moretum* too: Macrobius, who quotes eight lines, calls it an idyll, further proof of the Theocritean affiliations of the type.[2] A Greek source may have been used: a poem about a salad (μυττωτός) is linked, somewhat dubiously, with Gallus' client Parthenius.[3] But mannerism of the kind found in our *Moretum* – a mixture of mime and pastoral – could have been an indigenous creation, in Ovid's time, at any rate. Virgilian, or early Augustan authorship is ruled out by the poem's vocabulary, and metrical fluency: there are no fewer than sixty-nine non-Virgilian words in the piece, amongst them *excubitor* (2), and only nineteen elisions in one hundred and twenty-two hexameters. Dating is more or less decided by an epigram of Martial, 13.13, where it is said that whereas our grandfathers ate lettuce at the end of a meal, now it is consumed at the beginning. Since *Moretum* 76, *grataque nobilium requies lactuca ciborum*, agrees with the earlier habit, the poem cannot be later than the reign of Nero – especially if, as has been argued, Columella used it – and, on a stricter interpretation of Martial's *auorum*, is probably closer to the turn of the century. In the *Copa*, an invitation to drink occasioned by thoughts of human mortality, Propertian elegy consorts with pastoral. It has been disputed whether the bucolic debt is to Virgil or Theocritus – the *Copa* echoes the second *Eclogue*, and beyond that, *Idylls* 7 and 11 – but our most likely candidate is Virgil.[4] Imitations of Propertius' fourth book date the piece after 16–15 B.C., and therefore after Virgil's death.[5] We need not look much later: polysyllabic pentameter endings indicate a poet unconcerned about Ovidian elegiac technique, a conscious archaist who wished to adapt pastoral formulae to the uneven Propertian couplet.

Callimachus and Euphorion, with their curse poems, Ἀραί and Ἀραὶ ἢ Ποτηριοκλέπτης – Ovid's *Ibis* is a later example of the type – are the formal antecedents of the Virgilian *Dirae*: not that the poem is by Virgil himself. But

[1] See Hollis (1970) ad loc.

[2] See *FPL* 53; Macrob. 3.18.11. For the poem's realism (e.g. its depiction of the old negress) cf. the epigrams of Leonidas of Tarentum, Gow–Page (1965) I 107–39 and II 307–98. For the element of parody, Ross (1975b) 254–63.

[3] By a fifteenth-century Ambrosian manuscript, which tells us *Parthenius moretum scripsit in Graeco quem Vergilius imitatus est.*

[4] See Drew (1923) 73–81, and (1925) 37–42.

[5] See Wilamowitz (1924) I 311–15. Note *Copa* 29 and Prop. 4.8.37, and especially 18–22, and 4.2. 13–16; also 15–16, and 3.13.29–30. *Cineri ingrato*, 35, is from Virg. *Aen* 6.213. Drew (above), like Drabkin (1930), with their conviction of Virgilian authorship, are forced into making Propertius the imitator.

unlike the *Copa* and *Moretum*, this piece should be regarded as a conscious variation on a theme from Virgil: another mixed composition, this time pastoral and curse, the *Dirae* borrows its theme from *Eclogues* 1 and 9, recounting to its addressee, Battarus, the depredations of one Lycurgus, a veteran newcomer. Virgil had supplied the hint: *quod nec uertat bene* (*Ecl.* 9.6). Varius has been claimed as its author, as well as Valerius Cato: but difficulty of construction, even given the state of the tradition, unconvincing pastoral mannerism, and passages of inapposite inflation rule out an accomplished craftsman. Since the question of the confiscations was of particular interest to later generations we cannot argue from simple topicality towards an early date; but the fact that our poet is not expressly creating Virgilian juvenilia – for which there was a demand once the poet achieved celebrity – at least leaves room for that. Response to Virgil's *Eclogues*, whether immediate or not, has left us with a mediocre exercise, devoid of bearing on actual events.

Our manuscripts make no distinction between the *Dirae*, and the eighty hexameters of pastoral love lament which follow. It is not clear whether the *Lydia* was written as a sequel to the *Dirae*, where the poet's mistress had the same name, or was accidentally appended to the curse poem through a process of association. If it is a sequel, the *Lydia* need have no more relationship to the *Dirae* than the *Dirae* to the *Eclogues*; it is certainly unnecessary to postulate that its author accepted the *Dirae* as Virgilian and inserted references there to his own Lydia, then, thirsty for anonymous fame, appended his love poem simply in order that Virgil's name might ensure its preservation. But apart from the name, which was common enough, there is little reason to link the two poems: since there is no external support for a Virgilian *Lydia*, the confusion with the *Dirae*, accidental or not, probably took place in antiquity. Valerius Cato has again been favoured for authorship: but his *Lydia*, one of the most celebrated products of Republican literature, would surely have maintained a separate identity. Our poem, with its refrains, spondaic hexameter endings, and measured repetitions looks reasonably early: it could be Augustan. Its Alexandrianism and pastoral colour align it generically with the *Copa*, *Moretum*, and *Dirae*: smoother and more accomplished than the latter, it was probably written around the turn of the century, towards the end of the wave of enthusiasm for neoteric poetry.

Donatus and Servius assign Virgil a *Ciris*, presumably ours. Another Alexandrian composition, this time of decidedly non-Virgilian colour, the *Ciris* cannot be authentic, not only because of the circumstances of its author – a retired politician dedicated to philosophy[1] – but also because everything points to its having imitated, not inspired, all three canonical works: when

---

[1] See 1ff., 14ff. In his middle years, Virgil was employed on the *Georgics* and *Aeneid*. Why our author chooses to supply this biographical information is unclear.

paralleled by the *Ciris*, Virgil is generally better, that is – for poetry of this kind – earlier.[1] Furthermore, its clumsy imitations of Catullus and Lucretius are improbable a mere decade after publication: fifty years later, they might make sense.[2] Our author also seems to have imitated Ovid, and maybe Manilius: but once we pass A.D. 8, we run into problems over the identity of the poem's addressee – Messalla, the patron of Tibullus, who died in that year.[3] After that, we must find some descendant: Messalinus, born 42 B.C., has been canvassed, but it is not very likely that the *Ciris* was composed after Messalla's death. A date roughly contemporary with Ovid's *Metamorphoses* is probably our best choice. The poem's style is remarkably consistent with that of the Republican epyllion: spondaic line endings (e.g. *Amphitrites* 72, *latratus* 82, *ulciscendum* 158) are frequent, as are diminutives (*hortulus* 3, *paruulus* 138 and 479, *tabidulus* 182, *frigidulus* 251 and 348, *nutricula* 257 and 277, *lectulus* 440, *labella* 496: an especially non-Virgilian characteristic), excess in the use of colour terms (e.g. *purpureos…soles* 37), invocations, digressions (e.g. on the different versions of the myth, 54ff.: a very Alexandrian touch), exotic geographical and aetiological allusions, explanatory parentheses, long, ramshackle sentences – twice the average length of Virgil's – and congested speeches. Uneven and archaistic in his style, the author's morbid subject matter and quirky narrative technique are likewise throwbacks: Scylla's betrayal of her father, unrequited love for Minos, and final metamorphosis are indirectly and disjointedly recounted with the static pathos and histrionic gestures of Catullus in his sixty-fourth poem and presumably a dozen neoteric contemporaries.[4] Yet amidst these hallmarks of Republican Alexandrianism are embedded the tell-tale imitations of later work.[5] Our author does not impersonate Virgil; nor is he a *Vergilianus poeta*.[6] What we have in the *Ciris* is a genuine neoteric

[1] For example, cf. *Ciris* 59ff. and *Ecl.* 6.74ff., 538–41 and *Geo.* 1.406–9, 402–3 and *Aen.* 2.405–6, 474 and *Aen.* 3.74. *Ciris* 280 '*aut ferro hoc*': *aperit ferrum quod veste latebat*, is an interesting line, easier and more obvious than *Aen.* 6.406 '*at ramum hunc*': *aperit ramum qui ueste latebat*: perhaps a common source?

[2] Cf. *Ciris* 1ff., and Catull. 65.1ff.; 16ff., and Lucr. 2.9ff.

[3] Note that *Catalepton* 9 is likewise addressed to Messalla: though that is probably mere coincidence, despite the arguments of P. Jahn (1908), who wants a common author.

[4] In particular, note Ovid's version of the story of Io in *Met.* 1, probably in imitation of Calvus.

[5] After Virgil, the most frequent imitations are of Ovid: note, for instance, *Ciris* 285 *questus anilis* and *Met.* 9.276; also the frequency of Ovidian words absent from Virgil – though found in other writers – for example, *charta, libido, ocellus, releuo, tribuo.* In all, 142 non-Virgilian terms have been counted, many of them Ovidian: note for instance *alumna*, used a surprising twelve times. But the negative argument fails to convince. Manilius 5.569 *felix ille dies*, if it is the source and not the progeny of *Ciris* 27, begins to point to a later date, although the phrase looks formulaic. Obviously much depends on Stat. *Silv.* 1.4.120ff., if that is the source of *Ciris* 478–80; but there again Statius could be the imitator. Lyne (1971) has collected a great deal of first-century A.D. material, while arguing for a later date, but much of it could be common stock, or else inspired by our poem. An Augustan dating is not in principle necessary – after all epyllion was still being written in the time of Persius – but the identity of the addressee then poses real problems.

[6] For the term, see Lee *ap.* Herescu (1958) 457–71.

survival, written according to the principles of Catullus, probably before the death of Messalla, another chapter in the history of Alexandrianism, and archaism, at Rome.

We are left with the *Culex*, a humorous pseudo-narrative displaying some features of epyllion technique – unlike the *Ciris* it does pretend to be by Virgil – and the *Catalepton*, a collection of fifteen epigrams some of which may in fact be authentic. The only substantial forgery of the *Appendix*, the *Culex* was written to parallel the supposedly Homeric *Battle of frogs and mice*, a *praelusio* to greater work. Obvious echoes of the *Aeneid*, an unlikely prophecy of more important work to come, and a mock address to Octavian, the future Augustus, combine to indict this second-rate poem as the work of a *Vergilius personatus*, some schoolboy or grammarian who wished to align Virgil's early career with that of Homer. Yet Lucan, Statius, Martial, and Suetonius were all deceived: libraries must have been careless, critical examination scant. Not much happens during the course of the poem. A gnat warns a sleeping shepherd of the onslaught of a monstrous snake, is killed for its pains, appears, like the ghost of Patroclus, from the nether world, tells of its experiences there, in a long, inapposite νέκυια (the Roman heroes of the *Aeneid* have no bearing on the theme) and is awarded a tumulus for its merits. Catalogues abound; the narrative is static, the texture of the writing too smooth for the pretended date. Phrases occur which are otherwise first attested in the *Aeneid*, for example *hinc atque hinc*;[1] also, Ovid is imitated: *Culex* 133 *perfide Demophoon*, corresponds to *Rem. Am.* 597.[2] We cannot say much more than that our poet wrote before Lucan, and after Ovid – and, since time was needed for the acceptance of the impersonation, that a late Augustan date is more likely than early Imperial.

Virgilian authorship is claimed by external sources for the whole *Catalepton* – a title used, incidentally, by Aratus for a collection of short poems – and the testimony for the second piece – Quintilian, *Inst.* 8.3.27–9 – is relatively early. We can eliminate the final poem, which also makes that claim (*illius haec quoque sunt diuini elementa poetae*, 15.5), on the grounds that Virgil would hardly have produced such a poem so late in his career – after the unfinished *Aeneid* – as his last word on a body of material, some of which is demonstrably unauthentic, or else the kind of thing he would probably not have wished on posterity. The fifteenth poem is clearly the work of an editor, the man who brought the collection together, from whatever sources. Another forgery is 14, which purports to have been written while the *Aeneid* was still being composed, a vow of dedication to Venus if ever the epic is finished, suspect for the blandness of its style and unlikely psychology. Stylistic grounds also disqualify

---

[1] Twice in the *Culex*, eight times in the *Aeneid*, but we have lost much Latin poetry.

[2] Note also that *letare, Cul.* 325, is not used in Latin poetry until Ovid, and that *Cul.* 181 *sanguineae guttae* probably depends on *Met.* 2.358ff., although the phrase could be a formula.

the third poem, a wooden piece on the mutability of fortune, probably the thirteenth, an epode in the Horatian manner, and most certainly the ninth, a laborious, ill-structured panegyric of Messala. Of these, the last two are Augustan, but un-Virgilian: poem 3, on the other hand, is severe and prosaic in style, insufficiently ornate to be early, and rhetorical enough to belong to the first century. Alexander is not its subject: he was never exiled (line 8). Phraates and Mithridates were hardly world-conquerors (line 3): so perhaps we should opt for a Roman magnate – Pompey, preferably. Antony needs special pleading – he was not exactly exiled – even though he was more of a menace to Rome.

If the thirteenth poem had been included in Horace's *Epodes*, nobody would have been surprised. Its metre – alternating trimeter and dimeter – is Horatian, as much as its realistic vocabulary and scurrilous tone: its twenty-four non-Virgilian words are not the best argument against authenticity in view of its genre,[1] but if Virgil had ever written such an anomalous piece we would probably have heard so; and Virgil, unlike the author of the epigram, was never a soldier. No firm date can be assigned; even the name of its addressee is in doubt – Bücheler's suggestion, *Lucienus*, does not help in dating – and although the *collegia compitalia*, referred to in line 27, were disbanded in 46 B.C., they were restored by Augustus. All we can say is that since the poem must have been written after the *Epodes*, it must therefore follow the restoration of the *collegia*; also that its skilful author's relationship to Horace is similar to that of the writer of the *Dirae* to Virgil. A recently established form provides the impulse for an excursion into fashionable territory.

Messalla's triumph over the Aquitani, the event eulogized in *Catalepton* 9,[2] and known only too well from Tibullus, took place in 27 B.C.: since forgery and hence backdating are not in question, we may assign the piece to that year. Virgil is ruled out by the poem's extreme clumsiness,[3] his lack of connexion with the protagonist, and the fact that the author intends to turn some of Messalla's Greek pastorals into Latin:[4] now engaged on the *Aeneid*, Virgil would hardly have thought of being sidetracked into such a venture. The writer has learned something from Propertius – particularly noteworthy is the long, obscurely-phrased list of heroines beginning at line 25 – and besides the *Eclogues* and *Georgics* he knows Catullus, and the pseudo-Tibullan *Panegyricus*

---

[1] *inedia* and *turgidos*, l. 40, for example, have an iambic colour. Carcopino (1922) 164, notes that *Thybris*, l. 23, is a form which occurs 17 times in the *Aeneid*, but never in the *Eclogues* or *Georgics*: if it is a Virgilian epic innovation then we should begin our searches later on. But there is no reason to turn to Ovid, as do Hubaux (1930) and Radford (1928).

[2] The author knows the rules for Panegyric, as at, e.g. *Rhet. ad Her.* 3.11ff.

[3] Note the coincidence of the poem's opening with that of *Ecl.* 10 and the parallel between 17 and *Ecl.* 1.1.

[4] Strangely, Messalla seems to have written in Attic, not Doric; l. 14. He also translated Hyperides into Latin.

Messallae of 31 B.C.[1] A high proportion of his pentameters end in convenient polysyllables, and sometimes contain elisions; his structure is fluid and incoherent – the end of the poem is particularly loose – and his vocabulary is sparse, repetitive, and prosaic.[2] Our author is as inept as he is anonymous: better, then, not to insult Ovid, Propertius, or even Lygdamus, with claims for authorship.[3]

Next, a group of poems directly addressed to three of Virgil's associates: Octavius Musa, a historian who was involved in the land disputes around Mantua, and Varius and Tucca, Virgil's later editors. Given their themes, as well as their addressees, we can tentatively assume these poems to be genuine, part of Virgil's output in the forties. For none of them, apart from 4, is especially ambitious; none of them handles obvious or expected material.[4] The first, to Tucca, and the seventh, to Varius, are light, erotic pieces: the first is based on some local scandal, its point at first sight somewhat unclear: the seventh, in a context of homosexual love, raises the question whether Latin poetry should admit Greek words. Strict topicality is the key: a forger would hardly have bothered to invent so obscure an occasion for the epigram to Tucca, or so trivial and local a point for the poem to Varius. Octavius Musa, the little-known recipient of epigrams 4 and 11, was not the obvious choice: nothing is said about his *History*, nothing about his connexions with Mantua. A forger would have been more likely to choose Pollio or Varus. In all four poems, everything squares with authenticity: the metrical technique is early, the style mainly unassuming and akin to that of Catullus. And in particular, as we have said, no forger worth his salt would have dared provide an inquisitive audience with so little information about Virgil's youth. Our sole hesitation might be over the possibility that the verses were composed by a contemporary of Virgil with common associates, to be later reassigned by some well-meaning scholar or editor.

Epigrams 5, in scazons, and 8, in couplets, are more obviously autobiographical, therefore the more likely to have been forged. Siro, Virgil's teacher, figures in both. But this time, the contexts are expected, the style more elaborate and daring: in 5, 'Virgil' bids farewell to rhetoric and poetry in favour of philosophy; in 8, Siro's villa is hailed as a refuge from the evictions. Immediate suspicion is provoked by the subject matter of 8, and to a lesser degree by that of 5: the poems could all too easily be by a youthful Virgil – but there is no final court of appeal. The second epigram, on the other hand, can hardly be

[1] For the Tibullan parallel, see Sonner (1910).
[2] In particular, our author overworks *carmen, maximus,* and *uincere*; amongst his prosaisms, note 7 *nec minus idcirco*; 14 *cum...tum*; 24 *altera non...dixerit*; 56 *quin ausim hoc etiam dicere*.
[3] See Westendorp Boerma's commentary (1949) for details.
[4] A forger would hardly have resisted reference to the land confiscations in the epigrams to Musa, nor to their editorial activities in the poems to Varius and Tucca.

a forgery – though it need not be by Virgil – referring as it does to the archaizing fad of the forties, and in particular, to the taste for Thucydides which emerged at that time. We have no special reason to link Virgil with Annius Cimber, the poem's offending and criminal rhetorician: but at least we have a genuine, if obscure, product of the forties.

Catullus is the main influence on the sixth and twelfth epigrams, as on the tenth, a parody of the *phaselus* poem, number 4 in our collection. In the first two, fairly straightforward abusive exercises, a certain Noctuinus is assailed: once more obscurity of occasion perhaps rules out a forger – although it does not guarantee Virgilian authorship. And if Sabinus, the muleteer recipient of the parody *Catalepton* 10, is Ventidius Bassus, that poem too belongs to the forties: Bassus, friend of Caesar and *consul suffectus* in 43, was lampooned as an upstart by Cicero, Plancus, and the populace at large (Cic. *Fam.* 15.20 and Gell. 15.4). We are left with the insignificant 13, an epitaph on a literary man, of uncertain date, and three Priapic poems. Although Donatus and Servius may have thought Virgil wrote the whole of the *Priapea*, an entirely separate collection, probably compiled by one author in the late first century A.D.,[1] the three poems in question were chosen in antiquity for inclusion with the *Catalepton*. Their main distinguishing characteristic is their bucolic colour, taken from the *Eclogues*:[2] probably Augustan, they are unlikely to be the work of Virgil himself.

Tradition further ascribes a pair of elegies on the death of Maecenas, neither of them the work of any great talent: Scaliger is responsible for first noticing that the continuous elegy of the manuscripts should be divided into two. Whoever composed the first poem had also written an *epicedion* for some young man:

defleram iuuenis tristi modo carmine fata:
sunt etiam merito carmina danda seni.   (*Eleg. Maec.* 1.12)

My saddened muse of late had mourned a young man's death: now to one ripe in years also let songs be duly offered. (Tr. J. Wight Duff)

An obvious, but not inevitable, candidate for the *iuuenis* is Drusus, whose death in 9 B.C. antedated that of Maecenas by a year. Virgil, who died in 19 B.C., has never been a serious contender for the poem – at least not since the Middle Ages. But what of Ovid? That question is, unfortunately, posed by the couplet just quoted, since under Ovid's name has been transmitted a *Consolatio ad Liviam*, a lament on the death of Drusus. Though tedious, the *Consolatio* is better than either of the *Elegiae*, and is most unlikely to be the *epicedion* of the first elegy's first couplet. It could be the work of an Ovid composing in more official vein – but we need posit no more than influence: in terms of its conceits, its rhetorical deployment of ideas, the poem prefigures Lucan.

[1] See Buchheit (1962) and Kenney's review (1963).   [2] See Galletier (1920) 25f.

The *elegiae*, on the other hand, are not especially Ovidian, and the patchwork mythology at the end of the first is clearly the work of a bungler.[1] In neither case can we really talk of deliberate imitation: there is no conscious attempt to produce a particular style or tone, no feeling for language or metre, no ability to control a conceit, or work from within the material chosen.

Were it not for the reference at 1.9–10 to Lollius, Consul in 20 B.C., dead in 1 B.C., there would be little reason for adhering to an Augustan date.[2] Indeed, the depiction of the *princeps* at 1.163–4 smacks more of early Imperial hindsight than of the times of Augustus himself:

> Caesar amicus erat: poterat uixisse solute,
> cum iam Caesar idem quod cupiebat erat.

The Emperor was Maecenas' friend: so he was free to live a life of ease when the Emperor was all he longed to be.

Moreover, the portrait of Maecenas is very much a stereotype, the kind of thing an aspiring poet might find in a textbook – so much so, that it has been argued that the poem is a rebuttal of Seneca's charges in the rhetorical picture of his one hundred and fourteenth letter.[3] But then again, myths were fast to grow in Rome, and the life style of Maecenas was notorious in his own day.

Another point needs making: whoever wrote the first elegy did not necessarily write the second. Indeed, the second poem – a monologue by the dying Maecenas which looks for all the world like a fragment of something longer[4] – is more rhetorical, somewhat more obscure, and altogether more sparse and prosaic in its style. There is nothing to link it to names or events. The fact that the phrase *Caesaris illud opus*, line 6, also occurs at line 39 of the *Consolatio* says nothing about authorship. As in the case of the cliché shared by *Eleg.* 1.7 and *Cons.* 372, *illa rapit iuuenes*, the parallel could be the result of imitation, or even a formula of common stock; there is certainly no point in pressing verbal similarity to yield a common author. It seems most likely that both the *Consolatio* and the first elegy are genuine products of occasion, no matter how far they differ in terms of literary quality, while the second elegy may be no more than an exercise of the schools, of uncertain date at that.

Another poem transmitted as being by Ovid is the *Nux*, a complaint by a nut tree of its ill-omened fertility. Our piece is quite well managed, an expansion

---

[1] Bickel (1950) goes so far as to conclude that the end of the first elegy, from 107ff., is a separate poem.

[2] Unless, of course, we are dealing with a different Lollius; in which case we could give more weight to 'parallels' with Ovid's poetry of exile.

[3] See, e.g., Haupt (1875) I 347, developed by Birt (1877) 66, and Steele (1933).

[4] *sic est Maecenas fato ueniente locutus* is a strangely abrupt way to begin a poem.

from an epigram in the *Greek Anthology* where a nut tree tells how it is perpetually bombarded by greedy passers-by. It is most unlikely that the lament in any way reflects on Ovid's fate – undeservingly suffering punishment in exile. But the question of allegory apart, the author of the *Nux* can on occasions sound very much like the genuine Ovid, as, for instance, at lines 107–8:

> fructus obest, peperisse nocet, nocet esse feracem;
> quaeque fuit multis, ei mihi, praeda mala est.

My fruit is my bane, it is harmful to bear, it is harmful to be fertile; gain, which has hurt many, has hurt me too. (Tr. J. H. Mozley)

But as Lee points out in his article on authenticity, the author is more likely to be an *Ovidianus poeta* – a conscious imitator of a distinctive style – than Ovid himself.[1] Criteria are unstable: Lee demonstrates that 'un-Ovidian' diction is to be found in the genuine Ovid, hence the thirteen 'singletons' of the *Nux* should not sway the argument; likewise, un-Ovidian phrasing is of little help – except in the case of the poem's 'high frequency of *at*, the prosaic use of *aliquando*...the use of *quilibet* in a series of distributive clauses, and of *sic*...*sic*...*sic ego* in a series of comparisons, possibly too *aliquis*...*hic*... *hic*...*est quoque*'.[2] We are on slightly firmer ground when it comes to imitation: as Lee shows, *Met.* 8.747 and 14.663–4 are more likely to be the origin than the progeny of *Nux* 35–6, which in turn is more likely to be the work of an anonymous imitator, since it uses two expressions in a non-Ovidian way, than the work of Ovid himself. Similar conclusions are to be drawn from the parallelism between *Tristia* 5.5.17–18 and *Nux* 165–6 – the latter a conceit about the beaver's self-castration – though less should be made of *Heroides* 1.55 and *Nux* 127–8. Finally, there is the parallel between Silius 15.484–7 and the passage about the beaver, where probabilities are loaded in favour of Silius' priority. In the *Nux*, then, we have an accomplished poem, the work of someone who had mastered Ovid's style, who most likely lived towards the end of the first century A.D.

In the field of erotic elegy, it is not only the work of Gallus that we have lost. C. Valgius Rufus, *consul suffectus* in 12 B.C., besides his treatises on herbs and grammar, wrote lachrymose elegies, only to be recommended the epic: Horace's invitation is backed up by the *Panegyricus Messallae*, which implies that Valgius actually tried the grand manner. Of his dirges on the boy Mystes we know no more than is implied by Hor. *Odes* 2.9 – that they were plaintive, and somewhat dreary. But that he was not simply a second Tibullus, intent solely on his love, is shown by the most important fragment, fr. 2, which praises the poetry of Codrus, the shadowy bard of the *Eclogues*:

[1] Lee, *ap.* Herescu (1958) 457–71.
[2] Ibid. 463–4.

Codrusque ille canit, quali tu uoce canebas
atque solet numeros dicere, Cinna, tuos,
dulcior ut numquam Pylio profluxerit ore
Nestoris aut docto pectore Demodoci

. . .

. . .

falleris insanus quantum si gurgite nauta
Crisaeae quaerat flumina Castaliae.

*Codrus sings with the strains that you once used, and the measures that Cinna favoured,
the like of which never flowed more sweetly from the mouth of Pylian Nestor or the
breast of learned Demodocus . . .*

*You are wrong and mad, as if a sailor were to seek the waters of Castalia in the depths
of the sea.*

Like Propertius, Valgius shows that he can handle afresh the water imagery of
Callimachus, recreating the atmosphere of Alexandria in the midst of Augustan
Rome. Our other two elegiac fragments deal with a journey down a river. We
also have a snatch of abrasive hendecasyllables, and two apparently bucolic
hexameters, which look later than the *Eclogues*, but earlier than Ovid. His
connexion with Horace and Virgil shows that it was Propertius, rather than
elegy as such, which was out of tune with the literary mainstream; and the
prose works suggest a gentleman and a courtier, not an obsessed lover.[1]

Domitius Marsus may have written elegies, although *fusca Melaenis*, his
mistress, might just as well have figured in his collection of epigrams, the
Cicuta. In its most important fragment Virgil's enemy, Bavius, is arraigned in
the Catullan fashion: Marsus does not worry about polysyllabic pentameter
endings, and his language is prosaic. On several occasions Martial claims him
as his master, also providing evidence for a connexion with Maecenas.[2] Ovid
knew him, and Augustus' teacher, Apollodorus, corresponded with him. It
looks as if he belonged to the group around Maecenas, a contemporary of
Virgil and Horace, though living longer than they: yet the fragment to Epirota,
another figure from that circle, could be sarcastic,[3] and if Haupt is right,[4]
Horace pokes fun at his *Amazonis*, no doubt an unfortunate venture,[5] in the
difficult passage at *Odes* 4.4.18. At any rate, Horace never refers to him by
name, and this, as in the case of Propertius, is suspicious. He also wrote
Fabellae, and a prose work, entitled *De urbanitate*, for which he receives the
epithet *eruditissimus* from Quintilian. Another scholar like Valgius, he too

---

[1] See Appendix.
[2] See Mart. 7.29.5 *et Maecenati Maro cum cantaret Alexin | nota tamen Marsi fusca Melaenis erat.*
On the basis of such evidence, Virgil might just as easily be claimed for elegy as Marsus.
[3] See fr. 3, *Epirota tenellorum nutricula uatum*, with its somewhat ambiguous diminutives.
[4] Haupt (1876) III 333.
[5] Note Mart. 4.29.7 *leuis in tota Marsus Amazonide.*

shows how Romans had become more adventurous in letters, more resourceful and catholic than the previous generation.

Maecenas himself was a poet, writing occasional verse along the lines of Catullus, but taking his neoteric mannerisms to excess. We have fragments with contrived, affected diction, in hexameters, glyconics, hendecasyllables, galliambics, trimeters: but none of this was really *avant-garde*. Laevius had trifled in the same way fifty years before, and similar preciosities were to emerge in the second century A.D. Mannerism of this kind is germane to Roman literature, and though no doubt Alexandrian in origin, does not warrant the invocation of Greek models on its each and every occurrence. Augustus and Seneca were amused or appalled by his affectations: but such Asianism was probably common coinage. Maecenas also tried prose, writing *Dialogi*, one of which was a *Symposium* at which Horace, Virgil and Messalla were the guests.

Less needs to be said of Servius Sulpicius, a friend of Horace, who, according to Ovid, wrote *improba carmina*, and appears in a long list of erotic poets in Pliny. Other minor talents of a slightly later date are Proculus, who followed Callimachus, writing elegies; Alfius Flavus, a declaimer, and probably author of amatory trifles; Sabinus, who composed appropriate replies to Ovid's *Heroides* (Ov. *Am.* 2-18.27–34), an epic of uncertain name, and a *Fasti*; Fontanus, probably a bucolic poet; the elegist Capella; Tuscus, who wrote about Phyllis; M. Aurelius Cotta, perhaps an epigrammatist; Horace's addressee, Julius Florus; the brothers Visci; and Montanus, an elegist and, probably, writer of epyllia. Seneca preserves two hexameter fragments, descriptions of dawn and dusk, topics of which he was a devotee. Lyric is sadly represented: we only hear of Perilla, a pupil of Ovid, addressed in *Trist.* 3.7; and Titius and Rufus, imitators of Pindar, mentioned by Horace and Ovid – who may have been one and the same person.

Didactic remains the most neglected area of Latin literature. We still need a study of the formal characteristics of the genre; and general discussions tend too often to be limited to Lucretius and Virgil. Yet we have complete or fragmentary didactics by Cicero, Varro Atacinus, Columella, Nemesianus, Q. Serenus and Avienius – as well as three relatively extensive works from the early first century: the *Astronomica* of Manilius, the *Aratea* of Germanicus, and the *Cynegetica* of Grattius. Not only do these poems contribute to our knowledge of the contemporary world view; they also show how one of the favourite Alexandrian forms had become the property of Rome. Unfortunately we have lost the most important didactic poets of the age – after Virgil, that is. Aemilius Macer, who belonged to the older generation of Augustans, and is to be distinguished from the later epicist of the same name, was famed for his *Ornithogonia*, *Theriaca*, and *De herbis*. Ov. *Trist.* 4.10. 43:

saepe suas uolucres legit mihi grandior aeuo
quaeque nocet serpens, quae iuuat herba, Macer.

Often Macer, my elder, read to me his birds,
poisonous serpents, and medicinal herbs.[1]

It has been argued with some cogency that the *Theriaca* and *De herbis* belong to one and the same work – that Macer followed his model Nicander in writing one book on bites and a second on remedies.[2] His *Ornithogonia*, although inspired by the Greek poet Boios, contained Italian legends, for instance that of Picus, found also in Virgil and Ovid (fr. 1: cf. *Aen.* 7.189ff., *Met.* 15.320). But, as Bardon notes, there is a certain monotony in his verses:

tum sacrae ueniunt altis de nubibus Ibes

then from the high clouds come the sacred ibises;

auxilium sacrae ueniunt cultoribus Ibes   (frs. 5 and 6 M)

to the help of the cultivators come the sacred ibises.

Too much of that would easily have palled. Varius, like Macer, is half Republican, slightly old-fashioned in tone, but with more movement. Older than Virgil, he too adopted the didactic genre, writing a *De morte*, of which Macrobius, with his eye on Virgilian parallels, gives us a few lines. Fragment 2, which shows the influence of diatribe, was imitated by Virgil in the *Georgics*:

incubet ut Tyriis atque ex solido bibat auro

to sleep on purple and drink from solid gold,

and

ut gemma bibat et Sarrano dormiat ostro   (*Geo.* 2.506)

to drink from jewelled goblets and sleep on foreign purple.

Fragment 3 is Virgilian in movement, with a hint of Lucretius:

quem non ille sinit lentae moderator habenae
qua uelit ire, sed angusto prius ore coercens
insultare docet campis fingitque morando.

Pulling in the supple reins he does not let him go the way he wants, but checking him
with the narrow bit he makes him gallop on the plain and wins the mastery by
slowing him down.[3]

Hunting is Grattius' theme, the stars that of Manilius and Germanicus: their common aim is successful poetic arrangement of recalcitrant material, according to principles laid down in Hellenistic times, when interest in the

---

[1] As Hollis (1973) 11 points out, *grandior* seems to be in some sort of balance with *Macer*, the verbal play depending upon the idea of size.
[2] Bardon (1956) II 45–6, following Schulze (1898) 541–6.
[3] The *De morte* has been claimed for epic, but the title stands against that view.

form revived. Aratus, acclaimed by Callimachus for his polish and lightness of touch,[1] is the ancestor of a series of Roman imitations, some of them considerably altered: as Latin verse technique became standardized, interest gravitated towards adaptation and moral colouring, away from poetic finish – which, by the time of Germanicus (15 B.C.–A.D. 19) had become more or less a matter of course. Not that this is any detraction from his work, an accomplished composition, written slightly after Augustus' death. Like Manilius, he displays a certain Ovidian finesse, but is less pointed and rhetorical; he corrects Aratus' mistakes quite freely, and supplies his own insertions at will. One instance of his freedom of treatment is his depiction of Astraea's dereliction of the world: the passage relies on personification, moralistic comment, and concrete detail, where the original was colourless and abstract – a typically Roman expansion from source. Grattius, an acquaintance of Ovid (*Pont.* 4.16.34), is likewise not averse to the moralizing digression: but this time we have no Greek model against which to judge him – at least if, as has been argued, he did use a Greek source, none of it remains. Less accomplished than Germanicus, his main debt, though not as obvious as sometimes claimed, is to Virgil, and, to a much lesser degree, Lucretius:[2] it is unlikely that Manilius drew on him. Rare technical terms and *hapax legomena* – *plagium, metagon, praedexter, perpensare, offectus, cannabinus, nardifer, termiteus* – contribute to his reader's problems. But it is not in the technical sections, which maintain a certain degree of fluency, that he is most difficult. In the digressions – the double proem, the invective against luxury, the excursus on the Sicilian cave[3] – he is at his worst: misplaced grandiosity, vague prosaic phrasing, and unclear progressions of thought make him least attractive at precisely those points where a didactic poet might be expected to shine.

Of Manilius the man we know nothing: there is no external testimony; he gives us no personal information, and, apart from an invocation to Caesar at 1.7, has no addressee. A late Augustan date for Books 1 and 2 is indicated by a reference at 1.899 to the disaster of Varus which took place in A.D. 9, and by various passages which assume Augustus to be still alive. Housman has argued that the difficult passage at 4.764 implies that Augustus is dead: but that is not the only possible interpretation.[4] More than that we cannot say: Books 3 and 5 have no indication of date. The poem is something of a mystery. It is also probably unfinished: Book 5 breaks off abruptly, and there are places in the poem where Manilius promises material which does not appear.[5] Book 1

---

[1] Callim. *Epigr.* 29. See *CHCL* I.

[2] See the introduction to Enk's commentary (1918), and Pierleoni (1906).

[3] It is tempting to ask if Grattius used Augustus' poem on Sicily.

[4] See Housman (1903–30) I lxixff., marshalling the various pieces of evidence. The problem at 4.764 is that Tiberius is called *recturus*, then *lumen magni sub Caesare mundi*; is he therefore still heir apparent, a secondary light to Augustus, or already on the throne, the only light of the world?

[5] For example, 2.965, promising an account of the planets: see Housman, ibid. lxxii.

concerns the origins of astrology and the appearance of the heavens – their various zones and circles – concluding with a Virgilian finale, on the ability of the planets to presage the future. Book 2, after a proem which pays homage to Homer, Hesiod and other didactic poets, is devoted to the signs of the zodiac; the proem to Book 3 again concerns poetry, this time the difficulty of his theme compared to those of earlier writers, the bulk of the book being occupied by a treatment of the twelve *athla* which correspond to the signs. Book 4 begins in Lucretian vein, inveighing against our mortal cares, then moves on to the power of fate in history, and thence to the character traits connected with the signs, the geographical regions which they govern, the ecliptic signs, and finally, a vindication of the view that the heavens foretell the future. Book 5, without more ado, launches into a discussion of the *paranatellonta*, the signs which appear at the same time as the constellations of the zodiac, but outside the zodiac itself: it finishes suddenly, after a comparison between the earthly order and the order of the heavens.

Manilius' stylistic masters are Lucretius,[1] Virgil and Ovid. The old prosaic connectives are fully in evidence – *ergo age, perspice nunc, quin etiam, accipe, nunc age,* but there is a new polish, a new fluency, and a love of point, antithesis and word play: in terms of the rhetorical qualities of his verse, Manilius stands half way between Ovid and Lucan. He knows the imagery of the Callimachean poetic, but when he writes of untrodden paths, trite epic themes, and the struggle to create,[2] he reflects not the master himself, but the mainstream Latin tradition: the Callimachean programme was now itself banal.[3] Virgil is most obviously laid under contribution at the end of Book 1, where Manilius imitates the close of the first Georgic, incorporating echoes of the *Furor* ἔκφρασις from *Aeneid* 1:

> iam bella quiescant
> atque adamanteis Discordia uincta catenis
> aeternos habeat frenos in carcere clausa. (1.922ff.)

Now let wars end and Discord, tied with chains of adamant, be bound forever, coerced within a prison.

Yet even here there is a suspect facility, a non-Virgilian ease, which is the legacy of Ovid. Ovidian influence, visible throughout, is clearest in the Andromeda digression of Book 5. 549ff.:

[1] He worries less than Lucretius about using Greek terms, simply prefacing them with an apology, as at 2.693, 830, 897 and 3.41.
[2] Note *luctandum,* 2.34: cf. the Callimachean πόνος, Latin *labor.*
[3] See Wimmel (1960) 105–6, and Newman (1967) 196ff., 418ff. Manilius' claim to isolation (2.136ff.) may be no more than a variant on the Callimachean exclusiveness topic. He makes the conventional boast of originality at 1.4, 113, 2.57 and 3.1. The rejection of myth in favour of science, as at 3.5ff., is a commonplace of didactic.

at, simul infesti uentum est ad litora ponti,
mollia per duras panduntur bracchia cautes;
adstrinxere pedes scopulis, iniectaque uincla,
et cruce uirginea moritura puella pependit.
seruatur tamen in poena uultusque pudorque;
supplicia ipsa decent, niuea ceruice reclinis
molliter ipsa suae custos est uisa figurae,
defluxere sinus umeris fugitque lacertos
uestis et effusi scapulis haesere capilli.
te circum alcyones pinnis planxere uolantes
fleueruntque tuos miserando carmine casus
et tibi contextas umbram fecere per alas.
ad tua sustinuit fluctus spectacula pontus
adsuetasque sibi desit perfundere rupes,
extulit et liquido Nereis ab aequore uultus
et, casus miserata tuos, rorauit et undas.
ipsa leui flatu refouens pendentia membra
aura per extremas resonauit flebile rupes.

But when they came to the edge of the hostile sea, they stretched her soft arms across the harsh crag, bound her feet to the rock, and enchained her: the doomed maiden hung from her virgin cross. Despite the torture she kept her modest looks. The punishment became her: gently inclining her white neck she guarded her body. Her garments slipped from her shoulders, her robe slid down her arms and her hair, shaken out, spread close to her shoulders. Around her the sea birds flew and wailed, lamenting her fate in a song of misery, giving her shade from their intertwined wings. The sea stopped its waves to watch her, forsaking its usual rocky haunts; the Nereids raised their faces from the limpid waters, and pitying her plight, dropped tears on the waves. The breeze fondled her hanging limbs, and whistled sadly around the edges of the rocks.

This erotic sentimentalism, heavily reliant on the pathetic fallacy, with its coy rococo touches and rhetorical conceits, apart from occasional congestion, approaches the very essence of Ovid's *Metamorphoses*: never before had didactic so blatantly departed from its seriousness of intent.

But elsewhere, Manilius behaves with more dignity, his Stoicism precluding frivolity. Like Lucretius and Virgil before him, he goes to the diatribe in search of moral lessons, as in the proem to Book 4.[1] And like other didactic poets, he is concerned to set forth the *ratio* of this world,[2] and the place of his subject within it. There is an order within the universe, like the political order on earth – and both must be preserved if the machine is to function properly, 5.734ff.:

[1] Cf. 2.596ff., reminiscent also of Lucan's proem, especially 601ff., *et fas atque nefas mixtum, legesque per ipsas | saeuit nequities.*

[2] Note especially the expressions of his pantheistic beliefs at 1.247–54 and 2.60ff.: cf. Grattius on *ratio* in his proem.

utque per ingentis populus discribitur urbes,
principiumque patres retinent et proximum equester
ordo locum, populumque equiti populoque subire
uulgus iners uideas et iam sine nomine turbam,
sic etiam magno quaedam res publica mundo est
quam natura facit, quae caelo condidit urbem.
sunt stellae procerum similes, sunt proxima primis
sidera, suntque gradus atque omnia iusta priorum.
maximus est populus summo qui culmine fertur;
cui si pro numero uires natura dedisset,
ipse suas aether flammas sufferre nequiret
totus et accenso mundus flagraret Olympo.

And as a people is distributed through great cities – the senators hold the topmost position, the equestrian order the next; after the equites come the people, and after the people the lazy mob and then the nameless dregs – so in the cosmos at large there is a political order, the creation of nature, who has founded a city in the heavens. The constellations are the nobility, there are stars which are next in order, there are degrees and prerogatives: if nature had given sovereignty proportionate to their numbers to the greatest multitudes which revolve in the topmost zone, the aether would be unable to hold up the fiery stars which it supports, and the whole universe would go up in flames, setting light to the sky.

It would be hard to find a better example of Stoic Roman conservatism. Dorcatius remains, an uninteresting figure who wrote on ball games, mentioned by Ovid, and the author of two lines preserved by Isidore; also Plotius Crispinus, who, according to the scholia on Horace, versified the Stoic doctrine.

Names of authors and titles of works are more or less all that we have of Augustan mythological epic. We know of a Ponticus, who wrote a *Thebaid*, possibly in imitation of Antimachus; of a Homeric essay, the story of Nausicaa, by a friend of Ovid, Tuticanus; of an *Heracleid* by Carus, educator of Germanicus' children; of epics on Antenor's settlement in Gaul – like Aeneas' in Latium – by Largus, on Hercules' taking of Troy by Camerinus, on the *nostos* of Menelaus and Helen by Lupus, and of an anonymous *Perseid*. Iullus Antonius, son of Marcus, wrote a *Diomedēa* in twelve books, some time before 13 B.C., the date of Hor. *Odes* 4.2; the recipient of Propertius 2.24, Lynceus – perhaps a pseudonym – wrote a *Thebaid* and *Heracleid*; and Arbronius Silo was heard by Seneca the Elder reciting a poem on the Trojan war. We have two lines:

ite, agite, o Danai, magnum paeana canentes:
ite triumphantes: belli mora concidit Hector.

Come, come together, Greeks, singing a loud song of praise: come in triumph: Hector, their bulwark in war, has fallen.[1]

---

[1] Silo's phrase *belli mora* seems to have been the source of Sen. *Ag.* 211 *Danais Hector et bello mora*, and Lucan 1.100 *Crassus erat belli medius mora*, but cf. Virg. *Aen.* 10.428. Seneca discusses the phrase at *Suas.* 2.19.

Sabinus may have written an epic on the city of Troesmes: that depends on an emendation of Ov. *Pont.* 4.16.13. Numa and Priscus are mere names, perhaps epicists. This leaves us with Ovid's friend Macer, a poet of the Trojan cycle. At *Am.* 2.18, he is said to have dealt with material prior to the Trojan War; and *Pont.* 2.10.13 could perhaps be pressed to yield a *Posthomerica*. Sparse though the evidence may be, it is at least clear that the oldest form of poetry lost none of its attractions, despite the Roman adoption of Callimachean theory, with its many reservations about full scale epic.

Tragedy did not fare quite so well, but we do know of seven or eight writers who handled the genre – Varius, Gracchus, Pupius, Turranius and Ovid, as well as Pollio, and the *princeps* himself. Varius' *Thyestes*, produced in 29 B.C., survives in one alliterative, rather precious fragment:

> iam fero infandissima
> iam facere cogor.

Now my lot is unspeakable; now I must do unspeakable things.

Gracchus, mentioned at Ov. *Pont.* 4.16.31, seems to have treated the same myth. We have one line of his *Thyestes*:

> mersit sequentis umidum plantis humum

the soft ground hid the tracks of the pursuer,

as well as a grandiose snatch from his *Atalanta*:

> sonat impulsu regia cardo

the regal door sounded beneath the shock.

He also wrote a *Peliades*, of which a dimeter survives. Pupius and Turranius are just names, and Ovid's famous *Medea*, a work of his middle period, is only known in two lines, cited by Quintilian and Seneca. Pollio is a greater loss: we do not have much more than the tributes from Virgil and Horace, and the criticism of Tacitus. We cannot specify in what way his tragedies were 'modern' – as Virgil implies, perhaps with metre in mind[1] – but he was undeniably an important figure for the earlier group of Augustan poets, a survivor from the late Republic, who knew Catullus, Calvus, and Cinna. Suetonius informs us of an *Ajax* by Augustus; but again, we have no fragments.

---

[1] *Pollio et ipse facit noua carmina, Ecl.* 3.86. Virgil may have regarded Pollio's use of the trimeter (see Hor. *Sat.* 1.10.43, and cf. *A.P.* 251ff.) as an advance on senarii, but the epithet *nouus* still strikes one as strange: perhaps we are too accustomed to associating 'New Poetry' with the type of composition which Catullus and Calvus wrote. Certainly the grandiose image of the bull which prefaces the allusion to Pollio's *noua carmina* seems to designate tragedy. If there is a connexion between the present use of *nouus* and the literary pretensions of the previous generation, then what we have here is yet another instance of the increasingly loose interpretation of Callimachus' ideals; and perhaps it is significant that Pollio knew Calvus, was mentioned by Catullus, and was the recipient of a *propempticon* by Cinna.

Rome, it seems, never lost her taste for the grandiose, even at a time when many vaunted the ideals of Alexandria.

Surdinus and Statorius Victor were also dramatists, whether tragic or comic we cannot say; the son of Arbronius Silo wrote pantomimes; and Aristius Fuscus, the friend of Horace, wrote comedies. Fundanius and Melissus were more important, the first writing *palliatae* about Greek society, on which Horace complimented him, the second the author of *trabeatae*, a new form of comedy with the equestrian class as its subject – also of *Ineptiae* 'witty sayings', later retitled *Ioci*, maybe a work on grammar, and perhaps a natural history. We also hear of an Antonius Rufus, author of *praetextae* and *togatae*.

In the field of historical epic, one problem is that of finding precursors to Lucan: is he writing in a tradition, or is the *Bell. Civ.* an isolated phenomenon? Petronius' classicizing objections, albeit composed in a spirit of parody, might imply that he was an outrageous *Wunderkind*, a rebel against the absolute dominion of Virgil; but equally they could be taken as evidence for no more than a classicizing trend, which emerges in the preferences of Quintilian and the practice of the Flavians, Valerius, Statius and Silius. That the latter is the case is suggested by the nature of pre-Neronian epic: Cornelius Severus in particular, Albinovanus Pedo to some extent, and maybe Sextilius Ena and Rabirius, show that in terms of style at any rate, Lucan was not alone. Two parallel traditions existed in epic: first, the Virgilian, with its roots in Homer, and, to some degree, Ennius; second, the historical, a more sparse, abstract, and prosaic mode.

True, historical epic could have a Homeric slant, foreshadowing or reflecting Virgil's own conflation of Homer and history – in Callimachean terms, of heroes and kings. History was Homerized before Augustan times, Virgilianized afterwards: Ennius and Cicero employ *deorum ministeria*, and their style is a fusion of Greek and Roman; Petronius recasts Lucan in a Virgilian mould. But classicizing historical epic was not the same as that of Lucan, nor did it dominate the scene before him. Hellenistic *epos* was not all Homeric, and parts of Ennius' *Annales* – where the interest is contemporary and political – foreshadow the more prosaic methods of Severus and his like. Later Republican epic was presumably similar: for Homer could be too distant, or too elevated a model for contemporary themes. Varius Rufus, Rome's first epicist in 35 B.C. (Hor. *Sat.* 1.10.43), editor of the *Aeneid* in 19, and still a major force, along with Virgil, at the time of the *Ars Poetica* (541) has, in his lines on Antony, the familiar unpoetic ring of diatribe:

> uendidit hic Latium populis agrosque Quiritum
> eripuit, fixit leges pretio atque refixit.

This man sold Latium to the nations[1] and took away the fields from the citizens, meddling with the laws for money.

[1] See Hollis (1977) 188, interpreting the words as a reference to Antony's extension of Latin rights.

Epic or didactic, and presumably the latter, Varius' *De morte*, the origin of these lines, like the political sections of Lucretius' *De rerum natura*, shows the trend towards the abstract, undecorated manner of Lucan: Virgil's imitation at *Aen.* 6.621f. is an epic impulse to reincorporate its own – that is, if such material reached didactic via Ennius. But of Varian *forte epos* – epic as such – we have nothing.[1]

Rabirius and Sextilius Ena both chose civil war for their theme. Described by Ovid as *magni...oris* (*Pont.* 4.16.5), classed with Virgil by the soldier-critic Velleius (2.36.3), and relegated by Quintilian to the rank of Pedo (*Inst.* 10.1.90: before faint praise of Lucan), Rabirius shows, in three fragments of his anonymous epic on the war between Antony and Octavian, an unpolished affinity with the *Bellum civile*. Fragment 2:

> hoc habeo quodcumque dedi

What I have is what I have given

a motto from Antony's suicide – which also foreshadows the early Imperial Herculaneum papyrus on the Egyptian war – is reminiscent of the Stoic sentiments of Lucan's Vulteius episode in the fourth book, or Cato's pre-suicide ruminations in the ninth. Scientific colour brings the fourth fragment

> in tenerum est deducta serum pars intima lactis

the essence of the milk was reduced to a soft curd

into line with the didactic aspect of the *Bellum civile*; and Lucan rewrote fragment 3

> ac ueluti Numidis elephans circumdatur altus

and as a massive elephant is surrounded by Numidians

during his account of Scaeva's single combat, 6.208,

> sic Libycus densis elephans oppressus ab armis

so a Libyan elephant overwhelmed by many weapons,

a simile not so novel as sometimes claimed.[2] For the rest, Rabirius is Virgilian, or incomprehensible. Fr. 3,

> portarumque fuit custos Erucius

Erucius was the guardian of the gates

directs us to *Aen.* 9. 176:

> Nisus erat portae custos acerrimus armis

Nisus eager for war was the guardian of the gate

---

[1] All the fragments seem to be from the *De morte*, or the dubious *Panegyricus Augusti* (Porph. on Hor. *Epist.* 1.16.27–9, where Horace supposedly recasts Varius). See Norden (1926) 3 on *Aen.* 6.621 for fr. 1.

[2] Discussed by Aymard (1951).

while fr. 1,

Idaeos summa cum margine colles

Idean hills with their topmost verge

is conventional in word-order, as well as diction. Civil war reappears as an epic theme at Ov. *Pont.* 4.16.21 and 23, *ueliuolique maris uates*, and *quique acies Libycas Romanaque proelia dixit*, the latter, a poem on the campaigns in Africa, perhaps a source for Lucan Book 9, the former, probably an epic on Sicily or Actium. Next, more substantially, Cornelius Severus and Albinovanus Pedo.

One significant thing about their fragments is that they are embedded in the *Suasoriae* – and that Seneca adduces both as instances of a poet capping the *prosateurs*. The line between prose and verse has become blurred. If an epicist is comparable to a rhetorician or a historian, an epicist is discussable in terms appropriate to prose: and the terms appropriate to declamation and history are only occasionally appropriate to Virgil. We therefore have an alternative epic tradition: Lucan did not write in magnificent isolation. True, the Petronian parody, the debate reflected by Martial ('some say I'm not a poet'), and the criticisms of Quintilian ('the *Bellum civile* is stuff for orators, not for poets') show that Lucan caused a stir in his own day: and today he still has a reputation for extremism. But studied against the background of the fragments of Augustan historical epic his extremes are not only the extravagances of a youth in love with rebellion: and after all, when even younger, Lucan was a 'Neoteric'.

Severus' fragment on the death of Cicero is prosy, cold, logical – the work of a writer arranging words around ideas. Sextilius Ena's single line:

deflendus Cicero est Latiaeque silentia linguae

tears for Cicero and the silence of the Latin tongue,

hardly as ingenious as Seneca would have us believe, disappoints by contrast. One of Severus' phrases (8–9 *ille senatus | uindex*) crops up in Lucan: but common stock may explain the parallel as easily as imitation. His historical *exempla* reflect the trend which produced the handbook of Valerius Maximus; his declamatory negligence of historical detail shows that Lucan was not the first to be offhand with events: disregard for narrative – abridgement, curtailment, or total neglect – a factor common to both poets, leads to insistence on, and rationalistic hypertrophy of, the rhetorical moment. It cannot be said with certainty that Cornelius dispensed with the Olympians: but Jupiter would have looked decidedly unhappy in such surroundings.

Scope is uncertain: conflating the three ancient titles – *res Romanae, carmen regale, bellum Siculum* – we are left with an epic on Roman history, part of which may have consisted of an account of the regal period, and part, of the war with Sextus Pompeius around Sicily. Evidence for a regal section is tenuous: Ovid's phrase at *Pont.* 4.16.9, *carmen regale*, does not necessarily involve the kings of Rome; one need only compare Horace's allusion to Pollio's *regum facta* at *Sat* 1.10.42. But Quintilian's liking for the first book ('its style, if applied throughout the *Bellum Siculum*, would have won Severus second place to Virgil', 10.1.89) might, given his preferences, imply a consistently elevated, classicistic Virgilian colour, more suitable for the early kings than for the great men of the recent Republic. Certainly, a grandiose, archaizing manner is attested by fragments such as *stabat apud sacras antistita numinis aras*, and *pelagum pontumque moueri*[1] (frs. 4 and 1). As for the title *Bellum Siculum*, Quintilian probably had in mind the best part, or best known part, of a longer *res Romanae*: a book, or series of books, which, if written in one rather than two or several styles, would have earned Severus a higher place in epic. Conceivably, though not necessarily, a separate publication, this part of the epic fell short of the homogeneity of the first book, the postulated *carmen regale*. The fragments are, in fact, considerably uneven. In addition to the prosaic quality of the passage on the death of Cicero, and the archaizing colour of fragments 1 and 4, there is the average poetic manner of fragment 11 *stratique per herbam | 'hic meus est' dixere 'dies. . .'*,[2] as also of fragment 3 *huc ades Aonia crinem circumdata serta*,[3] fragment 5 *ignea iam caelo ducebat sidera Phoebe | fraternis successor equis*, and fragments 7 *flauo protexerat ora galero*, and 8 †*therua purpureis gemmauit pampinus uuis*. In the same category we can place fragments 6 *et sua concordes dant sibila clara dracones*, 9 *pomosa lentos seruabat in arbore ramos*, and 10 *pinea frondosi coma murmurat Appennini*. But this time we can adduce Lucan himself, who likewise occasionally employed standard poetic language: with fragments 6 and 9 we can compare the ornamental Hesperides excursus, 9.348ff., and with fragment 10, the similar spondaic ending of 2.396 *umbrosis mediam qua collibus Appenninus*, another epic usage of an effeminate neoteric device.[4] Closer to the essential Lucan are the moralizing fragments 2 *ardua uirtuti longeque per aspera cliua | eluctanda uia est: labor obiacet omnis honori*,[5] and 12 *luxuriantur opes atque otia longa grauantur*, the first perhaps a comment on the destiny of Rome, the second, a description of the causes of civil war. Quintilian himself implies the connexion with Lucan: Severus, he writes, was a better versifier than poet.[6] Ovid, significantly, was rather more complimentary.

[1] Probus, *GLK* IV 208 notes that fr. 1 comes from the first book; the other fragments are not allocated.

[2] Cf. Lucr. 2.29; Virg. *Georg.* 2.527; *Aen.* 9. 104; Sen. *Med.* 1017. Sen. *Suas.* 2.12 criticizes the lines.

[3] From a proem: for *huc ades* cf. Virg. *Ecl.* 9.39, and Caesius Bassus fr. 2.1.

[4] Cf. Hor. *Epod.* 16.29; Ov. *Met.* 2.266; Pers. 1.95; Quint. *Inst.* 9.4.65 *est permolle. . .cum uersus clauditur 'Appennino' et 'armamentis'.*

[5] Cf. Lucan 9.402, where the schol. quotes the passage of Severus.

[6] Quint. *Inst.* 10.1.19. Grenade (1950) discusses the influence of Severus on Lucan.

Pedo is more Virgilian. Usually seen as a forerunner of Lucan, his fragment on the voyage of Germanicus is, ironically, full of small-scale parallels, well integrated on the whole, from the *Eclogues*, the *Georgics*, as well as the *Aeneid*:

> iam pridem post terga diem solemque relictum
> †iamque uident†,[1] notis extorres finibus orbis,
> per non concessas audaces ire tenebras
> ad rerum metas extremaque litora mundi.
> nunc illum, pigris immania monstra sub undis
> qui ferat, Oceanum, qui saeuas undique pristis
> aequoreosque canes, ratibus consurgere prensis
> (accumulat fragor ipse metus), iam sidere limo
> nauigia et rapido desertam flamine classem,
> seque feris credunt per inertia fata marinis
> a ! non felici laniandos sorte relinqui.
> atque aliquis prora caecum[2] sublimis ab alta
> aera pugnaci luctatus rumpere uisu,
> ut nihil erepto ualuit dinoscere mundo,
> obstructa in talis effundit pectora uoces:
> 'quo ferimur? fugit ipse dies orbemque relictum
> ultima perpetuis claudit natura tenebris.
> anne alio positas ultra sub cardine gentes
> atque alium nobis[3] intactum quaerimus orbem?
> di reuocant rerumque uetant cognoscere finem
> mortales oculos: aliena quid aequora remis
> et sacras uiolamus aquas diuumque quietas
> turbamus sedes?'

For some time now sun and daylight have been behind them, exiles from the earth they knew, who dare to travel through illicit darkness to the verge of existence and the final shores of the world. At one moment they think that Ocean – the home of monstrous beasts beneath its sluggish waves, of sea dogs and savage monsters in profusion – rises to overwhelm their boats, their fears increased by the crashing breakers; at another, they think their ships are foundering on mud, that their fleet is abandoned by the rapid winds, and that they are to suffer the awful plight, the impotent death of being left as prey to the ferocious animals of the deep. And now some sailor high on top of the prow tries to thrust his vision into the impenetrable fog, but fails to see anything in a world beyond his reach. 'What is our course?', he chokes from his tightened lungs, 'Day has fled and outermost nature encloses the world we have left in everlasting shadows. Do we travel in search of nations living far beneath another pole and another world as yet unknown to man? The gods recall us and forbid our mortal eyes to know the end of things. For what reason do our oars violate foreign seas, and forbidden waters, why do we disturb the silent seats of the gods?'[4]

[1] Possibly *respiciunt*. The text I print is my own. I am pleased to find it does not differ substantially from that of Winterbottom (1974) II 502–4.

[2] Possibly *densum*.

[3] Suggested by R. G. M. Nisbet in a private communication; better than Haupt's *flabris*.

[4] I revise Kent's translation (1912).

But echoes from Virgil apart,[1] Albinovanus is still a declaimer's poet (although less fussy than they), the general shape of the fragment being determined by the rhetorical scheme for descriptions of Ocean: the prose deliberations of Alexander, later used of Caesar crossing the Channel,[2] have here been more aptly transferred to Germanicus' voyage across ·the North Sea – and this in epic verse.

His sentences have an analogous movement to, although greater length than, those of Lucan, while his conceits and wording – the former are neither bizarre, nor especially pointed: the latter sees a considerable amount of reduplication and variation[3] – have some of Lucan's abstraction, but some of Virgil's congestion: in the speech of his frightened sailor, less fanciful, but still similar to that of Cato's men at *Bell. Civ.* 9.848f.,[4] he is closest to Neronian epic. Once more the gods would have looked uncomfortable. And again, Quintilian, unlike Ovid, was not enthusiastic (10.1.90). Tacitus may have known him,[5] but the schools might be all they have in common.

From the mixed quality of most of this material, considered against Lucan's later innovations, we might conclude that his place in historical epic was similar, if not in intention, at least in effect, to that of Ovid in the mythological:

[1] Since most of the points of contact with Virgil, definite or doubtful, have gone unnoticed, they are listed here: *Ecl.* 6.47 and 52 *a!* . . . *infelix*, and 6.77 *a! timidos nautas canibus lacerasse marinis* ~ Pedo, l. 11 *a! non felici* (supporting the exclamation supplied by Gertz); ibid. *canibus* . . . *marinis* ~ 7 *aequoreosque canes*, and 10 *feris marinis*; *lacerasse* ~ 11 *laniandos*; *timidos nautas*, and *Aen.* 7.587f. *ut pelagi rupes magno ueniente fragore | quae sese multis circum latrantibus undis | mole tenet* ~ 8 *accumulat fragor ipse metus* (on writing *canes*, Pedo makes an associative transition from the Scylla of the sixth *Eclogue* to the seventh *Aeneid* – in effect, from dogs to barking waves – and as a result remembers *fragor*, the word there taken up by *latrantibus?*); *Geo.* 2.122–3 *extremi sinus orbis* ~ 4 *extremaque litora*; 2.503 *sollicitant alii remis freta caeca* ~ 21–2 *aliena quid aequora remis | et sacras uiolamus aquas*; 2.512 *atque alio patriam quaerunt sub sole iacentem* ~ 18–19 *anne alio positas ultra sub cardine gentes | atque alium nobis intactum quaerimus orbem* (but cf. Hor. *Odes* 2.16.18f. *quid terras alio calentes | sole mutamus*); *Aen.* 1.88 *eripiunt subito nubes caelumque diemque* ~ 1 *diem solemque*, and 14 *erepto mundo*; 2.724 *ferimur per opaca locorum* ~ 16 *quo ferimur?*, and the ensuing description of darkness; 3.583 *immania monstra* ~ 5 *immania monstra*; 4.241 *rapido* . . . *flamine*, 5.832 *flamina classem*, and 5.612 *desertosque uidet portus classemque relictam* ~ 9 *rapido desertam flamine classem*; 4.616 *finibus extorris* ~ 2 *extorres finibus*; 5.482 *effundit pectore uoces* (cf. 5.723, 8.70, 11.377 and 840) ~ 15 *obstructa in tales effundit pectora uoces*; 6.729 *fert monstra sub aequore* ~ 5–6 *monstra sub undis | qui ferat*; 10.447 *truci* . . . *uisu* ~ 13 *pugnaci* . . . *uisu* (*uisu*, in mitigation of *erepto* . . . *mundo*, which is equivalent to *erepto oculis prospectu mundi*, not *nisu*: *Aen.* 1.88, above, continues *Teucrorum ex oculis*, and cf. 8.254 *prospectum eripiens oculis*). For some possible imitations of Ovid, see Bardon (1956) 72 n. 1.

[2] Quint. *Inst.* 7.4.2 *Caesar deliberat, an Britanniam impugnet*; the other world motif crops up in this context at Vell. 2.46.1.

[3] Witness *diem solemque* 1; *immania monstra, saeuas undique pristes, aequoreosque canes* 5–7; *nauigia et* . . . *classem* 9; *sublimis ab alta* 12; *anne alio* . . . *gentes | atque alium* . . . *orbem* 18–19. But also note nonchalance about repetition: *dies* and *relictum* occur at 1 and 16, *relinqui* at 11; *orbis* at 2, 16 and 19; *tenebrae* at 3 and 17; *mundus* at 4 and 14.

[4] Note *segnia fata* 849, and *inertia fata* 10; *claustra ferit mundi* 865, and *ad rerum metas extremaque litora mundi* 4; *euoluimur orbe* 876, and *notis extorres finibus orbis* 2. But against direct imitation here, cf., with *imus in aduersos acies*, 876, and *anne alio positas ultra sub cardine gentes* 18, *Bell. Civ.* 8.335–7 *quid transfuga mundi | terrarum totos tractus caelumque perosus, | auersosque polos alienaque sidera quaeris?*

[5] See Tac. *Ann.* 2.23, describing the same storm.

another area of Latin literature met its master, and refused future development. Retrogression was the only solution. For after Ovid, mythological epic reverted to the Virgilian mode in the works of Valerius and Statius; and after Lucan, whose innovations served, amongst other things, to diminish the Homeric and Virgilian affiliations of the genre, there is only Silius – the victim of a poetic which sought salvation in an unimaginative classicism from the generic changes threatened a generation ago.

2. PROSE

Apart from Justin's epitome of Pompeius Trogus' *Historiae Philippicae*, we have little Augustan historiography: Livy, of course, excepted. Pollio, Fenestella, and a considerable number of important memoirs and contemporary histories are known merely by name, or a few scrappy fragments. We do, however, possess Augustus' record of his own achievements, the *Res gestae Divi Augusti*, and some works of a technical nature: the medical part of Celsus' Encyclopaedia, the *De architectura* of Vitruvius, and an abridgement – albeit at two removes – of Verrius Flaccus' *De verborum significatu*. Of Augustan oratory we have almost nothing.

Trogus, a writer of Gallic origin with Sallustian affiliations, set out to rival Livy in scope, dealing with the history of the Near East in forty-four books: beginning with the legendary Ninus of Babylon, he takes us through Macedonian history – hence the title, used by Theopompus and Anaximenes of Lampsacus for their histories of Philip II – into Roman times, closing his account with the year 20 B.C. It is not clear which sources he used: Timagenes has been a favourite candidate, but scholars have also canvassed Herodotus, Ctesias, Dinon, Ephorus, Timaeus, Phylarchus, Polybius, Clitarchus, Posidonius and Livy, as well as Theopompus. Justin's abridgement, of uncertain date, does not give us much of the original. But we do have a speech of Mithridates, at 34.4–7, quoted *in extenso* to give an idea of Trogus' style: wordier and flatter than that of Sallust, but more antithetical and less bland than that of Livy. Like Caesar, he favoured *oratio obliqua* in his speeches, censuring the direct discourse of Livy and Sallust. He also wrote on botany and zoology, providing material for the elder Pliny.

Pollio's *Historiae* are a greater loss: not only for their scope – they covered the period from 60 B.C., perhaps down to Philippi – but also for their style. Pollio began to write his History around 35 B.C., the year of Sallust's death – he inherited Sallust's learned freedman, Ateius Philologus – after an important political career, first as a Caesarian, and then as a supporter of Antony. He had retired after his consulate of 40 B.C. and triumph of 39,[1] to devote himself to letters – oratory, poetry and criticism, as well as historiography. He made quite

---

[1] 38 B.C. is also a possible date.

an impact by his criticisms of other writers (Caesar wrote without due diligence and regard for truth; Sallust was too archaic, obscure, and figurative; Cicero was faulty, Livy provincial), also by his own peculiar manner of writing, characterized by later estimates as rugged, ascetic and dry. But in the one long fragment which we have, on the death of Cicero, there is no archaism, no perversity. His word order is difficult, and there is a certain starkness – a lack of *nitor* and *iucunditas*, as Quintilian noted. Pollio is certainly an Atticist: but he is no eccentric Thucydidean. Horace tantalizes with his description of the histories in *Odes* 2.1, whence we gain the impression of a pathetic, rhetorical manner, not far distant from the methods of the dramatic historiography of Hellenistic times. Such rhetorical colouring and emotionality, combined with the ideals of the Roman Atticists – an abrupt *Latinitas* and a dour propriety – would have produced a truly remarkable work. Since the last century, much labour has been expended on the question whether he provided a source for Plutarch and Appian in their accounts of the civil war: it seems that he did, but only at second hand, through a Greek intermediary.[1] Fenestella was quite different, an antiquarian in spirit, who wrote an annalistic history of Rome in over twenty-two books. He is quoted for the information he gives on customs and society, not political events. His style is bare and matter-of-fact, ideal for the material he chooses to convey. Not a competitor with Livy, Fenestella is closer to Varro than mainstream historiography.

L. Arruntius is a lesser figure, but of some interest for the history of the Sallustian manner in Rome. According to Seneca his history of the Punic wars brimmed with the more perverse of his predecessor's mannerisms: *bellum facere, hiemauit annus, ingentes esse famas de Regulo*. Clodius Licinus, a contemporary of Ovid and Iulius Hyginus, likewise went to the earlier Republic for his matter, composing a *Res Romanae*, from the third book of which Livy quotes an event for the year 194 B.C., and Nonius one from the twenty-first book, perhaps for the year 134 B.C.: but that is all we know of its scope, and nothing of its style.

Octavius Ruso may be an invention of Porphyrio, but L. Furnius, a friend of Horace, is real enough, although we know no details, as once again in the case of Octavius Musa, the recipient of two poems in the *Catalepton*. We reach contemporàry history with Q. Dellius, who dealt with the Parthian wars of Antony, and a group of five historians who wrote about Augustus: Iulius Marathus, the secretary of the *princeps*, C. Drusus, Julius Saturninus, Aquilius Niger, and Baebius Macer. Suetonius mentions the first four: Servius the fifth. In addition, there were memoirs: Augustus himself wrote *Commentarii*, in thirteen books, dealing with his life up to the war in Spain, 27–24 B.C. Our sole original fragment deals with the star which heralded Caesar's

---

[1] See Gabba (1956), esp. 83–8, 230–49.

apotheosis in a stiff, rather official style, Atticist and laboured. Agrippa also wrote an autobiography – this, in addition to his cartographical enterprise: in letters, according to Pliny the Elder, he was rustic. Messalla published pamphlets, and, more likely than not, memoirs. Cicero praised his oratory: for Tacitus, he was *Cicerone mitior...et dulcior et in uerbis magis elaboratus*, a verdict substantiated by the fragment in Suetonius, which offers Augustus the title of *pater patriae*. A classicist through and through: Appian, as well as Suetonius, seems to have used his autobiography in Book 5 of the *Civil war*. Maecenas too may have written memoirs, but of this we cannot be certain.

According to Suetonius, Augustus had no time for affectation and archaism; he was equally dismissive of the very different styles of Maecenas, Tiberius and Antony; and Sallust's thefts from Cato were as objectionable to him as the volubility of the Asianists. His own style was

chaste and elegant, avoiding the variety of attempts at epigram and an artificial order, and as he himself expresses it, the noisomeness of far-fetched words, making it his chief aim to express his thoughts as clearly as possible. With this end in view, to avoid confusion and checking his reader or hearer at any point, he did not hesitate to use prepositions with names of cities, nor to repeat conjunctions several times, the omission of which causes some obscurity, though it adds grace.

Not to say that Augustus had no quirks: Suetonius tells us that he was sometimes popularist in questions of orthography, and had an eccentric preference for *baceolus* over *stultus*, for *uacerrosus* over *cerritus*, for *betizare*, a facetious coinage, over *languere*, and for *uapide se habere* instead of *male se habere*. In his letters, too, he shows an individuality which is hardly a sign of the purist. But the *Res gestae*, a list of Augustus' exploits and achievements, was written to be set up as an inscription; and as we might expect, the manner is official, cold and formal. There is no doubt that in Augustus we have lost a stylist of some interest and accomplishment: but that judgement must be based upon the fragments and what we glean from the critics, not the inscription from Ancyra.

Augustan oratory, despite the impression given by the elder Seneca's collection of specimens, was not all puerile brilliance: the generation prior to the declaimers, and of it, notably Messalla, showed that the style of Cicero – or at least a version of it – was a viable alternative to the follies and extravagances of the schools. Renowned in antiquity for the purity of his manner, Messalla was a moderate, a classicist who translated Hyperides, and wrote on philology. A Republican of the civil war period, he attracted a circle of writers, including Tibullus, thus continuing the system of patronage which appertained in pre-Augustan times.

Vitruvius, the author of ten books on architecture, left style to the experts and schools. A practical fellow, he did not find it easy to write, and he tells us as much. Often obscure, his pages are full of Grecisms, most of them necessitated by his subject matter, but he maintains an admirable objectivity. Antiquity had no specialized scientific or technological idiom, and writers of textbooks and tracts were for the most part at the mercy of rhetoric. Celsus is more stylistically accomplished than Vitruvius but now of greater interest to historians of medicine than students of literature. The eight books we possess constitute the medical section of a larger encyclopaedia, which went by the title of *Artes*. Behind such productions we catch glimpses of an urge to match Greece in scholarship, to fill in cultural gaps – the concept of the complete man is now fully entrenched at Rome. Grammatical and literary studies also had their audience: Hyginus, friend of Ovid, and librarian of the Palatine; Q. Caecilius Epirota, commentator on Virgil; Cloatius Verus, who wrote on the debt of Latin to Greek; Sinnius Capito, grammarian and literary historian; Crassicius, commentator on Cinna, and a philosopher to boot; Scribonius Aphrodisius, writer on orthography; Verrius Flaccus, author of a *De verborum significatu*, a *De obscuris Catonis*, and an *Etruscan antiquities* – such men, too often slighted by literary history, helped Romans feel true rivals to Greece, continuing a trend that Varro had made respectable, after the earlier opposition offered by figures like the elder Cato.

APPENDIX OF
AUTHORS AND WORKS

VERGILIUS MARO, PUBLIUS

LIFE

b. 15 October 70 B.C. at Andes near Mantua. If (which is doubtful) the ancient sources may be trusted, father was a prosperous self-made man of modest origins, mother possibly well-connected. Educ. Cremona, Milan and Rome. Chronology of early life uncertain; renunciation of rhetoric for philosophy and adherence to Epicurean circle under Siro at Naples rests on dubious authority (*Catal.* 5). Story (current early in antiquity) that family estate was involved in confiscations after Philippi and restored by Octavian is ostensibly supported both by poems (*Catal.* 8, *Ecl.* 9, 1) and by Servius *auctus* (*Ecl.* 9, 10; cf. L. P. Wilkinson, *Hermes* 94 (1966) 320–4), but this too may be plausible fiction. With pub. of *Ecl.* passed from ambit of C. Asinius Pollio to that of Maecenas (to whom he introd. Horace) and Octavian. Rest of life uneventful; d. 20 September 19 B.C. at Brundisium (Brindisi) on way back from Greece. Buried at Naples. Main sources: poems, esp. *Catal.* 5, 8; *Ecl. passim*; *Geo.* 3.1–48; Horace, esp. *Sat.* 1.5; ancient *Vitae* (ed. J. Brummer, BT, 1912; C. Hardie, OCT 2nd ed., 1957) and commentators (Servius ed. G. Thilo–H. Hagen, 3 vols., Leipzig 1881–7; E. K. Rand et al., Harvard–Oxford 1946–); cf. Büchner, under *Studies* below, 1–41 (pagination of independently printed ed. of *RE* article).

WORKS

Juvenilia: of the poems in the so-called *Appendix Vergiliana* (q.v., pp. 859–61) one or two of the short pieces in various metres entitled *Catalepton* (= κατὰ λεπτόν 'miniatures', 'trifles') have been identified as V.'s. See (ed.) R. E. H. Westendorp Boerma, 2 vols. (Assen 1949–63). *Eclogues* (*Bucolica*): book of ten pastorals generally accepted as having been written and pubd c. 42–37, but precise order and dating still controversial. See G. W. Bowersock, *H.S.C.Ph.* 75 (1971) 73–80; W. Clausen, ibid. 76 (1972) 201–6; R. J. Tarrant, ibid. 82 (1978) 197–9; Bowersock, ibid. 201–2. *Georgics*: didactic poem in four books, seven years in the writing, completed by 29 B.C. (*Vit. Don.* 85). *Aeneid*: epic in twelve books begun immediately after *Geo.* (*Vit. Don.* 85), incomplete at V.'s death; pubd on Octavian's orders by his literary executors Varius and Tucca 'lightly corrected' (*summatim emendata*: see *Vit. Don.* 140–65, raising controversial problems).

BIBLIOGRAPHY

(see Williams (1967) under *Studies* (1) below; *ANRW* II 31.1, 2 (1981))

TEXTS AND COMMENTARIES: TEXTS: O. Ribbeck (Leipzig 1859–68; 2nd ed. 1894–5); E. de Saint-Denis, H. Goelzer, R. Durand, A. Bellessort (Budé, 1925–56); H. R. Fairclough, 2nd ed. (Loeb, 1934–5); R. Sabbadini (Rome 1930), repr. with minor alterations L. Castiglioni (Paravia, 1945–52); M. Geymonat (Paravia, 1973); R. A. B. Mynors (OCT, 1969; 2nd ed. 1972), replacing F. A. Hirtzel (OCT, 1900). For Servius' commentary see under *Life*. COMMENTARIES: (1) Complete. J. L. de la Cerda (repr. Cologne 1642); C. G. Heyne, G. P. E. Wagner, 4th ed. (Leipzig 1830–41); J. Conington, H. Nettleship, F. Haverfield (London 1858–98); T. E. Page (London 1894–1900); F. Plessis, P. Lejay (Paris 1919); R. D. Williams (London 1972–9). (2) Individual works. *Aeneid*: J. Henry (London, Edinburgh and Dublin 1873–89); J. W. Mackail (Oxford 1930). *Aen.* 1: R. G. Austin (Oxford 1971). *Aen.* 2: idem (Oxford 1964). *Aen.* 3: R. D. Williams (Oxford 1962). *Aen.* 4: A. S. Pease (Cambridge, Mass. 1935); R. G. Austin (Oxford 1955). *Aen.* 5: R. D. Williams (Oxford 1960). *Aen.* 6: E. Norden, 3rd ed. (Stuttgart 1926); F. Fletcher (Oxford 1941); R. G. Austin (Oxford 1977). *Aen.* 7–8: C. J. Fordyce (Oxford 1977). *Aen.* 8: P. T. Eden (Leiden 1975); K. W. Gransden (Cambridge 1976). *Aen.* 12: W. S. Maguinness (London 1953). *Georgics*: W. Richter (Munich 1957). *Georg.* 1 and 4: H. H. Huxley (London 1963). *Eclogues*: R. Coleman (Cambridge 1977).

TRANSLATIONS: J. Dryden (1697); C. Day Lewis (1940–63). *Eclogues*: P. Valéry, *Oeuvres* I (1962) 207–22; G. Lee, *Virgil's Eclogues* (Liverpool 1980).

STUDIES. (1) GENERAL, and dealing particularly with *Aeneid*. C. A. Sainte-Beuve, *Étude sur Virgile* (Paris 1857); W. Y. Sellar, *The Roman poets of the Augustan age: Virgil* (Oxford 1877; 3rd ed. 1897); D. Comparetti, *Vergil in the middle ages*, tr. E. F. M. Benecke (London 1885); R. Heinze, *Virgils epische Technik* (Leipzig 1903; 3rd ed. 1915); T. R. Glover, *Virgil* (London 1904; 7th ed. 1942); H. W. Prescott, *The development of Virgil's art* (Chicago 1927); R. S. Conway, *The Vergilian age* (Harvard U.P. 1928); R. M. Henry, 'Medea and Dido', *C.R.* 44 (1930) 97–108; C. S. Lewis, *A preface to Paradise Lost*, ch. 6 (Oxford 1942); W. F. J. Knight, *Roman Vergil* (London 1944; 2nd ed. 1966); E. Paratore, *Virgilio* (Rome 1945; 2nd ed. 1954); C. M. Bowra, *From Virgil to Milton* (London 1945); T. S. Eliot, *What is a classic?* (London 1945); V. Pöschl, *Die Dichtkunst Virgils: Bild und Symbol in der Aeneis* (Innsbruck 1950; tr. Seligson, Michigan 1962); B. M. W. Knox, 'The serpent and the flame: the imagery of the second book of the Aeneid', *A.J.Ph.* 71 (1950) 379–400; A. M. Guillemin, *Virgile* (Paris 1951); J. Perret, *Virgile, l'homme et l'oeuvre* (Paris 1952; 2nd ed. 1965); R. A. Brooks, 'Discolor aura: reflections on the Golden Bough', *A.J.Ph.* 74 (1953) 260–80; E. M. W. Tillyard, *The English epic and its background* (London 1954); K. Büchner, *RE* VIIIA (1955–8) 1021–1486, separately pubd Stuttgart 1961; G. B. Townend, 'Changing views of Vergil's greatness' *C.J.* 56 (1960–1) 67–77; M. Coffey, 'The subject matter of Virgil's similes', *B.I.C.S.* 8 (1961) 63–75; J. Lockwood, 'Virgil and his critics', *P.V.S.* 2 (1962–3) 1–8; A. Parry, 'The two voices of Virgil's Aeneid', *Arion* 2 (4), (1963) 66f.; V. Buchheit, *Vergil über die Sendung Roms* (Heidelberg 1963); Brooks Otis, *Virgil: a study in civilised poetry* (Oxford 1963); W. V. Clausen, 'An interpretation of the Aeneid', *H.S.C.Ph.* 68 (1964) 139–47; M. C. J. Putnam, *The poetry of the Aeneid* (Harvard 1965); (ed.) Steele Commager, *Virgil, Twentieth-Century Views* (New Jersey 1966); R. D. Williams, *Virgil, G.&R., New surveys in the classics* 1 (1967; repr. with Addenda 1978); F. Klingner, *Virgil* (Zurich 1967); K. Quinn, *Virgil's Aeneid, a critical description* (London 1968); R. G. Austin, '*Virgil*, Aeneid 6.384–476' *P.V.S.* 8 (1968–9) 51–60; (ed.) D. R. Dudley, *Virgil* (Studies in Latin literature and its influence, London 1969); G. K. Galinsky, *Aeneas, Sicily and Rome* (Princeton 1969); W. A. Camps, *An introduction to Virgil's Aeneid* (Oxford 1969); A. G. McKay, *Virgil's Italy* (Bath 1970); G. Highet, *The speeches in Virgil's Aeneid* (Princeton 1972); W. R. Johnson, *Darkness visible* (Berkeley 1976).

(2) 'ECLOGUES': (*a*) GENERAL: G. Jachmann, 'Die dichterische Technik in Vergils Bukolika', *N.J.A.* 49 (1922) 101–20; H. J. Rose, *The eclogues of Vergil* (Berkeley 1942); K. Büchner, *P. Vergilius Maro* (Stuttgart 1960) 160–243 = *RE* VIIIA.1 (1955) 1180–1264; V. Pöschl, *Die Hirtendichtung Virgils* (Heidelberg 1964); F. Klingner, *Virgil* (Zurich 1967) 9–174; G. Williams, *Tradition and originality in Roman poetry* (Oxford 1968: for *index locorum* see p. 801); T. G. Rosenmeyer, *The green cabinet* (Berkeley 1969); M. C. J. Putnam, *Virgil's pastoral art* (Princeton 1970); R. Kettemann, *Bukolik und Georgik* (Heidelberg 1977). (*b*) INDIVIDUAL ECLOGUES: 1 (or 1 and 9): F. Leo, *Hermes* 38 (1903) 1–18; R. Coleman, *G.&R.* 13 (1966) 79–97; P. Fedeli, *G.I.F.* n.s.3 (1972) 273–300; W. Clausen, *H.S.C.Ph.* 76 (1972) 201–5. 2: E. Pfeiffer, in *Virgils Bukolika* (Stuttgart 1933) 1–34; O. Skutsch. *H.S.C.Ph.* 74 (1968) 95–9. 4: E. Norden, *Die Geburt des Kindes* (Leipzig 1924); W. W. Tarn, *J.R.S.* 22 (1932) 135–60; G. Jachmann, *A.S.N.P.* 21 (1952) 13–62; H. C. Gotoff, *Philologus* 111 (1967) 66–79; G. Williams, in (edd.) A. J. Woodman and D. West, *Quality and pleasure in Latin poetry* (Cambridge 1974) 31–46. 5: A. G. Lee, *P.C.Ph.S.* n.s.23 (1977) 62–70. 6: G. Jachmann, *Hermes* 58 (1923) 288–304; O. Skutsch, *Rh.M.* 99 (1956) 193–201; Z. Stewart, *H.S.Ph.* 64 (1959) 179–205; J. P. Elder, *H.S.Ph.* 65 (1961) 109–25; D. O. Ross, in *Backgrounds to Augustan poetry* (Cambridge 1975) 18–37; W. Clausen, *A.J.Ph.* 97 (1976) 245–7. 8: G. W. Bowersock, *H.S.C.Ph.* 75 (1971) 73–80. 10: F. Skutsch, in *Aus Vergils Frühzeit* (Leipzig 1901) 2–27; idem, in *Gallus und Vergil* (Leipzig 1906) 155–92; D. O. Ross, in *Backgrounds to Augustan poetry* (Cambridge 1975) 85–106· (*c*) STRUCTURE: C. Becker, *Hermes* 83 (1955) 314–28; J. van Sickle, *T.A.Ph.A.* 98 (1967) 491–508; O. Skutsch, *H.S.C.Ph.* 73 (1968) 153–69; idem, *B.I.C.S.* 18 (1971) 26–9; N. Rudd, in *Lines of enquiry* (Cambridge 1976) 119–44; J. van Sickle, *The*

design of Virgil's Bucolics (Rome 1978). (*d*) THEOCRITUS: A. S. F. Gow, *Theocritus* (Cambridge 1952: with tr.); K. J. Dover, *Theocritus* (London 1971); S. Posch, *Beobachtungen zur Theokritnachwirkung bei Vergil, Commentationes Aenipontanae* 19 (Innsbruck 1969); L. E. Ross, *S.I.F.C.* n.s.43 (1971) 5–25. (*e*) PASTORAL LANDSCAPE: B. Snell, in *The discovery of the mind*, tr. T. G. Rosenmeyer (Cambridge, Mass. 1953) 281–303; G. Jachmann, *Maia* 5 (1952) 161–74; A. M. Parry, *Y.Cl.S.* 15 (1957) 3–29.

(3) 'GEORGICS'. T. Keightley, *Notes on the Bucolics and Georgics of Virgil* (London 1846); T. F. Royds, *The beasts, birds and bees of Virgil* (Oxford 1914); G. Wissowa, 'Das Prooemium von Vergils Georgica', *Hermes* 52 (1917) 92–104; J. Sargeaunt, *The trees, shrubs and plants of Virgil* (Oxford 1920); W. E. Heitland, *Agricola* (Cambridge 1921: in English); R. Billiard, *L'agriculture dans l'antiquité d'après les Géorgiques de Virgile* (Paris 1928); E. Burck, 'Die Komposition von Vergils Georgica', *Hermes* 64 (1929) 279–321; H. M. Fraser, *Beekeeping in antiquity* (London 1931); L. A. S. Jermyn, 'Weather-signs in Virgil', *G.&R.* 20 (1951) 26–37, 49–59; H. Altevogt, *Labor improbus* (Münster, Westfalen 1952: in German): H. Dahlmann, *Der Bienenstaat in Vergils Georgica* (Wiesbaden 1955); F. Klingner, *Vergils Georgica* (Zurich 1963); E. Abbe, *The plants of Virgil's Georgics* (Ithaca, New York 1965); L. P. Wilkinson, *The Georgics of Virgil* (Cambridge 1969); M. C. J. Putnam, *Vergil's poem of the earth* (Princeton 1979); G. B. Miles, *Virgil's Georgics: a new interpretation* (California 1980).

(4) CONCORDANCE: H. H. Warwick (Minnesota 1975).

HORATIUS FLACCUS, QUINTUS

LIFE

b. 8 Dec. 65 B.C. at Venusia in Apulia, son of a freedman. Educ. at Rome by Orbilius, and later at Athens. Appointed *tribunus militum* by Brutus 43 B.C.; after defeat at Philippi received pardon and purchased position of *scriba quaestorius*. Acquainted with Virgil, Maecenas, and Augustus, whose offer of a secretaryship he refused. d. 27 Nov. 8 B.C. Buried on Esquiline. Main sources: ancient *Vita* (printed in Klingner (BT), under *Texts* below; tr. by J. C. Rolfe, *Suetonius* (Loeb, 1914) vol. II); Hor. *Epist.* 2.1.71 (Orbilius), 2.2.41ff. (education), 1.20.20ff., *Sat.* 1.6.45ff. (introduction to Maecenas and father's supervision of education). See J. F. d'Alton, *Horace and his age* (London 1917), E. Fraenkel, *Horace* (Oxford 1957) 1–23.

WORKS

Satires 1, 35–34 B.C.; *Satires* 2, 30–29 B.C.; *Epodes*, 30–29 B.C.; *Odes* 1–3, 23 B.C.; *Epistles* 1, 20–19 B.C.; *Epistles* 2.2, 19–18 B.C.; *Carmen saeculare*, 17 B.C.; *Epistles* 2.1, c. 15 B.C.; *Odes* 4, 13 B.C. or later; *Ars poetica*, either between 23 and 17 B.C. or after *Odes* 4. See C. O. Brink, *Horace on poetry* 1 (Cambridge 1963) 239–43, G. Williams, *Horace, G.&R.*, *New surveys in the classics* 6 (1972) 38–48.

BIBLIOGRAPHY

(see W. S. Anderson, *C.W.* 50 (1956) 33–40 and 57 (1964) 293–301; R. J. Getty, *C.W.* 52 (1959) 167–88 and 246–7; *ANRW* II 31.3 (1981))

TEXTS AND COMMENTARIES: TEXTS: E. C. Wickham, 2nd ed. rev. H. W. Garrod (OCT, 1912); F. Klingner, 3rd ed. (BT, 1959); M. Lenchantin de Gubernatis and D. Bo, 1st–2nd edd. (Paravia, 1958–60: with indexes, metrical and linguistic data). COMMENTARIES: Pomponius Porphyrio (3rd c. A.D.) ed. A. Holder (Innsbruck 1894); pseudo-Acro (5th c. A.D.) ed. O. Keller (BT, 1902–4); R. Bentley (Cambridge 1711); J. G. Orelli and J. G. Baiter, 4th ed. rev. W. Hirschfelder and W. Mewes (Berlin 1886–92); E. C. Wickham (Oxford 1891–6); A. Kiessling, rev. R. Heinze, 5th–10th edd. (Berlin 1957–61: all with bibliographies by E. Burck). *Odes* and *Epodes*: T. E. Page (London 1895); J. Gow (Cambridge 1895). *Odes*: P. Shorey and G. J. Laing (Chicago 1910); H. P. Syndikus (Darmstadt 1972–3). *Odes* 1–2: R. G. M. Nisbet and M. Hubbard (Oxford 1970–8). *Odes* 3: G. Williams (Oxford 1969). *Satires* and *Epistles*: E. P. Morris (New York 1909–11). *Satires*: A. Palmer (London 1891); J. Gow (Cambridge 1901–9); P. Lejay (Paris 1911). *Epistles*: A. S. Wilkins (London 1896). *Epistles* 1: O. A. W. Dilke, 3rd ed. (London 1966). *Ars poetica*: C. O. Brink (Cambridge 1971).

TRANSLATIONS: E. C. Wickham (Oxford 1903); C. E. Bennett and H. R. Fairclough (Loeb, 1927–9). *Odes*: J. Michie (Penguin, 1967). *Satires* and *Epistles*: N. Rudd (Penguin, 1979).

STUDIES: (1) GENERAL: W. Wili, *Horaz und die augusteische Kultur* (Basel 1948); E. Fraenkel, *Horace* (Oxford 1957); C. Becker, *Das Spätwerk des Horaz* (Göttingen 1963); C. O. Brink, *Horace on poetry* (Cambridge 1963); A. la Penna, *Orazio e l'ideologia del principato* (Turin 1963); J. Perret, *Horace l'homme et l'oeuvre*, Eng. tr. B. Humez (New York 1964); K. J. Reckford, *Horace* (New York 1969); (ed.) H. Oppermann, *Wege zu Horaz* (Darmstadt 1972); (ed.) C. D. N. Costa, *Horace* (London 1973). (2) 'ODES': L. P. Wilkinson, *Horace and his lyric poetry*, 2nd ed. (Cambridge 1951); S. Commager, *The odes of Horace* (London 1962); G. Pasquali, *Orazio lirico*, ed. A. la Penna (Florence 1964); E. Doblhofer, *Die Augustuspanegyrik des Horaz* (Heidelberg 1966); D. A. West, *Reading Horace* (Edinburgh 1967); V. Pöschl, *Horazische Lyrik* (Heidelberg 1970); K. E. Bohnenkamp, *Die horazische Strophe* (Hildesheim 1972). (3) 'EPODES': V. Grassman, *Die erotischen Epoden des Horaz* (Munich 1966); R. W. Carruba, *The Epodes of Horace* (The Hague 1969). (4) 'SATIRES': N. O. Nilsson, *Metrische Stildifferenzen in den Satiren des Horaz* (Uppsala 1952); N. Rudd, *The Satires of Horace* (Cambridge 1966); C. A. van Rooy, 'Arrangement and structure of satires in Horace, Sermones Book I', *Acta Classica* 11 (1968), 13 (1970), 14 (1971), 15 (1972). (5) 'EPISTLES': E. Courbaud, *Horace, sa vie et sa pensée à l'époque des Épîtres* (Paris 1914); M. J. McGann, *Studies in Horace's first book of Epistles*

(Brussels 1969). (6) 'ARS POETICA': W. Steidle, *Studien zur Ars Poetica des Horaz* (Hildesheim 1967).

CONCORDANCES: L. Cooper (Washington 1916); D. Bo (Hildesheim 1965).

LOVE-ELEGY

GENERAL WORKS

Day, A. A., *The origins of Latin love-elegy* (Oxford 1938).

Luck, G., *The Latin love elegy*, 2nd ed. (London 1969).

idem, *ANRW* 1.3 (1973) 361–8.

Platnauer, M., *Latin elegiac verse. A study of the metrical uses of Tibullus, Propertius and Ovid* (Cambridge 1951).

Ross, D. O., *Backgrounds to Augustan poetry: Gallus, elegy and Rome* (Cambridge 1975).

Sellar, W. Y., *Horace and the elegiac poets*, 2nd ed. (London 1899).

Stroh, W., *Die römische Liebeselegie als werbende Dichtung* (Amsterdam 1971).

Sullivan, J. P. (ed.), *Elegy and lyric* (London 1962).

Wilkinson, L. P., *Golden Latin artistry* (Cambridge 1963).

Williams, G., *Tradition and originality in Roman poetry* (Oxford 1968).

GALLUS, GAIUS CORNELIUS

LIFE

b. 70/69 B.C. at Forum Iulii (mod. Fréjus) in Gaul, of humble birth; later rose to equestrian rank. Educ. at Rome by same teachers as Virgil, thenceforth a close friend. Fought in Civil War on Octavian's side from 43 B.C. to Actium; appointed first prefect of Egypt 30 B.C. Vaunted his achievements in an inscription (*ILS* 8995), fell into disgrace and committed suicide 26 B.C. Sources: Jerome, *Chron.* (birth); Probus, Thilo–Hagen III. 2.328 (education); Suet. *Aug.* 66, Dio Cass. 53.23.5ff. (military career and death). See also Ovid, *Am.* 3.9.63f., *Trist.* 2.445f. On his birthplace and background see R. Syme, *C.Q.* 32 (1938) 39ff.; on the inscription E. Hartman, *Gymnasium* 72 (1965) 1–8, and H. Volkmann, ibid. 328–30.

WORKS

Four books of elegies, of which one pentameter (*FPL* 99) and some ten other lines survive, the latter first pubd by R. D. Anderson, P. J. Parsons, R. G. M. Nisbet, 'Elegiacs by Gallus from Qaṣr Ibrîm', *J.R.S.* 69 (1979) 125–55. Cf. Prop. 2.34.91f., Ovid, *Am.* 1.15.30, *Ars Am.* 3.537, Mart. 8.73.6. Some lines echoed in Virg. *Ecl.* 10

(Serv. *ad loc.*); on G.'s relation to Virgil see F. Skutsch, *Aus Vergils Frühzeit* (Leipzig 1901); idem, *Gallus und Vergil* (Leipzig 1906); R. Coleman, 'Gallus, the Bucolics, and the ending of the fourth Georgic', *A.J.Ph.* 83 (1962) 55–71.

BIBLIOGRAPHY

STUDIES: E. Bréguet, 'Les élégies de Gallus', *R.E.L.* 26 (1948) 204–14; Bardon II 34–44; J.-P. Boucher, *Caius Cornélius Gallus* (Paris 1966); indexes to Ross and Stroh under *General works* above.

TIBULLUS, ALBIUS

LIFE

b. *c.* 55 B.C. of equestrian rank, possibly in Gabii (cf. *v.l.* in *Vita Tib.*). Lived between Praeneste and Rome in the *regio Pedana*. Closely connected with circle of M. Valerius Messalla Corvinus, with whom he campaigned in Aquitania in 27 B.C. d. as *iuuenis* (i.e. before age 46) either in same year as Virgil (19 B.C.) or shortly after (2.5 shows influence of *Aeneid*, pubd soon after V.'s death). Sources: anonymous *Vita* (birth); Ovid, *Trist.* 4.10.45ff. (chronological list of Roman poets); Tib. 1.7.9ff (campaign); epigram by Domitius Marsus, *FPL* 111 (death; cf. M. J. McGann, *Latomus* 29 (1970) 774ff.); Hor. *Epist.* 1.4, *Odes* 1.33.

WORKS

(1) GENUINE: First two books of *Corpus Tibullianum* (sixteen elegies). Bk 1 pubd *c.* 27 B.C. (1.7 describes Messalla's triumph), 2 at unknown later date. (2) DUBIOUS OR SPURIOUS: Remainder of the Corpus, comprising: six elegies written by a 'Lygdamus'; a *Panegyricus* of Messalla in hexameters; five anonymous elegies on the love of Sulpicia for Cerinthus; six short elegies by Sulpicia herself; one elegy whose author calls himself Tibullus; one four-line epigram. Majority of these probably written by minor poets of Messalla's circle. On Lygdamus see B. Axelson, 'Lygdamus und Ovid', *Eranos* 58 (1960) 92–111.

BIBLIOGRAPHY

(see H. Harrauer, *A bibliography to the Corpus Tibullianum* (Hildesheim 1971))

TEXTS AND COMMENTARIES: TEXTS: E. Hiller, in *Corpus poetarum Latinorum* (London 1894); J. P. Postgate (Loeb, 1913); idem, 2nd ed. (OCT, 1915); F. W. Lenz (BT, 1937); M. Ponchont, 6th ed. (Budé, 1967); F. W. Lenz, 3rd ed. rev. G. K. Galinsky (Leiden 1971); A. G. Lee, bks 1–2 (Cambridge 1975: with tr.). COMMENTARIES: K. F. Smith, complete except for Lygdamus and *Panegyricus* (New

York 1913; repr. Darmstadt 1964). Bk 1: J. André (Paris 1965); P. Murgatroyd (Pietermaritzburg 1980). Bks 1–2: M. C. J. Putnam (Norman, Oklahoma 1973).

STUDIES: (1) GENERAL: A. Cartault, *A propos du Corpus Tibullianum* (Paris 1906); M. Schuster, *Tibull-Studien* (Vienna 1930); J. P. Elder, 'Tibullus: tersus atque elegans', in (ed.) Sullivan, under *General works* above; F. Solmsen, 'Tibullus as an Augustan poet', *Hermes* 90 (1962) 295–325; A. W. Bulloch, 'Tibullus and the Alexandrians', *P.C.Ph.S.* n.s.19 (1973) 71–89; F. Cairns, *Tibullus: a Hellenistic poet at Rome* (Cambridge 1979). (2) INDIVIDUAL POEMS: See Harrauer above and the following: J. H. Gaisser, *A.J.Ph.* 92 (1971) 202–16 (1.6); eadem, *C.Ph.* 66 (1971) 221–39 (1.7); A. G. Lee, in (edd.) A. J. Woodman and D. West, *Quality and pleasure in Roman poetry* (Cambridge 1974) 94–114 (1.1).

CONCORDANCE: E. N. O'Neil (Ithaca, N.Y. 1963).

PROPERTIUS, SEXTUS

LIFE

b. *c.* 50 B.C. of equestrian family in Umbria, probably (cf. correction at 4.1.125) in Assisi; part of his family estate confiscated 41/40 B.C. When still young rejected rhetoric in favour of poetry; closely associated with Ovid. d. not much later than A.D. 2. Of the names ascribed to him by MSS – Propertius Aurelius Nauta – the second is impossible and the third based on a corruption in 2.24b. 38; the *praenomen* Sextus has ancient testimony (Donat. *Vita Verg.*). Sources: own works, esp. 1.21–2 (discussed by Williams, *TORP* 172ff.) and 4.1.127–34. Other testimonia in Butler and Barber, under *Commentaries* below.

WORKS

Four books of elegies: bk 1 pubd in or before 29 B.C. (2.31, datable to 28 B.C., not included); 2 *c.* 26 B.C. (Gallus recently dead at 2.34.91); 3 between 23 and 20 B.C.; 4 *c.* 16 B.C. (death of Cornelia described in 4.11).

BIBLIOGRAPHY

(see H. Harrauer, *A bibliography to Propertius* (Hildesheim 1973))

TEXTS AND COMMENTARIES: TEXTS: J. P. Postgate, in *Corpus poetarum Latinorum* (London 1894); H. E. Butler (Loeb, 1912); M. Schuster and F. Dornseiff, 2nd ed. (BT, 1958); E. A. Barber, 2nd ed. (1960). COMMENTARIES: Complete: H. E. Butler and E. A. Barber (Oxford 1933); W. A. Camps (Cambridge 1961–7). Bks 1–2: P. J. Enk (Leiden 1946–62). Bk 1: P. Fedeli (Florence 1980). Bk 4: idem (Bari 1965).

STUDIES: (1) GENERAL: A. W. Allen, 'Sunt qui Propertium malint', in (ed.) Sullivan, under *General works* above; J.-P. Boucher, *Études sur Properce* (Paris 1965); E. Lefèvre, *Propertius ludibundus* (Heidelberg 1966); M. E. Hubbard, *Propertius* (London 1974); J. P. Sullivan, *Propertius: a critical introduction* (Cambridge 1976). (2) ON BK 4: C. Becker, *Hermes* 99 (1971) 449–80. (3) INDIVIDUAL POEMS. See Harrauer above and the following: R. O. A. M. Lyne, *P.C.Ph.S.* n.s.16 (1970) 60–78 (1.3); F. Cairns, *C.Q.* n.s.21 (1971) 455–60 (2.29a); idem, *C.Q.* n.s.24 (1974) 94–110 (1.1); J. Bramble, in (edd.) A. J. Woodman and D. West, *Quality and pleasure in Roman poetry* (Cambridge 1974) 81–93 (1.20). (4) TEXT AND INTERPRETATION: D. R. Shackleton Bailey, *Propertiana* (Cambridge 1956); G. Luck, *A.J.Ph.* 100 (1979) 73–93. (5) MANUSCRIPTS: A. E. Housman, *J.Ph.* 21 (1893) 101–97, and 22 (1894) 84–128 = *Classical papers* 232–304, 315–47.

CONCORDANCE: B. Schmeisser (Hildesheim 1972).

OVIDIUS NASO, PUBLIUS

LIFE

b. 20 March 43 B.C. at Sulmona (Abruzzi), of equestrian family. Sent to Rome as a boy to study rhetoric under Arellius Fuscus and Porcius Latro. Visited Athens and travelled in Greek lands. Held minor judicial posts, but abandoned official career for literature; cultivated society of poets, esp. those in circle of M. Valerius Messalla Corvinus. Thrice married. In A.D. 8 banished by Augustus on account of the *Ars Amatoria* and another cause, never specified, to Tomis (mod. Constanţa, Romania), where he d. A.D. 17. Main source for life his own works, esp. *Trist.* 4.10; also Sen. *Contr.* 2.2.8–12, 9.5.17 (rhetorical studies); Jerome, *Chron.* (death; cf. Ovid, *Fast.* 1.223–4 and Bömer, under *Commentaries* below, *ad loc.*); R. Syme, *History in Ovid* (Oxford 1978). On his official career see E. J. Kenney, *Y. Cl. S.* 21 (1969) 244–9; on his exile J. C. Thibault, *The mystery of Ovid's exile* (Berkeley 1964).

WORKS

(1) EXTANT: (All in elegiac couplets except *Met.*) *Amores*: three books totalling fifty elegies (15 + 20 + 15); in this form pubd shortly before *Ars Am.* (q.v.). *Heroides* or *Epistulae Heroidum* (G. Luck, *Die römische Liebeselegie* (Heidelberg 1961) 223–4): single letters (1–14) pubd between the two edd. of the *Amores* (*Am.* 2.18); double (16–21) written before A.D. 8 but possibly not pubd until after O.'s death. For *Ep. Sapph.* (15) see under (3) below. *Medicamina Faciei Femineae*: fragment of 100 vv. on cosmetics, pubd. before *Ars Am.* 3 (ibid. 205–6). *Ars Amatoria* (see Sen. *Contr.* 3.7, *GLK* v 473.5): bks 1–2 pubd not before 1 B.C. (*Ars Am.* 1.171ff.), bk 3 added later (*Ars Am.* 2.745–6). *Remedia Amoris*: mock recantation in one book; no indication of

date. (On the chronology of the early works see discussion and previous literature cited by H. Jacobson, *Ovid's Heroides* (Princeton 1974) 300–18; Syme, under *Life* above, 1–20.) *Metamorphoses*: epic in fifteen books of hexameters; substantially complete by A.D. 8. *Fasti*: calendar poem planned in twelve books, one per month; only bks 1–6 (Jan.–June) completed by A.D. 8, but some revision at Tomis (*Fast.* 1.3, 2.15). *Tristia*: bks 1, 3–5 are made up of short poems to various addressees (unnamed except for his wife and Augustus); bk 2 is a single continuous poem, an apologia for his poetry addressed to Augustus. Individual books sent to Rome at intervals during A.D. 9–12. *Epistulae ex Ponto*: as *Trist.* 1, 3–5, but to named addressees. Bks 1–3 compiled from poems of various dates (*Pont.* 3.9.53) and pubd A.D. 13; bk 4 probably posthumous. *Ibis*: pubd *c.* A.D. 11.

(2) LOST: *Amores* (version in five books): his first attested work, pubd in his early twenties (*Trist.* 4.10.55–60). Relationship with three-book ed. obscure: see Jacobson under (1) above. *Medea*: his only tragedy: *Am.* 2.18, 3.1, *Trist.* 2.553–4, Quint. 10.1.98, Tac. *Dial.* 12.6. Other lost works included epigrams and an abbreviated tr. of Aratus' *Phaenomena*. Fragments and testimonia: Owen, *Tristia* (OCT), Lenz, *Halieutica* etc. (Paravia), Postgate (*Corpus*), under *Texts* below.

(3) DUBIOUS OR SPURIOUS: *Heroides*: 9 (Deianira): D. W. T. C. Vessey, *C.Q.* n.s.19 (1969) 349–61. 15 (*Epistula Sapphus*): Jacobson (see *Works* (1) above) 277–99; H. Dörrie, *P. Ovidius Naso. Der Brief der Sappho an Phaon* (Munich 1975); R. J. Tarrant, *H.S.C.Ph.* (forthcoming). 16–21: B. Latta, *Die Stellung der Doppelbriefe (Heroides 16–21) im Gesamtwerk Ovids* (diss. Marburg 1963); E. Courtney, *B.I.C.S.* 12 (1965) 63–6; (on 16.39–144, 21.145–248) U. Fischer, *Ignotum hoc aliis novavit opus* (Augsburg 1969); E. J. Kenney, *C.Q.* n.s.29 (1979) 394–431. *Priapeum* 3: ascribed to O. on the strength of Seneca (*Contr.* 1.2.22), but see V. Buchheit, *Studien zum Corpus Priapeorum* (Munich 1962) 15–18. Certainly not by O. *Somnium* (*Am.* 3.5): E. J. Kenney, ΑΓΩΝ 3 (1969) 1–14. *Halieutica*, on sea-fishing: A. E. Housman, *Classical papers* 698–701; B. Axelson, *Eranos* 43 (1945) 23–35. *Nux*: A. G. Lee, in *Ovidiana*, under *Studies* below, 457–71. *Consolatio ad Liviam* (see pp. 474–5).

BIBLIOGRAPHY

(see R. J. Gariepy, *C. W.* 64 (1970) 37–56; Barsby, *Studies* below; *ANRW* II 31.4 (1981))

TEXTS AND COMMENTARIES: TEXTS: (1) Complete works: R. Ehwald, F. Lenz, F. Levy, W. S. Anderson, E. H. Alton, D. E. W. Wormell, E. Courtney (BT, 1916–78); E. J. Kenney, S. G. Owen (OCT, 1915–); J. H. Mozley, G. Showerman, F. J. Miller, A. J. Wheeler, (Sir) J. G. Frazer (Loeb, 1916–29: *Am.* and *Her.* rev. G. P. Goold 1977); A. Palmer, G. M. Edwards, G. A. Davies, S. G. Owen, A. E. Housman, J. P. Postgate, in *Corpus poetarum Latinorum* (ed. Postgate), vol. 1 (London 1905). (2) Individual works: *Amores*: A. G. Lee (London 1968: with tr.); F. Munari, 5th ed. (Florence 1970: with Italian tr.). *Heroides*: H. Sedlmayer (Vienna 1886); H. Dörrie

APPENDIX OF AUTHORS AND WORKS

(Berlin 1971). *Metamorphoses*: H. Magnus (Berlin 1914); cf. D. A. Slater, *Towards a text of the Metamorphosis of Ovid* (Oxford 1927). *Tristia*: S. G. Owen (Oxford 1889). COMMENTARIES. *Amores*: P. Brandt (Leipzig 1911); F. W. Lenz, 3rd ed. (Berlin 1976: with German tr.). Bk 1: J. A. Barsby (Oxford 1973: with tr.). *Heroides*: A. Palmer, 2nd ed. by L. C. Purser (Oxford 1898: with Greek prose tr. of M. Planudes). *Ep. Sapph.*: H. Dörrie (Munich 1975). *Med. Fac.*: A. Kunz (Vienna 1881). *Ars Amatoria*: P. Brandt (Leipzig 1902); F. W. Lenz (Berlin 1969: with German tr.). Bk 1: A. S. Hollis (Oxford 1977). *Remedia Amoris*: (with *Med. Fac.*) F. W. Lenz, 2nd ed. (Berlin 1968: with German tr.); A. A. R. Henderson (Edinburgh 1979). *Metamorphoses*: M. Haupt, O. Korn, R. Ehwald, 10th ed. rev. M. von Albrecht, 2 vols. (Zurich 1966); F. Bömer (Heidelberg 1969–). Bk 1: A. G. Lee (Cambridge 1953). Bks 6–10: W. S. Anderson (Norman, Oklahoma 1972). Bk 8: A. S. Hollis (Oxford 1970). *Fasti*: (Sir) J. G. Frazer, 5 vols. (London 1929: with tr.); F. Bömer, 2 vols. (Heidelberg 1957–8: with German tr.). *Tristia*: G. Luck, 2 vols. (Heidelberg 1967–77: with German tr.). Bk 2: S. G. Owen (Oxford 1924: with tr.). Bk 4: T. J. de Jonge (Groningen 1951). *Epistulae ex Ponto*: Bk 1: A. Scholte (Amersfurt 1933). *Ibis*: R. Ellis (Oxford 1881); A. la Penna (Florence 1957). [*Halieutica*: J. A. Richmond (London 1962); F. Capponi, 2 vols. (Leiden 1972). *Nux*: S. Wartena (Groningen 1928). *Cons. ad Liviam*: A. Witlox (Groningen 1935).]

TRANSLATIONS: H. T. Riley, 3 vols. (Bohn, 1852–9); Loeb (under *Texts* (1) above). M. Planudes: (*Heroides*) A. Palmer (under *Commentaries* above); M. Papathomopoulos, 2nd ed. (Joannina 1976); (*Ars Am., Am., Rem.*) P. E. Easterling and E. J. Kenney, *Ovidiana Graeca, P.C.Ph.S.* suppl. 1 (Cambridge 1965); (*Metamorphoses*) J. F. Boissonade (Paris 1822).

STUDIES: (1) GENERAL: E. Martini, *Einleitung zu Ovid* (Prague 1933); W. Kraus, 'Ovidius Naso', in von Albrecht and Zinn, *Ovid* (see below) 67–166 = rev. version of *RE* XVIII (1942) 1910–86; H. Fränkel, *Ovid: a poet between two worlds* (Berkeley 1945); L. P. Wilkinson, *Ovid recalled* (Cambridge 1955); J.-M. Frécaut, *L'esprit et l'humour chez Ovide* (Grenoble 1972); J. Barsby, *Ovid, G.&R., New surveys in the classics* 12 (Oxford 1978). (2) MISCELLANIES: (ed.) N. I. Herescu, *Ovidiana: recherches sur Ovide* (Paris 1958); *Atti del Convegno internazionale Ovidiano*, 2 vols. (Rome 1959); (edd.) M. von Albrecht and E. Zinn, *Ovid* (Darmstadt 1968); (ed.) J. W. Binns, *Ovid* (London 1973). (3) INDIVIDUAL WORKS: *Heroides*: H. Jacobson, *Ovid's Heroides* (Princeton 1974). *Metamorphoses*: B. Otis, *Ovid as an epic poet*, 2nd ed. (Cambridge 1970); G. K. Galinsky, *Ovid's Metamorphoses: an introduction to the basic aspects* (Berkeley 1975). (4) SURVIVAL: W. Stroh, *Ovid im Urteil der Nachwelt* (Darmstadt 1969); (*Heroides*) H. Dörrie, *Der heroische Brief* (Berlin 1968). (5) CONCORDANCE: R. J. Deferrari, M. Inviolata Barry, M. R. P. McGuire (Washington 1939).

LIVIUS, TITUS

LIFE

b. 59 B.C. in Patavium, d. A.D. 17 (Jerome, *Chron. ann. Abr.* 1958). A case has been made by R. Syme (*H.S.Ph.* 64 (1959) 27ff.) for a life-span five years earlier. For his activities in Rome see Pliny, *Epist.* 2.3.8; Suda s.v. 'Κορνοῦτος'; Quint. 1.5.56, 8.1.3; Tac. *Ann.* 4.34; Suet. *Claud.* 41.1.

WORKS

Ab urbe condita libri: history of Rome from foundation to 9 B.C., originally in 142 books (perhaps 150 were planned), of which 1–10 and 21–45 survive. Of the lost books there are fragments preserved by grammarians and others (including a passage from bk 120 on Cicero's death) and summaries (*Periochae* of whole work preserved in MSS and a 3rd c. papyrus from Oxyrhynchus containing epitomes of bks 37–40 and 48–55); see Mart. 14.190.1; Suet. *Dom.* 10.3. There is no trace of the philosophical dialogues which he wrote in his youth (Sen. *Epist.* 100.9), but the excursus on Alexander (9.17–18) possibly betrays the style of his youthful declamations.

BIBLIOGRAPHY

TEXTS AND COMMENTARIES: TEXTS: W. Weissenborn, M. Müller and W. Heraeus (BT, 1887–1908: bks 21–2 rev. T. A. Dorey 1971); R. S. Conway, C. F. Walters, S. K. Johnson, A. H. McDonald and R. M. Ogilvie (OCT, 1919–74: bks 1–35 so far pubd); J. Bayet and P. Jal (Budé, 1940–79: bks 1–7, 41–2, 45 and frs. so far pubd). COMMENTARIES: W. Weissenborn and H. J. Müller, 4th ed. (Berlin 1910). Bks 1–5: R. M. Ogilvie, 2nd ed. (Oxford 1969). Bks 31–7: J. Briscoe (Oxford 1973–81).

STUDIES: (1) GENERAL: P. G. Walsh, *Livy, his historical aims and methods* (Cambridge 1961); (ed.) E. Burck, *Wege zu Livius* (Darmstadt 1967); (ed.) T. A. Dorey, *Livy* (London 1971); P. G. Walsh, *G.&R.*, New surveys in the classics 8 (1974); T. J. Luce, *Livy: the composition of his history* (Princeton 1977). (2) LIFE AND CONNEXIONS: R. Syme, 'Livy and Augustus', *H.S.Ph.* 64 (1959) 27–76; H. Petersen, 'Livy and Augustus', *T.A.Ph.A.* 92 (1961) 440ff.; H. J. Mette, 'Livius und Augustus', *Gymnasium* 68 (1961) 278ff.; T. J. Luce, *T.A.Ph.A.* 71 (1965) 209ff.; E. Mensching, *M.H.* 24 (1967) 12ff. (3) ATTITUDE: E. Burck, 'Livius als augusteischer Historiker', *Die Welt als Geschichte* 1 (1935) 448ff.; I. Kajanto, *God and fate in Livy* (Turku 1957); M. Mazza, *Storia e ideologia in Livio* (Catania 1966); W. Liebeschütz, 'The religious position of Livy's history', *J.R.S.* 57 (1967) 45ff. (4) SOURCES: H. Nissen, *Kritische Untersuchungen über die Quellen der vierten und fünften Dekade des Livius* (Berlin 1868); A. Klotz, *Livius und seine Vorgänger* (Leipzig–Berlin 1940–1); R. M. Ogilvie, 'Livy, Licinius Macer and the Libri Lintei', *J.R.S.* 48 (1958) 40ff. (5) COMPOSITION AND STYLE: K. Witte, 'Über die Form der Darstellung', *Rh.M.* 65 (1910)

270ff., 359ff.; E. Burck, *Die Erzählungskunst des T. Livius* (Berlin 1934; 2nd ed. 1964); idem, *Einführung in die dritte Dekade des Livius* (Heidelberg 1950); A. H. McDonald, 'The style of Livy', *J.R.S.* 47 (1957) 155ff.; J.-P. Chausserie-Laprée, *L'expression narrative chez les historiens latins* (Paris 1969). (6) LANGUAGE: E. Wölfflin, *Livianische Kritik und livianischer Sprachgebrauch* (prog. Winterthur 1864); S. G. Stacey, 'Die Entwicklung des livianischen Stiles', *Arch. Lat. Lex.* 10 (1896) 17ff.; K. Gries, *Constancy in Livy's Latinity* (New York 1947); H. Tränkle, 'Beobachtungen und Erwägungen zum Wandel der livianischen Sprache', *W.S.* n.s.2 (1968) 103ff.

CONCORDANCE: D. Packard (Cambridge, Mass. 1968).

APPENDIX VERGILIANA

Collection of poems in various metres; so called, since Scaliger, from being printed as an appendix to the three canonical works of Virgil. At the most, a few epigrams in the *Catalepton* are genuine. In the case of the *Culex* and some of the *Catalepton*, demand for juvenilia created forgeries; elsewhere, ascription of extant works supplied the need. In the following list, D, S, and M denote ascriptions to Virgil by Donatus' *Vita Vergilii*, by the *Vita Servii*, or by the 9th- c. Murbach catalogue alone. For the *Vitae* see H. Nettleship, *Ancient lives of Vergil, with an essay on the poems of Vergil* (Oxford 1879); E. Norden, 'De Vitis Vergilianis', *Rh.M.* 61 (1906) 166–77; E. Diehl, *Die Vitae Vergilianae und ihre antiken Quellen* (Bonn 1911: Kleine Texte 72); A. Rostagni, *Suetonio: De poetis e biografi minori* (Turin 1944); OCT by C. Hardie, 2nd ed. (1957).

Moretum (M): description of country life; pre-Neronian (Mart. 13.13). *Copa* (S; cf. Charisius, *GLK* I 63.11): an invitation to drink, written after pub. of Prop. bk 4. *Dirae* (D, S), a farmer's curse, and *Lydia*, a love lament: not distinguished as two poems until discovery by F. Jacobs in 1729 that *Dirae* 104 marked beginning of a new poem in a Vatican MS. *Ciris* (D, S): Epyllion relating story of Scylla. *Culex* (D, S): mock-epic on death of a gnat; see Suet. *Vita Luc. ad init.* (cf. Stat. *Silv.* 2.7.73); Stat. *Silv.* I praef.; Mart. 8.56.20, 14.185; Nonius 211. *Catalepton* (D, S, mentioned along with *Epigrammata*): fifteen poems in various metres, the second accepted as V.'s by Quint. 8.3.27–9. *Priapea* (D, S): three poems, perhaps alluded to by Pliny, *Ep.* 5.3.6. *Elegiae in Maecenatem* (M): distinguished as two poems by Scaliger. *Aetna* (D, expressing doubt, S): see pp. 629–30 and 886.

BIBLIOGRAPHY

(1) General

TEXTS: R. Ellis (OCT, 1907); H. R. Fairclough, *Virgil* (Loeb, 1954) vol. II; R. Giomini (Florence 1962: with tr. and bibliography); W. V. Clausen, F. R. D. Goodyear, E. J. Kenney, J. A. Richmond (OCT, 1966).

SURVEYS: R. Pichon, *Journal des Savants* n.s.9 (1911) 113–25; G. D. Hadzsits, *C.W.* 15 (1922) 106–21; H. W. Prescott, *C.J.* 26 (1930) 49–62; R. Henry, *A.C.* 6 (1937) 357–95; G. E. Duckworth, *Vergilius* 1 (1938) 44–6, 3 (1939) 33–4, 6 (1940) 49–50; idem, *C.W.* 51 (1958) 92, 116–7; N. I. Herescu, *Bibliographie de la littérature latine* (Paris 1943) 159–65.

STUDIES: F. Skutsch, *Aus Vergils Frühzeit* (Leipzig 1901); idem, *Gallus und Vergil* (Leipzig 1906); H. R. Fairclough, 'The poems of the Appendix Vergiliana', *T.A.Ph.A.* 53 (1922) 5–34; A. Rostagni. *Virgilio minore, saggio sullo svolgimento della poesia virgiliana* (Turin 1933); E. H. Clift, *Latin pseudepigrapha* (Baltimore 1945); K. Büchner, *RE* VIIIA.1 (1955) 1061–1180; R. E. H. Westendorp Boerma, 'L'énigme de l'appendix Vergiliana', in (edd.) H. Bardon and R. Verdière, *Vergiliana* (Leiden 1971).

(2) Individual works

'MORETUM': F. L. Douglas, *A study of the Moretum* (New York 1929); R. B. Steele, 'The authorship of the Moretum', *T.A.Ph.A.* 61 (1930) 195ff.; W. Kroll, *RE* XVI (1933) 298–9; D. O. Ross, 'The Culex and Moretum as post-Augustan literary parodies', *H.S.C.Ph.* 79 (1975) 235ff. For Parthenius' doubtful *Moretum*, see R. Sabbadini, *R.F.* 31 (1903) 472. 'COPA': Commentary: E. H. Blakeney (Winchester 1933: with *Moretum*). Studies: M. Haupt, *Opuscula* I (Berlin 1875) 143ff.; F. Vollmer, *Rh.M.* 55 (1900) 527ff.; D. L. Drew, *C.Q.* 17 (1923) 73–81 and 19 (1925) 37–42; U. von Wilamowitz-Moellendorff, *Hellenistische Dichtung* II (Berlin 1924) 311–15; I. E. Drabkin, *The Copa* (Geneva–New York 1930); R. E. H. Westendorp Boerma, *Mnemosyne* 11 (1958) 331ff.; idem, *Hermeneus* 29 (1958) 114ff. 'DIRAE' AND 'LYDIA': Commentary: C. van der Graaf (Leiden 1945). Studies: W. M. Lindsay, *C.R.* 32 (1918) 62f. (ascribed to Cato), answered by R. P. Robinson, *T.A.Ph.A.* 54 (1923) 98–116; P. J. Enk, *Mnemosyne* n.s.47 (1919) 382–409 (ascribed to Varius); R. B. Steele, *The authorship of the Dirae and Lydia* (Nashville 1930); E. Fraenkel, *J.R.S.* 56 (1966) 142–55, answered and modified by F. R. D. Goodyear, *P.C.Ph.S.* n.s.17 (1971) 30–43. 'CIRIS': Commentaries: M. Lenchantin de Gubernatis (Turin 1930); R. Helm (Heidelberg 1937); H. Hielkema (diss. Utrecht 1941); D. Knecht (Bruge 1970); R. O. A. M. Lyne (Cambridge 1978). Studies: F. Leo, 'Vergil und die Ciris', *Hermes* 37 (1902) 14–55; R. F. Thomason, 'The Ciris and Ovid', *C.Ph.* 18 (1923) 239–62 (survey of earlier views), also ibid. 334–44, and 19 (1924) 147–56; F. Munari, 'Studi sulla Ciris', *Atti Accad. d. Italia, sci. mor. e stor.* 7.4 (1944) 273–314; F. Ehlers, 'Die Ciris und ihre Original', *M.H.* 11 (1954) 65–88; R. O. A. M. Lyne, 'The dating of the Ciris', *C.Q.* 65 (1971) 233–53. 'CULEX': Commentaries: F. Leo (Berlin 1891); C. Plésent (Paris 1910); C. Curcio (Turin 1928: with *Ciris*). Studies: D. L. Drew, *Culex* (Oxford 1925); R. S. Radford, 'The Culex and Ovid', *Philologus* 86 (1930) 18–66; E. Fraenkel, 'The Culex', *J.R.S.* 42 (1952) 1–9; R. Helm, 'Beiträge zum Culex', *Hermes* 81 (1953) 49ff.; D. Güntzschel, *Beiträge zur Datierung des Culex* (Münster–Aschendorff 1972); D. A. Ross (see above on *Moretum*). 'CATALEPTON' AND 'PRI-

APEIA': Commentary: R. E. H. Westendorp Boerma, 2 vols. (Assen 1949–63). Studies: E. Galletier, *Epigrammata et Priapea* (Paris 1920); idem, *R.Ph.* 50 (1926) 153–72; J. Carcopino, *R.Ph.* 46 (1922) 156–84; R. S. Radford, 'Ovid's carmina furtiva', *Ph.Q.* 7 (1928) 45–59; R. B. Steele, *The Catalepta of the Virgilian Appendix* (Nashville 1936). *Catalepton* 9: P. John, *Rh.M.* 63 (1908) 100; P. Sonner, *De P. Virgili Maronis Catalepton carminibus quaestionum capita tria* (diss. Halle 1910). *Catalepton* 13: G. Némethy, *De epodo Horatii Cataleptis Virgilii inserto* (Budapest 1908); J. Hubaux, 'Une épode d'Ovide', in *Serta Leodiensia* (Liège 1930) 187–245; idem, *A.C.* 7 (1938) 77–80.

VALGIUS RUFUS, GAIUS

LIFE

Consul *suffectus* 12 B.C. (Prosop. 3.382.N.169); mentioned at Hor. *Sat.* 1.10.82, and the recipient of *Odes* 2.9. Refs. in the fragments to Codrus and Cinna imply an early Augustan dating: no reason to suppose he was younger than Horace.

WORKS

Elegiac laments (Hor. *Odes* 2.9); hendecasyllables (preserved by Charisius, *GLK* I 108.7); bucolic hexameters (quoted by Philargyrius *ad* Virg. *Geo* 3.177); book on herbs (Pliny, *N.H.* 25.4); translation of Apollodorus' *Rhetoric* (Quint. 3.1.18, 5.17, 5.104); etymological work (Gell. 12.3.1, Charisius, *GLK* I 108.28). Fragments in *FPL* 105–6. See Schanz–Hosius II 172–4; Bardon II 19–22.

DOMITIUS MARSUS

LIFE

Dead at time of Ovid, *Pont.* 4.16.5, but still alive in 19 B.C. (date of lines on deaths of Virgil and Tibullus). For his connexion with Maecenas see Mart. 5.29.5, 8.56.23. Also mentioned at Mart. *praef.* 1, 2.71.3, 2.77.5, 5.5.5, 7.99.7.

WORKS

Epigrams: probably represented by frs. 3 (Epirota), 4 (Horace's schoolmaster Orbilius), 5 (*hircum et alumen olens*), and 7 (Virgil and Tibullus). Philargyrius (*ad* Virg. *Ecl.* 3.90) attests the title *Cicuta*: since, however, it implies something rustic, it might have been a collection within a collection; cf. Martial's *Liber spectaculorum*. Elegies (?): *fusca Melaenis* mentioned at Mart. 7.29.5, although she could have figured in the epigrams. Also an epic, *Amazonis* (4.29.7), *Fabellae* (Charisius, *GLK* I 72.4), and a prose work *De urbanitate* (Quint. 6.3.102, 104ff.). Fragments in *FPL* 110–11. See Schanz–Hosius II 174–6, Bardon II 52–7.

AEMILIUS MACER

LIFE

b. in Verona (Serv. *ad Ecl.* 5.1, identifying him with Mopsus), d. in Asia 16 B.C. (Jerome, *Chron. ann. Abr.* 2001). An acquaintance of Tibullus (Tib. 2.6.1).

WORKS

Didactic poems on birds, serpents and herbs (Ovid, *Trist.* 4.10.43), the last two possibly belonging to one work. Diomedes (*GLK* I 374.21) and Nonius (220.18 and 518.32) attest the title *Ornithogonia*; Charisius (*GLK* I 81.18) attests a *Theriaka*, in two books, as shown by *Comm. Bern. ad* Lucan 9.701. *Dist. Cat.* 2, *praef.* 2 is of dubious value for the *De herbis*. Boios has been claimed as source for *Ornithogonia* by G. Knaack, *Analecta Alexandrino-Romana* (Greifswald 1880) 11, and G. Lafaye, *Les métamorphoses d'Ovide* (Paris 1904) 43: ref. to *pictas uolucres* at Manil. 2.43 is probably to Boios, not Macer. Quint. 10.1.56 notes M.'s unsuccessful imitation of Nicander (in his *Theriaka*), for which see also R. Unger, *De Aemilio Macro Nicandris imitatore* (Friedland 1845), Schneider's edition of Nicander (Leipzig 1856) 74, Knaack (above), and K. P. Schulze, *Rh.M.* 53 (1898) 543. Quintilian calls his style *humilis* at 10.1.87.

BIBLIOGRAPHY

Fragments in *FPL* 107–10. Discussions in Teuffel II 22–3, Schanz–Hosius II 164–5, Bardon II 44–7.

VARIUS RUFUS

LIFE

A contemporary of Virgil and Horace (Jerome, *Chron. ann. Abr.* 2000), but older than they (Virg. *Ecl.* 9.35, bracketing him with Republican poet Cinna), he introduced Horace to Maecenas (Hor. *Sat.* 1.6.55), and is mentioned several times in the *Satires* (1.5.40 and 93, 1.9.23, 1.10.81, 2.8.21 and 63). Editor with Tucca of Virgil's *Aeneid*, on the author's death (Quint. 10.3.8, Donat. *Vita Verg.* 39, Jerome, *Chron.* above, Serv. *praef.*).

WORKS

De morte (title attested by Macr. *Sat.* 2.19.20, 6.1.39–40): most probably a didactic with Epicurean flavour (on V.'s philosophy see Quint. 6.3.78); appears to have attacked Antony. Some critics identify it with the *forte epos* of Hor. *Sat.* 1.10.43, changing its title to *De morte Caesaris*: but the preposition *de* implies didactic, and no ancient epic has a similar title. Fr. 1 imitated at Virg. *Aen.* 6.621, 2 at *Geo.* 2.506, 3 at *Geo.* 3. 115 and 4 at *Ecl.* 8.88. Of Varian epic we have nothing: *recusatio* at Hor. *Odes* 1.6 implies that V. is a suitable author for Agrippa's exploits, also that he contemplated a *Diomedea*, but no more. A tragedy, *Thyestes*: produced at games for Actium 29 B.C. (Parisinus 7530); see Quint. 10.1.18, 3.8.45. Valgius Rufus and the Varus of the *Eclogues* have been claimed for authorship, but Tac. *Dial.* 12 and Quint. 3.8.45 and 11.3.73 are quite clear on the name. Bardon (II 82) claims other tragedies for V., perhaps correctly. *Panegyricus Augusti*: attested by Porph. and ps.-Acron *ad* Hor. *Epist.* 1.16.27–9, which has been claimed as a recasting of the original; the rhythm, at any rate, is clearly that of Horace. Elegies mentioned at Porph. *ad Odes.* 1.6.1 have no other ancient testimony and are therefore suspect. Fragments in *FPL* 100–1.

BIBLIOGRAPHY

R. Unger, *Varii de Morte eclog. reliqu.* (Halle 1870); A. E. Housman, 'The Thyestes of Varius', *C.Q.* 11 (1917) 42–8; Schanz–Hosius II 162–4; A. Momigliano, 'Epicureans in revolt', *J.R.S.* 31 (1941) 151–7; E. Bickel, *S.O.* 28 (1950) 100ff.; Bardon II 28–34; Nisbet and Hubbard (1970) on Hor. *Odes* 1.6; H. D. Jocelyn, *C.Q.* n.s. 30 (1980) 387–400.

GRATTIUS

LIFE

Wrote before A.D. 8 (Ovid, *Pont.* 4.16.34) and is often assumed to have come from Falerii (see v.40). *Bella ferarum* at Manil. 2.43 is an allusion to a Greek *Cynegetica*, not to G.

WORKS

An incomplete *Cynegetica*, in 536 lines, with five fragments. For his improbable bucolics (on the basis of Ovid, *Pont.* 4.16.33) see Bardon II 58.

BIBLIOGRAPHY

TEXTS AND COMMENTARIES: TEXTS: *PLM* I 29–53; J. W. and A. M. Duff, *Minor Latin poets*, 2nd ed. (Loeb, 1935). COMMENTARIES: P. J. Enk (Zutphen 1918); R. Verdière, 2 vols. (Wetteren 1964).

STUDIES: M. Fiegl, *Des Grattius Faliscus Cynegetica, seine Vorgänger und seine Nachfolger* (Görz 1890); G. Pierleoni, 'Fu poeta Grattius?', *R.F.* 34 (1906) 580ff.; P. H. Damsté, 'Ad Grattium notulae'. *Mnemosyne* 53 (1925) 299ff., J. Tolkiehn, Bursian 153 (1911) 95, and 171 (1915) 5; M. Schuster, ibid. 212 (1927) 82.

GERMANICUS IULIUS CAESAR

LIFE

b. 15 B.C., adopted by his uncle Tiberius A.D. 4; served under him in Pannonia and Germany (7–11), consul 12, proconsul in Gaul and Germany from 13. d. A.D. 19.

WORKS

Aratea: 686 lines (in MSS, *Claudi Caesaris Arati Phaenomena*), an adapted translation of Aratus' *Phaenomena*. Apostrophe to Augustus at 558 implies he is dead: *genitor* at 2 is Tiberius. Domitian, who also took title Germanicus, has been unnecessarily canvassed for authorship. Epigrams: *Anth. Lat.* 708, which has a Greek version (*Anth. Pal.* 9.387), *Anth. Lat.* 709 (= *Anth. Pal.* 7.542), *Anth. Pal.* 9.17–18 (see also Pliny, *N.H.* 8.55). Greek comedies (Suet. *Cal.* 3.2, *Claud.* 11.2). Ovid addresses him at *Fast.* 1.19, *Pont.* 2.5.55 and 4.8.67ff.

BIBLIOGRAPHY

TEXTS AND COMMENTARY: TEXTS: A. Breysig (Berlin 1867: with scholia); idem (BT, 1899); *PLM* 1; A. le Boeuffle (Budé, 1975). COMMENTARY: D. B. Gain (London 1976).

STUDIES: J. Frey, *De Germanico Arati interprete* (Culm 1861); G. Sieg, *De Cicerone Germanico, Avieno Arati interpretibus* (Halle 1886); J. Maybaum, *De Cicerone et Germanico Arati interpretibus* (Rostock 1889); A. E. Housman, 'The Aratea of Germanicus', *C.R.* 14 (1900) 26ff.; J. Tolkiehn, Bursian 153 (1911) 102, and 171 (1915) 14; M. Gelzer and W. Kroll, *RE* x (1919) 435–64.

MANILIUS, MARCUS

LIFE

No external testimonia, though he was imitated by, e.g., Lucan. Wrote his poem under Augustus (and Tiberius?): internal evidence for dating discussed by Housman (under *Texts* below: 1903, lxix ff. and 1930, 111ff.). 5.513 (so Housman, *ad loc.*) is not an allusion to the burning of Pompey's theatre in A.D. 22. For his name see Housman (1930, 108ff.).

WORKS

Astronomica in five books, probably unfinished: Housman asks if there originally may have been eight books (1903, lxxii).

BIBLIOGRAPHY

TEXT AND COMMENTARIES: TEXT: A. E. Housman (Cambridge 1932); G. P. Goold (Loeb, 1977). COMMENTARIES: A. E. Housman, 5 vols. (London 1903–30; repr. in two vols. Hildesheim 1972). Bk 2: H. W. Garrod (Oxford 1911: with tr.).

STUDIES: G. Lanson, *De Manilio poeta eiusque ingenio* (Paris 1887); A. Kraemer, *De Manilii qui feruntur astronomicis* (Marburg 1890); R. Ellis, *Noctes Manilianae* (Oxford 1891); C. Hosius, 'Lucan und seine Quellen', *Rh.M.* 48 (1893) 393ff.; F. Cumont, *Astrology and religion among the Greeks and Romans* (New York 1912); F. Schwemmler, *De Lucano Manilii imitatore* (Giessen 1916); R. B. Steele, 'The Astronomica of Manilius', *A.J.Ph.* 53 (1932) 320.

RABIRIUS, GAIUS

LIFE AND WORKS

Author of an epic on the civil war between Antony and Octavian. Most important notices are Ovid, *Pont.* 4.16.5, Vell. Pat. 2.36.3, Sen. *Ben.* 6.3.1 (ascribing fr. 2 to the dying Antony) and Quint. 10.1.90. Rightly, Bardon (II 69) sees him as a precursor of Lucan, and denies (73–4) that he is the author of the Herculaneum Papyrus on the Egyptian war: community of subject matter has encouraged the ascription; see Bardon loc. cit. and 136–7, Schanz-Hosius II 267–8. M. Alfonsi, 'Nota a Rabirio', *Aegyptus* (1944) 196ff., has credited him with the supposedly Virgilian lines on the Egyptian war mentioned by the humanist Decembrius, *armatum cane, Musa, ducem belloque cruentam Aegyptum*: see R. Sabbadini, *Le scoperte dei codici latini e greci ne' secoli XIV e XV* (Florence 1905) 138–9. For the elephant simile see J. Aymard, *Quelques séries de comparaisons chez Lucain* (Montpellier 1951). Fragments in *FPL* 120–1.

CORNELIUS SEVERUS

WORKS

Epic on Roman history, scope uncertain: Ovid attests the '*carmen regale*' (*Pont.* 4.16.9, cf. 4.2.1 and 11), Quintilian the '*bellum Siculum*' (10.1.89), Probus the *res Romanae* (*GLK* IV 208.16). Sen. *Suas.* 6.26 preserves fragment on death of Cicero; Sen. *Epist.* 79.5 mentions a description of Etna. See Schanz–Hosius II 268–9; Bardon II 61–4; P. Grenade, 'Le mythe de Pompée et les Pompéiens sous les Césars', *R.E.A.* 52 (1950) 28–67 (influence on Lucan).

ALBINOVANUS PEDO

LIFE

Contemporary of Ovid (*Pont.* 4.16.6), who calls him *sidereus* (an adulatory epithet, cf. Colum. 10.434 of Virgil; not implying a *De sideribus*); probably the *praefectus equitum* of Tac. *Ann.* 1.60; coupled by Quint. (10.1.90) with Rabirius. Called *fabulator elegantissimus* at Sen. *Epist.* 122.15 (cf. Sen. *Contr.* 2.10.12).

WORKS

Poem on Germanicus' expedition in North Sea A.D. 16 (fr. preserved by Sen. *Suas.* 1.15); an epic, *Theseis* (Ovid, *Pont.* 4.10.71); epigrams (Mart. *praef.* 1, 2.77.5, 5.5.5, 10.19.10). See R. G. Kent, *C.R.* 17 (1903) 311ff.; Bardon II 69–73.

POMPEIUS TROGUS

LIFE AND WORKS

For his Gallic ancestry, see Justin 43.5.11; his cursory treatment of early Italian history, 43.1.2.; his censure of direct discourse, 38.3.11. *Historiae Philippicae* (44 bks): history of Near East down to 20 B.C., extant only in fragments and in Justin's epitome. Scientific works attested by Charisius, *GLK* I 102.10 and 137.9, Pliny, *N.H.* 17.58.

BIBLIOGRAPHY

TEXTS: Fragments: O. Seel (BT, 1956). Justin's epitome: idem (BT, 1972).

STUDIES: H. Peter, *Die geschichtliche Literatur über die römische Kaiserzeit bis Theodosius I und ihre Quellen* (Leipzig 1897); Schanz–Hosius II 319–77; W. Kroll, *RE* X (1919) 956; E. Norden, *Die antike Kunstprosa*, 4th ed. (Leipzig–Berlin 1923) 300; A. Momigliano, 'Livio, Plutarco.e Giustino su virtu e fortuna dei Romani', *Athenaeum* (1934) 45–56; M. Rambaud, 'Salluste et Trogue-Pompée', *R.E.L.* 26 (1948) 171ff.; O. Seel, *Die Praefatio des Pompeius Trogus* (Erlangen 1955); A. D. Leeman, *Orationis ratio* (Amsterdam 1963) 244–7 (T. a *Sallustianus*, his predilection for *oratio obliqua* perhaps deriving from Caesar); O. Seel, *Eine römische Weltgeschichte, Studien zum Text der Epitome des Justinus und zur Historik des Pompeius Trogus* (Nuremberg 1972).

VITRUVIUS POLLIO

LIFE

A late Republican, early Augustan date is usually given: he addresses Augustus in his proem, but does not mention any of the important buildings of the reign.

WORKS

De architectura in ten books. See Schanz–Hosius II 386–95.

BIBLIOGRAPHY

TEXTS: V. Rose, 2nd ed. (Leipzig 1899); F. Krohn (BT, 1912); F. Granger (Loeb, 1931); C. Fensterbusch (Darmstadt 1964).

CELSUS, AULUS CORNELIUS

WORKS

Artes: encyclopaedia, possibly composed under Tiberius, dealing with agriculture, medicine, the military arts, rhetoric, philosophy and jurisprudence (see Quint. 12.11.24); medical section alone survives, in eight books. Alternative title suggested by schol. Plaut. *Bacch.* 69, *Celsus libros suos a uarietate rerum 'cestos' uocauit.* Sources include the Hippocratic Corpus, Asclepiades, Heraclides of Tarentum, Erasistratus, Philoxenus and Meges of Sidon.

BIBLIOGRAPHY

TEXTS: E. Milligan, 2nd ed. (Edinburgh 1831: with index); S. de Renzi (Naples 1851: with lexicon); C. Daremberg (BT, 1859), rev. F. Marx, *Corp. Med. Lat.* 17 (Leipzig 1915); W. G. Spenser (Loeb, 1935). Bks 1–4: F. Serra (Pisa 1976).

STUDIES: Schanz–Hosius II 722–9; J. Scarborough, *Roman medicine* (Ithaca, N.Y. 1969); *OCD* s.v. 'Medicine'; J. Ilberg, in (ed.) H. Flashar, *Antike Medizin, Wege der Forschung* 221 (Darmstadt 1971); E. D. Phillips, *Greek medicine* (London 1973).

SENECA, LUCIUS ANNAEUS

LIFE AND WORKS

LIFE: b. of equestrian family at Corduba in Spain, probably in 50s B.C. Divided his time between Rome and Spain (dates uncertain). *Condiscipulus* and lifelong friend of

Porcius Latro, but not a rhetorician himself. Three sons: Novatus (later Junius Gallio), Seneca (the philosopher), and Mela (Lucan's father). d. before A.D. 41. See Fairweather, under *Studies* below, 3–26. WORKS: (1) Extant: *Oratorum et rhetorum sententiae divisiones colores* (completed after A.D. 34 (*Suas.* 2.22), possibly in Caligula's reign): one book of seven *Suasoriae* (more were planned, *Contr.* 2.4.8), and ten, each with preface, of *Controversiae* (only bks 1–2, 7, 9–10 survive; 4th–5th c. abridgement supplies two missing prefaces and excerpts from lost books). (2) Lost: History from beginning of civil wars to his own times; see younger Seneca fr. 98 Haase.

BIBLIOGRAPHY

TEXTS AND COMMENTARY: TEXTS: A. Kiessling (BT, 1872); H. J. Müller (Vienna 1887); M. Winterbottom (Loeb, 1974). COMMENTARY: *Suas.*: W. A. Edward (Cambridge 1928).

STUDIES: H. Bardon, *Le vocabulaire de la critique littéraire chez Sénèque le Rhéteur* (Paris 1940); L. A. Sussman, *The elder Seneca* (Leiden 1978); J. A. Fairweather, *Seneca the elder* (Cambridge 1981).

SURVEYS: J. E. G. Whitehorne, *Prudentia* 1 (1969) 14ff.; forthcoming articles by Sussman and Fairweather in *ANRW*.

METRICAL APPENDIX

(1) BASIC PRINCIPLES
(A) STRESSED AND QUANTITATIVE VERSE

In metres familiar to speakers of English, rhythm is measured by the predictable alternation of one or more stressed syllables with one or more unstressed syllables (distinguished by the notation – and ᴗ, or ′ and ˣ). Consequently, it is word-accent that determines whether or not a word or sequence of words may stand in a certain part of the verse. Thus the word *classical* may occupy the metrical unit represented by the notation –ᴗᴗ by virtue of the stress imparted to its first syllable in everyday pronunciation. In contrast, the rhythms of classical Latin metres are measured by the predictable alternation of one or more 'heavy' syllables with one or more 'light' syllables (defined below, and distinguished by the notation – and ᴗ), so that in the construction of Latin verse the factor of primary importance is not word-accent but syllabic 'weight'. Thus the word *facerent*, although accented in normal speech on the first syllable, consists for metrical purposes of two light syllables followed by one heavy syllable, and for this reason can only occupy the metrical unit ᴗᴗ–. Verse constructed upon this principle is conventionally designated *quantitative*: it should be emphasized that this term refers to the quantity (or 'weight') of syllables, and that throughout this account such quantity is described by the terms 'heavy' and 'light' to distinguish it from the intrinsic length of vowels; unfortunately, both syllabic weight and vowel-length are still generally denoted by the same symbols, – and ᴗ.

(B) SYLLABIFICATION

A syllable containing a long vowel or diphthong is heavy (e.g. the first syllables of *pacem* and *laudo*).

A syllable containing a short vowel is light if it ends with that vowel (e.g. the first syllable of *pecus*), but heavy if it ends with a consonant (e.g. the first syllable of *pectus*).

To decide whether or not a short-vowelled syllable ends with a consonant (and thus to establish its quantity), the following rules should be observed:[1] (i) word-division

---

[1] The resulting division is practical only; for the difficulties involved in an absolute definition of the syllabic unit see Allen (1973) under (4) below, esp. 27–40.

should be disregarded; (ii) a single consonant between two vowels or diphthongs belongs to the succeeding syllable (thus *pecus* →*pe–cus*; *genus omne* →*ge–nu–som–ne*); (iii) of two or more successive consonants, at least one belongs to the preceding syllable (thus *pectus* →*pec–tus*; also *nulla spes* →*nul–las–pes*, though short final vowels are normally avoided in this position), except as allowed for below.

Note: for this purpose *h* is disregarded; *x* and *z* count as double consonants, 'semi-consonantal' *i* and *u* as consonants (except in the combination *qu*, regarded as a single consonant).

To (iii) there is an important exception. In the case of the combination of a plosive and liquid consonant (*p, t, c, b, d, g* followed by *r* or *l*), the syllabic division may be made either between the consonants (e.g. *pat–ris*) or before them (e.g. *pa–tris*), resulting in *either* a heavy *or* a light preceding syllable. However, when two such consonants belong to different parts of a compound or to two different words, the division is always made between them, giving a heavy preceding syllable (e.g. *ablego* → *ab–lego*, not *a–blego*; *at rabidae* →*at–rabidae*, not *a–trabidae*). Lastly, when, after a short final vowel, these consonants begin the next word, the division is nearly always made before them, giving a light preceding syllable (e.g. *plumbea glans* →*plum–be–a–glans*).

(C) ACCENT

The nature of the Latin word-accent (whether one of pitch or stress) and its importance in the construction of verse are both matters of controversy: for a clear discussion of the basic problems see Wilkinson under (4) below, 89–96, 221–36. By way of practical guidance in reading Latin verse, all that may be said is that for the present-day English speaker, accustomed to a naturalistic manner of reading poetry, it will sound as strange (and monotonous) to emphasize the heavy syllables of a metrical structure ('Quális Théseá iacuít cedénte carína') as it does to read Shakespearian verse with attention only to its iambic structure ('Now ís the wínter óf our díscontént'); furthermore that, even in giving stress to the word-accent in Latin verse, heavy syllables will generally coincide with accented syllables with sufficient frequency to ensure that the metre is not forgotten – particularly at the beginning and end of many metres, as in the hexameter quoted above. It should be remembered, however, that what sounds natural is not thereby authentic, and that poetic delivery is highly susceptible to whims of fashion, idiosyncrasy and affectation. Even now it is not uncommon criticism of a Shakespearian actor that he 'mutilates' the shape of the verse by reading it as prose, while recordings of Tennyson and Eliot reading their poetry already sound bizarre (in different ways) to the modern ear.

(2) TECHNICAL TERMS

Anceps ('unfixed'): term used to describe a metrical element which may be represented by either a heavy or a light syllable. The final element of many Latin metres is regularly of this nature, but not in certain lyric metres in which there is metrical continuity (*synaphea*) between as well as within lines.

Brevis brevians, or *the law of iambic shortening*: in comedy and other early Latin verse a heavy syllable may be lightened if it directly follows a light syllable and is adjacent to an accented syllable.

Caesura ('cutting') and *diaeresis*: division between words within a verse is termed *caesura* when occurring inside a metrical foot, or *diaeresis* when occurring at the end of a foot. The varied distribution of these plays an important part in avoiding monotony in the structure of verse; in particular, the caesura prevents a succession of words co-extensive with the feet of a metre (as found in Ennius' hexameter, 'sparsis hastis longis campus splendet et horret').

Elision and *hiatus*: a vowel (or vowel + *m*) ending a word is generally suppressed or *elided* when immediately preceding another vowel or *h*. When it is not elided in these circumstances (a phenomenon most frequently found in comedy), it is said to be in *hiatus*; by the rare process of *correption* a long vowel or diphthong in hiatus may be scanned short to make a light syllable. *Prodelision* (or *aphaeresis*) signifies the suppression of *e* in *est* after a final vowel or *m*, *hypermetric elision* the suppression of a vowel between lines (nearly always that of –*que*).

Resolution: the substitution of two light syllables for a heavy one.

(3) COMMON METRES

For the sake of simplicity only the most basic characteristics of each metre are given here. For the numerous divergencies regarding anceps, resolution, position of caesura etc., see Raven under (4) below.

(a) Stichic verse (constructed by repetition of the same metrical line)
Iambic senarius (or trimeter):

$$\underset{\smile}{-}\,\smile\,-\,|\,\underset{\smile}{-}\,\smile\,-\,|\,\underset{\smile}{-}\,\smile\,\underset{\smile}{}$$

(commonest dialogue metre in early Roman drama; also used in Seneca's tragedies, Phaedrus' *Fables*, and, in alternation with an iambic dimeter (= $\underset{\smile}{-}\,\smile\,-\,|\,\underset{\smile}{-}\,\smile\,-$), Horace's *Epodes* 1–10)
Iambic septenarius (or tetrameter catalectic):

$$\underset{\smile}{-}\,\smile\,-\,|\,\underset{\smile}{-}\,\smile\,-\,|\,\underset{\smile}{-}\,\smile\,-\,|\,\smile\,-\,\underset{\smile}{}$$

(common dialogue metre of comedy)

Trochaic septenarius (or tetrameter catalectic):

$$-\cup-\underset{\smile}{\cup}\,|\,-\cup-\underset{\smile}{\cup}\,|\,-\cup-\underset{\smile}{\cup}\,|\,-\cup\underset{\smile}{\cup}$$

(very common dialogue metre in early Roman drama)

Hexameter:

$$-\underset{\smile\smile}{}\,|\,-\underset{\smile\smile}{}\,|\,-\underset{\smile\smile}{}\,|\,-\underset{\smile\smile}{}\,|\,-\cup\cup\,|\,-\underset{\smile}{}$$

(regular metre for epic, satiric, pastoral and didactic poetry)

Pentameter:

$$-\underset{\smile\smile}{}-\underset{\smile\smile}{}-\,|\,-\cup\cup-\cup\cup\underset{\smile}{}$$

(following the hexameter this forms the elegiac couplet, which is regarded as an entity and hence as stichic; regular metre for love-poetry and epigram)

Phalaecean hendecasyllables:

$$\underset{\smile}{\circ}\,|\,-\cup\cup-\,|\,\cup-\cup-\underset{\smile}{}$$

(i.e. first foot may be a spondee, iamb or trochee; used by Catullus, Martial and Statius)

(b) Non-stichic verse (constructed by combination of different metrical lines)

Alcaic stanza:	$--\cup--\,|\,-\cup\cup-\,|\,\cup\underset{\smile}{}$	(twice)
	$--\cup---\cup-\underset{\smile}{}$	
	$-\cup\cup-\cup\cup-\,|\,\cup-\underset{\smile}{}$	
Sapphic stanza:	$-\cup--\,|\,-\cup\cup-\,|\,\cup-\underset{\smile}{}$	(three times)
	$-\cup\cup-\,|\,\underset{\smile}{}$	(adonean)
Third asclepiad:	$--\,|\,-\cup\cup-\,|\,\cup\underset{\smile}{}$	(glyconic)
	$--\,|\,-\cup\cup--\cup\cup-\,|\,\cup\underset{\smile}{}$	(lesser asclepiad)
Fourth asclepiad:	$--\,|\,-\cup\cup--\cup\cup-\,|\,\cup\underset{\smile}{}$	(lesser asclepiad, three times)
	$--\,|\,-\cup\cup-\,|\,\cup\underset{\smile}{}$	(glyconic)
Fifth asclepiad	$--\,|\,-\cup\cup--\cup\cup-\,|\,\cup\underset{\smile}{}$	(lesser asclepiad, twice)
	$--\,|\,-\cup\cup-\,|\,\underset{\smile}{}$	(pherecratean)
	$--\,|\,-\cup\cup-\,|\,\cup\underset{\smile}{}$	(glyconic)

(the First and Second asclepiad consist, respectively, of the lesser and greater asclepiad only; the latter $= --\,|\,-\cup\cup--\cup\cup--\cup\cup-\,|\,\cup\underset{\smile}{})$

All the above found in Horace's *Odes*; some in Catullus and Statius.

(4) BIBLIOGRAPHY

Allen, W. S., *Vox Latina*, 2nd ed. (Cambridge 1978).

idem, *Accent and rhythm* (Cambridge 1973).

Raven, D. S., *Latin metre* (London 1965).

Wilkinson, L. P., *Golden Latin artistry* (Cambridge 1963) 89–134 and *passim*

ABBREVIATIONS

Anth. Lat.	A. Riese–F. Bücheler–E. Lommatzsch, *Anthologia Latina Latina* (Leipzig, 1894–1926). (Cf. *CLE*)
ANRW	H. Temporini, *Aufstieg und Niedergang der römischen Welt* (Berlin, 1972–)
Bardon	H. Bardon, *La littérature latine inconnue* (Paris 1951–6)
BT	Bibliotheca Scriptorum Graecorum et Romanorum Teubneriana (Leipzig & Stuttgart)
Budé	Collection des Universités de France, publiée sous le patronage de l'Association Guillaume Budé (Paris)
Bursian	Bursian's *Jahresbericht über die Fortschritte der klassischen Altertumswissenschaft* (Berlin, 1873–1945)
CAF	T. Kock, *Comicorum Atticorum Fragmenta* (Leipzig, 1880–8)
CAH	*The Cambridge Ancient History* (Cambridge, 1923–39)
CAH²	2nd ed. (Cambridge, 1961–)
CC	*Corpus Christianorum.* Series Latina (Turnholt, 1953–)
CGF	G. Kaibel, *Comicorum Graecorum Fragmenta* (Berlin, 1899)
CGFPap.	C. F. L. Austin, *Comicorum Graecorum Fragmenta in papyris reperta* (Berlin, 1973)
CIL	*Corpus Inscriptionum Latinarum* (Berlin, 1863–)
CLE	F. Bücheler–E. Lommatzsch, *Carmina Latina Epigraphica* (Leipzig, 1897–1930). (= *Anth. Lat.* Pars II)
CRF	O. Ribbeck, *Comicorum Romanorum Fragmenta*, 3rd. ed. (Leipzig, 1897)
CSEL	*Corpus Scriptorum Ecclesiasticorum Latinorum* (Vienna, 1866–)
CVA	*Corpus Vasorum Antiquorum* (Paris & elsewhere, 1925–)
Christ–Schmid–Stählin	W. von Christ, *Geschichte der griechischen Literatur*, rev. W. Schmid and O. Stählin (Munich, 1920–1924) 6th ed. (Cf. Schmid–Stählin)
DTC	A. W. Pickard-Cambridge, *Dithyramb, tragedy and comedy*. 2nd ed., rev. T. B. L. Webster (Oxford, 1962)
DFA	A. W. Pickard-Cambridge, *The dramatic festivals of Athens*. 2nd ed., rev. J. Gould–D. M. Lewis (Oxford, 1968)

ABBREVIATIONS

DK	H. Diels–W. Kranz, *Die Fragmente der Vorsokratiker*. 6th ed. (Berlin, 1951)
EGF	G. Kinkel, *Epicorum Graecorum Fragmenta* (Leipzig, 1877)
FGrH	F. Jacoby, *Fragmente der griechischen Historiker* (Berlin, 1923–)
FHG	C. Müller, *Fragmenta Historicorum Graecorum* (Berlin, 1841–70)
FPL	W. Morel, *Fragmenta Poetarum Latinorum* (Leipzig, 1927)
FPR	E. Baehrens, *Fragmenta Poetarum Romanorum* (Leipzig, 1886)
FYAT	(ed.) M. Platnauer, *Fifty years (and twelve) of classical scholarship* (Oxford, 1968)
GLK	H. Keil, *Grammatici Latini* (Leipzig, 1855–1923)
GLP	D. L. Page, *Greek Literary Papyri* (Cambridge, Mass. & London, 1942–)
Gow–Page, *Hell. Ep.*	A. S. F. Gow–D. L. Page, *The Greek Anthology: Hellenistic Epigrams* (Cambridge, 1965)
Gow–Page, *Garland*	A. S. F. Gow–D. L. Page, *The Greek Anthology: The Garland of Philip* (Cambridge, 1968)
Guthrie	W. K. C. Guthrie, *A History of Greek Philosophy* (Cambridge, 1965–81)
HRR	H. Peter, *Historicorum Romanorum reliquiae* (Leipzig, 1906–14)
HS	J. B. Hofmann, *Lateinische Syntax und Stilistik*, rev. A. Szantyr (Munich, 1965)
IEG	M. L. West, *Iambi et Elegi Graeci* (Oxford, 1971–2)
IG	*Inscriptiones Graecae* (Berlin, 1873–)
ILS	H. Dessau, *Inscriptiones Latinae Selectae* (Berlin, 1892–1916)
KG	R. Kühner–B. Gerth, *Ausführliche Grammatik der griechischen Sprache: Satzlehre*. 4th ed. (Hannover, 1955)
KS	R. Kühner–C. Stegmann, *Ausführliche Grammatik der lateinischen sprache: Satzlehre*. 3rd ed., rev. A. Thierfelder (Hannover, 1955)
Leo, *Gesch.*	F. Leo, *Geschichte der romischen Literatur*. I *Die archaische Literatur* (all pubd) (Berlin, 1913; repr. Darmstadt, 1967, w. *Die römische Poesie in der sullanischen Zeit*)
Lesky	A. Lesky, *A History of Greek Literature*, tr. J. Willis–C. de Heer (London, 1966)
Lesky, *TDH*	A. Lesky, *Die tragische Dichtung der Hellenen*, 3rd ed. (Göttingen, 1972)
LSJ	Liddell–Scott–Jones, *Greek–English Lexicon*, 9th ed. (Oxford, 1925–40)
Loeb	Loeb Classical Library (Cambridge, Mass. & London)
MGH	*Monumenta Germaniae Historica* (Berlin, 1877–91)
OCD²	*Oxford Classical Dictionary*, 2nd ed. (Oxford, 1970)

ABBREVIATIONS

OCT	Scriptorum Classicorum Bibliotheca Oxoniensis (Oxford)
Paravia	Corpus Scriptorum Latinorum Paravianum (Turin)
PIR	E. Klebs–H. Dessau, *Prosopographia Imperii Romani Saeculi I, II, III* (Berlin, 1897–8), 2nd ed. E. Groag–A. Stein (Berlin & Leipzig, 1933–)
PL	J.-P. Migne, *Patrologiae cursus completus* Series Latina (Paris, 1844–)
PLF	E. Lobel–D. Page, *Poetarum Lesbiorum Fragmenta* (Oxford, 1963)
PLM	E. Baehrens, *Poetae Latini Minores* (Leipzig, 1879–83), rev. F. Vollmer (incomplete) (1911–35)
PLRE	A. H. M. Jones–J. R. Martindale–J. Morris, *The prosopography of the later Roman Empire* (Cambridge, 1971–)
PMG	D. L. Page, *Poetae Melici Graeci* (Oxford, 1962)
PPF	H. Diels, *Poetarum Philosophorum Graecorum Fragmenta* (Berlin, 1901)
Pfeiffer	R. Pfeiffer, *A history of classical scholarship* (Oxford, 1968)
Powell	J. U. Powell, *Collectanea Alexandrina* (Oxford, 1925)
Powell–Barber	J. U. Powell–E. A. Barber, *New chapters in the history of Greek Literature* (Oxford, 1921), 2nd ser. (1929), 3rd ser. (Powell alone) (1933)
Preller–Robert	L. Preller, *Griechische Mythologie*, 4th ed., rev. C. Robert (Berlin, 1894)
RAC	*Reallexicon für Antike und Christentum* (Stuttgart, 1941–)
RE	A. Pauly–G. Wissowa–W. Kroll, *Real-Encyclopädie der klassischen Altertumswissenschaft* (Stuttgart, 1893–)
ROL	E. H. Warmington, *Remains of old Latin* (Cambridge, Mass. & London, 1935–40)
Roscher	W. H. Roscher, *Ausführliches Lexicon der griechischen und römischen Mythologie* (Leipzig, 1884–)
SEG	*Supplementum Epigraphicum Graecum* (Leyden, 1923–71; Alphen aan den Rijn, 1979–)
SVF	H. von Arnim, *Stoicorum Veterum Fragmenta* (Leipzig, 1903–)
Snell	B. Snell, *Tragicorum Graecorum Fragmenta* (Göttingen, 1971–)
Schanz–Hosius	M. Schanz–C. Hosius, *Geschichte der römischen Literatur* (Munich, 1914–1935)
Schmid–Stählin	W. Schmid–O. Stählin, *Geschichte der griechischen Literatur* (Munich, 1929–1948)
Spengel	L. Spengel, *Rhetores Graeci* (1853–6); I ii rev. C. Hammer (Leipzig, 1894)
Teuffel	W. S. Teuffel, *Geschichte der römischen Literatur* (Leipzig & Berlin, 1913–1920)

ABBREVIATIONS

TGF	A. Nauck, *Tragicorum Graecorum Fragmenta*, 2nd ed. (Leipzig, 1889)
TLL	*Thesaurus Linguae Latinae* (Leipzig, 1900–)
TRF	O. Ribbeck, *Tragicorum Romanorum Fragmenta*, 3rd ed. (Leipzig, 1897)
Walz	C. Walz, *Rhetores Graeci* (Stuttgart, 1832–6)
Williams, *TORP*	G. Williams, *Tradition and originality in Roman Poetry* (Oxford, 1968)

WORKS CITED IN THE TEXT

Allen, W. S. (1973). *Accent and rhythm: prosodic features of Latin and Greek.* Cambridge.

Altevogt, H. (1952). *Labor improbus.* Münster, Westf.

Anderson, W. B. (1933). 'Gallus and the Fourth Georgic', *C.Q.* 27: 36–45, 73.

Austin, R. G. (1961). 'Virgil, *Aeneid* 2.567–88', *C.Q.* n.s. 11: 185f.

   (1964). (ed.). *P. Vergili Maronis Aeneidos Liber secundus.* Oxford.

Axelson, B. (1958). 'Der Mechanismus des ovidischen Pentameterschlusses: eine mikrophilologische Causerie', in Herescu (1958) 121–35.

Aymard, J. (1951). *Quelques séries de comparaisons chez Lucain.* Montpellier.

Bailey, C. (1935). *Religion in Virgil.* Oxford.

Bardon, H. (1956). *La littérature latine inconnue.* II. *L'époque impériale.* Paris.

Barnes, J. W. B. and Lloyd-Jones, H. (1963). 'Un nuovo frammento papiraceo dell' elegia ellenistica', *S.I.F.C.* 35: 205–27.

Bayet, J. (1930). 'Les premières "Géorgiques" de Virgile', *R.Ph.* 3me sér. 4: 128–50; 227–47.

   (1955). 'Un procédé virgilien: La déscription synthétique dans les Géorgiques', in *Studi in onore di G. Funaioli* 9–18. Rome.

Bickel, E. (1950). 'De elegis in Maecenatem, monumentis biographicis et historicis', *Rh. Mus.* 93: 97–133.

Birt, T. (1877). *Ad historiam hexametri latini symbola.* Diss. Bonn.

Bowersock, G. W. (1971). 'A date in the Eighth Eclogue', *H.S.C.Ph.* 75: 73–80.

Bowra, C. M. (1929). 'Some Ennian phrases in the Aeneid', *C.Q.* 23: 65f.

   (1933–4). 'Aeneas and the Stoic Ideal', *G. & R.* 3: 8f.

Brunt, P. A. (1963). Review of H. D. Meyer, *Die Aussenpolitik des Augustus und die Augusteische Dichtung* (Cologne 1961). *J.R.S.* 53: 170–6.

Buchheit, V. (1962). *Studien zum Corpus Priapeorum.* Zetemata XXVIII. Munich.

Büchner, K. (1955). 'P. Vergilius Maro', *RE* VIIIA. Sep. publ. 1956.

Bulloch, A. W. (1973). 'Tibullus and the Alexandrians', *P.C.Ph.S.* n.s. 19: 85ff.

Burck, E. (1929). 'Die Komposition von Vergils Georgica', *Hermes* 64: 279–321.

Cairns, F. J. (1969). 'Propertius 1.18 and Callimachus' *Acontius and Cydippe*', *C.R.* n.s. 19: 131–4.

Cameron, A. (1976). *Circus factions. Blues and Greens at Rome and Byzantium.* Oxford.

Camps, W. A. (1954). 'A note on the structure of the *Aeneid*', *C.Q.* n.s. 4: 214f.
  (1959). 'A second note on the structure of the *Aeneid*', *C.Q.* n.s. 9: 53f.
Carcopino, J. (1922). 'Vergiliana. A propos du *Catalepton*', *R.Ph.* 46: 156–84.
Clausen, W. V. (1964). 'Callimachus and Latin poetry', *G.R.B.S.* 5: 181–96.
  (1972). 'On the date of the First Eclogue', *H.S.C.Ph.* 76: 201–5.
  (1976). 'Virgil and Juvenal', *H.S.C.Ph.* 80: 181–6.
Coleman, R. G. G. (1962). 'Gallus, the Bucolics, and the ending of the Fourth Georgic', *A.J.Ph.* 83: 55–71.
Costa, C. D. N. (1973). (ed.). *Horace*. London.
Crump, M. M. (1920). *The growth of the Aeneid*. Oxford.
D'Alton, J. F. (1931). *Roman literary theory and criticism*. London.
Day Lewis, C. (1966). *The Eclogues, Georgics and Aeneid of Virgil*. (Trans.) Oxford.
Dickinson, R. J. (1973). 'The *Tristia*: poetry in exile', in J. W. Binns (ed.), *Ovid* 154–90. London.
Doblhofer, E. (1966). *Die Augustuspanegyrik des Horaz in formalhistorischer Sicht*. Heidelberg.
Douglas, F. L. (1929). *A study of the Moretum*. New York.
Drabkin, I. E. (1930). *The Copa*. New York.
Drew, D. L. (1923). 'The Copa', *C.Q.* 17: 73–81.
  (1925). 'The Copa – II', *C.Q.* 19: 37–42.
Duckworth, G. E. (1954). 'The architecture of the Aeneid', *A.J.Ph.* 75: 1f.
  (1957). 'The *Aeneid* as a trilogy', *T.A.Ph.A.* 88: 1f.
  (1959). 'Virgil's *Georgics* and the *Laudes Galli*', *A.J.Ph.* 80: 225–37.
  (1962). *Structural patterns and proportions in Vergil's Aeneid*. Michigan.
  (1969). *Vergil and classical hexameter poetry: a study in metrical variety*. Ann Arbor.
Du Quesnay, I. M. Le M. (1976). 'Vergil's Fourth *Eclogue*', *Papers of the Liverpool Latin Seminar 1976. ARCA 2*. Liverpool.
Edwards, M. W. (1960). 'The expression of Stoic ideas in the *Aeneid*', *Phoenix* 14: 151f.
Enk, P. J. (1918). (ed.). *Gratti Cynegeticon quae supersunt*. 2 vols. Zutphen.
  (1919). 'De Lydia et Diris carminibus', *Mnemosyne* n.s. 47: 382–409.
Fairclough, H. R. (1934). (ed.). *Virgil* II: *Aeneid VII–XII and the minor poems*. Loeb. London & Cambridge, Mass.
Fraenkel, E. (1937). Review of Pasquali (1936), in *J.R.S.* 27: 262ff.
  (1957). *Horace*. Oxford.
  (1964). *Kleine Beiträge zur klassischen Philologie*. 2 vols. Rome.
  (1966). 'The Dirae', *J.R.S.* 56: 142–55.
Frank, T. (1928). *Catullus and Horace*. Oxford.
Froesch, H. H. (1968). *Ovids Epistulae ex Ponto I–III als Gedichtsammlung*. Diss. Bonn.
Frost, R. (1946). *The poems of Robert Frost*. New York.
Gabba, E. (1956). *Appiano e la storia delle guerre civili*. Florence.

Galinsky, G. K. (1975). *Ovid's Metamorphoses: an introduction to the basic aspects.* Berkeley & Los Angeles.

Galletier, E. (1920). *Epigrammata et Priapea.* Paris.

Goold, G. P. (1970). 'Servius and the Helen Episode', *H.S.C.Ph.* 74: 101f.

Gow, A. S. F. (1950). (ed.). *Theocritus.* 2 vols. Cambridge.

(1952). (ed.). *Theocritus.* 2 vols. 2nd edn. Cambridge.

Gow, A. S. F. and Page, D. L. (1965). (eds.). *Hellenistic epigrams.* 2 vols. Cambridge.

Grenade, P. (1950). 'Le mythe de Pompée et les Pompéiens sous les Césars', *R.E.A.* 52: 28–67.

Griffin, J. (1979). 'The Fourth Georgic, Virgil and Rome', *G. & R.* n.s. 26: 61–8.

Grisart, A. (1959). 'La publication des "Métamorphoses": une source du récit d'Ovide (*Tristes* 1, 7, 11–40)', in *Atti del convegno internazionale ovidiano* II 125–56. Rome.

Harding, D. P. (1962). *The club of Hercules.* Urbana.

Haupt, M. (1875). *Opuscula* I. Leipzig.

(1876). *Opuscula* III. Leipzig.

Henry, J. (1873–89). *Aeneidea, or critical, exegetical, and aesthetical remarks on the Aeneis.* 4 vols. London, Edinburgh & Dublin.

Herescu, N. I. (1958). (ed.). *Ovidiana: recherches sur Ovide.* Paris.

Highet, G. (1972). *The speeches in Vergil's Aeneid.* Princeton.

Holleman, A. W. J. (1971). 'Ovid and politics', *Historia* 20: 458–66.

Hollis, A. S. (1970). (ed.). *Ovid, Metamorphoses Book VIII.* Oxford.

(1973). 'Aemilius Macer, Alexipharmaca?', *C.R.* n.s. 23: 11.

(1977). 'L. Varius Rufus, *De Morte* (Frs. 1–4 Morel)', *C.Q.* n.s. 27: 187–96.

Hornsby, R. A. (1970). *Patterns of action in the Aeneid.* Iowa.

Housman, A. E. (1903–30). *M. Manilii Astronomicon Libri.* 5 vols. Cambridge. (Repr. in 2 vols. Olms 1972.)

(1972). J. Diggle and F. R. D. Goodyear. (eds.). *The classical papers of A. E. Housman.* 3 vols. Cambridge.

Hubaux, J. (1930). 'Une Epode d'Ovide', *Serta Leodiensia* 187–245. Liège.

Jahn, P. (1908). 'Vergil und die Ciris', *Rh. Mus.* 63: 79–106.

Johnson, W. R. (1973). 'The emotions of patriotism: Propertius 4.6', *California Studies in Classical Antiquity* 6: 151–80.

Kenney, E. J. (1963). Review of Buchheit (1962), in *C.R.* n.s. 13: 72–4.

(1965). 'The poetry of Ovid's exile', *P.C.Ph.S.* n.s. 11: 37–49.

(1970). 'Love and legalism: Ovid, *Heroides* 20 and 21', *Arion* 9: 388–414.

(1973). 'The style of the *Metamorphoses*', in J. W. Binns (ed.), *Ovid* 116–53. London.

(1976). 'Ovidius prooemians', *P.C.Ph.S.* n.s. 22: 46–53.

Kidd, D. A. (1977). 'Virgil's voyage', *Prudentia* 9: 97–103.

Kirkwood, G. M. (1961). 'The authorship of the Strasbourg Epodes', *T.A.Ph.A.* 92: 267–82.

Klingner, F. (1963). *Virgils Georgica.* Zurich & Stuttgart.

Knauer, G. N. (1964). *Die Aeneis und Homer.* Göttingen.

Knight, W. F. Jackson (1939). *Accentual symmetry in Vergil*. Oxford.

   (1966). *Roman Vergil*. 2nd edn. London.

Kost, K. (1971). *Musaios, Hero und Leander*. Bonn.

La Cerda, I. L. de (1608). *P. Vergilii Maronis Bucolica et Georgica*. Frankfurt am Main.

Leo, F. (1906). 'Diogenes bei Plautus', *Hermes* 41: 441–6 (= *Ausgewählte Kleine Schriften* 1, Rome 1960, 185–90).

Luck, G. (1959). *Die römische Liebeselegie*. Heidelberg.

   (1974). 'The woman's role in Latin elegiac poetry', in G. K. Galinsky (ed.), *Perspectives of Roman poetry* 23ff. University of Texas.

Ludwig, W. (1961). 'Die Anordnung des vierten Horazischen Odenbuches', *Mus. Helv.* 18: 1–10.

Lyne, R. O. A. M. (1971). 'The dating of the *Ciris*', *C.Q.* n.s. 21: 233–53.

Mackail, J. W. (1930). *The Aeneid of Virgil*. Oxford.

Martini, E. (1933). *Einleitung zu Ovid*. Prague.

Maurois, A. (1957). *Les trois Dumas*. Paris.

Meuli, K. (1955). 'Altrömische Maskenbrauch', *Mus. Helv.* 12: 206–35.

Nettleship, H. (1890). 'Literary criticism in Latin antiquity', *Journal of Philology* 18: 225–70.

Newman, J. K. (1967). *Augustus and the New Poetry*. Collection Latomus LXXXVIII. Brussels.

Nisbet, R. G. M. and Hubbard, M. (1970). *A commentary on Horace: Odes Book I*. Oxford.

Norden, E. (1913). *Agnostos Theos*. Berlin.

   (1915). *Ennius und Vergilius. Kriegsbilder aus Roms grosser Zeit*. Leipzig & Berlin.

   (1926). (ed.). *P. Vergilius Maro, Aeneis Buch VI*. 3rd edn. Leipzig & Berlin.

   (1934). 'Orpheus und Eurydice', *Sitzb. d. Preuss. Akad.* Phil.-hist. Kl. 1934, 626–.83 = *Kleine Schriften zum klassischen Altertum*, Berlin 1966, pp. 468–532.

Ogilvie, R. M. (1965). *A commentary on Livy Books 1–5*. Oxford.

Otis, B. (1959). 'Three problems of *Aeneid* 6', *T.A.Ph.A.* 90: 165f.

   (1963). *Virgil: a study in civilized poetry*. Oxford.

   (1966). *Ovid as an epic poet*. Cambridge.

Packard, D. W. (1968). *A concordance to Livy*. 4 vols. Cambridge, Mass.

Page, D. L. (1950). (ed.). *Select papyri* III. *Literary papyri: poetry*. Revised repr. Loeb. London & Cambridge, Mass.

   (1972). 'Early Hellenistic elegy', *P.C.Ph.S.* n.s. 18: 63–4.

Pasquali, G. (1936). *Preistoria della poesia romana*. Florence.

Pierleoni, G. (1906). 'Fu poeta Grattius?', *Rivista di Filologia e di Istruzione Classica* 34: 580–97.

Platnauer, M. (1951). *Latin elegiac verse. A study of the metrical usages of Tibullus, Propertius & Ovid*. Cambridge.

Posch, S. (1969). *Beobachtungen zur Theokritnachwirkung bei Vergil*. Comm. Aenipont. XIX. Innsbruck.

Pöschl, V. (1950). *Die Dichtkunst Virgils: Bild und Symbol in der Aeneis*. Innsbruck; tr. G. Seligson, Michigan 1962.

Putnam, M. C. J. (1965). *The poetry of the Aeneid*. Harvard.

Quinn, K. (1963). *Latin explorations*. London.

(1965). 'The Fourth Book of the *Aeneid:* a critical description', *G. & R.* n.s. 12: 16f.

Radford, R. S. (1928). 'Ovid's *Carmina furtiva*', *Phil. Quart.* 7: 45–59.

(1930). 'The *Culex* and Ovid', *Philologus*. 86: 18–66.

Ribbeck, O. (1865). *Der echte und der unechte Juvenal*. Berlin.

(1866). *Prolegomena critica ad P. Vergili Maronis opera maiora*. Leipzig.

Richter, W. (1957). (ed.). *Vergil, Georgica* (edn. with commentary).

Ricks, C. (1968). (ed.). *A. E. Housman*. New Jersey.

Robinson, R. P. (1923). 'Valerius Cato', *T.A.Ph.A.* 54: 98–116.

Ross, D. O. jr. (1975*a*). *Backgrounds to Augustan poetry: Gallus, elegy and Rome*. Cambridge.

(1975*b*). 'The *Culex* and *Moretum* as post-Augustan literary parodies', *H.S.C.Ph.* 79: 235ff.

Rudd, N. (1960). 'Patterns in Horatian lyric', *A.J.Ph.* 81: 373–92.

(1976). *Lines of enquiry: studies in Latin poetry*. Cambridge.

Saint-Denis, E. de (1956). *Virgile, Géorgiques* (Budé). Paris.

Sassoon, S. (1945). *Siegfried's journey 1916–1920*. London.

Scazzoso, P. (1956). 'Reflessi misterici nelle Georgiche', *Paideia* 11: 5–28.

Schöpsdau, K. (1974). 'Motive der Liebesdichtung in Vergils Dritter Ekloge', *Hermes* 102: 268ff.

Schulze, K. P. (1898). 'Ovid *Trist.* IV.10.43f.', *Rh. Mus.* 53: 541–6.

Segal, C. (1966). 'Orpheus and the Fourth Georgic', *A.J.Ph.* 87: 307–25.

Slater, D. A. (1912). 'Was the Fourth Eclogue written to celebrate the marriage of Octavia to Mark Antony?', *C.R.* 26: 114.

Small, S. G. P. (1959). 'The Arms of Turnus: *Aeneid* 7. 783–92', *T.A.Ph.A.* 90: 243f.

Solmsen, F. (1948). 'Propertius and Horace', *C.Ph.* 43: 105–9.

Sonner, P. (1910). *De P. Vergili Maronis carminibus capita tria*. Diss. Halle.

Sparrow, J. (1931). *Half-lines and repetitions in Virgil*. Oxford.

Steele, R. B. (1933). *The Nux, Maecenas and Consolatio ad Liviam*. Nashville.

Stroh, W. (1968). 'Ein missbrauchtes Distichon Ovids', in M. von Albrecht and E. Zinn (eds.), *Ovid* 567–80. Darmstadt.

(1971). *Die römische Liebeselegie als werbende Dichtung*. Amsterdam.

Syme, R. (1939). *The Roman revolution*. Oxford.

(1958). *Tacitus*. 2 vols. Oxford.

Tarn, W. W. (1932). 'Alexander Helios and the golden age', *J.R.S.* 22: 135–60.

Tyrrell, R. Y. and Purser, L. C. (1933). *The correspondence of Cicero* VI. 2nd edn. Dublin.

Valéry, P. (1962). 'Variations sur les *Bucoliques*', *Oeuvres* I: 207–22.

van de Woestijne, P. (1929). 'Haud mollia iussa', *R.B.Ph.* 8: 523–30.

Van Sickle, J. (1975). 'The new erotic fragment of Archilochus', *Quadri Urbinati di cultura classica* 20: 123–56.

Vessey, D. W. T. C. (1973). *Statius and the Thebaid*. Cambridge.

Warmington, B. H. (1957). *Remains of Old Latin* III: *Lucilius, The Twelve Tables*. 2nd edn. Loeb. London & Cambridge, Mass.

Westendorp Boerma, R. E. H. (1949). (ed.). *P. Vergili Maronis Catalepton*. 2 vols. (vol. II 1963). Assen.

   (1958). 'Virgil's debt to Catullus', *Acta Classica* 1: 55f.

Wiedemann, T. (1975). 'The political background to Ovid's *Tristia* 2', *C.Q.* n.s. 25: 264–71.

Wilamowitz-Moellendorff, U. von (1924). *Hellenistiche Dichtung*. 2 vols. Berlin.

   (1928). *Erinnerungen 1848–1914*. Leipzig.

Wili, W. (1947). 'Die literarischen Beziehungen des Properz zu Horaz', *Festschrift Tièche*. Bern.

Wilkinson, L. P. (1955). *Ovid recalled*. Cambridge.

   (1963). *Golden Latin artistry*. Cambridge.

   (1969). *The Georgics of Virgil: a critical survey*.

Williams, G. W. (1968). *Tradition and originality in Roman poetry*. Oxford.

Williams, R. D. (1960). (ed.). *Virgil, Aeneid V*. Oxford.

   (1962). (ed.). *Virgil, Aeneid III*. Oxford.

   (1963). 'Virgil and the *Odyssey*', *Phoenix* 17: 266f.

   (1972). 'The pageant of Roman heroes', in *Cicero and Virgil: Studies in honour of Harold Hunt*. Amsterdam.

Wimmel, W. (1960). *Kallimachos in Rom*. *Hermes* Einzelschrift XVI. Wiesbaden.

Winterbottom, M. (1974). (ed.). *The Elder Seneca. Declamations*. 2 vols. Loeb. London & Cambridge, Mass.

Wissowa, G. (1917). 'Das Prooemium von Vergils Georgica', *Hermes* 52: 92–104.

INDEX

Main references are distinguished by figures in bold type. References to the Appendix (which should normally be consulted for basic details of authors' lives and works, and for bibliographies) are given in italic figures.

Aeschylus, 28, 44
Agrippa, M. Vipsanius, 67, 197
Albinovanus Pedo, 189, 191, **193–4**, *218*
Alcaeus, 81, 91, 93
Alfius Flavus, 182
Anacreon, 82, 91, 93
Anaximenes (historian), 195
Annius Cimber, 178
Anser, 122
Antimachus, 190–10, 187
Antipater (epigrammatist), 100
Antonius, Iullus, 171, 187
Antonius, M. (Mark Antony), 24, 75, 102, 112, 115; Virgil and, 19, 20, 39; subject of *Catalepton* 3 (?), 176; criticized by Varius, 189; Rabirius on, 190; Dellius on, 196; style criticized by Augustus, 197
Antonius Rufus, 189
Aphrodisius, Scribonius, 198
Apollonius of Rhodes, 22, 45, 158
Appendix Vergiliana, 122, **171–9**, *211–13*
Appian, 196, 197
Aquilius Niger, 196
Aratus of Soli: influence on Virgil, 25, 29; model for Ovid, 133; *Catalepton* of, 175; translated by Germanicus, 184
Arbronius Silo (epic poet), 187
Arbronius Silo (son of preceding, pantomimist), 189
Archilochus, 76, 79–80
Aristius Fuscus, 189
Aristophanes (comic poet), 140
Aristotle, 84, 164, 166, 167
Arruntius, L., 196
Artemidorus of Tarsus (grammarian), 9
Ateius Philologus, 195
Atticus, T. Pomponius, 164
Augustine, 57
Augustus (Octavian), 176; Virgil and: (*Aeneid*),

37–43, 48, 54, 56, 62, 63, 138; (*Eclogues*), 13, 16–20 *passim*; (*Georgics*), 24, 25, 27, 29, 30–1, 36; patronage under, 3–4; Ovid and, 114, 122, 145, 146–51 *passim*, 155–6, 157, 161; Livy and, 162, 163; Horace and, 41–2, 74, 75, 77, 85–6, 91, 92–3, 96–7, 102–7 *passim*, 138, 149; love-elegists and, 114; Messalla and, 115; in *Appendix Vergiliana*, 175, 179; criticism of others' styles, 182, 197; Manilius and, 184; histories about, 196
 works: poem on Sicily, 184n.; tragedies, 188; *Res gestae*, 195, 197; *Commentarii*, 196–7; style, 197

Bacchylides, 82
Baebius Macer, 196
Bassus (iambic poet), 117
Bavius, 181
Bion, 9
Boios, 183
Brutus, M. Junius (tyrannicide), 74, 75, 112

Caecilius Epirota, Q., 181, 198
Caesar, C. Julius, 105, 114, 164; in Ovid, 136, 138, 146
Callimachus, 2, 3, 8, 113, 184
 influence: on Virgil, 21–3; on Horace, 81, 85; on Gallus, 115; on Proculus, 122, 182; on Ovid, 129, 132–3, 136–7, 141, 158; on *Appendix Vergiliana*, 171, 172; on Valgius, 181
Callinus, 109
Calvus, C. Licinius: as poet, 122, 171, 174n.; Pollio and, 188 and n.
Camerinus, 187
Camillus, 166
Capella, 182
Carus (epic poet), 187
Catalepton, 174n., **175–8**, *211–13*

INDEX

Horace (*cont*.)
85, 92; (2.2), 83; *Epodes*: (7 and 16), 41–2;
(8), 75–6; *Odes*: (1.3), 78–9; (1.4), 100; (1.5),
90; (1.9), 99–100; (1.11), 99; (1.31), 106;
(1.37), 93; (1.38), 93; (2.3), 76–7; (2.13),
90–1; (2.15), 94; (3.1), 94; (3.4), 104–5; (3.11),
91–2; (3.19), 77; (3.21), 92; (3.25), 77; (4.2),
92–3; (4.4), 98–9; (4.6), 106; (4.7), 101
Hostia, *see* 'Delia'
Hyginus, C. Julius, 196, 198
Hyperides, 176n., 197

Julius Caesar, *see* Caesar
Julius Florus, 63, 182
Julius Marathus, 196
Julius Saturninus, 196
Justinus, M. Junianus (Justin), 195
Juvenal, 160
'Juventius', 113

Laevius, 182
Largus, 187
Leonidas (epigrammatist), 100
'Lesbia', 111–13
Livy, 1, 42, 73, **162–70**, 196, *210–11*; Augustus
and, 162, 163; ancient views on, 168, 170, 195,
196; structure of work, 162; historical
techniques, 164–8; style, 168–70
Lollius, M., 179
Lucan, 175, 178, 186n., 194–5; debt to Ovid,
160; relation to Virgil, 160, 189; Petronius
and, 189, 191; models for historical epic, 189–
95
Lucilius, 80, 83, 126
Lucretius, 28, 67, 69
    influence: on Ovid, 144; on Virgil, 26,
    45–6; on *Ciris*, 174; on Grattius, 184; on
    Manilius, 185
Lupus, 187
'Lycoris', 112, 115
Lydia, 171, **173**, *211–13*
Lygdamus, **115–16**, 124, *205–6*
Lynceus, 187

Macer (epic poet), 188
Macer, Aemilius (didactic poet), **182–3**, *214*
Macer, C. Licinius (annalist), 163, 165
Macrobius, 44, 46, 67, 172
Maecenas, C.: as patron, 3, 118; style and
writings, 182, 197; Horace and, 75, 79, 95,
96, 103, 106, 108; Virgil and, 8, 19, 24, 25, 27
29; Propertius and, 114, 118; elegies on death
of, 178–9; Dom. Marsus and, 181
Manilius, *216–17*, 174; *Astronomica*, 171, 182,
183, **184–7**
'Marathus', 113, 116
Marcellus, M. Claudius (Augustus' nephew), 118

Marius, C., 165
Martial, 175, 191; cited, 172; models, 159–60,
181
Maximian (6th c. A.D. elegist), 123
Meleager (and *Garland* of), 81, 100, 109
Melissus (dramatist), 189
Menippus, 83
Messal(l)a Corvinus, M. Valerius: as patron,
115; Tibullus and, 114, 115; addressee of
Ciris (?), 174; praised in *Catalepton* 176; in
Maecenas' *Symposium*, 182; as orator, 197
writings, 176 and n., 197
Messal(l)a Messal(l)inus, M. Valerius, 174
Mevius, 80
Mimnermus, 109
Montanus, 122, 182
Moretum, 171–2, **173**, *111–13*
Moschus, 9
Musaeus (5th c. A.D. poet), 130

'Neaera', 112
'Nemesis', 112, 116
Neoptolemus of Parium, 84
Nicander, 25, 137, 183
Nonius Marcellus, 196
Numa (epic poet?), 188
Nux, 179–80; Appendix as for Ovid

Octavian, *see* Augustus
Octavius Musa, 177, 196
Octavius Ruso, 196
Orpheism, 65
Ovid, 2, 63, 109, 114, 120–2, **124–61**, 171, *207–9*;
Augustus and, 3, 4, 114, 122, 145, 146–51
passim, 155–6, 157, 161; Lucretius and, 144;
style and metre, 66, 69, 147, 159–60; Tibullus
and, 112, 116, 120, 121; on homosexuality,
113; Quintilian on, 115, 125, 136; Lygdamus
and, 115–16; Propertius and, 117, 119, 120,
121, 126, 132–3; contemporaries, 122–3, 181,
182, 184, 187, 188, 196, 198; relation to Virgil,
126, 128–9, 133, 135–9 *passim*, 144–5, 154,
156n., 160–1; relation to Callimachus, 129,
132–3, 136–8, 141, 158; on Rabirius, 190; on
Corn. Severus, 192
    influence, 159–60; on Martial, 159–60; on
Juvenal, 160; on Lucan, 160; on Silius, 160;
on Statius, 160; on Claudian, 160; on *Ciris*,
174 and n.; on *Culex*, 175 and n.; on Manilius,
185–6
    works: *Amores*, 112, **120–1**, *124–5*, 127,
128, 152, 159; *Ars amatoria*, 120, **121–2**, 125,
127, 128, 129, 134–5, 146, 150, 159, 161;
Epistulae ex Ponto, 157–8; *Fasti*, 115, **132–4**,
135, 149, 158; *Heroides*, 120, 125, **126–32**,
135, 147, 159; *Ibis*, 134, **158–9**, 172; *Medea*,
120, **125**, 132, 188; *Medicamina fac. fem.*, 121;

237

INDEX